Criminology: Principles and Concepts

Criminology: Principles and Concepts

Dr. G.S. Rajpurohit

RANDOM

RANDOM PUBLICATIONS

NEW DELHI (INDIA)

Criminology: Principles and Concepts

ISBN 978-93-5111-907-4

Published in 2016 in India by

RANDOM PUBLICATIONS

4376-A/4B, Gali Murari Lal, Ansari Road
New Delhi-110 002
Phone : +9111-43580356, 011-23289044, 011-43142548
e-mail: sales@randompublications.com,
info@randompublications.com, randomexports@gmail.com

Reprinted 2026

Type Setting by : Friends Media, Delhi-110089

Preface

Criminology is the body of knowledge regarding the social problem of crime. It includes information regarding the nature and extent of crime and the policies used in dealing with crime and criminals. Criminology is sometimes defined more narrowly to include only the information regarding the characteristics of criminals; the policies are then called penology. But the broader definition is justified both in etymology and usage and is preferable to this narrower definition both because it is desirable to have one term to refer to the whole field of crime and also because the term "penology" is obviously unsatisfactory as a name for the policies, since many of these policies are not penal.

Crime is an important area of research and study because it raises the fundamental questions about civil liberties and the power of the state. Besides this, criminological studies reveal several facts which help is understand the human behaviour in general. Criminology as a subject at the postgraduate level is gradually becoming popular in many universities. Very few empirical studies have been conducted in this discipline in our country.

Criminology is the scientific study of the nature, extent, causes and control criminal behavior in both he individual and in society. Criminology is an interdisciplinary fielding the behavioral sciences, drawing especially upon the research of sociologists (particularly in the sociology of deviance) and social anthropologists as well as on writing in law.

Criminologyy is concerned with crime as a personal and group phenomenon. As such it is primarily sociological. It draws information, to be sure, from a great variety of specialized investigation physiological, psychological, legal, chemical, economic, statistical, educational and sociological. Many of these investigations are not, in themselves, sociological; legal chemistry, for instance, is not criminology, for it is concerned with crime only in one of its impersonal aspects.

The book is written in a very lucid and simple language so that it can be useful not only for academician, students and research scholars but equally important for social thinkers and common man.

– Author

Contents

1

Meaning and Definition of Criminology

DEFINITIONS OF CRIME

The following section examines the three major approaches to defining crime. This is not to say that these are the only approaches, or even the best approaches; rather that they are the most widespread. New ways of viewing crime are continually being developed, such as the critiques presented from a feminist perspective. However, for the present purpose the three main approaches will suffice. *The consensus view* The consensus approach to defining crime stems from the functionalist school within sociology. The basic tenet of this school of thought is that society functions as an integrated structure, its stability depending upon agreement, or consensus, among its members about the norms, rules, and values which are to be uniformly respected. Thus, a society's legal system is a reflection of the consensus of what, within that particular society, will and will not be tolerated as acceptable conduct. A crime is therefore a violation of the criminal law, an act which meets with the disapproval of the majority.

A definition of crime following this tradition would be of the style exemplified by Williams: 'A crime is an act that is capable of being followed by criminal proceedings, having one of the types of outcome known to follow these proceedings'.

This definition clearly has a number of important consequences. First and foremost an act has to be committed before a crime can be said to have occurred; thought without some action is not a crime. Further, the act must be legally forbidden; 'antisocial' behaviour in itself is not a crime unless specifically and explicitly prohibited by law.

In keeping with this, in the majority of instances the individual must also have had criminal intent in committing the act, the exception being crimes of *strictliability* such as health and safety regulations. An interesting discrepancy arises here between what might seem *morally* wrong, as opposed to 'wrong' in the legal sense. Racism and sexism, for example, may raise great moral issues, but are not well established in criminal law.

This is not to preclude the possibility that they might: criminal law has to have the flexibility to accommodate shifting societal values. Sutherland and Cressey illustrate this latter point, noting that at various times in the past activities such as printing a book, having gold in one's house, or driving with reins have all been criminal acts. More recently abortion, suicide, and consenting homosexual behaviour in adults over the age of 21 years have all been removed from the criminal law domain. The reverse can also happen: acts once not punishable by law are turned into crimes. In the USA it was perfectly legal to own and sell marijuana until the federal law was amended in 1937. In this country changes have been made regarding the sale of solvents to certain age groups, criminalizing a once legal activity— within, of course, the specific boundaries of the law itself. In other instances, technological advances are at present proving challenges to the law-makers: video piracy and computer fraud are contemporary acts which criminal law is having to address. While there are those acts which may pass in and out of criminal law, and can be thought of as 'statutory' crimes, there are other acts which are almost universally deemed 'wrong' or 'bad in themselves'.

Such acts would include those which inflict harm on another's person, for example murder, assault, and rape; or would inflict harm on the other person's property, for example burglary, malicious damage, and trespass. Thus the function of criminal law is to ensure the maintenance of these agreed aims of society, that is to protect the individual's person and property. However, as N.Walker points out, criminal law adopts a wider brief in seeking to achieve this aim. Laws also exist for the defence of the Realm, and to prevent public acts which might shock, corrupt, or deprave. It can be seen that such laws can be comfortably accommodated within a consensus framework: they act to preserve the stable society within which the individual lives and his or her possessions exist. An important part of criminal law is the delivery of retribution to those who transgress the commonly agreed boundaries of acceptable conduct.

The concept of punishment is not a simple one, raising many practical, legal, and ethical issues. For example, most people would agree that not all crimes merit the same punishment. Some system is needed which can differ between crimes of varying severity and magnitude. The tradition in this country is to distinguish between serious offences, sometimes referred to as *indictable* or *notifiable* offences, such as theft, fraud, and violence against the person; and less serious, or *non-indictable* or *summary,* offences such as minor traffic offences and petty damage to property. This dichotomy of serious and non-serious offences can be broken down still further: for example Siegal summarizes findings from the American National Survey of Crime Severity of public perceptions of crime seriousness. In this survey the five most serious crimes, as nominated by a sample from the American public, were all crimes of violence against the person. The most serious of all was: 'Planting a bomb in a public building. The bomb explodes and twenty people are killed.' The crimes judged least serious were being drunk in public, trespass, and least serious of all the 204 crimes in the survey was a 'youngster under sixteen years plays hooky from school'. If criminal law reflects the consensual views of society, then the punishments it delivers must also reflect the consensual view of the seriousness of different types of crime.

THE CONFLICT VIEW

The conflict view of crime stands directly opposed to the consensus view. It argues that rather than functioning as an integrated unit, society is best seen as a collection of competing diverse groups—professional bodies, unions, students, industrialists, and so on. These groups are in conflict with each other on a range of fronts as, given the unequal distribution of wealth and power within society, some are poor and dissatisfied while others are wealthy and powerful. This inequality in the distribution of power creates a social atmosphere based on conflict, which in turn, it is argued, promotes crime. The conflict view of crime grew in both popularity and sophistication in the late 1960s and early 1970s. It is most closely associated with the writings of criminologists such as Turk, Quinney, and Chambliss and Seidman; although the contribution of earlier writers such as Vold and Dahrendorf should not be neglected.

The conflict view of crime developed into a distinct branch of criminology with the introduction of Marxist theory, a merger generally credited to the book *The New Criminology* by I.Taylor, Walton, and Young. Specifically Marxist or new criminology views crime as a function of a capitalist system which produces those who have wealth and power and those who do not. While each group, or class, within society commits crimes, the type of crime is dictated by the system: the poor commit crimes within their scope, such as theft, murder, and burglary; the middle class commit typical 'white-collar' crimes such as tax evasion and theft from employers; while the wealthy and powerful upper class indulge in activities such as exploitation, profiteering, and environmental pollution and damage—acts which are not accorded the status of crime. As theories based on conflict are clearly political and economic in orientation, the function of the criminal justice system is viewed in very much the same terms.

Criminal laws exist for the express purpose of protecting the rich and powerful from the remainder of the population. In Marxist terms, the 'justice' system exists to preserve capitalist interests —that is the interests of the capitalist bourgeoisie—ensuring power remains with the wealthy and not the proletariat. Thus inequalities in sentencing can be used to support the position of conflict theories. Laws which exact harsher penalties for offences against property rather than against people, and cases in which the poor are imprisoned for minor offences while the rich receive lesser sentences for more serious crimes, appear to offer evidence for a conflict view of crime. Conflict theories have attracted a great deal of criticism. Klockars has pointed specifically to a number of gaps and flaws in Marxist theories: for example the neglect of individual differences—why do not all people within a capitalist system commit crimes? It should be noted that Marxists have responded to these criticisms and are seeking to refine their theories of criminology.

The Interactionist View

While the consensus and conflict view of crime stand directly opposed, the interactionist view falls between these two camps. With its beginnings in a school of thought within sociology known as *symbolic interactionism*, this view of crime rests on a number of critical assumptions. The first of these assumptions is that each individual's behaviour is guided by their interpretation of reality and the meaning which events hold for them. The second assumption has its focus on the learning of meaning, a process seen as resulting from the way in which other people react, either positively or negatively, towards any given individual or situation. Finally, the third assumption holds that the evaluation of one's own behaviour is made just as to the meanings learned and acquired from other people. In focusing so sharply on meaning, the interactionist view of crime moves away from the moral stance of 'right' and 'wrong' central to the consensus view. Thus, while taking the life of another person is a criminal act, this does not *always* have to be the case: self-defence, in battle during war, and state execution are examples of 'legitimate' killing. The decision as to when an act becomes a crime is not a matter of consensus, rather a statement of the preferences of those who hold social power and are able to impose their preferred definition on society. However, unlike the conflict views of crime, the interactionist view does not suggest that economic and political considerations are the driving motivations for those in power. Becker used the term 'moral entrepreneurs' to describe those individuals who advance to positions in society which allow them to influence the rule making process. Thus the interactionist view is concerned with the way in which changing moral standards—not therefore seen as fixed or absolute—relate to changes in legal standards. Interactionist views were at their most influential in the 1960s but have rather declined in popularity since then within the criminological community. Some of those who held interactionist views have moved to a conflict position while others shifted to a consensus view: it is probably true to say that in the 1980s the conservative consensus view is once again gaining the ascendancy.

THEORIES OF CRIMINOLOGY

The three views have clearly placed very different constructions around the phenomenon of crime. The view taken by the individual criminologist, together with his or her own background in sociology, psychology, and so on, will influence the way in which research evidence is gathered, data interpreted, and theories constructed. The following section briefly examines how the three views have been translated into theories of crime.

CLASSICAL AND POSITIVIST THEORIES

The consensus view of crime is linked to two schools of thought within criminology. The *classical* theorists hold central the concept of free will in explaining why a person commits a crime. When the opportunity for crime arises, the individual has a free choice between criminal and non-criminal behaviour. If the payoffs for the criminal act are greater than the retribution it will bring, so the probability of a crime increases. At its most basic this suggests that severe retribution will deter people from any criminal act. Indeed, this simple philosophy was one which guided the process of justice through to the mid-1700s and even into the early 1800s, when acts such as stealing or vagrancy were punishable by severe physical punishment such as flogging or even death.

The eighteenth-century Italian economist Cesare Beccaria was in accord with the general view of the time that humans are rational beings, able to choose and control their behaviour. Beccaria was also concerned that the punishment should fit the crime and so argued, with eventual success, that extreme measures are unnecessary and, indeed, may be counter-productive. There is more than a grain of truth in the saying that 'it is as well to be hung for a sheep as a lamb'. Around the turn of the eighteenth century, the British philosopher Jeremy Bentham similarly argued that a balance between profit and pain guided the free choice of a criminal act. Bentham formulated a number of rules by which to regulate the administration of punishment; with the justification for punishment always presented in terms of its preventing a greater evil than it creates.

Classical theory, as presented by Beccaria and Bentham, was the dominant force in Europe and America in the late eighteenth and nineteenth centuries, guiding both judicial philosophers and criminal justice system of the time. With the advent of positivist theories the classical school waned in popularity and influence throughout the twentieth centry. However, the 1970s and 1980s have seen a renewed interest in classical criminology. The *neo-classical* or *conservative* criminologists have emerged as a strong voice in contemporary theorizing. Fuelled by a general failure of positivist theories to discover the causes of crime and to develop effective strategies for controlling crime, some of the basic ideas associated with classical theories are beginning to return. The call for greater deterrence in the form of longer prison sentences, the return of the death penalty, and the notion of 'just deserts' for lawbreakers, has been heard increasingly over the past decade.

The *positivist* theorists, while sympathizing with the consensus view of crime, differ from classical theorists with respect to the role of free will in determining behaviour, including criminal behaviour. Positivist theories grew from the arguments, advanced from the mid-nineteenth century onwards, that influences outside the realm of free will are the most important in determining behaviour. As theories have advanced and fallen so these influences have ranged from biological factors such as genetic transmission, to psychological constructs such as personality, learning, and moral development. While from a more sociological perspective, there are *social structure* theories which emphasize concepts such as 'anomie', and 'strain' which result from class structure and poverty; and *social process* theories which focus on the effects of, for example, education, peer relationships, and the family. Positivist theories are generally seen as more liberal in orientation, with their suggestions that some form of helpful intervention—be it welfare at a social level or treatment at an individual level—is the optimum strategy for reducing crime.

RADICAL CRIMINOLOGY

While conflict views of crime encompass a range of opinions, it was those theorists who emphasized the Marxist position who advanced the framework for a new model within criminology. The new criminology promised by I.Taylor *et al.* quickly became more popularly known as radical criminology. It is incorrect to say that radical criminology represents a unified theory; rather since 1973 it has put forward a series of associated coherent statements which combine to form a body of knowledge and opinion. While radical criminology has its roots in the writings of Marx and Engels, it was theorists such as Willem Bonger who began to formulate a full Marxist critique of crime. In contrast to classical theories it is proposed that no act in itself is naturally immoral or criminal; definitions of crime are socially determined, reflecting current social values. This emphasis on social determination also runs counter to those positivist theories which incorporate genetic or other biologically based explanations of crime.

Within a radical framework, criminal law is designed to suit the purposes of the dominant ruling class, those within society who hold wealth and power. In a capitalist system, the unequal distribution of wealth means that those without finance have to resort to crime to enjoy the luxuries and advantages seen to be enjoyed by others. Crime therefore is in some instances a function of poverty. The rich also commit crimes for the purpose of gaining further wealth and power. However, as the rich control the means of regulating crime, their legal sysem will discriminate against the poor. So while the poor, the proletariat, may commit the same number of crimes as the wealthy, the bourgeoisie, they are arrested and punished with much greater frequency. A number of modern writers have clarified, elaborated, and extended the position defined by Bonger and articulated by I.Taylor *et al.*

In terms of a solution for crime, radical criminology suggests that changes must occur at economic, political, and social levels. Specifically if progress from the present capitalist system to monopoly capitalism can be made, then redistribution of wealth can take place. It is argued that crime will then no longer be necessary; any crimes which do occur will be the result of individual psychopathology. T.Platt presents a blueprint for the formulation of alternatives to the present system of 'law and 'order' which follow a radical criminological approach. Radical criminology has been subjected to fierce criticism, with some carefully constructed commentaries and others with more than a touch of naivety.

LABELLING THEORY

The interactionist view of crime gave rise to a theory of criminology which relies on a mixture of social and semantic processes to explain deviance. In common with conflict theories, labelling theory suggests that the law is applied to the benefit of those who hold social and economic power. Thus disadvantaged groups within society, such as the lower socioeconomic classes and minority groups, are more likely to be prosecuted and to receive harsher penalties. An individual becomes a criminal when the people who hold power—judges, parents, police, teachers, etc. —decide to confer the label 'criminal'. As Becker notes: 'Deviant behaviour is behaviour that people so label'.

Here there is a clear contrast with a moral view: behaviour is not seen as 'right' or 'wrong', rather 'deviant behaviour' is a judgement by certain sections of society towards certain classes of behaviour. This argument does not, of course, apply only to criminal behaviour: the same reasoning has been used to explain the creation of groups variously labelled 'alcoholic', 'mentally ill', 'sexually deviant', and so on. While writers such as Gove have offered explanations within a labelling theory framework to account for the involvement of people in criminal acts, the main force of labelling theory has been to examine the consequences of labelling. Two consequences are emphasized—the creation of stigma and modification of self-image. The term *stigma* refers to the public attitude of condemnation of the deviant and the associated exclusion of the labelled individual from some parts of society.

The label 'criminal' is associated with undesirable traits and so, in the public eye, the criminal is a person to be avoided and treated with suspicion. Thus the criminal will find that he or she is barred from certain types of employment; the young offender may find that their school or their family is unwilling to offer a welcome; those with criminal records may attract an undue amount of attention from the police. The force of these social pressures can lead to the second major consequence of the label: the individual comes to believe society's judgement and so modifies his or her self-image to match the label. The prophecy becomes self-fulfiling: the individual becomes the person described by the label. As the label becomes a role for the labelled individual, so the role is reinforced so that the person's life changes to suit the role. More crimes are committed, the peer group changes to others playing the same role, the person's identity becomes that of a 'criminal' with all its associated values, attitudes, and beliefs. Lemart calls this process *deviance amplification*.

The irony of any attempt at intervention, either by punishment or treatment, is that it serves only to reinforce the individual's self-perception of him- or herself as a criminal. Like all other theories of crime, labelling theory has its critics. There are a range of objections from a failure to specify why some individuals set off on a path of crime, to a failure to acknowledge that some crimes such as murder and rape are universally judged as 'wrong'.

As Siegal points out, several criminologists who were at one time strong advocates of labelling theory have in the 1970s and 1980s shifted ground to favour more radical theories, principally the conflict theories. In summary, it can be seen that the three influential theories explain crime in very different ways. It is true that there is a degree of overlap between certain aspects of some theories, which has been examined by experimental methods but in the main the theories remain independent of each other. While these theories offer explanations for crime, they do not inform us as to the numbers of crimes committed.

Knowledge of the numbers of crimes committed is important both theoretically and practically: if crime is a low frequency behaviour then criminals may differ in some important way from those who do not perform such acts; if on the other hand it is a high frequency behaviour this may mean quite the reverse. The practical reasons are concerned with the allocation of finance to those establishments concerned with controlling crime: if there is a great deal of crime, and it is society's wish to control it, then the forces of law and order will demand a proportion of the public purse—the higher the frequency of crime, the greater the demand on the purse.

ORGANIZED CRIME

Organised crime is the name for illegal acts committed by a criminal organisation or group, working together to achieve a common goal—usually to make money. For many people, organised crime stirs TV and movie images of gangsters from the Italian and Sicilian mafia in the five major crime families identified in New York City by the Federal Bureau of Investigation. Real-life organised crime, however, also includes mobsters from Russia and Eastern Europe. Organised crime rings from African and Asian countries are involved in everything from prostitution and trafficking people and drugs to pornography, financial scams, computer crimes, genocide, and terrorism. The FBI estimates these groups of organised criminals around the world annually earn $1 trillion US Dollars in profits. In some places, organised crime has infiltrated legitimate businesses and industries, such as construction and garbage disposal. The legitimate businesses are often used to launder money and help cover up illegal activities. Organised criminals in Italy have been known as the mafia since the

1800s. These criminal organisations have been in the United States since the early 1900s. One of the most famous of the Italian mobsters in the US was Charles "Lucky" Luciano, who came from Sicily in 1907, when he was still a boy. He is credited with helping establish the modern mafia, or La Cosa Nostra, which is the organisation of Italian and Sicilian crime families that operate mainly in US cities on the East Coast. Since the early 1990s, organised criminals have been coming to the United States from countries that comprised the former Soviet Union. Their activities include human smuggling and prostitution, fraud, money laundering, drug trafficking, auto theft, and extortion. In Russia, they have been regarded as the leading threat to national security because of the threat they pose to political institutions and the economy. Asian groups of organised criminals have been active in the United States since the early 1900s. In addition to China and Japan, most of these gangsters have ties to Korea, Thailand, the Philippines, Cambodia, Laos, and Vietnam.

They have begun to participate in white-collar crime and use legitimate businesses to cover their criminal activity. They are involved in crimes ranging from gambling and prostitution, to smuggling aliens, and trafficking heroin and methamphetamine. They are also known to commit financial fraud and produce counterfeit computers and clothing. Of the organised groups of criminals from African countries, those in Nigeria are considered the most significant threat. They operate in more than 80 countries, including the United States. Much of their criminal activity is centred around drug trafficking and financial fraud.

ORGANIZED CRIME, INTERNATIONAL CRIME, AND TERRORISM

Crime is often seen in highly individual and informal terms, though we have tried to emphasize the ways in which it is generated in and through cultural and subcultural forms of social organization related to class, gender, and ethnic differences. It is important, however, to recognize that much criminality is professionally organized, and we have, again, tried to indicate some of the ways in which this is socially organized.

In the next part, we turn to an examination of these issues of the formal social organization of crime in much greater detail. We look, in particular, at crime as a business, organized nationally and internationally in ways that challenge conventional businesses in the scale of their activities. We trace how processes of globalization have produced extensive transnational criminal organizations. We look also at the growing significance of international terrorism—the use of criminal acts for political purposes—and trace some of the parallels and connections between terrorism and organized crime.

ORGANIZED CRIME

We have looked at certain forms of professional but we have not discussed what is commonly referred to as 'organized crime'. This can be defined as that form of criminal activity that is organized as a business enterprise through the systematic use of administrative mechanisms, formal coordination, alliances, and joint ventures, and do so in relation to a range of markets for goods and services. Organized crime is criminal activity that goes beyond the relatively smallscale professional and gang activity considered so far.

Like these, it has its roots in the specific subcultures of criminality that comprise the underworld, but it also has quite distinctive causes and conditions. Where organized crime exists, it affects the whole pattern of crime within a society. In this part as suggested, look at the common characteristics of organized crime in the United States, Russia, Japan, and Hong Kong, commonly seen as the foci of 'Mafia' style criminality in the world today.

Mafia and Cosa Nostra

Public recognition of something called the Mafia or Cosa Nostra in the United States dates largely from the 1950s and 1960s, when a series of Senate hearings brought the activities of a number of leading Italian-American criminals to public attention. The most influential model of 'Mafia' organization is that depicted by Donald Cressey, originally produced in association with a Presidential Task Force on organized crime. Cressey presented a picture of a huge national confederation involved in fraud, drugs, prostitution, corruption, gambling, and violence, but also using its funds in conventional business operations such as property, finance, clubs, and restaurants.

Its methods had come to parallel those of other business enterprises and it was impossible to disentangle illegal from legal activities and profits. This type of organized crime may never have been quite as tight and centralized as they seemed to the public and as they were portrayed in such films as The Godfather, but it was, in many ways, a distinctive form of criminal activity. Such organized crime became a prominent feature of major American cities in the 1920s and 1930s.

It is often seen as a direct outgrowth of the rural networks of support and control that proliferated in Sicily and other isolated parts of Italian society in the nineteenth century and that were transplanted to the United States by migrants from these areas. These were loose networks of friends and relations, rather than secret societies, and were organized around the 'honour' of family and locality and were involved in a wide range of neighbourhood and regional activities. The true origins of organized crime are more recent and more complex. It arose in its contemporary form after the great waves of European migration to New York, Chicago, and other American cities and was an outgrowth of the very specific conditions of the 1920s and 1930s.

The urban slums gave rise to many loosely organized groups that were rooted in their distinctive subcultures. We have already shown how similar gangs also emerged in districts of London. The emergence of such gangs can be explained by the distinctive subcultures found in lowerclass areas of large cities and the corresponding differential association in which this results. It depends also, however, on the attractiveness of an 'innovative' response to the anomie found in such areas.

The gangs of the major US cities became especially involved in the production and sale of 'bootleg' alcohol, made profitable by the 'Prohibition' legislation of the American state. The central participants in the bootlegging of whiskey were European immigrants and the descendents of immigrants, and both Italians and Sicilians were prominent. They were actively involved in a range of criminal activities within their neighbourhoods and became drawn into intensive conflict for customers. Debt bondage traps women when a parent or husband sells them into indentured labour, and they are then required to work as prostitutes to pay back the "debt" from the cost of travel, payoffAn alliance of Sicilian and Italian gangs was forged in 1930–31 and came to be known by outsiders as the Mafia.

Far from being a direct descendent of the rural neighbourhoods, then, the gang grouping of the 1930s was a new phenomenon and a distinctive product of American society. It is true, nevertheless, that many of the leading figures in the emerging criminal gangs were recent migrants who had fled the clampdown on the Italian mafia by Mussolini's Fascist regime in the late 1920s.

For all these reasons, Cressey rejected the 'mafia' label, holding that it is inaccurate and was not used by the participants themselves. Participants themselves preferred such impersonal terms as the 'organization', 'business', or 'firm', and sometimes 'Cosa Nostra'. The organization existed, Cressey argued, as a federation of separate and autonomous family-based gangs, each of which defended its particular territory and held that it had a legitimate claim on the support of its local population.

In acting 'honourably' towards 'their' people, providing them with the political influcnce and personal welfare they were denied by the city and national authorities, they earned the respect of people living in their neighbourhoods. This was reinforced by a structure of coercion that ensured that no one in the locality would challenge the right of the gang to monopolize its profitable ventures. Typical of such territorial groups was the Capone Mob of 1930s Chicago.

By the 1960s, Cressey argued, there were over thirty such family mobs. Each family boss—or 'Don'—had absolute authority in his territory. Through a series of cross-cutting alliances designed to protect the territorial claims of each of the gangs, a vast national organization had been built. The Organization itself had no single leader, but was run by a committee of major mobsters known as the 'Commission'. Cressey held that, by the late 1960s, the Organization was dominated by nine powerful families: three from New York, three in the surrounding cities of Buffalo, Newark, and Boston, and one each in Philadelphia,

Detroit, and Chicago. The various families recognized the role of the Commission in resolving disputes and coordinating activities at a national level. The criminal activities of a family were typically organized through a hierarchy of executive positions, running from the Don through his deputy and advisers to the 'Buffer', who acts as the interface or intermediary between the senior family members and the lower-level operatives. The Buffer had various 'Lieutenants' responsible for particular operating units, each of which had its Chief to liaise with the 'Soldiers' who actually operate particular activities—money lending, lotteries, vending machine rackets, protection, and so on.

Beyond the level of the Soldiers, numerous non-Italians were employed or contracted for specific purposes at street level to take bets, answer telephones, sell narcotics, collect protection money, and so on. Cressey further claimed that the Organization and its families operated just as to a strict code of behaviour that governs all their activities.

This code comprises five principles:

1. *Loyalty*: This is the basic injunction to respect the interests of other families and to keep silent about family activities.
2. *Rationality*: This is the requirement to act coolly and calmly in pursuit of the family's business: not to take drugs, not to get into fights, and to follow orders as a good team player.
3. *Honour*: This is tied to ideas of masculinity and patriarchalism, involving respect for women and for the senior members of the family.
4. *Courage:* Family members are to withstand pressure and punishment without complaint. This is, again, tied to a strong ethos of masculinity.
5. *Commitment*: Family members are to uphold their way of life without being drawn into the conventions of regular employment or social conformism.

Joseph Albini has warned that the Organization must be regarded not as a bureaucratic enterprise but as a looseknit system of patron–client or network relationships. As such, its structure is constantly in flux and no rigid model can describe its shape at any particular time. It is clear, nevertheless, that Cressey highlighted the ways in which such a loose-knit structure can coordinate and control the actions of its constituent gangs through both formal and informal mechanisms.

Other Organized Crime

Much discussion of organized crime in the United States has been concerned with that of Italian Americans, but a number of sociologists have pointed to the existence of many other forms of organized crime. Robert Davidson has documented the rise of Asian-American gangs in Chicago and other cities. Those from China, the Philippines, India, Korea, and other parts of Asia now form a significant part of the US population.

In a number of areas of Asian settlement, there has been a growth of criminal involvement in drug trafficking, especially the trade in heroin from South East Asia. Organized gangs in American cities use their connections with Chinese triads operating from Hong Kong to obtain heroin for re-sale in the United States.

Actual sales to users are handled by street gangs, but the bulk trade itself is a highly organized business. Outside the United States, evidence for strong organized criminal gangs has been found in Japan, Russia, and other parts of Eastern Europe. Organized crime had begun to develop in the final twenty years of Communism in Russia, when corrupt and self-serving politicians used illegal means to further their own interests, but it was the collapse of Communism that really stimulated its growth.

The disappearance of the strong, totalitarian state in Russia and the consequent privatization of state economic assets allowed many private individuals to amass considerable wealth through dealing in state assts. Many former Communist politicians were able to use their knowledge and connections to build up personal fortunes themselves and to join this emerging Russian 'mafia'. Organized crime has proliferated because of the economic dislocations that followed the ending of Communism, as this allowed the criminal syndicates to obtain and monopolize scarce resources from which they could benefit.

Russian organized crime, like its American counterpart, is organized through loose 'syndicates' that operate on the basis of patron–client relationships. In these relationships, a person of power or wealth helps or protects specific others, who, in return, perform services for their patron. The relationship is not a contractual, employment relationship but rests on informal patterns of trust and obligation. Hierarchies of patron–client relationships form networks of reciprocity and obligation centred on the most powerful individuals.

Those involved in these networks are engaged in a range of illegal activities. Although Russia has virtually no bank robberies, bank fraud is rife and banks pay high levels of protection money to avoid becoming the targets of robberies. Forging of documents is widespread, as is illegal arms trading, including dealing in nuclear materials, prostitution, drug smuggling, money laundering, and illegal imports. Crime is so closely integrated with conventional business that it has been argued that there is a 'shadow economy' of marginal and unregulated business with its 'black market' for distributing goods.

There are high levels of political corruption, giving the criminal syndicates considerable influence over the state. Organized crime in Hong Kong and mainland China originated in the 'triad' secret societies, though it now reaches beyond them. Triads are a long-standing feature of traditional Chinese society and prospered in Hong Kong during its separation from the rest of China. A triad is a family- and neighbourhood-based grouping that provides support and services for its members and organizes its activities on the basis of secrecy and elaborate rituals of membership. Acting outside, and often against, the central state, triads became involved in a range of legal and illegal activities. Triad activity in Hong Kong grew after the Communist revolution in China, when many prominent leaders were expelled from the mainland. The economic success of Hong Kong since the 1960s provided many opportunities for triads to expand their involvement in prostitution, gambling, and drugs. Thus, while there is continuity between the traditional triads and those of today, systematic involvement in organized crime is a recent and more specific phenomenon.

Triads tend to be organized as loose networks of independent gangs that regard themselves as part of a larger 'family' or clan in which there is a decentralized structure of command. The various gangs are loosely ranked as 'Red Pole', 'Blue Lantern', and ordinary. Although they cooperate for common purposes, they are also involved in recurrent and intense conflict over the pursuit of their interests.

Organized crime in Japan originated in gambling groups and itinerant dealers who banded together for mutual protection and were given official encouragement to organize markets at shrines and temples and to regulate the supply of labour for public works constriction. By the early twentieth century, they were a strongly entrenched feature of Japanese society and had come to be known as Yakuza. They were used as government tools for strikebreaking and for fighting left-wing political groups and they had strong links with right-wing political leaders.

The Yakuza took their present form, however, after the Second World War. Industrial reconstruction and slow political liberalization created opportunities for profitable enterprise in the black markets and in the supply of labour for construction and dock work. They moved into the growing entertainment industry of bars, prostitution, and pachinko, and they extended their protection and extortion activities. Intense conflict among Yakuza led to the emergence of a small number of major syndicates, paralleling the structure of business groups that had developed in the conventional economy. Despite a police clamp down in the 1960s, organized crime in Japan remains highly concentrated. Hill has established that there are currently about 90,000 men involved in organized crime in Japan and that about 40 per cent are involved in gangs affiliated to one of the three big syndicates: Yamaguchi-gumi, Iwagawa-kai, and Sumiyoshi-kai.

The syndicates have great similarities to Cressey's model of the Cosa Nostra and are organized in ways that draw on the idea of the traditional family household, with its paternalistic and authoritarian patterns of control by the 'father' over junior members.Formal administrative mechanisms are also used, however, and the syndicates are organized into series of ranks such as 'boss', executive, soldier, and trainee.

A Yakuza syndicate and its affiliated groupings are organized in relation to a tight discipline and obedience, embodied in a strict code of behaviour that is enforced, when necessary, through violence. Yakuza are currently involved in protection rackets, the supply of drugs, gambling, the sale of festival trinkets, prostitution, debt collection, loan sharking, rent collection, and the supply of labour through sub-contractors.

In many of these areas they act under commission from conventional businesses and public authorities, which rely on the ability of the Yakuza to manage and manipulate their employees, shareholders, and voters through blackmail and coercion.

INTERNATIONAL CRIME

Organized crime, we have suggested, has certain similarities with conventional business activity. Like many businesses, those involved in organized crime have expanded their activities to an international level. Organized criminal gangs in the United States, China, Russia, and elsewhere have been involved in extensive international transactions and have increasingly begun to organize their activities on a global scale.

State borders have always provided opportunities for, as well as barriers to, criminal activity. Within the United States, organized crime has been able to operate under different state jurisdictions, as laws vary from one part of the country to another, and it has been only a small step further to operate across international state borders. Providing goods and services that are legal in one state but illegal in another provides great opportunities for such operations.

The smuggling of alcohol and tobacco, because of variations in tax levels, is one example of such international crime that has existed for a very long time. The growing complexity of legal regulations and of the economic and political interdependence of nation states has created the immense opportunities that organized crime groups have been able to exploit. It has been argued that the globalization of the political economy has resulted in a globalization of crime.

Causes and Consequences

The most obvious and important criminal activity is smuggling, and this has always existed alongside and interdependently of legal international trade. The liberalization of international trade, creating global markets and encouraging business enterprises to operate freely and without regard for national borders has created a situation in which smuggling operations come to be seen, almost, as forms of 'free trade' activity. International smugglers can present themselves as providing commodities that market restrictions prevent from flowing freely across the world.

Although smuggling is often thought of in terms of a tourist carrying a few hundred cigarettes or a bottle of whiskey, the scale of smuggling is immense and it is highly organized. It has been estimated that smuggling is a major global business, valued at more than $600 billion a year, especially through money-laundering operations that are closely tied to established banking and financial activities.

The transformation of the transport industry with the rise of large container ships and juggernaut lorries, has transformed the methods of smuggling. Previously, drugs such as marijuana and cocaine were smuggled into the United States in small planes and speedboats, but organized criminal groups are now transporting larger consignments in sealed containers alongside conventional cargos. Containers and sealed lorries are also used to smuggle migrants across national borders. These mechanisms are anonymous and impersonal, making it more difficult for states to trace those responsible.

The flow of goods from Mexico to the United States, for example, combines both legal and illegal commodities. Drug traffickers have established factories and distribution centres in northern Mexico and have taken advantage of the deregulated trucking industry to transport their drugs into the United States alongside legitimate trade in fruit and vegetables. Within the European Union, the opening-up of national borders has made it easier for lorries to transport economic migrants, asylum seekers, and drugs into Germany, France, and Britain.

The liberalization of financial markets was intended to promote the transnational flow of capital, but it has also promoted a huge growth in money laundering. This is the process through which the proceeds from illegal activities can be converted into legal—and untraceable—financial assets through the use of multiple international bank accounts and investments in tax havens and other financial centres. This has been particularly important for organized criminal groups from Russia and Colombia. The transformation of the international financial system has also created opportunities for new forms of crime.

The almost exclusive reliance on credit cards for consumer purchases has made the copying of credit cards and the 'skimming' of credit details from them into a major criminal activity. Information from cards skimmed in a London restaurant can be used to produce cards that can, within hours, be used to make purchases in New York, Athens, or Rome. The technology required makes this an obvious area for the involvement of organized criminal groups, which have increased their level of investment in technologies for fraud in the face of the growth on international credit card trading.

Criminal Organizations

The actors involved in international crime are many and diverse. Organized crime groups vary from one country to another, and even within countries. They are not organized in precisely the same way as large-scale business enterprises engaged in conventional activities, but they do have certain common characteristics as international actors and they use many of the same mechanisms as those conventional businesses. Criminal groups from numerous countries extend their international scope and combine with other criminal groups in a number of ways. At its loosest, there may be a recognition of the respective spheres of influence and territories of each group, but these easily give way to mutual supplier relationships that may persist over time. Colombian drug producers, for example, have established stable supply linkages with Italian organized criminal groups, and the latter are given exclusive rights to redistribute the drugs across western Europe. The Russian organized crime groups have established links with organized criminal groups in the Netherlands and Japan for supplying women from Eastern Europe for prostitution.

Such supply relations may involve barter rather than money transactions: guns may be exchanged for drugs, for example. Stronger forms of transnational organization occur when groups form what Williams has called tactical and strategic alliances. Short-term tactical cooperation may lead to longer-term strategic alliances that allow systematic and extensive cooperation. Drug trafficking into the United States, for example, has involved the establishment of strong strategic linkages between Colombian producers and dealers in the Dominican Republic, these links being built as their earlier reliance on Mexican intermediaries became less profitable.

Most recently, the Colombian dealers have built strategic alliances with Russian groups to handle distribution through eastern and central Europe. If there are no transnational bureaucratic criminal organizations, the loose networks do, nevertheless, have certain formal mechanisms of cooperation. It has been reported that summit meetings of major criminal groups have been used to regulate spheres of influence and to plan joint ventures. Although the participants are not, in any sense, representatives or leaders of whole national criminal gangs, the meetings do bring together many of the important criminal groups and bring some stability to international criminal activity.

These meetings are complemented by bilateral meetings and by continued contacts through intermediaries. Some criminal groups, it has been suggested, have made such mediation and courier business their main activity. Much discussion has focused on the idea that the Chinese triads of Hong Kong have expanded through the overseas Chinese communities to establish transnational triad organizations. Hong Kong has been seen as the directing centre for such global criminal activities, and the drive to globalization has been strengthened since the 1997 return of Hong Kong to rule—and strong political control—from Beijing. While Chinese organized criminal groups have certainly established strong links across national borders, there is no global triad structure. Chinese communities are diverse in their ethnicity and there is little basis for dominance by Hong Kong migrants. Chinese criminal gangs have become very active in drug smuggling and people smuggling, but they do so as parts of the larger growth in global criminal activity that has been described.

TERRORISM

Terrorism is political action against a state and its citizens that pursues its goals through extreme violence, often on a spectacular or mass scale, and that is generally criminalized through legislation, proscription, and exclusion. It has become, since the 1960s, one of the most important targets for police and security service operations and it has entered the public consciousness as a major—and perhaps permanent—source of concern at work, in travel, and during leisure. X-ray and security checks at airports and other public places have become an accepted, if unwelcome, weapon in what many politicians describe as 'the war against terrorism'.

Violent political conflict has a history as long as the human species. Its organized form as the internal opposition of political groups to state authorities has a history almost as long. Eric Hobsbawm has termed this 'social banditry' when it takes the form of redistributive political action pursued through violent acts that are criminalized by the state. Social bandits engage in a range of criminal activities in support of their political aims, and their overall political strategy and tactics are labelled as criminal by the state that they attack.

In rural societies, social banditry is generated by a sense of grievance and wrong-doing and a desire to secure vengeance and justice. Examples of such social banditry include the idealistic robber of the Robin Hood myth, the guerrilla or resistance fighter, and the violent avengers who terrorize their opponents.

Pacification of their societies by industrializing states, especially those that established liberal and democratic structures, greatly reduced the level of social banditry and institutionalized the legitimate and non-violent opposition of political parties. Even in these societies, however, criminalized forms of political violence could still erupt. Many European governments of the nineteenth century were concerned about the activities of 'anarchists', who were widely seen as motivated by the French revolution. Anarchists were seen as forming secret societies and organizations through which they could plot acts of violence, and a number of bombings and assassinations did take place in this period.

The most protracted forms of political violence, however, have been linked with separatist and nationalist claims, as in the Irish Republican Army in the United Kingdom from the late nineteenth century until the establishment of the Republic of Ireland in 1922. The IRA attacked political or military targets and saw itself as engaged in a war against an imposed state. From the 1960s, these forms of political violence were renewed, but they also began to be transformed as dispossessed groups generated by international conflicts began to take their struggles to the metropolitan and colonial states that they saw as responsible for their oppression.

This was the beginning of that form of violent political conflict described as terrorism. The violent political organizations of the late 1960s and 1970s—

groups such as the IRA, the Red Army Faction, the Red Brigade, and ETA—were formed, like the IRA of fifty years earlier, as highly centralized and tightly coordinated organizations with a structure of command modelled on that of conventional armies. Indeed, many used militaristic terminology in their names and in their tactics.

They emerged in the political upheavals of the 1960s and saw themselves pursuing radical, leftist policies through violent means because they were unable to pursue their goals through conventional political means. They often saw themselves as part of an international struggle, though their international links were limited and each group tended to operate on a national basis. Their targets were politicians and businessmen, embassies and banks, and national airlines.

2

Criminology and Criminogenic Traits

INTRODUCTION

Who commits crime? Our picture of the typical offender depends on how broad a brush we use to paint the answer. With too fine a brush, only the accidents of single lifetimes become salient-a harsh parent, an evil influence, a bad break or two that tipped the balance the wrong way. We may look at this picture and say that there is no typical offender, only atypical ones, each atypical in his or her own way. At the other extreme, with too broad a brush, only the general sociological forces emerge-poverty, inequality, oppression, racism and the like. In this picture, an offender is typical only to the extent that he or she has been buffeted by those social forces. But between these two levels of description lies evidence showing offenders to be, on the average, something other than a random sampling of the population at large or of the populations subjected to the sociological forces. The focus of on this intermediate level of description, where we seek the distinguishing individual traits of the average offender.

To the extent that this intermediate level differs from the two on either side of it, the traits of the typical offender cannot be assumed to be caused either by how he or she was treated by society-by the educational system, by the job market, by the political system, by the law-or by accidental circumstances having led the offender astray. Social institutions, families, friends, even random events, matter, but they do not tell the whole story about the average criminal life.

The average offender is psychologically atypical in various respects, not necessarily to a pathological degree, but enough so that the normal prohibitions against crime are relatively ineffective. In designing public policy, we must bear in mind that a society that successfully keeps 80 to 90 percent of its population on the right side of the law may find that it needs other measures to deter the remaining 10 to 20 percent, for reasons that have more to do with individual criminogenic traits than with defects in policy.

ORIGIN OF CRIMINOLOGY

The word "criminology" suggests studies that have relation to crimes and to criminals. Definitions of the terms *crime* and *criminal* are as desirable as those of any other concepts that are the subjects of serious discussion. At the same time, exact definitions to begin with are not absolutely essential. It is one of the functions of science to arrive at definitions. In order to attain this end the student must often explore whatever portion of his total problem appears most promising for the time being in the expectation that as he and perhaps others after him proceed, one avenue after another will open up and that ultimately fundamentals will be uncovered underneath the whole area. Then a definition of a scientific character can be offered. In the meantime he must be content with tentative and partial or approximate delimitations. To haggle over definitions at the outset is to invite stagnation. This applies to the terms "crime," "criminal," "criminology," and many other terms in daily use.

Crime is both a social and an individual phenomenon. Some of the main characteristics of a crime and of a criminal may be made clear by examining one or two hypothetical situations, and they, instead of more precise statements, may serve a good purpose. One cannot conceive of crime in a world in which but one person is living. Such a lonely one certainly could injure no one but himself and there would be neither statute law nor common law for him to transgress. It is true that we can conceive of his developing a moral code for himself. He might, for example, develop a sense of responsibility for the lower animal and plant life with which he is surrounded. He might even write definite statements in some form to indicate precisely what his responsibility is in particular relations. In such a case, he would be very likely to think of injury to himself, or of taking his own life as at the very apex of forbidden forms of behaviour, because such actions would leave his plants and animals in the lurch. But crime, as we think of it, could not be said to exist.

Let us conceive, however, of a world in which there are two or more persons. Provided they have access to one another, we then have a situation in which there may be what we today think of as crimes and criminals. They may injure one another in manifold ways. In addition, the greater the number of such persons, and the more densely they are concentrated here and there, the greater are the possibilities of mutual interference and injury.

Now, if we follow up our hypothetical situation, we may be able to get some other characteristics into relief. Assume a given concentration of primitive people: a tribe, if you please. In the neighborhood of their camp is a pack of hungry and ferocious wolves. The animals are on their way towards the camp and a struggle is immediately impending. The members of the tribe are coming together for defence, and all are needed for the purpose. But one of them climbs a tree or hides himself and will not come forward to coöperate with his fellows. In such a case, his neighbors, (whether they call him a "criminal" or not is of no consequence) will inevitably consider him as a creature who, at best, has no claim upon them for equal advantages with themselves, and feelings of revulsion and hatred will be engendered against him. He is not contributing to public safety. He is endangering it.

In another situation, he may be thoroughly contemned. In the hypothetical situation we have described, he has only subtracted his own skill and brawn from the sum total of the equipment of the tribe and has weakened their effectiveness perhaps in only a minimal degree. His act is fraught with danger to the group, not only because it has somewhat weakened the whole body, but chiefly because his example may be contagious. Let us suppose that instead of merely absenting himself from the fray, he actually stole away with the weapons of his companions. He has thus made it impossible for them to defend themselves to their full bent. Only less serious would be the same sort of interference with one of his companions. In a similar category would be his making away with any tool or article in common use by one of his neighbors, even though it may interfere but a little with that neighbor's effectiveness in his daily labour to provide the necessaries of life for himself and for those who depend upon him. Let him but interfere with his neighbor's reputation for honesty and thereby with his effectiveness. By doing so, he once again places himself in the criminal class, whether he is marked by such a name or not. In a greater or less degree he is here too, putting public safety and weal in jeopardy. The situation is not essentially different if he commits an injury to the person of his neighbour or takes his life. By doing so, he creates at least an interference with the injured one's customary round of activities and, in the extreme case, he deprives others of their accustomed support and of some of their cherished satisfactions. At the same time, he is depriving the group of some of its strength.

The point of all this is that the behaviour of our hypothetical offender derives its character from the fact that he is living with others, each of whom, like himself, is pressed by certain primary needs that are coextensive with life itself. In other words, a crime and a criminal have an essentially social character. The relation is never to an individual solely, but to the group, also, of which he is a part.

But more may be said about this hypothetical offender against his neighbour as an individual, and, consequently, against the group to which he belongs. He may possess characteristics by virtue of which the revulsion of feeling against him is mitigated, and in another case, his characteristics may intensify these reactions. In the past, he may have been extraordinarily useful to others and to the group as a whole. He may have committed his hostile deed in a moment of intense anger; in a state of drunkenness; in one of frequently recurring fits of madness, such as lead sophisticated folk of our generation to talk about epileptic seizures. He may be a stupid or peculiar fellow who is known by his neighbors never to have been able to fit in with his neighbors and to plan a course of conduct. In any of these hypothetical situations, he may be spared some of the revulsion of feeling that, in other circumstances, would be directed towards him. It may, indeed, come to pass that in a primitive society, what we today popularly describe as a simpleton or a madman may be deified and put upon a pedestal. In any case of mitigation of revulsion of feeling, or in case of its never appearing in the picture, obviously what is to be done about it may be more or less profoundly altered.

On the other hand, a given offence may have been repeated until his otherwise lenient neighbors, as a consequence of something like a summation of stimuli, have reached the limit of forbearance. The end of tolerance is at hand and their revulsion is complete. What shall be done in the case is then a question only of the utmost that can be done.

All this argues that this primitive society will, almost insensibly at first, have developed what we call a code; unwritten at the outset, only later to be committed to some permanent form. And a form of machinery will be developed to regulate the application of the code as a mode of control. This is a system of law and of procedure. It will define the criminal and the criminal act. It will embody "thou shalts" and "thou shalt nots." It will prescribe the methods by which the offender may be dealt with, whether for his own building up so that he may not again be a transgressor, or primarily for the protection of the whole body against the contaminating influence of his presence in it.

Furthermore, when, whatever the circumstances, what we call crime and criminals have become numerous and troublesome; when there has been an accumulation of knowledge relating to human and lower forms of animal life and behaviour; when for any reason it has been forced upon our attention that human beings do not all behave according to a pattern even though their surroundings and the circumstances of their lives may be similar in high degree; when, moreover, techniques or methods for studying the behaving organism have been developed; when all these situations have come to pass it is inevitable that crimes and criminals should be conceived not only as social but as psycho-physical phenomena; that the criminal is one who is on a hair-trigger, so to speak, whose behaviour is set off by a situation in his environment; the behaviour of the honest individual on the other hand, is not set off by the same situation. His hairtrigger is in a different relation. Between the one and the other is an inaccurately graded scale of behaviors, from the most offensive in the eye of the controlling group to the opposite extreme. Our ideal in whatever we do about criminals is to arrange the complex situation so that their behaviour patterns may be kept moving up the scale.

POSSIBLE FIELDS FOR EMPHASIS

The foregoing remarks suggest certain lines of procedure to the student of crime and criminals in our day and civilization. One may observe the occurrence of various categories of crime in every describable social environment and compare the frequencies of their occurrence; their times and seasons; the economic conditions in which they occur; the religious and economic atmospheres in which they are found in varying degrees of frequency. One may compare the legal and other systems of control of the societies in which crimes of this and that category occur. An almost infinite array of correlations may be computed between the occurrence of criminals and the crimes they commit, on the one hand, and social factors on the other.

Thus criminology may be sociologic and legalistic in its emphasis. And it cannot be denied that this emphasis where it has occurred has profoundly improved our grasp of the crime problem and has affected for the better our attitude towards the practical question: "What are we going to do about it?" No one can write or think about these problems successfully while entirely neglecting the emphasis we have referred to.

But there is another procedure that is valid too: one that has equally proven its usefulness. It is directed towards the "hairtrigger" situation. What is the nature of the organism by reason of which the behaviour is what we describe by the term "criminal"? The student of criminology may emphasize the study of this organism itself. What are the characteristics of a particular organism by reason of which it responds to a situation in a form of criminal activity whereas another reacts otherwise?

The question incites the student to describe the offender's personality; to consider his condition of physical and mental health; his acquired attitudes; to make measurements upon him from the viewpoints of physical anthropology and psychology. The programme that this suggests is a challenging one.

We have chosen in this book to place our emphasis here rather than more distinctly upon sociologic, economic, and tellurian factors. The individual will be the central feature. From this standpoint we are interested in him as a psycho-physical organism — but principally as a psychological problem. Sociological and other conditions may be the stimuli or situations among others that in time occasion criminal predispositions and behaviour. In that case it is altogether pertinent to point out the fact.

Problems of detection and apprehension by the police, and of legal procedure against those who are charged with crime are more incidental in this text because we are inquiring into the nature of individual offenders; not in detail into our officials' technique in relation to them. Questions of penology are somewhat closer to us than those of detection, apprehension and court procedure; but in this relation, too, details belong to an independent study.

It is possible to place this limitation upon the scope of such a text as this because attention to the subject matter has already had a long history of great activity beginning in the hazy past that antedated scientific method. And in common with every other department in the whole area of scientific inquiry, criminology has developed through several periods of scientific awakening and enlargement and has profited by each of them.

A PRIMITIVE CONCEPTION OF THE CRIMINAL

In the hypothetical situation with which we launched this chapter we pointed out the emergence of the criminal in a primitive society: one who has violated a written or unwritten code. In contrast with our own there was an age in which superstition loomed relatively large. The violator of the code was one possessed by a more or less virulent evil spirit. It was the problem of leaders to consider means whereby the demon might be cast out, whether by fire or water or exposure and privation or the infliction of extreme and acute bodily suffering by any means whatsoever.

In this situation one who sits in judgement becomes an ingenious specialist in devising cruelties and inflicting them upon the violator because only so can the evil spirit be put to flight. Thus: "Damn that boy," said Mr. Squeers, "he's always up to something of that sort.""I say it's obstinacy," said Mrs. Squeers: "I'd beat it out of him." The violator as a complex of flesh and blood before the judgement seat is of the least importance. The spirit (it might be only personified "obstinacy" as in the mouth of Mrs. Squeers) is everything and everywhere but particularly in those beings that seem to behave spontaneously and of their own free will. This was particularly the lot of those who today would be described as mentally diseased. But likewise of the criminal, for it is his *behaviour*, just as in relation to the mentally afflicted, that marks him as a mischief-maker in his milieu. It is the devil in him, and the devil was personified. He might be frightened away by hurling an inkstand at his head as Martin Luther is said to have attempted to do it — but probably more strenuous measures would need to be invoked.

It might require drowning or ducking in salt water; torture by fire; exposure to the weather; infliction of pain, whatever the method. For it is possession by a demon that accounts for the criminal act and demons flee before rough treatment. This suggests the root of the ascetic's self-inflicted punishment — St. Simeon Stylites voluntarily upon the top of a column, naked, exposed to all weather, fed upon water and a crust of bread, all to purify his soul.

Extraordinary as it appears in our century, that conception of a mischief-making spirit as responsible for the violation of a code of behaviour accounts for many a dumb animal being solemnly charged with offence, tried, and punished; mayhap a hog for rooting up the turnips; and probably many an ox likewise for goring his master's neighbour. For: "If an ox gore a man or a woman that they die, then the ox shall be surely stoned and his flesh shall not be eaten; but the owner of the ox shall be quit."

Thus unutterable cruelties and absurdities were committed in the name of social protection and to maintain the code; all because of a particular conception applied to one who violates the code. Moreover justice, in the application of this conception, was defeated by the absence of the semblance of uniformity in dealing with offenders. Variations in this respect were as wide as the difference among those who judged and enforced judgments.

ATTEMPTING ESCAPE FROM VARIATIONS IN TREATMENT

Here attention shifts from the offender to what he has done. "What is the degree of gravity of each form of violation?" and "What should be exacted of one in return for each type of violation in the category?" These questions presuppose a series of crimes, graduated according to their heinousness, each one possessing a definable existence of its own; and the object is to correlate all with a corresponding series of penalties or exactions that the criminal should be required to pay. For each person, violator of a code or not, is assumed to possess complete freedom of will and action at all times and in all circumstances and as a consequence to be able to act or to refrain according to his choice. Individual differences were not the vogue, as far as this point was concerned.

Under the inspiration of this viewpoint it became a nice academic problem to equate offenses and penalties, so that there should be no guess work and no inequalities in practical relations between public authorities and offenders.

For every criminal violation there is something to pay; precisely as there is something to pay if one accidentally breaks one's neighbor's window. What is to be paid is the value of the window or the cost of replacing it. It matters not whether the unfortunate one who breaks the glass is sick or well, imbecilic or normal, old or young. The value of the window is uniform in all circumstances. If the damage is done maliciously the argument is the same as in the accidental situation.

Likewise if one in a vicious brawl breaks one's companion's tooth, or puts out an eye, or if one slanders a neighbour there is a fixed amount to be paid whether in the form of money as damages, restriction of freedom, or life itself. And because, once more, in every situation one is absolutely free to choose and to act or to forbear, guilt is equal and punishment — what is to be paid — is equal. Moreover the payor had some rights, too. He had the right to be protected against paying more than others paid in like circumstances.

THE STAGES OF A CRIMINAL LIFE

Some people find it hard to imagine criminogenic traits at all, independent of social forces. Aren't crimes, they say, crimes only because society says so? The answer is yes, but that does not mean that everyone is equally likely to violate the social and legal constraints on our behaviour. Whatever else criminal behaviour may be, it is distinctive in being illegal. The very fact that it is illegal may affect different people differently, depending on their psychological makeup. For example, in the nineteenth century, when the use of opium and morphine was legal, the typical addict was an upper or middle class, middle-aged woman. After the drugs became controlled substances and their use illegal, their price skyrocketed; but the typical opiate addict became a young, lower class man, someone who could afford it less than a middle or upper class woman. Making it illegal evidently deterred the earlier population of users; the current population of illegal users differs from the earlier one in its individual characteristics as well as in its sociological ones.

The most serious crimes are, in addition, not just arbitrarily so. They are not like the consumption of opium, which is illegal now but was routinely recommended by physicians a century ago. Most serious crimes are activities that no human society has ever tolerated. Rape, murder, robbery, arson and theft are among the crimes that are criminal because they strike most people in most societies as sufficiently wrong to warrant restraint by the weighty arm of the law. Virtually by definition, acts that most people are disposed to do are not going to fall into this category of male in se-crimes that are wrong in themselves. It should come as no surprise that the small minority of people who kill, steal, rape, or burn for their own evil purposes are unlike the rest of us. The typical offender today, like the typical addict, is a young male, probably between the ages of fifteen and twenty-four. Age and sex are, in fact, among the most predictive variables we know of for criminal behaviour, but there are other distinctive factors, which consider in due course. Age and sex, as criminogenic variables, serve to illustrate what is meant by saying that offenders are not a random selection of the population: the average person is not a young male, but the average criminal.

Many youngsters, especially males, break the law during their teens and early twenties, but most of them quit soon thereafter. Younger than that, boys may be boys, but they are too small, too much under the control of grownups and not interested enough in sex, money, mayhem and fast cars to wreak much damage. Older, the processes of socialization, or a regular paycheck, tame most of them. This tells us that the typical offender is young not just because habitual criminals are active in their late teens and early twenties but because a few crimes are committed at this age by many people who will not be habitually criminal at other times of their lives.

For example, almost all male college undergraduates (a population which, we hope, is not distinctive for its criminal tendencies) admit (or boast about) committing a few crimes-underage drinking, falsifying drivers' licenses, driving while intoxicated, illegally using controlled substances, shoplifting and various other manifestations of adolescence. A much smaller proportion of the general population starts offending even earlier than in mid-adolescence and continues doing so at high rates until well into adulthood. But even though some low level of occasional criminality during male adolescence is the rule more than the exception, most of the personally threatening crime around us is committed by a small fraction of the population. What is this small fraction like? One way to find out is from longitudinal studies, which pick a sample of people at one point in their lives, then follow them long enough to see who breaks the law, how they break it and how much they do so. Or, alternatively, they may pick a sample of offenders and then try, retrospectively, to reconstruct the events or characteristics that foreshadowed the criminal behaviour.

Longitudinal studies tell us that juvenile offenders are at risk to become adult offenders. And vice versa: adult offenders are likely to have been juvenile offenders. In a large sample of men born in Philadelphia, for example, then followed in a longitudinal study that covered several decades, the ones who had been arrested as juveniles were more than four times as likely to be arrested as adults as the ones not arrested as juveniles. Similarly, those arrested as adults were almost three times as likely to have been arrested as juveniles as the men who had not been arrested as adults. Although the precise ratios vary, thc pattern is firmly established in other longitudinal studies.

It would an overstatement to say "once a criminal always a criminal," but it would be closer to the truth than to deny the evidence of a unifying and long-enduring pattern of encounters with the law for most serious offenders. We cannot, however, accept this unifying pattern uncritically, for it is possible that being labeled a criminal by the criminal justice system marks a person for further arrests and convictions and that that, rather than any personal trait, explains the apparent continuity of criminal lives. Or, perhaps, a person who has been caught breaking the law resigns himself to a life of crime, believing that the odds of a happy, law-abiding life have become hopelessly stacked against him.

These alternative explanations probably have some validity; but they cannot fully, or even nearly, account for the enduring patterns of behaviour suggested by the evidence. Even among males who have never been arrested or convicted, those who characterize themselves (on anonymous questionnaires) as offenders in youth are more likely to do so in adulthood than those who did not do so earlier and those who so describe themselves in adulthood were likewise more likely to have done so as youngsters.

Longitudinal studies uncover other traces of the continuity of criminal behaviour. The probability of first arrests is smaller than that of second arrests, which, in turn, is smaller than that of third arrests and so on. In the Philadelphia study mentioned earlier, about 35 percent of the men had a first arrest. Among these men, about 54 percent had a second arrest. The trend continues upward: for men arrested six times, about 80 percent had a seventh arrest. Other studies have found the risks of arrest rising even higher for those with long arrest records. The average seriousness of the crime similarly rises with each successive arrest.

If each arrest reduced the risk of further arrests, we could conclude that encounters with the criminal justice system deterred further offending, or at least that criminals learn to become shrewder about their crimes after they've been caught a few times. What does the reverse trend, which is so strongly present in the data, mean? One possibility is that encounters with the criminal justice system literally increase a person's tendency to break the law or decrease his ability to get away with it. But a simpler explanation is that each successive arrest isolates a population at increasingly high risk for being arrested, so that by the time a person has been arrested, say, eight or nine or ten times, he (or, infrequently, she) falls into a category of people whose behaviour is so strongly tipped towards whatever it is that gets one arrested that future arrests are almost certain. What is it that gets one arrested? Perhaps part of it is that each successive arrest isolates a less competent group of offenders, one that is more likely to get caught for its crimes. But it would be extremely odd if breaking the law were not at least one of the factors that get a person arrested.

The rising risk of arrest and the increasing gravity of the offenses suggest that within the population as a whole is a subpopulation of repeating, perhaps close to incorrigible, serious offenders. Each successive arrest draws an ever tighter loop around this highly criminal population, by filtering out the people with weaker tendencies to break the law and get arrested. The 5 to 7 percent of the population failing into the category of habitual offenders is responsible for no less than half of all arrests or police contacts. For example, 70 percent of all convictions by 1981 of English men born in 1953 were of the 5.5 percent who had six or more convictions. Comparable concentrations of crime have turned up in Scandinavian statistics as well. Everything points towards there being a small (in percentage terms) population of chronic offenders who are committing most of the serious crime that has inflated the crime statistics, frightened people off our streets and filled up the prisons since 1960. The sharp concentration of crime among a relatively small fraction of the population has been used to argue for selective detention and incapacitation, but here I note it simply as a fact about who breaks the law.

For more insight into who these chronically criminal people are, we turn to one of the leading contemporary studies, still under way and already invaluable to students of criminal behaviour. The Cambridge Study of Delinquent Development started in 1961-62 with a survey of 411 boys, ages eight to nine, living in working class neighborhoods in London within a one-mile radius of a research office that had been established for the study. The sample comprised all the boys of their age attending six local primary schools (399) plus, in order to make the group more representative cognitively, a dozen boys from a local school for the educationally subnormal. Eighty-eight percent of the boys were whites whose parents had been raised in Great Britain; 3 percent were blacks with at least one parent from the West Indies or Africa; the rest of the sample included a smattering of other ethnic and national backgrounds. Compared with the British population at this time, the sample was disproportionately working class, white and urban. A deluge of publications-by the original director, Donald West and his successor, David Farrington and their associates-continues to flow from this sample of youngsters as they have grown into adulthood. At this writing, the sample has been interviewed eight times, starting at the age of eight, most recently at thirty-two. It has been repeatedly tested psychologically. The families have been visited by social workers and interviewed. The boys' schoolteachers at several grade levels filled out questionnaires. Their classmates were asked for ratings of the boys-for their popularity, aggressiveness and other behavioral traits. Official police and court records for the boys and their families have been obtained, along with self-reports of criminal and non-criminal behaviour. Data were assembled on school performance, employment, sexual experiences and family life. The follow-up has been singularly effective. Every man from the original 411 was accounted for at the age of thirty-two. Eight had died; of the 403 still alive, almost 94 percent have been interviewed or have responded to questionnaires.

By the age of thirty-two, the sample had suffered 683 convictions of 153 of the men, for crimes more serious than petty violations of law. Although only 12 percent of the convictions were for violent offenses, a third of the men convicted for any crime had at least one conviction for a violent crime. Twenty-two of the men had 9 or more convictions. Almost one-half of the offenses ever committed by all 411 men were the work of this most chronically criminal 5 percent of the men. The serious offenders had started breaking the law early and often and were still at it in their early thirties. The signs of chronic adult criminal behaviour were already in evidence before the boys reached the age of ten. This, along with other information.

These men were almost five times as likely to have been rated as aggressive between the ages of eight and ten as to have been rated as non-aggressive. That ratio is plotted as the first of the three columns in this group. Those who would become adult chronic offenders were six times as large a proportion of those rated aggressive between the ages of twelve and fourteen as those rated non-aggressive. The ratio increased further, to seven to one, when they were between sixteen and eighteen. Chronic adult offenders, in other words, are disproportionately recruited from the population of children and teenagers who are aggressive early in life. The several other adult behaviors that were similarly foreshadowed by aggressiveness in childhood-whether they were ever (that is, by the age of thirty-two) convicted at all (first group of three columns), whether they had been unemployed for more than ten months (fourth group of columns) and whether they described themselves as heavy drinkers (fifth group) or as offenders (final group). Among these categories, childhood aggression is least predictive of not owning a home (third group of three columns); but even here, the predictiveness reaches statistical significance. Presumably home ownership measures, not only economic resources, but something about rootedness in the community. The men who do not develop this rootedness were disproportionately aggressive in childhood. We may take it as self-evident that the most deviant behaviour was the chronic offending of the most criminal 5 percent, which was best predicted by childhood aggression; the least deviant behaviour in the figure-the 52 percent who do not own their own homes-is least well predicted.

But, across the board, childhood aggression is predictive of adult antisocial or criminal behaviour. The generally rising heights of the columns say that the older the boy is, the more predictive his childhood aggressiveness was of his adult antisocial or asocial behaviour.

Aggression was not the only childhood behaviour that foreshadowed later criminality. At the fifty-seven men in the sample who, by the age of thirty-two, had at least one conviction for burglary. Because most habitual offenders commit a variety of crimes, the convicted burglars turn out to have been engaging in other crimes as well. The age of fourteen, these men had manifested various signs of antisocial or unconventional behaviour, such as sheer troublesomeness, thievery, bullying and so on.

The ratio in the figure is obtained by dividing into the proportion of burglars who engaged in the childhood activity the proportion of non-burglars who had. Thus, the ratio of over eight for sexual activity says that over eight times as many of those who were convicted of burglary by the age of thirty-two had been sexually active by the age of fourteen, compared with those who were not convicted.

The five childhood behaviors that are most strongly associated with becoming an adult burglar are sexual activity, disobedience, truancy, thievery and lying. Less predictive are childhood anger and bullying. But all of the plotted ratios in the significantly above one, indicating their association with adult burglary.

The Cambridge study leaves little doubt that adult criminal behaviour is part of a broader category of uncivil or antisocial behaviour that reaches back to childhood. A sample of over 200 American boys pushes the foreshadowing of such behaviour still earlier into childhood. These boys were recruited from two school districts in an unidentified small metropolitan area when they were between ten and sixteen years old, then followed up for five years. They were questioned about their behaviour, delinquent and otherwise. Their parents, peers, teachers and others who knew them were also interviewed.

The mothers were questioned about the boys prior to the first interviews. How hard had the boys been to raise? mothers were asked. Were they problem children; were the mothers ever worried about their sons' behaviour or adjustment and why? The answers provided various measures of psychological trouble reaching back into the boys' second year of life and afterwards. Mothers were also asked about their (and their spouses') parental styles. Besides the answers the mothers gave, the interviewers were trained to take note of the way the mothers and sons behaved with each other.

From official records and self-reports a picture could be drawn of the boys' delinquency, the seriousness of their offenses and the frequency of offenses up to the latest point in the survey, when they were between fifteen and twenty-one years old. The survey ranged widely enough to show whether, in addition to offending, the boys pursued "the delinquent lifestyle," as it has been called-use of alcohol and drugs, frequent fighting, or otherwise raising hell. The study does not give us a full picture of lifetime criminality, because it terminates so early in the boys' lives, but it shows the precursors of at least the beginnings of criminal behaviour in adolescence and early adulthood. Inasmuch as we know that almost all chronic adult offenders were in some kind of trouble by late adolescence, we can assume that the variables in this study foreshadow chronic criminality to some extent.

The boys who were hardest to raise between the ages of one and five started offending earlier than the boys who were easier to raise. They were likely to be arrested younger and they committed more and more serious, crime. Boys who were hard to raise when they were toddlers were more than four times as likely to be multiple offenders as boys who were easy to raise. Their thefts were of larger amounts; their aggressions were more severe; and the variety of their criminal offenses, more diverse. The boys who were identified as aggressive, hyperactive, impulsive and lacking in attention span when they were between ten and sixteen years old were more likely to have been problem children between one and five years old. Thus, troublesomeness in infancy unfolded into hyperactive aggressiveness and impulsiveness in childhood, thence into delinquency and crime in the teens.

The sequence is not rigid or unvarying, inasmuch as it often varies in one respect or another from boy to boy, but it is a prototypical pattern, observed with at least statistical regularity. in this particular study, not much effect on later delinquency could be traced to parental behaviour, although one has turned up in other studies. For example, in the Cambridge study, among the five major predictors of chronic offending that were available when the boys were not yet ten years old, one was parenting that was inconsistent, indifferent, or harsh, along with troublesome childhood behaviour, low tested intelligence, poor economic conditions and parents with criminal records.

Troublesome toddlerhood as a predictor of later delinquency was unearthed only in mothers' memories both in the Cambridge study and in the American study just described. It may therefore be suspect. After all, a mother with an uncontrollable adolescent son may simply be misremembering the boy's infancy as being more difficult than it actually was. This interpretation is refuted by yet another major and still ongoing, longitudinal study, involving over 1,000 boys and girls born in 1972 and 1973 in a small city in New Zealand, almost all of whom were of European ancestry. Several dozen physiological and psychological measures were obtained when the children were three years old, supplemented by data available from records back to their births. Ratings and objective assessments of the children for various kinds of psychological difficulty-from interviews and questionnaires administered to the children, to parents and to teachers-were repeatedly obtained until they were thirteen years old, at which point it was possible to state which children had developed a psychological disorder and which ones had not. The disorders have themselves been broken down further into antisocial disorders or "other" disorders (for example, anxiety, phobias, depression). The early precursors of these disorders can be extracted. In addition, the boys and girls have been asked for self-reports of their behaviour, including delinquent behaviour, at the age of fifteen. Police records are also available.

Boys were more than twice as likely to develop psychological difficulties as girls. But antisocial boys were four times as large a proportion of the boys as antisocial girls were of the girls, while being only 1.67 times as likely as girls to suffer from other disorders. The early predictors of antisocial disorders in later childhood were essentially the same for boys as for girls, except that boys were generally at greater psychological risk. At the age of three, the statistically significant precursors of antisocial disorder at the age of eleven included poor motor control, low scores on the Peabody Picture Vocabulary Test (a measure of general cognitive ability), hyperactivity and inattentiveness and being rated as "difficult to manage" At the age of five, the precursors included low IQ scores, problems with sleep and a high frequency of "bad" behaviour. The parents' ratings of their children at the age of three or five were among the best predictors of antisocial disorder at the age of eleven, but their ratings were echoed in the results of various objective indexes of behaviour.

Psychological disorders-both antisocial and otherwise-at the age of eleven were predicting both self-reported crimes and contacts with the police by the age of fifteen. For the children with two or more police contacts-the clear recidivists, in other words-antisocial disorder was by far more predictive than other disorders, or than no disorders at all. Most of the children identified as having antisocial disorders at eleven were not demonstrably delinquent at fifteen. However, most of the delinquents at age fifteen were identifiable from variables gathered in their preschool years. This is a recurrent pattern in the technical literature. Most individuals with the early precursors of criminal behaviour do not become serious offenders, but most (albeit not all) serious offenders have shown the precursors earlier in life. How shall we interpret this?

For one thing, the pattern suggests that we do not know all of the precursors. There may be signs in early life or in the individual's background that would, if we knew about them, make the predictions more accurate. It's not hard to believe that our knowledge is incomplete, but another explanation is also doubtless correct to some degree. To the extent that offending depends on events that arise later on in life, it is going to be unpredictable from early precursors. One study, for example, suggests that later offending is dependent to a degree on prior offending per se, as if the breaking of the law somehow disinhibits additional acts of crime. More obviously, circumstances not yet taking their toll on an individual-such as success or failure in school or at work-affect whether or not his or her predisposing traits will show up in criminal behaviour.

THE BIOLOGY OF CRIMINALITY

Some theorists criticize the search for the psychological characteristics of chronic offenders. Doing so, they imply, is like the wise men describing the elephant, each sedulously describing the trunk or the tail or the tusks or the ears, but all missing the beast. Instead, they suggest, we should be looking at the propensity for breaking the law, "criminality," as a trait in its own right.

Yet, there are good pragmatic reasons for teasing out the specific psychological correlates. For one thing, there are established ways for measuring them. Insofar as "criminality" differs from the behaviour of breaking the law, it is not obvious how to measure it. For another, we know something about the origins of intelligence, personality and temperament. The evidence for a substantial heritability for IQ is no longer seriously in doubt. Personality has likewise been shown to have significant genetic involvement, although probably less so than IQ. Inasmuch as criminal behaviour is associated with intelligence and personality and inasmuch as personality and intelligence have genetic influences on them, then it follows logically, as night follows day, that criminal behaviour has genetic ingredients.

However ironclad the logic, it is reassuring to have it confirmed by data. In some of the longitudinal studies we mentioned, the criminal behaviour (or other forms of antisocial behaviour) of parents is one of the primary risk factors for criminal behaviour in their children. It may seem that this is more readily explained environmentally than genetically, but it is also true for children who are raised in adoptive homes by foster parents who are not offenders. Adopted children resemble their natural parents in their offending more than they resemble their foster parents. The more serious an offender a biological parent is, the greater the risks of crime in his or her adopted-away child. The more serious the offending of the adopted offspring, the more likely it is that there is an offender among the natural parents.

The data on adopted children resonate with the data on twins. If one twin is an offender, his or her co-twin is at risk for being one, too. If the twins are identical, then the correlation between them is significantly larger than if they are fraternal. Since identical twins share all their genes, while fraternal twins share about one half, a difference between fraternals and identicals in the correlation is evidence for a genetic ingredient in offending. The evidence has frequently been disputed on the grounds that it is the greater similarity of environments for identical twins that makes them resemble each other in antisociality, rather than all the genes they share.

As a general argument against twin studies, this one has been largely refuted. The greater similarity among identical twins in personality and in intelligence is evidently caused primarily by their greater genetic overlap, not because they are treated similarly or share a family environment. One of the more unexpected discoveries of human behaviour genetics of the past decade has been that the family environment develops psychological differences among the children growing up in it, rather than resemblances. Identical twins, in other words, resemble each other psychologically so much, not because of the family environment, but in spite of it.

On the other hand, recent data seem to indicate that this general finding may need to be qualified for criminal activities specifically. Lawbreaking activities are somewhat contagious, as anyone who has witnessed the looting and vandalizing mobs in urban riots should realise. On a microscopic scale, something similar may go on within families. Siblings (including twins) influence each other's tendency to break the law. If one sibling uses illegal drugs or commits other crimes, the chance that the other one will as well depends on how close a relationship and on how many mutual friends the siblings have. One plausible (though not the only) interpretation is that siblings reinforce or inhibit each other's behavioral dispositions towards criminal behaviour, the more so the closer their relationship with each other.

Let us summarize by saying that the cognitive and personality dispositions towards antisocial behaviour may be less influenced by the family environment than the acting out of the behaviour itself. But this is not the same as saying that only the environment matters in determining behaviour, as distinguished from dispositions. In adoption data, blood relatives act criminally in similar ways even though they have not shared a family environment.

Some commentators argue that behaviour is too ephemeral to have genetic roots. This argument arises in a misunderstanding of how inheritance works, but perhaps such critics will be helped by the evidence of physical correlates of criminal behaviour. No one doubts that physical traits may have genetic influences on them.

It has been shown repeatedly that offender populations are moderately atypical in physique. They are more likely to be mesomorphic (*i.e.*, muscular, large-boned) and less likely to be ectomorphic (*i.e.*, tall, linear bodies) than the population at large. Even among childhood delinquents, who are disproportionately non-ectomorphic mesomorphs (*i.e.*, chunky, large-boned and muscular), the ones who go on to adult criminal behaviour are still more disproportionately non-ectomorphic mesomorphs. Why? One reason is that physique is correlated with personality and temperament and that non-ectomorphic mesomorphs are likely to have the traits associated with offending in higher frequency than the population at large. Another may be that children like this are generally more effective in acting out their frustrations and desires than delicately built children. Yet another may be the stereotypic expectations of people, based on their appearance. A strong-looking, large-boned youngster may simply look tougher to adults and his or her peers. He or she then learns to live up to the expectations and vice versa for a delicate-looking youngster. Many chunky people, of course, do not become criminals, but the elevation of the risk among them is easy to substantiate, if not to interpret.

A growing scientific literature is replete with other evidence of correlations between offending or antisocial behaviour and physical traits. I will run through a few of them, but note, first, that most of these correlations are weaker than the correlations with psychological traits. It has been shown that offenders have, on the average, lower heart rates than non-offenders and lower nervous system responsiveness to sudden stimuli. Their brain waves are more likely to have had atypical patterns in childhood. Neurological, biochemical and metabolic abnormalities, some of which may be caused by abuse, injury, or disease, rather than genes, turn up disproportionately in offenders who are especially brutal or violent. An expected correlation has not been clearly substantiated: although a good many studies show some weak association between male hormones and criminal behaviour or antisociality, many do not.

An association between criminal behaviour and hormones was expected because few variables correlate as strongly with criminal behaviour as sex, in our society and in every other one for which data are available. The changing woman's role in America has just barely narrowed the huge disproportion between male and female crime. The next section further discusses the sex difference in offending; it is noted here as yet another example of a physical variable that correlates with criminal behaviour.

FEMALES, MALES AND SUPERMALES

The disproportion in offending across the sexes varies with the crime, but it ranges from barely two to one for certain property offenses and vagrancy to well over fifty to one for overtly violent crimes. Men outnumber women in prisons by more than twenty to one and in jails by almost ten to one. As a rule, the more heinous the crime or more chronic the criminal, the greater the disproportion between males and females. The only major category of crime with an excess of female perpetrators is prostitution, which may say more about sexual behaviour and about a criminal justice system that considers the seller of a commodity more culpable than the buyer than it does about criminal tendencies. While some have argued that the disproportionate antisocial behaviour of males is a result of culture and learning pure and simple, by far the majority of experts grant that it has some genetic foundation. The sheer universality of the difference across time and place makes the purely cultural explanation implausible on its face. Yet, it has not been easy to pinpoint wherein the fundamental psychological differences reside, beyond noting that it is more likely to be in something that distinguishes the typical personalities of males and females than in their intelligence. The average female offender is more deviant psychologically than the average male offender, for a given level of criminal behaviour.

Whatever differentiating genetic factor makes men more likely to be antisocial than women, it must ultimately arise in the chromosome pair that determines genetic sex. This pair is called XX in women and XY in men, referring to what the chromosomes look like microscopically. If one Y chromosome increases the tendency towards offending, it seems plausible that two should increase it more. Thus, it is not surprising that the discovery of XYY males in the 1960s prompted talk of "supermales" who were supposedly prone to frighteningly violent criminal behaviour.

The picture of an XYY male conjured up in the popular media looked like Boris Karloff playing Frankenstein's monster. This was certainly overdrawn, but now the pendulum has swung too far back. It has become commonplace to deny any correlation at all between the XYY syndrome and criminal behaviour. In fact, there is a clear elevation of criminal behaviour among the tiny population of XYY males. But the crime is, as far as has been shown in aggregate studies, usually fairly ordinary, not excessively or preternaturally violent.

At the least the extra Y chromosome reduces IQ and thereby elevates the risk of criminality. However, studies of other species have shown that the level of aggression displayed by males can be traced to genes on the Y chromosome. it therefore remains possible that an extra Y chromosome does something to personality and temperament to increase the tendency to break the law, as well as to IQ. The practical significance of the XYY syndrome is negligible, since it is so rare (probably fewer than 1 per 1,000 men). The theoretical significance is not small.

Here is a genetic contributor to crime that is not hereditary, in the sense that it does not run in families; it pops up randomly across social classes and races, as far as is known. It increases the risk of criminal incarceration by a factor of about ten: the proportion of XYY male prisoners is about 1 per 100. The XYY syndrome is thus a natural experiment separating genetic from environmental factors and the results of this experiment show decisively that criminal behaviour can have genetic roots.

There is, in short, a scientific consensus that criminal and antisocial behaviour have genetic, as well as environmental, sources. The disagreements among experts concern the size of the genetic factor. Some say it is negligible; others, that it may account for as much as 50 percent or more of the variance in criminal behaviour. I will make no attempt to set a figure on the heritability of criminality or criminal behaviour. For the purposes of this essay, it is enough to show that individual traits play a significant role in criminal behaviour. For that proposition, it seems to me, there can be no doubt.

A Case History

The case of Arthur Shawcross, a serial killer currently serving a 250-year sentence, illustrates the power of criminogenic traits. Ordinarily, case histories are of limited value beyond describing the cases themselves. But when the individual's criminal history is as egregious as Shawcross's has been, then it could help identify the variables that have large effects on the kinds of criminal behaviour involved in the case. We have the benefit of detailed forensic/ psychiatric accounts of this frighteningly dangerous person.

Shawcross is in prison for murdering eleven adult females. The crimes were committed in and around Rochester, New York, in the late 1980s, where, in his early forties, he had been released on parole after having been in prison for fifteen years for the manslaughter of two children. He had been released early for the two manslaughters because he was considered a model prisoner.

Mutilated bodies of women started being found in the Rochester area within months of his release. When confronted by police, Shawcross confessed to the killings, blaming them on a hatred for his mother and on incestuous impulses towards a younger sister. He also blamed feelings of sexual inadequacy and uncontrollable rages. Shawcross told the interviewing psychiatrist that he had always felt so different from the rest of his family that he believed himself to have been a "doorstep baby," a foundling left to be raised by strangers.

For being a foundling, there is no substantiation. Shawcross was the eldest of four children born into a stable family, rooted in a small community in New York State named after his forebears (Shawcross Corners) and still populated by relatives. He was raised on land owned by his family, in a house built by his father. His father had stable employment throughout his working life; his three siblings suffer no known psychopathology or criminal-ity. There are no other known instances in his immediate family of criminal violence or mental illness. Nor is there any evidence that he was abused, neglected, or unloved in childhood.

Shawcross's mother is unable to account for her eldest child's bitter hostility towards her, describing him as having been a good and beautiful baby. Nor is she able to account for the behavioral troubles that started turning up when Shawcross was six years old. He began running away from home and cutting himself off from other children and his parents. When he was seven, he was referred to a mental health clinic for having threatened other children on a school bus with an iron pipe. Descriptions of Arthur at this time characterize him as hostile, untruthful, unreliable, unable to form an identification with either parent or to internalize moral standards. He was, however, also described as a well-dressed, neat and clean child, further testifying to the evident desire of his parents to take care of him.

He lost interest in school in the second grade; by fourth grade, he was failing to get promoted. He quit school by the ninth grade. Before he was ten, his mother recalls, he was stealing money from his teachers. Family members and acquaintances remember the teenage Arthur to be strange, moody, hostile, dishonest and dull. Out of school and on his own, he had trouble holding a job and was prone towards injuries at work. Each of his first three wives described him similarly angry, triggertempered, moody, taciturn and adrift in his own world. When he talked to his wives, it was frequently about his resentment of his mother and alienation from his father and about his sense of not belonging in his family. He occasionally noted that he even looked different from his relatives and one of his wives concurred.

He started getting into trouble with the law soon after leaving school, getting convicted for several burglaries and for arson in the space of a few years. An examining prison physician after one of the arson convictions cautioned about what he considered to be Shawcross's homicidal inclinations. Nevertheless, he was placed on probation for the burglaries and arsons, during which time Shawcross was arrested for killing an eight year old child. He eventually confessed to two child killings while he had been on probation, These crimes finally caused him to be imprisoned for an extended period.

What can we say about this person, described in an early parole report as a "psychosexual maniac," one "whose inner workings are probably completely beyond comprehension?" When he was released after serving fifteen years of his sentence for the child slayings, a local parole officer wrote, "At the risk of being dramatic, the writer considers this man to be possibly the most dangerous individual to have been released to this community in many years" A few weeks later, a woman complained to the parole office that Shawcross had robbed her and had made unwelcome sexual advances. Within seven months he started killing women.

Shawcross had none of the socioeconomic or home life disadvantages often blamed for criminal behaviour. His family was not poor and suffered no alcoholism; he is not a member of a minority group; he had the benefit of professional counseling early in life; and he probably had abundant whole-some role models. His personal history does contain several circumstantial factors that could, conceivably, have been involved in his descent into crime. Twice during adolescence, he sustained head injuries bad enough to leave permanent traces of a healed skull fracture and of scar tissue over his brain, but not bad enough to result in seizure disorders. The brain injuries are medically classified as "mild" In addition, he served thirteen months in a combat unit in Vietnam, which he characterized (without independent confirmation) to his wives as brutal and traumatic, involving not only killings but cannibalism. A recent medical assessment of him found no evidence of post-traumatic stress disorder nor of any identifiable psychosis. The primary criminogenic traits are evidently found elsewhere in the accounts of this case. Shawcross's full-scale IQ is 95; his verbal IQ, which is generally more predictive of crimi-nal behaviour, is 88. His personality is similarly inclined towards the criminogenic. Clinical evaluation characterizes him as quick to anger, intolerant of frustration, deficient in abstract thinking and as having an antisocial personality with "episodic acting out" and "a truly amazing failure to look at what (he is) doing"

He is a large man-six feet tall and 250 pounds-as is typical of the XYY syndrome that was first diagnosed at his latest arrest. This may account in part for his atypical appearance in his family, but it had evidently never been suspected until it came to light in his trial for the recent murders. The syndrome was dismissed in court as being of no relevance. It may be immaterial legally, but hardly to our understanding of his behaviour. The lower-than-average IQ, the distortions of personality and temperament and perhaps even the sense of not belonging to his biological family, are all more readily understood in the context of a chromosomal anomaly that may have a broad range of physical and psychological consequences.

In addition to the XYY syndrome, Shawcross has now been found to suffer from a possibly genetic metabolic disorder that is often associated with psychiatric, as well as physiological, symptoms. An elevated risk of episodic violence is one of the symptoms of this disease.

In summary, a lifelong tendency towards antisocial behaviour; alienation from his family and community; a verbal IQ well below average; brain trauma; an extra Y chromosome; a psychiatrically relevant metabolic disorder; and, according to his own account, harrowing experiences of brutality as a soldier in Vietnam constitute an extraordinary aggregation of circumstantial and risk factors for criminal behaviour. That the person who suffered from this incalculably improbable collection of risks developed into an offender of comparably incalculable dangerousness is less mystifying than the bald facts of his crimes suggest.

It has become almost a cliché to say that criminal dangerousness is, to all intents and purposes, virtually unpredictable. Most of the youngsters who show one or another of the statistical precursors of criminal behaviour do not, in fact, become criminals. Also, most of the people judged dangerous by the criminal justice system do not commit further violent crimes. But the cliché of unpredictability is wrong. Most of the people at risk for offending are only slightly at risk. They may, for example, have low verbal IQs, but not the antisocial personality traits that are associated with criminal behaviour; they may be non-ectomorphic mesomorphs with high IQs and shy, non-aggressive personalities. They may have the impulsiveness of the typical of fender, but not the cruelty nor the emotional detachment from friends and family. They may have been convicted for a crime, but have no other known risk factor for future offending. We need only assume that the likelihood of committing crimes rises in an orderly fashion with the number and intensity of the risk factors that a person has to make sense of the large number of "false alarms" in the literature on criminal dangerousness. As the risk factors move further out into the tail of the distribution of dangerousness, the risk of offending similarly rises. Arthur Shawcross is a living example of the princi-ple. His risks were extreme and when he succumbed to them, his crimes were extreme, too.

The Causes of Criminal Behaviour

Who commits crime? which I have attempted to answer in a limited way, at the individual level and in the probabilistic terms that the data provide. Age, sex, intelligence, personality and a history of previous criminal or antisocial behaviour are among the overlapping individual variables that affect the probability that a person will break the law.

Now let us to turn to a different question: What causes crime? I am asked this question in one form or another by non-specialists more often than the one I tried to answer, but it is too hard for me. My purpose in this final section is to make the case that the question is not only hard but ill-framed.

Criminal behaviour is behaviour. It is not necessary to prove that human behaviour is multiply determined, for it is obvious. Nothing we do, not even coughing or sneezing, has just one governing antecedent condition. The more complex the set of antecedent conditions, the less sense it makes to frame questions about behaviour in terms of causes. We will never be able to say what caused Arthur Shawcross to murder no fewer than thirteen people, let alone to have predicted in advance that he would do so; but we can say why he was more likely to have done so than almost anyone else.

And even with the benefit of all that science can tell us about the variables that predispose people towards crime, we may not be able to say whether someone at his high risk for criminal behaviour will murder one or two or ten people or content himself with assaults, batteries, muggings, arsons and rapes. Accidents, situations and social forces do, after all, take their toll. They modulate the criminogenic factors that have been reviewed here.

Let us assume that a behaviour occurs because there is an occasion for it and because it has some probability of earning a currently desired conse-quence. It also has a cost, both current and deferred. The consequence may be economic for example, money or goods in a burglary or more personal and idiosyncratic-for example, seeing a building go up in flames or wreaking revenge for old grievances, as in the case of Shawcross. The costs, too, have a calculus of their own. They comprise a mixture of the objective, risks of getting caught and the subjective penalties of conscience. The people who commit a lot of crime are, simply, people for whom the positive side of the ledger sufficiently outweighs the negative side and who have the opportunity for breaking the law. Their appetites for the fruits of crime may be very strong or their perceptions of the risk of getting caught and of feeling the sting of conscience, very small.

The risk factors that turn up at the intermediate level of analysis exemplify the personal and idiosyncratic elements in the conse quences and costs of criminal behaviour. They concern people's appetites for violence and cruelty, their capacity for internalizing abstract rules of conduct, their degree of presentorientation, their anger at society, their sexual impulses, their attitudes towards conventional morality. None of these things causes crime, for each can only operate in contexts that provide opportunities for getting the desired consequences and that minimize paying the costs of punishment. But then, the opportunities do not cause crime either. One cannot mug an elderly person on a dark street if dark streets contain no elderly persons, but we are not likely to say that muggings are caused by elderly persons venturing out of their homes at night.

If talking about causes of crime is misguided, so is talking about public policy in terms of causes (more familiarly, "root causes"). Just as the data push us to see criminal behaviour within the framework of risk factors, so they should push public policy. The evidence about individual precursors of criminal behaviour reach back, not only to childhood and infancy, but to parental traits as well. Within the constraints of due process and of a decent regard for individual freedom and privacy, society needs to consider taking heed of the evidence concerning criminogenic traits and of how these traits vary from person to person when it is seeking ways to solve the problem of crime.

PREPARATIONS FOR POSITIVISM IN CRIMINOLOGY

Long before Lombroso brought the attention of many scholars away from abstract considerations and fixed it upon the characteristics of the individual delinquent, Gall in 1825 wrote of criminals who are controlled-or rather upset-by passion and those who are driven blindly to their deeds by their innate instinctive nature. This suggests a consideration of criminals and consequently of their acts on the basis, not of mere abstractions, but of observations of psychologic nature. A little later (1836) two French students, Toulmouch and Diey, were probably the first to conceive of ignorance, poverty, passion and evil example on one hand and originally vicious nature on the other as determining conditions of criminal acts. Here we may say are psycho-social criteria or characteristics by which these men believed that criminals might be distinguished.

In 1840 Fregier distinguished thieves on the basis of their greater and less repugnance to the shedding of blood in connection with their thefts; a psychologic distinction. And contemporary with Lombroso's active life several others had taken steps away from abstract conceptions towards considerations of concrete conditions in the constitution of the criminal. Among these are Despine, Thomson, Nicholson and Maudsley. These works are indications of a trend that was very evident more than a half century ago. In these writings there is proof enough that the authors had a notion of classes of offenders who were incorrigible in every circumstance and unyielding to the treatment that the times had devised; because the basis of incorrigibility lay deep in the psychologic or psycho-physical constitution of the individual. Indeed in 1856, Rossi, an Italian criminologist, had stated a theory (or restated an older one) that in men there are strata of original nature corresponding at least to primitive racial society and to the higher level of civilization upon which the individual himself grew. There are, he thought, at least these two levels and possibly intermediate ones. This is a conception of elements in human nature that have been inherited by each of us from more or less remote ancestors who lived in the dawning ages of race history.

Rossi thought of the residuum from the ancients that has been referred to as something boiling and seething underneath and now and again bursting its bounds and mobilizing the energies even of the occasional criminal. In the habitual criminal this inherited nature has not only broken out, but the weight of more recent acquisitions is not sufficient to push it down again. All this is neighbour to the educational doctrine very recently in vogue, that the individual has gathered up in himself the history of the race and that this history is a powerful determinant of what the individual will do.

The foregoing are indications, some of them, of steps that were taken, even before Lombroso, towards making the criminal and his traits concrete: towards pulling them out of the realm of abstractions and doctrinal disputations-not that there was an end to disputations nor to doctrines.

Here are indications of the intellectual atmosphere of Lombroso's time that created the background for thinking intently of the biological basis of all human behaviour. And the times were changed, too, with Darwin and the doctrine of evolution and with Haeckel's law of recapitulation whereby the individual recapitulates the biological history of the race.

But there were probably in the early days of Lombroso even greater influences than these upon an eager young man of his profession and interests. Physiologists had set a tide towards mechanism in psychology. And for half a century before Lombroso's infancy and as long thereafter, the physiological literature of Europe was crowded with animated discussions of the mechanistic principle in animal and human behaviour. The theory of the specific energy of the nerves, first expressed by Charles Bell in 1811, was, in 1836, young enough to excite debate. Marshall Hall and the German Kuerschner, opposed by Volkmann and others were carrying on their scientific debates. A little later, in the decade of the 1830's, Goltz was conducting his arresting experiments on the spinal cord, chiefly of the frog, in an effort to determine between "soul" and mechanism. And Broca, in 1860, had discovered the cortical localization of the motor speech function in the cortex, which encouraged the hypothesis that functional cortical areas in detail would ultimately be found.

As early as 1842 Longet had shown that the coördination of muscular activity is provided by sensations of movement themselves. Apparently we in our times have little conception of the warmth respecting problems scientific that was excited in the course of Lombroso's earlier years among the followers of scientific research. And the pros and cons were still vigorously being kept to the fore in the years of Lombroso's prime when he was doing his greatest work and when Lewis in his "Physical Basis of Mind" in 1877 came out in support of Lotze's theory of 1853 of a qualified mechanism. It was a stirring period.

CESARE LOMBROSO: HIS CONTRIBUTION

Without this preparation of the times, Lombroso could hardly have written as vigorously as he did in support of his theory that there is a physical criminal type: that criminals can be distinguished by their facial and other bodily features. It was a bold conception and one that, measured at least by the indirect or incidental results, was abundantly worth fighting for. And because of it Lombroso will always justifiably have a great place in the history of Criminology and among the great pioneers in scientific research. He is one of a relatively few, the results of whose life work have proved that the promotion of a great idea may be of greater value than the complete proof of its validity.

Lombroso's conception of the criminal grew out of his physiological and anatomical studies. He was originally a physician by profession. In his earlier years he was, as we have shown, under the influence of the enthusiasm for those sciences like neurology, anatomy and physical anthropology that have their bases more particularly in biology. He first conceived of criminals as illustrating a physical type.

And he meant, at the outset of his career at least, that the criminal can be recognized by his physical conformation-as one recognizes a dog and distinguishes an Airedale from a Boston terrier. Not, however, that the distinction of a criminal, as Lombroso saw him, was so clear and unmistakable, but yet he regarded certain physical characteristics as symbols of the criminal character.

Much that he had to say suggests Rossi's "strata of original nature" The notion of criminal type, it is fair to say, is one of the abstractions that he invented. It has its physical or somatic aspect and its psychologic aspect also. In relation to the former, he was voluminous in describing but not so in measuring. It is to a consideration of the physical features of the "type" that we now turn our attention.

His very earliest glimpse of the great idea out of which his life work grew occurred in 1864 when he was a young army physician. He became interested in the tattoos upon the arms and chests of soldiers. Some of these were elaborate and others quite simple. Some were coarse and indecent while others were quite inoffensive. He observed that the indecent ones were upon the bodies of troublesome, dishonest soldiers who, by reason of their irregularities, were now and again before the military courts, whereas those of inoffensive character marked the steady-going, honest soldier.

This observation suggested a key to the situation. The pictures that the individual makes upon his own person are, willingly or unwillingly, an indication of his own nature. This was not a physico-anthropological, but a psychological conception. And it gave him the notion of a scientific psychiatry as well as criminology.

Statistics of 13,666 individuals of whom 4376 were honest, 6347 criminal and 2943 insane seemed to Lombroso a strong support for an association between criminality and tattooing. But tattoos were not only symbolic of inner nature as already suggested. They are indications of a great degree of physical insensibility. And he concluded that moral insensibility is a result of physical insensibility. It was in connection with his post-mortem examination of the brain of a brigand, as he says, that his eyes were opened to the meaning of the data of criminal physical anthropology that he later accumulated. He found in the brigand's brain an enormous occipital fossa and an hypertrophied vermis like that in lower vertebrates. At the sight of these anomalies, he saw, as on a wide plain, the solution of the problem of the criminal and his origin. In him are reproduced the characteristics of primitive man and of lower animals. The criminal is atavistic.

In the earlier years of his professional career, especially, Lombroso made much use of the word "atavism" and its derivatives in discussing the physical characteristics of criminals. The term suggests a reversion to a lower type of animal. Thus the low receding forehead is a reminder of our early Simian ancestors. Similarly the prognathous jaw. The criminal in certain respects has suffered an arrest of development. At certain points he has stopped low down on the animal scale. This, in Lombroso's opinion, makes it a very pertinent question-the one already quoted-whether one who possesses many of these stigmata can possibly have the "sentiments" of normally developed men.

He may reasonably be expected to retain in his make-up a considerable admixture of lower animal traits. This alone suggests a psychological consideration of the criminal to which we turn later. Indeed it is only a fight against the outer works to attack Lombroso's "physical type" and that alone. The essence of the thing is within. It is the lower animal nature, the complex of "sentiments" peculiar to lower orders of beings behind these outward signs, that is of real significance.

The dust and furor relating to the physical type is really on the question whether the criminal can be recognized by his physical appearance in advance of his committing an offence.Following upon his observation of the brigand's brain, Lombroso ran over a wide range of physical characteristics, picking up analogies between the criminal and lower animals.Among the characteristics that Lombroso considered most worthy of mention in this connection are the following: prognathism or prominent lower jaw; wooly hair; scant beard; oxycephaly (the cranium pointed at the crown); obliquely set eyes; prominent cheek bones; prominent supra-orbital arches or ridges immediately above the eyes; receding forehead; unusually large or small cranium; unusually long or narrow cranium; asymmetries of skull, face, or body, or of all three; high pointed palate; approximation as to physical form between the sexes; enormous ears. It will be observed that these are for the most part cranial, physiognomic and other somatic characteristics.

Some of them Lombroso regards as more significant than others. And when several are found together upon one person, the situation is particularly meaningful.Data such as the following are typical of the earlier Lombrosian archives. He is reporting upon his observations of 383 skulls of criminals:

- 58.2 per cent displayed prominent superciliary arches.
- 44.6 per cent showed evidence of anomalies in the development of wisdom teeth.
- 32.5 per cent of the skulls were of small capacity.
- 22 per cent included Wormian bones.
- 18.4 per cent had unusually simple sutures between skull plates.
- 16.6 per cent of occipital protuberances were unusually prominent.
- 13.2 per cent of occipital regions were flattened.

A union of many of the above named anomalies occurred in 43 per cent of the 383 skulls and a single anomaly occurred in but 21 per cent.

"Can such individuals," he asks "have normal sentiments?"

It is evident that tabulations of this nature leave much to be desired. There is no discussion of the single or multiple racial affiliation of the 383 criminals from whom these skulls came and there is no attempt here to compare with the non-criminal groups. The readers left to guess at the frequency with which the features indicated occur in other than criminal groups. Results such as these were obtained by Lombroso and his associates from observations and measurements upon several thousand criminals.

PATHOLOGY SUPPLEMENTS ATAVISM

Of course, it did not in all relations escape Lombroso and his friends that malformations (stigmata) of the sort we have mentioned are to be found in the non-criminal as well as in the criminal population. It was their contention, however, that they are not numerous outside the criminal class. For example

Ferri, the great Italian Sociologist of Lombroso's time, compared 711 soldiers with 699 prison inmates.

Only 10 per cent of the prisoners were without stigmata while they were lacking in 37 per cent of the soldiers. There were never more than three or four on the person of an individual soldier, while six or seven or more were found upon the prisoner. It was declared by Benedikt in 1885 that the stigmata occur more frequently in notorious criminal characters than in the rank and file. By "notorious criminals" he meant those who have suffered capital punishment.

But the alleged facts that some criminals do not possess these characteristics while some non-criminals do have them, embarrassed the Lombrosians also. In the earlier days of the doctrine, the answer to these points ran thus: "It often requires an expert eye to discover the stigmata in the criminal.

When they are found in honest men and women, we may be dealing with criminal natures who have not yet committed the overt act because the circumstances in which they have lived protected them against temptation"- which many consider a tacit admission that there may be factors outside the criminal himself that work together with others to produce the malicious deeds of the criminal though they may have no effect upon his original nature. These factors Lombroso thought of as revealing but not producing the criminal.

At the same time the difficulties of the Lombrosian doctrine in the face of the too numerous phenomena that refused to come under the hypothesis of atavism led its promoter to acknowledge the force of a pathological condition in the human organism as a partial determiner of criminal behaviour. But what is the condition? Lombroso identified it with epilepsy. The identification of the criminal nature with forms of epilepsy was suggested to him by his study of a young soldier who had served for several years in the army without having displayed any unfavorable behavioristic symptoms. He was subject to epileptic seizures of a mild order.

One day, without serious provocation, he attacked and killed eight of his comrades and thereafter during many hours he was in a deep stupor. On regaining consciousness he had no recollection of what he had done. There were no pronounced atavistic signs upon him. As a result of observations of this nature Lombroso amplified his views of the nature of the criminal so that they included the pathological condition.

SYSTEMATIC COMPARISON OF CRIMINALS AND NON-CRIMINALS

In 1889, when the conflict between Lombroso and his opponents had been vigorous during several years, he proposed that his antagonists themselves select a group of criminals and an equal group of honest men, make measurements of their physical features in as much detail as they would and compare the two groups on the basis of these measurements with a view to arriving at definite, incontrovertible conclusions on the question of a "physical type" of criminal. This was a very sensible suggestion.

It would have been even more appealing to the anthropologist and to the statistician of today had Lombroso proposed the selection of much larger groups than he did: only 100 in each. But those who were interested arrived at no agreement as to the manner of selection and the method of procedure once the groups were ready. Nothing came from the proposal at once.

Twelve years later, however, the same suggestion in its general features was made in England by a prison physician, Dr. Griffiths, who had heard the original proposal. Action on the proposal at last fell into the hands of Dr. Charles Goring-Physician of His Majesty's Prisons. The eminent statistician Dr. Karl Pearson and others coöperated. Twelve years later Dr. Goring published a monumental work that grew out of the proposal and that represented an amazing amount of labour at measuring, computing and comparing. This publication appeared eight years after Garofalo had made the statement that we quoted above. On the side of physical anthropology it is an effective answer to the claims of Lombroso and the adherents to his doctrine.

Of all adverse criticisms of the Lombrosian views relating to the "physical type," this one by Dr. Goring is the most trenchant. On the side of criminal (compared with non-criminal) physical anthropology (we must be understood as thinking only of somatic characteristics) this work appears to leave no room for further argument. Goring and his associates had spent twelve years making greatly detailed studies of 3,000 prisoners. All the prisoners were recidivists, or repeaters.

They, if any therefore, according to Lombroso's view, should reveal the physical type. These studies included measurements in almost infinite detail of certain physical features of the prisoners and he worked out correlations between figures obtained from measurements on one group of prisoners and corresponding figures obtained from each of several other groups. The classification of convicts for this purpose was on the basis of the crimes of which they had been convicted: thievery, burglary, forgery, desertion of family, incendiarism, murder and others.

There were no striking differences to be found between those of one group and those of another. Such as were discovered could be attributed to the manner of life of the criminals (on the whole the forgers and burglars had doubtless lived in very different environment prior to incarceration) and to a natural selection among those who follow different occupations in normal life.

His correlations and measurements related to the following features: circumference of skull; height of skull above the centre of the meatus; facial length and breadth; cephalic index; occipital projection; chin projection; length of the right ear and the left; distance between the eyes; inclination of the nose;

shape of nose; shape of palate; asymmetry of the face and skull; acuity of vision and hearing. He described the colour of hair, facial pallor, concurrence of eyebrows and tendency to tattooing of various body surfaces such as the arms and chest. The evidence for a criminal "physical type," as already pointed out, based on anthropometric data relating to the skull and face and based, too, upon certain descriptive data concerning facial and other features, is nothing. No such physical characteristics can be accepted as signs of the criminal or of any sub-group of criminals.

With this view Havelock Ellis is in agreement. He believes that nothing very definite can be said of the significance of cephalic indices, *e.g.*, excepting that they are exaggerations of the characteristics of the race to which the criminal belongs. In a racially mixed population, unlike that with which Goring was concerned, this observation has especial weight. "The Corsican criminal," says Ellis, "is often very dolichocephalic and the Breton criminal often very brachycephalic" And Perrier after having examined the skulls of 859 prisoners at Nîmes has drawn attention to their racial characteristics that vary considerably according to the provinces and other regions from which they came. They do not justify drawing any conclusions as to cephalic differences between criminals and non-criminals.

Furthermore, one needs hardly to be reminded that recession of the forehead in a group of Negro criminals will be greater than the occurrence of the corresponding feature in a group of Anglo-Saxon criminals. Prognathism will occur more often in a northern European prison than in such an institution in southern Europe. The occipital region is relatively more prominent than the frontal among Mediterranean peoples, whereas the reverse is true of the Anglo-Saxons.

SKULL CAPACITY

But let it be granted that all the indications referred to are negative. How does the case stand in respect to skull capacity? Dr. Goring's answer is brief. Comparing convicts with Cambridge students, the difference is 33.8 c.cm. (1431 c.cm.-1397.2 c.cm.), the convicts' skulls having the smaller capacity. This difference corresponds to 21/2 m.m. which is the excess of head length of the student group compared with that of the convicts. The difference in capacity referred to, Dr. Goring regards as insignificant when considered in relation to the total magnitudes.

No other investigators of this problem have made a clear case for differences in skull capacity between criminals and other groups.

PHYSIQUE

Dr. Goring took notice also of the physique of criminals as Lombroso had done: their height and weight; span of arms; general health (robust, good, delicate); physical constitution (stout and strong; stout and weak; thin and muscular; thin and weak). When corrections were made for age, there were no significant correlations whatever between physique and kind of crime committed. He did find, however, a slight relation between health and muscularity on one hand and on the other hand crimes of violence, fraud, arson and stealing. Those who have been convicted on charges of personal violence are on the whole more healthy and muscular than those who are convicted of fraud, arson and stealing. He made no discovery of a relation between any characteristic of physique on the one hand and recidivism or repetition of convictions on the other.

Comparing with non-criminal groups, Dr. Goring's comparisons of his physical measurements of prisoners with corresponding measurements of large groups from the non-criminal population serve to clinch his argument. In these last, he included students from Oxford University, Cambridge University, Aberdeen University, the University of London and the teaching staff of the University of London and non-commissioned officers and men of the Royal Engineers. No important differences were found. Indeed it was easier to point out physical differences between Oxford and Cambridge students than between either of these groups and any sub-group of criminals. It was easier to determine, on the basis of physical measurement, that one was a Scottish or an English student than to determine whether he was a thief or a murderer.

Certain differences in physique, however, he did observe between criminals and non-criminals. Those of the fraudulent group are inferior in height to the non-criminals: 66.55 inches to 67.3 inches. Other groups of prisoners were found to be markedly inferior in both stature and weight-and weight had been in no way affected by imprisonment.

Thus Dr. Goring has piled up a deal of data from physical measurement and the net result of it all is that his crow-section of the prisoners of England, Scotland and Wales differs from that of the non-criminal population only in respect to height and weight. Similar results have come from Germany, reported by Baer. Lombroso and others of the Positive School in Italy declared that Italian prisoners are taller and heavier than non-criminals. Between one group of criminals and another, furthermore, there are only insignificant physical differences except that murderers are taller, heavier and stronger than others.

CONTRIBUTIONS OF ACTUARIAL STATISTICS

At this point it is worth drawing attention to actuarial statistics. If the average height of 221,819 Americans examined by forty-three life insurance companies represents the typical American height, the Wisconsin convict at Waupun is 1.8 in. too short. He is 1.3 in. shorter than the Federal soldiers in the Civil War. He weighs but little less than the non-criminal American. Weighing records of prospective purchasers of life insurance include "some clothing," whereas prisoners were weighed "without clothing" But after due allowance has been made for this difference, there remain several pounds of flesh and blood by which the non-criminal excels the prisoner.

NEW ANGLE OF APPROACH

In this connection it must not be overlooked that our own day is witnessing a movement among many Italian and other students that may be interpreted as a reëxamination of the Lombrosian doctrine and even as a support for it from a new viewpoint. Several Italians particularly have begun endocrinological studies of delinquents. They discuss the chemical functions that go on in certain glands of internal secretion (manufacturers of hormones) which regulate bodily growth and psychologic development. These functions are conceived as explaining the physical type, the psychologic character and temperament of the individual and bring into relief the relationship between the physical and the moral aspects of human nature.

Thus the extreme development of hair upon the body that Lombroso listed among his "stigmata" is associated with hyperthyroidism. Likewise the overdevelopment of the cheek-bones and the jaw, arms, hands and feet and the heavy, thick skin to all of which Lombroso has frequently drawn attention, are functions of hyperthyroidism or of extreme activity of the pituitary body. Even further than this Vidoni, for instance, claims to have had some success in correlating endocrinological disturbances with certain types or forms of delinquency. The general emotional quality and therefore character, differs, depending upon the dominating glandular function. When the pituitary action prevails there is an inferiority feeling and deviations of the moral sense, with tendencies to robbery, assault and homicide.

Thus the morphological, neuropsychic and temperamental phases of the individual are outgrowths of hormonic activity and a wellbalanced individual is a result of hormonic equilibrium. One and the same physiological mechanism is therefore conceived as guaranteeing an integration of the individual. In this light even somatic characteristics, theoretically, become meaningful in respect to character and behaviour.

And while we are upon this point it is worth bearing in mind that recent studies, such as have been made by Franz Boas indicate that racial features undergo changes in a new environment in the course even of a generation or two. This he has shown by means of measurements, especially of the cranial proportions of groups of Italian and Slavic immigrants into the United States. The round head tends to become long and vice versa. Consequently nationality as well as race must be considered in any refined study of criminal anthropology. So even as to this point the question has become very complicated.

But there are other puzzling complications on a par with these and that are incidental to technique (or the lack of it) quite different from that of physical anthropology. The physical features of criminals as they are found in prisons, for instance, must be compared with those that occur in the non-criminal population, precisely as Goring has done so thoroughly. The comparison, however, is of necessity made between those who are in prison on the one hand and on the other those who are not known to be criminals or to have committed crime. Furthermore, comparisons must be made race with race; nationality with nationality; age with age; social level with social level and the groups compared must also be of even intelligence level.

One very embarrassing situation here is that far short of 100 per cent of criminals are apprehended. In Cleveland, Ohio, for instance, from 1917 to 1921, only 25 per cent of reported felonies were followed by arrest. Arrests were made in 6 per cent of the felonies reported to the police in Rochester in 1921, 10 per cent in 1920 and 19 per cent in 1919. The Cleveland and Rochester figures are a fair sample of what is to be found in other cities of the United States.

What the corresponding figures in Europe are now or what they were when Lombroso, his contemporaries and followers, were comparing the criminal and the non-criminal as to their physical features, we do not know. But Garofalo says: "The fact is well known that not the half of those guilty of established crimes are brought to justice" So one may be comparing criminals and non-criminals, with criminals, or criminals in custody with unapprehended criminals.

INSTITUTIONAL TREATMENT OF CRIMINALS

What can prevent the enormous misuse of energy and the pain and degradation that is crime? What can remedy the warped character of the criminal so that he will not again commit crime? These are questions that have puzzled men since laws began. Indeed, these same questions, essentially, have been to the fore since family life and any other sort of group life came into existence.

3

Theories of Crime

INTRODUCTION

The three views have clearly placed very different constructions around the phenomenon of crime. The view taken by the individual criminologist, together with his or her own background in sociology, psychology, and so on, will influence the way in which research evidence is gathered, data interpreted, and theories constructed. The following section briefly examines how the three views have been translated into theories of crime.

CLASSICAL AND POSITIVIST THEORIES

The consensus view of crime is linked to two schools of thought within criminology. The *classical* theorists hold central the concept of free will in explaining why a person commits a crime. When the opportunity for crime arises, the individual has a free choice between criminal and non-criminal behaviour. If the payoffs for the criminal act are greater than the retribution it will bring, so the probability of a crime increases. At its most basic this suggests that severe retribution will deter people from any criminal act. Indeed, this simple philosophy was one which guided the process of justice through to the mid-1700s and even into the early 1800s, when acts such as stealing or vagrancy were punishable by severe physical punishment such as flogging or even death.

The eighteenth-century Italian economist Cesare Beccaria was in accord with the general view of the time that humans are rational beings, able to choose and control their behaviour. Beccaria was also concerned that the punishment should fit the crime and so argued, with eventual success, that extreme measures are unnecessary and, indeed, may be counter-productive. There is more than a grain of truth in the saying that 'it is as well to be hung for a sheep as a lamb'. Around the turn of the eighteenth century, the British philosopher Jeremy Bentham similarly argued that a balance between profit and pain guided the free choice of a criminal act. Bentham formulated a number of rules by which to regulate the administration of punishment; with the justification for punishment always presented in terms of its preventing a greater evil than it creates.

Classical theory, as presented by Beccaria and Bentham, was the dominant force in Europe and America in the late eighteenth and nineteenth centuries, guiding both judicial philosophers and criminal justice system of the time. With the advent of positivist theories the classical school waned in popularity and influence throughout the twentieth centry. However, the 1970s and 1980s have seen a renewed interest in classical criminology. The *neo-classical* or *conservative* criminologists have emerged as a strong voice in contemporary theorizing. Fuelled by a general failure of positivist theories to discover the causes of crime and to develop effective strategies for controlling crime, some of the basic ideas associated with classical theories are beginning to return. The call for greater deterrence in the form of longer prison sentences, the return of the death penalty, and the notion of 'just deserts' for lawbreakers, has been heard increasingly over the past decade.

The *positivist* theorists, while sympathizing with the consensus view of crime, differ from classical theorists with respect to the role of free will in determining behaviour, including criminal behaviour. Positivist theories grew from the arguments, advanced from the mid-nineteenth century onwards, that influences outside the realm of free will are the most important in determining behaviour. As theories have advanced and fallen so these influences have ranged from biological factors such as genetic transmission, to psychological constructs such as personality, learning, and moral development. While from a more sociological perspective, there are *social structure* theories which emphasize concepts such as 'anomie', and 'strain' which result from class structure and poverty; and *social process* theories which focus on the effects of, for example, education, peer relationships, and the family. Positivist theories are generally seen as more liberal in orientation, with their suggestions that some form of helpful intervention—be it welfare at a social level or treatment at an individual level—is the optimum strategy for reducing crime.

Radical Criminology

While conflict views of crime encompass a range of opinions, it was those theorists who emphasized the Marxist position who advanced the framework for a new model within criminology. The new criminology promised by I.Taylor *et al.* quickly became more popularly known as radical criminology. It is incorrect to say that radical criminology represents a unified theory; rather since 1973 it has put forward a series of associated coherent statements which combine to form a body of knowledge and opinion. While radical criminology has its roots in the writings of Marx and Engels, it was theorists such as Willem Bonger who began to formulate a full Marxist critique of crime. In contrast to classical theories it is proposed that no act in itself is naturally immoral or criminal; definitions of crime are socially determined, reflecting current social values. This emphasis on social determination also runs counter to those positivist theories which incorporate genetic or other biologically based explanations of crime.

Within a radical framework, criminal law is designed to suit the purposes of the dominant ruling class, those within society who hold wealth and power. In a capitalist system, the unequal distribution of wealth means that those without finance have to resort to crime to enjoy the luxuries and advantages seen to be enjoyed by others. Crime therefore is in some instances a function of poverty.

The rich also commit crimes for the purpose of gaining further wealth and power. However, as the rich control the means of regulating crime, their legal sysem will discriminate against the poor. So while the poor, the proletariat, may commit the same number of crimes as the wealthy, the bourgeoisie, they are arrested and punished with much greater frequency. A number of modern writers have clarified, elaborated, and extended the position defined by Bonger and articulated by I.Taylor *et al.*

In terms of a solution for crime, radical criminology suggests that changes must occur at economic, political, and social levels. Specifically if progress from the present capitalist system to monopoly capitalism can be made, then redistribution of wealth can take place. It is argued that crime will then no longer be necessary; any crimes which do occur will be the result of individual psychopathology. T.Platt presents a blueprint for the formulation of alternatives to the present system of 'law and 'order' which follow a radical criminological approach. Radical criminology has been subjected to fierce criticism, with some carefully constructed commentaries and others with more than a touch of naivety.

Labelling Theory

The interactionist view of crime gave rise to a theory of criminology which relies on a mixture of social and semantic processes to explain deviance. In common with conflict theories, labelling theory suggests that the law is applied to the benefit of those who hold social and economic power. Thus disadvantaged groups within society, such as the lower socioeconomic classes and minority groups, are more likely to be prosecuted and to receive harsher penalties. An individual becomes a criminal when the people who hold power—judges, parents, police, teachers, etc. —decide to confer the label 'criminal'. As Becker notes: 'Deviant behaviour is behaviour that people so label'.

Here there is a clear contrast with a moral view: behaviour is not seen as 'right' or 'wrong', rather 'deviant behaviour' is a judgement by certain sections of society towards certain classes of behaviour. This argument does not, of course, apply only to criminal behaviour: the same reasoning has been used to explain the creation of groups variously labelled 'alcoholic', 'mentally ill', 'sexually deviant', and so on. While writers such as Gove have offered explanations within a labelling theory framework to account for the involvement of people in criminal acts, the main force of labelling theory has been to examine the consequences of labelling. Two consequences are emphasized—the creation of stigma and modification of self-image. The term *stigma* refers to the public attitude of condemnation of the deviant and the associated exclusion of the labelled individual from some parts of society.

The label 'criminal' is associated with undesirable traits and so, in the public eye, the criminal is a person to be avoided and treated with suspicion. Thus the criminal will find that he or she is barred from certain types of employment; the young offender may find that their school or their family is unwilling to offer a welcome; those with criminal records may attract an undue amount of attention from the police. The force of these social pressures can lead to the second major consequence of the label: the individual comes to believe society's judgement and so modifies his or her self-image to match the label. The prophecy becomes self-fulfiling: the individual becomes the person described by the label. As the label becomes a role for the labelled individual, so the role is reinforced so that the person's life changes to suit the role. More crimes are committed, the peer group changes to others playing the same role, the person's identity becomes that of a 'criminal' with all its associated values, attitudes, and beliefs. Lemart calls this process *deviance amplification*.

The irony of any attempt at intervention, either by punishment or treatment, is that it serves only to reinforce the individual's self-perception of him- or herself as a criminal. Like all other theories of crime, labelling theory has its critics. There are a range of objections from a failure to specify why some individuals set off on a path of crime, to a failure to acknowledge that some crimes such as murder and rape are universally judged as 'wrong'.

As Siegal points out, several criminologists who were at one time strong advocates of labelling theory have in the 1970s and 1980s shifted ground to favour more radical theories, principally the conflict theories. In summary, it can be seen that the three influential theories explain crime in very different ways. It is true that there is a degree of overlap between certain aspects of some theories, which has been examined by experimental methods but in the main the theories remain independent of each other. While these theories offer explanations for crime, they do not inform us as to the numbers of crimes committed.

Knowledge of the numbers of crimes committed is important both theoretically and practically: if crime is a low frequency behaviour then criminals may differ in some important way from those who do not perform such acts; if on the other hand it is a high frequency behaviour this may mean quite the reverse. The practical reasons are concerned with the allocation of finance to those establishments concerned with controlling crime: if there is a great deal of crime, and it is society's wish to control it, then the forces of law and order will demand a proportion of the public purse—the higher the frequency of crime, the greater the demand on the purse.

THE VICTIMS OF CRIME

- *Classes of Victims:* The public is always the victim injurious to the public. The public may be the victim of crime either directly, as in cases of treason or destruction of public property, or indirectly in the form of expense of maintaining an organization to deal with crimes and criminals or in the form of fear and worry that crimes will be committed. In this sense every individual is a victim of crime. In addition, some individuals are victims of crime in one or both of the following ways:
  - — by acts of aggression directed against them, as in murder, burglary, assault, or rape;
  - — by the ruthless or reckless pursuit by others of interests which are at variance with the interest of the victims, as the pedestrian who is injured by a reckless driver of an automobile, or the dependents of a man who wastes his income in gambling or drinking, or the relatives of a prostitute who by her career brings shame and loss of status to her family, or the children hired by an employer in violation of law for his profit but for the ultimate loss of the children.

  It is impossible to determine accurately the comparative numbers of victims of these two types, but there is no doubt that the number of victims in the second class is immensely larger than the number in the first class and that the total losses suffered by them are much greater than those suffered by victims of the first class. Not more than one-fifth of the persons committed to penal and reformatory institutions in 1910 were convicted of crimes of aggression. Since we are more apt to imprison the criminal who commits crimes of aggression than other criminals, it is probable that the crimes of aggression are much less than one-fifth of all crimes. It is probable, also, that the average crime of aggression involves no more victims than does the average crime of the non-aggressive type.
- *Classes of Losses:* The victims of crime may lose anything that has value. Life and money are perhaps basic values because they contribute to the satisfaction of so many wishes. But there are many other values that are frequently neglected in the consideration of the losses from crime. Of these one of the very important is status in the group and it is most apt to affect those who suffer from crimes other than murder and burglary. The victim of rape, the victim of assault, the relatives of the prostitute, the relatives of one who

commits murder frequently suffer loss in this respect. The victim is sometimes fully conscious of the loss he has suffered; frequently he is not especially aware of it. The child who is employed in violation of the child-labour law, for instance, may be quite willing that the law be violated, but he may suffer a loss greater than many a bank burglary announced in big head-lines in the newspapers.

- *The Victims of Homicides:* Homicide statistics, though a very inadequate method of measuring murder and manslaughter, show beyond any doubt that the groups which suffer the largest losses in this respect are negroes, males, adults and Italians.

  During the decade 1911-1920 the death rate of negroes by homicide in the registration area of the United States was almost seven times as high as for whites. For a few cities the homicide rate of negroes has been enormous, going in at least one year during the decade above 100 per 100,000 population in four out of the thirteen cities listed in the mortality statistics.

  This is almost one hundred times as high as the death rate by homicide for the entire population of some of the New England states. The colored males insured in the industrial department of the Metropolitan Life Insurance Company during the same decade had a homicide rate ten times as high as the white males and colored women had a rate seven times as high as white women. Officials of that company state

  "Homicide ranked next to pneumonia and tuberculosis as a cause of death among young adult colored males" The mortality reports of the registration area of the United States show a decided decrease in homicide rates of negroes during the decade, but this is probably due to changes in the composition of the registration area, for the statistics of the Metropolitan Life Insurance Company show no appreciable change during the decade. Males in the registration area have a homicide rate about three times as high as females; this varies somewhat from section to section and is very much higher for negro males than for white males. The rate for negro females is almost three times as high as for white males.

  For both sexes and races the ages of greatest frequency of death by homicide are from 25 to 30 years. The whites have a much higher rate for infants (under one year of age) than do the negroes, which means that a larger proportion of whites suffer infanticide.

  While it is probable that many foreign-born groups have an unusually high death rate from murder and manslaughter, it is clear that the Italians have a rate far higher than the native-born and most of the other foreign-born groups. The evidence on this is particularly clear in Massachusetts.

The victim and the offender generally belong to the same group, with reference to colour, nationality and age. In Washington, D.C., during the period 1915-1919, 87 negroes were murdered, of whom 80 were murdered by other negroes, 7 by whites. In Chicago in 1921-1922, 41 negroes were murdered, of whom 33 were murdered by other negroes. The Italian victims of homicide in Massachusetts meet death almost entirely at the hands of other Italians. In Chicago in 1921-1922, 71 Italians were murdered, of whom 67 were murdered by other Italians. The nativity of murderers in St. Louis coincided almost exactly with the nativity of their victims.

Many persons are murdered when resisting burglary or robbery; 36.2 per cent. of those murdered in Chicago in 1920 were of this type. There is little other detailed information regarding the victims of homicide, but there are some types that appear frequently: one of two men interested in the same woman is killed by the other; two companions after drinking engage in an argument which develops into a quarrel in which one is killed; two workmen quarrel over a trivial detail of their work and one is killed; wives are killed by husbands in quarrels over money matters or the attentions of other men. One of the significant things about the homicides resulting from quarrels between lovers or between husband and wife is police of Chicago reported 26 murders of this kind in 1920 and the offenders committed suicide in 11 of the cases.

- *Financial Loss Suffered by the Individual Victims of Crimes of Aggression:* There is no accurate enumeration of the financial losses by crimes of aggression, but some more or less questionable estimates of details may be presented. The police of Detroit, Baltimore, Boston and Washington reported that the losses by thefts in each city amounted to more than a million dollars in 1920; the police of Chicago reported a loss by theft of more than four million dollars in 1920; and the police of Philadelphia in 1921 reported seven million dollars stolen, of which five million was in automobiles alone. W. J. Burns has estimated that railroads, express companies and other transportation companies lose about $100,000,000 a year by theft.

  In 1920 the claims paid by thirty insurance companies for burglary were a little over ten million dollars and for embezzlement a little over five million. The Advertising Clubs of the World state that in 1922 the people of the United States lost about $600,000,000 by swindles. W. B.

  It is clear that the economic loss as estimated may be grossly exaggerated and it is quite probable that the recovery of stolen property is not taken into account. For instance, the police of

Philadelphia in 1921 recovered automobiles amounting to 94 per cent. of the loss reported; 74 per cent. of the loss reported in all larcenies was recovered. Of the amount reported as stolen in 1920 in Chicago about one-third was recovered and in Rochester, New York, the stolen property recovered during 1916-1921 amounted to thirty per cent. of the loss reported. In general the theft of automobiles does not result in much loss, if the reports of police departments can be trusted, for they generally show that from 85 to 90 per cent. of the automobiles reported as stolen are recovered.

The direct loss suffered by the average victim of larceny seems to be small. The average loss per theft in Rochester (excluding automobile thefts) in 1916-1921 was $94 and of the total loss reported approximately one-third was recovered by the police. The average loss reported per theft in 1920 was $79 in Rochester, $63 in Detroit and $94 in Toronto.

- *Financial Loss to the Public:* Aside from the direct loss to the public due to the destruction of public property, forgery of government bonds and similar crimes, there is huge financial loss due to the fact that the public must pay the bill for whatever policy is used in dealing with the criminal. In general the expense may be listed as the original investment in lands, buildings and equipment, the current expenditures and the loss of the productive power of persons, lands and buildings. The lands and buildings include all the prisons, reformatories, penitentiaries, jails, workhouses and houses of detention and a large part of the lands and buildings for courts, probation and parole officers, state boards of correction, investigating committees, police departments, sheriffs and a smaller part of the space used for legislative bodies and executive officials and for fire departments and street-lighting systems. The current expenditures include salaries and some pensions for the entire list of police, sheriffs, marshals, factory inspectors, fish and game wardens, mine inspectors, bank inspectors, prison officials, probation and parole officers and a part of the salaries of mayors, governors, legislators, officers and clerks in state boards of corrections and investigating committees in this field. This expense is a rough measure of the loss of productive power of these men and these lands, buildings, etc., which if used for the purpose of dealing with crime or criminals cannot be used for other purposes. This enumeration should include, also, lawyers, judges, employees of insurance companies and similar persons and organizations concerned with the problem of crime.
- *Other Losses:* In addition to these direct losses mustbe included the social expenditures, whether public or private, for the maintenance

of the dependents of those held in penal institutions or of those injured by the crimes of others. It should include the indirect financial cost to private individuals in insurance against burglary, the cost of preventing crimes by safes, burglary-alarms, watchmen, guards and detectives and the expenses of prosecution. It is impossible to determine these items in detail, but they may be illustrated by the fact that the premiums for burglary insurance in nineteen principal insurance companies in 1919 amounted to $13,500,000. The non-economic losses to private individuals directly connected with the crimes committed have not been sufficiently investigated to justify anything more than the statement previously made. But it is evident that there is a great fear-and-worry loss from crime. There is probably no one who does nor suffer somewhat in this way. A great many people, perhaps women especially, are terrorized. Sometimes an entire community is terrorized by a series of robberies or burglaries.

- *Estimates of the Total Financial Cost of Crime:* It is quite apparent that many of the items considered cannot be reduced to dollars, but various efforts have been made to estimate the total financial loss. In 1900 Smith estimated the total cost of crime in the United States at $600,000,000 a year. Weir later fixed it at $1,370,000,000, Lydston at $5,000,000,000, Bushnell at $6,000,000,000 and the Institute of Economics at $5,000,000,000. Little dependence can be placed on any of these, but it seems probable, in view of the large number of items to be included and the immense losses of certain kinds that are known, that the highest of these is not too high. When we consider that the estimate of the direct cost of education is about one billion dollars a year, it is evident that crime is one of the big financial burdens on modern civilization.
- *The Value of Crime:* It is urged by some people that crime makes certain contributions that offset this loss to some extent. The contributions suggested are, first, notification of a maladjsutment and, second, increased, solidarity of the group. Just as pain is a notification to an organism of a maladjustment, so, it is asserted, crime is a notification that something is wrong and that modifications should be made. It is possible that without such opposition as comes from criminals our system might continue to perpetuate evils that can be eliminated by reason of attention attracted by crime.

  In addition, it is said that a group is held together by individuals who perform variant acts, just as the solidarity of a group is increased by enemies outside the group, as in war.

  Opposition in some cases, at least, welds the group together, whether the opposition be inside or outside the group. Opposition gives an opportunity for work for the group and for self-expression and enhances the feeling of self-esteem. In offering an opportunity for a group to take an organized attitude against something, crime has made a contribution which might conceivably be as large as or larger than the economic losses due to it.

But there are three respects in which this contribution of crime is not pure gain.

— Crime also decreases the solidarity of the group. The proposition may be considered specifically with reference to a small group, such as a college fraternity. Suppose a member of the fraternity begins to steal money belonging to other members. Every member becomes suspicious of the other members. It may be that several members stand together in the belief that a particular member is guilty; but several others are convinced that the suspected person is innocent and they, in turn, suspect someone else. The result is that the group is divided, suspicious and weakened. The same seems to be true of the larger groups. So far as solidarity does result, it is solidarity of one part against another part and this means internal division, dissension and discord.

— A very small part of the crimes contribute practically all of the increase in solidarity. Such violations as those against traffic regulations, park regulations, liquor laws, gambling laws, revenue laws, factory laws, child-labour laws, quarantine laws and compulsory school laws do not seem to arouse emotions or weld the group together. The victims of violations of such laws are apt to lose respect for the group which permits its leaders and other representatives to commit such crimes. Especially the violations of laws by persons sworn to enforce the laws make a distinct contribution to this destruction of solidarity. It is only the crimes such as murder and burglary that arouse the emotion of the group and produce the solidarity.

— The solidarity which is produced is rather impotent, especially in dealing with the problem of crime. The group opposition against those who commit crimes which are regarded as heinous drives those criminals from the society, makes outlaws of them, forces them into association with each other and thus makes a conflict group of them. This makes crime an organized business and prevents the reformation of the criminal. Consequently the increased solidarity is impotent to eliminate crime. Crime, in this respect, is like war in that it produces certain values that can be produced better in other ways. The elimination of crimes requires

> something else than this emotionally activated solidarity. An attitude of understanding, scientific approach and assistance, rather than an attitude of emotional opposition, is necessary. The juvenile court and the public schools are the best illustrations of the scientific approach to such problems. Because of the increased facility of communication, group solidarity is being developed without resorting to the internal enmity which crime has fostered. Opposition, self-expression, enhanced feeling of selfesteem can be attached to other objects than the criminal, such as poverty, bad housing conditions, unsanitary drainage systems, germs, lack of recreational facilities and a host of other things. There are plenty of objects in which a group can become interested in such ways as to produce solidarity.

DEFINITIONS OF CRIME

The following section examines the three major approaches to defining crime. This is not to say that these are the only approaches, or even the best approaches; rather that they are the most widespread. New ways of viewing crime are continually being developed, such as the critiques presented from a feminist perspective. However, for the present purpose the three main approaches will suffice. *The consensus view* The consensus approach to defining crime stems from the functionalist school within sociology. The basic tenet of this school of thought is that society functions as an integrated structure, its stability depending upon agreement, or consensus, among its members about the norms, rules, and values which are to be uniformly respected. Thus, a society's legal system is a reflection of the consensus of what, within that particular society, will and will not be tolerated as acceptable conduct. A crime is therefore a violation of the criminal law, an act which meets with the disapproval of the majority.

A definition of crime following this tradition would be of the style exemplified by Williams: 'A crime is an act that is capable of being followed by criminal proceedings, having one of the types of outcome known to follow these proceedings'. This definition clearly has a number of important consequences. First and foremost an act has to be committed before a crime can be said to have occurred; thought without some action is not a crime. Further, the act must be legally forbidden; 'antisocial' behaviour in itself is not a crime unless specifically and explicitly prohibited by law. In keeping with this, in the majority of instances the individual must also have had criminal intent in committing the act, the exception being crimes of *strictliability* such as health and safety regulations. An interesting discrepancy arises here between what might seem *morally* wrong, as opposed to 'wrong' in the legal sense. Racism and sexism, for example, may raise great moral issues, but are not well established in criminal law.

This is not to preclude the possibility that they might: criminal law has to have the flexibility to accommodate shifting societal values. Sutherland and Cressey illustrate this latter point, noting that at various times in the past activities such as printing a book, having gold in one's house, or driving with reins have all been criminal acts. More recently abortion, suicide, and consenting homosexual behaviour in adults over the age of 21 years have all been removed from the criminal law domain. The reverse can also happen: acts once not punishable by law are turned into crimes. In the USA it was perfectly legal to own and sell marijuana until the federal law was amended in 1937. In this country changes have been made regarding the sale of solvents to certain age groups, criminalizing a once legal activity— within, of course, the specific boundaries of the law itself. In other instances, technological advances are at present proving challenges to the law-makers: video piracy and computer fraud are contemporary acts which criminal law is having to address. While there are those acts which may pass in and out of criminal law, and can be thought of as 'statutory' crimes, there are other acts which are almost universally deemed 'wrong' or 'bad in themselves'.

Such acts would include those which inflict harm on another's person, for example murder, assault, and rape; or would inflict harm on the other person's property, for example burglary, malicious damage, and trespass. Thus the function of criminal law is to ensure the maintenance of these agreed aims of society, that is to protect the individual's person and property. However, as N.Walker points out, criminal law adopts a wider brief in seeking to achieve this aim. Laws also exist for the defence of the Realm, and to prevent public acts which might shock, corrupt, or deprave. It can be seen that such laws can be comfortably accommodated within a consensus framework: they act to preserve the stable society within which the individual lives and his or her possessions exist. An important part of criminal law is the delivery of retribution to those who transgress the commonly agreed boundaries of acceptable conduct.

The concept of punishment is not a simple one, raising many practical, legal, and ethical issues. For example, most people would agree that not all crimes merit the same punishment. Some system is needed which can differ between crimes of varying severity and magnitude. The tradition in this country is to distinguish between serious offences, sometimes referred to as *indictable* or *notifiable* offences, such as theft, fraud, and violence against the person; and less serious, or *non-indictable* or *summary,* offences such as minor traffic offences and petty damage to property. This dichotomy of serious and non-serious offences can be broken down still further: for example Siegal summarizes findings from the American National Survey of Crime Severity of public perceptions of crime seriousness. In this survey the five most serious crimes, as nominated by a sample from the American public, were all crimes of violence against the person. The most serious of all was: 'Planting a bomb in a public building. The bomb explodes and twenty people are killed.' The crimes judged least serious were being drunk in public, trespass, and least serious of all the 204 crimes in the survey was a 'youngster under sixteen years plays hooky from school'. If criminal law reflects the consensual views of society, then the punishments it delivers must also reflect the consensual view of the seriousness of different types of crime.

CRIME

Crime is the breach of rules or laws for which some governing authority can ultimately prescribe a conviction. Individual human societies may each define crime and crimes differently. While every crime violates the law, not every violation of the law counts as a crime; for example: breaches of contract and of other civil law may rank as "offences" or as "infractions". Modern societies generally regard crimes as offences against the public or the state, distinguished from torts. When informal relationships and sanctions prove insufficient to establish and maintain a desired social order, a government or a state may impose more formalized or stricter systems of social control.

With institutional and legal machinery at their disposal, agents of the State can compel populations to conform to codes, and can opt to punish or attempt to reform those who do not conform. Authorities employ various mechanisms to regulate certain behaviours in general. Governing or administering agencies may for example codify rules into laws, police citizens and visitors to ensure that they comply with those laws, and implement other policies and practices which legislators or administrators have prescribed with the aim of discouraging or preventing crime. In addition, authorities provide remedies and sanctions, and collectively these constitute a criminal justice system. Legal sanctions vary widely in their severity, they may include incarceration of temporary character aimed at reforming the convict. Some jurisdictions have penal codes written to inflict permanent harsh punishments: legal mutilation, capital punishment or life without parole. The sociologist Richard Quinney has written about the relationship between society and crime. When Quinney states "crime is a social phenomenon" he envisages both how individuals conceive crime and how populations perceive it, based on socictal norms.

The label of "crime" and the accompanying social stigma normally confine their scope to those activities seen as injurious to the general population or to the State, including some that cause serious loss or damage to individuals. Those who apply the labels of "crime" or "criminal" intend to assert the hegemony of a dominant population, or to reflect a consensus of condemnation for the identified behaviour and to justify any punishments prescribed by the State. Usually a natural person perpetrates a crime, but legal persons may also commit crimes.

The Conflict View

The conflict view of crime stands directly opposed to the consensus view. It argues that rather than functioning as an integrated unit, society is best seen as a collection of competing diverse groups—professional bodies, unions, students, industrialists, and so on. These groups are in conflict with each other on a range of fronts as, given the unequal distribution of wealth and power within society, some are poor and dissatisfied while others are wealthy and powerful. This inequality in the distribution of power creates a social atmosphere based on conflict, which in turn, it is argued, promotes crime. The conflict view of crime grew in both popularity and sophistication in the late 1960s and early 1970s. It is most closely associated with the writings of criminologists such as Turk, Quinney, and Chambliss and Seidman; although the contribution of earlier writers such as Vold and Dahrendorf should not be neglected.

The conflict view of crime developed into a distinct branch of criminology with the introduction of Marxist theory, a merger generally credited to the book *The New Criminology* by I.Taylor, Walton, and Young. Specifically Marxist or new criminology views crime as a function of a capitalist system which produces those who have wealth and power and those who do not. While each group, or class, within society commits crimes, the type of crime is dictated by the system: the poor commit crimes within their scope, such as theft, murder, and burglary; the middle class commit typical 'white-collar' crimes such as tax evasion and theft from employers; while the wealthy and powerful upper class indulge in activities such as exploitation, profiteering, and environmental pollution and damage—acts which are not accorded the status of crime. As theories based on conflict are clearly political and economic in orientation, the function of the criminal justice system is viewed in very much the same terms.

Criminal laws exist for the express purpose of protecting the rich and powerful from the remainder of the population. In Marxist terms, the 'justice' system exists to preserve capitalist interests —that is the interests of the capitalist bourgeoisie—ensuring power remains with the wealthy and not the proletariat. Thus inequalities in sentencing can be used to support the position of conflict theories. Laws which exact harsher penalties for offences against property rather than against people, and cases in which the poor are imprisoned for minor offences while the rich receive lesser sentences for more serious crimes, appear to offer evidence for a conflict view of crime. Conflict theories have attracted a great deal of criticism. Klockars has pointed specifically to a number of gaps and flaws in Marxist theories: for example the neglect of individual differences—why do not all people within a capitalist system commit crimes? It should be noted that Marxists have responded to these criticisms and are seeking to refine their theories of criminology.

The Interactionist View

While the consensus and conflict view of crime stand directly opposed, the interactionist view falls between these two camps. With its beginnings in a school of thought within sociology known as *symbolic interactionism*, this view of crime rests on a number of critical assumptions. The first of these assumptions is that each individual's behaviour is guided by their interpretation of reality and the meaning which events hold for them. The second assumption has its focus on the learning of meaning, a process seen as resulting from the way in which other people react, either positively or negatively, towards any given individual or situation. Finally, the third assumption holds that the evaluation of one's own behaviour is made just as to the meanings learned and acquired from other people. In focusing so sharply on meaning, the interactionist view of crime moves away from the moral stance of 'right' and 'wrong' central to the consensus view. Thus, while taking the life of another person is a criminal act, this does not *always* have to be the case: self-defence, in battle during war, and state execution are examples of 'legitimate' killing. The decision as to when an act becomes a crime is not a matter of consensus, rather a statement of the preferences of those who hold social power and are able to impose their preferred definition on society. However, unlike the conflict views of crime, the interactionist view does not suggest that economic and political considerations are the driving motivations for those in power. Becker used the term 'moral entrepreneurs' to describe those individuals who advance to positions in society which allow them to influence the rule making process. Thus the interactionist view is concerned with the way in which changing moral standards—not therefore seen as fixed or absolute—relate to changes in legal standards. Interactionist views were at their most influential in the 1960s but have rather declined in popularity since then within the criminological community. Some of those who held interactionist views have moved to a conflict position while others shifted to a consensus view: it is probably true to say that in the 1980s the conservative consensus view is once again gaining the ascendancy.

MORAL DEVELOPMENT AND CRIME

The process of socialization is linked with moral development in the theories of both Piaget and Kohlberg. There are various accounts of Piaget's theories on moral development and Aronfreed compares the views of Piaget and Kohlberg. However, Kohlberg has used his theory to develop an explanation for offending and therefore this particular theory is of interest here. Kohlberg, like Piaget, argues that moral reasoning develops in a sequential manner as the individual attains maturity. Kohlberg describes three levels of moral development, with two stages at each level.

At the lower stages moral reasoning is concrete in orientation, becoming more abstract at the higher stages and involving concepts such as 'justice', 'rights', and 'principles'. Offending, Kohlberg argues, is associated with a delay in the development of moral reasoning so that given the opportunity for offending the individual does not have the internal mechanisms to control and resist the temptation. A number of recent reviews have both elaborated this basic premise and discussed the empirical evidence. The main body of experimental evidence compares the moral judgements of delinquents and non-delinquents. The results are mixed with some studies finding that young offenders use less mature reasoning than non-offenders; others failing to show any distinction between the two groups.

There are two procedural explanations for these varied results: the first is the failure to control for behavioural and personality correlates of moral development; the second is the possibility of variations just as to the type of offence within the offender population. Indeed, Thornton and Reid reported that convicted criminals who had offended for no financial gain showed more mature moral judgement than those who offended for money. Thus, as Jurkovic notes: 'Not only do they vary from one another in stage of moral judgement, but they also fluctuate in their own reasoning level on different moral problems'. As both Ross and Fabiano and Arbuthnot and Gordon point out, the concept of moral development is not a simple one and a number of important distinctions require clarification within the overall framework. While research has focused on the *content* of the offender's moral code, that is the offender's beliefs and attitudes, this contextual aspect can be contrasted with the *process* of moral reasoning. It is an assumption that process is related to content: while delayed development may be the cause of an antisocial moral code, it is also possible that as Ross and Fabiano suggest: 'One can argue eloquently and convincingly about social/moral issues yet have a personal set of values which are entirely self-serving, hedonistic or anti-social'.

Further, the assumption of a relationship between moral reasoning, moral values, and behaviour must also be queried: several well-known experiments have shown that people will behave in ways which they believe or know to be wrong. In summary, there are a number of doubts about the general applicability of moral development theory to crime. A direct causal link between moral functioning and criminal behavour remains to be established.

Further, tests of moral development which assess answers to hypothetical moral and social issues have also been criticized as having little relevance to the type of thinking an offender engages in when deciding whether to commit a crime. Indeed, studies of thinking prior to offending show that the criminal is not concerned with moral issues, but rather with the likelihood of being successful. Cognitive, social, and moral development are the subjects of much recent research and it may be that these advances will be applied to delinquent populations in the future to respond to some of the doubts expressed.

Eysenck's Theory of Crime

Eysenck's theory, which is also a control theory, incorporates biological, social, and individual factors. The basis of the theory is that through genetic endowment some individuals are born with cortical and autonomic nervous systems which affect their ability to learn from, or more properly to *condition* to, environmental stimuli. An individual's behaviour, influenced by both biological and social factors, defines that person's *personality*. H.J.Eysenck defined two dimensions of personality, *extroversion* (E) and *neuroticism* (N); later work described a third dimension, *psychoticism* (P). Each of these dimensions is conceived as a continuum with most people falling in the middle range and, it follows, with comparatively few people at the extremes of each scale. Extraversion runs from high to low; similarly neuroticism runs from high to low; as also does psychoticism. The extravert is considered as cortically *under*aroused and therefore is continually seeking stimulation to maintain cortical arousal at an optimal level: thus the extravert is impulsive and seeks excitement.

The introvert is cortically *over*aroused and therefore tries to avoid stimulation to keep arousal levels down to a comfortable, optimal level: introverts are therefore characterized by a quiet, reserved demeanour. In terms of conditioning, that is learning by Pavlovian conditioning or association rather than operant conditioning the theory maintains that extraverts condition less efficiently than introverts. Neuroticism, sometimes called emotionality, is argued to be related to the functioning of the autonomic nervous system. Individuals at the high extreme of this continuum are characterized by a very labile ANS, which causes strong reactions to any unpleasant or painful stimuli: High N individuals display moody, anxious behaviour. Low N individuals have a very stable ANS and so display calm, eventempered behaviour even when under stress.

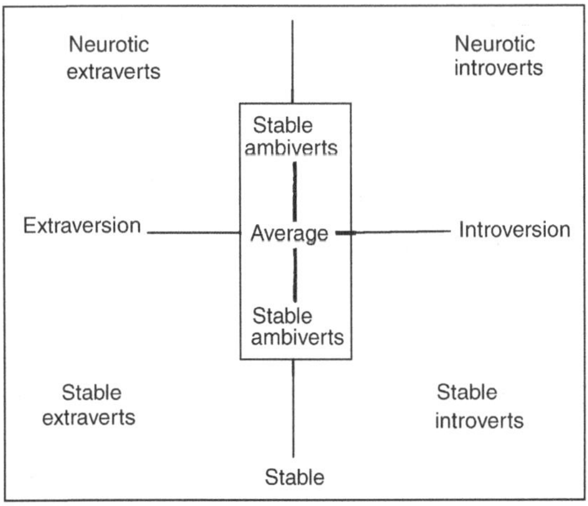

Fig. Eysenck's Personality Dimensions of Extraversion and Neuroticism.

As with E, N is also linked with conditionability: High N leads to poor conditioning because of the vitiating effects of anxiety; Low N leads to efficient conditioning. As assessed by standard psychometric tests, each individual scores on both E and N; therefore their position on these two dimensions of personality can be plotted as shown in Figure. As conditionability is related to levels of E and N it is further suggested that stable introverts will condition best; stable extraverts and neurotic introverts will be at some mid-point; while neurotic extraverts will condition least well.

The third personality dimension, psychoticism is not so well formulated as E and N: while maintaining a genetic basis for P, its biological basis has not been described in detail. Indeed, various descriptions of P have been offered: initially intended to distinguish the personality underlying psychosis, as opposed to neurosis, the suggestion was later made that P might better denote psychopathy than psychoticism. The P scale assesses attributes such as a preference for solitude, a lack of feeling for others, sensation-seeking, toughmindedness, and aggression. Although recently revised, there is still some doubt about what exactly the P scale is measuring.

The relationship between personality and crime has been described and refined by H.J.Eysenck, and recent summaries are available. The principal assumption is that children learn to control antisocial behaviour through the development of a 'conscience': this conscience, Eysenck maintains, is a set of conditioned emotional responses to environmental events associated with the antisocial behaviour. For example the child who misbehaves incurs parental wrath; the fear and pain this brings is associated with the antisocial act, and through this conditioning process the child becomes socialized. The speed and efficiency of social conditioning will mainly depend upon the individual's personality in terms of E and N. As the High E-High N combination leads to poor conditionablity then such individuals will be least likely to learn social control and therefore, it is predicted, will be over-represented in offender populations. Conversely Low E-Low N would lead to effective socialization, so that these individuals would be predicted to be under-represented in offender groups.

The remaining two combinations, High E-Low N and Low EHigh N, fall at some intermediate level and so would be expected in both offender and non-offender groups. The third personality dimension, P, is also argued to be strongly related to offending, particularly with crimes which involve hostility towards other people. H.J.Eysenck suggests that 'In general terms, we would expect persons with strong antisocial inclinations to have high P, high E, and high N scores'. It is important to note the use of the term *antisocial*: as H.J.Eysenck is at pains to point out, not all crimes are antisocial in the general sense of that term. There are politically motivated crimes, impulsive crimes, crimes committed by the intellectually disadvantaged, and so on. In other words, some allowance has to be made for the heterogeneity of the offender population. Eysenck's theory of crime has generated a great deal of empirical research and there are several reviews of the findings up to 1980.

The broad position is that there is unanimous support for the contention that offenders will score highly on P, and the majority of studies show that offender samples score highly on N. The evidence is mixed for E: some studies reported high E scores as predicted in offender samples, others found no difference between offender and non-offender samples, and a small number of studies reported *lower* scores in offender groups. The general pattern for P, E, and N is similar with both young and adult offender groups. In seeking to account for the discrepant findings for E, S.B.G.Eysenck and H.J.Eysenck suggested that E might be split into two subscales, Sociability and Impulsiveness, with only the latter related to offending. A study by S.B.G.Eysenck and McGurk confirmed that an offender sample scored higher than a non-offender sample on Impulsiveness, with no difference between the two samples on a measure of Sociability.

There are two important points to note with regard to these early investigations: the majority of studies have examined the personality traits singly rather than in combination; and few studies have attempted to control for the type of crime. It will be recalled that Eysenck's theory is specifically concerned with the combined effects of different personality traits and with antisocial crimes. A small number of studies have attended to these specific aspects of the theory. Two studies by Allsopp and Feldman suggested that P, E, and N in combination provided support for Eysenck's theory.

The most compelling evidence is presented in a more recent study by McGurk and McDougall. McGurk and McDougall report the results of a cluster analysis of the P, E, and N scores of 100 delinquents and 100 non-delinquent college pupils. The analysis showed four personality clusters in each group: both groups contained Low E-High N and High E-Low N clusters, but the clusters predicted to be related to criminal behaviour—High E-High N and High P-High EHigh N—were, indeed, found only in the delinquent sample. The Low E-Low N group, which the theory would predict to be highly socialized, was found only in the non-delinquent group.

McEwan attempted a similar analysis with a delinquent population and also found four personality clusters. With a more rigorous definition for 'high' and 'low', McEwan's analysis gave rather different clusters to McGurk and McDougall. While the High E-High N combination figures prominently, the other groups show varying degrees of dissimilarity with those reported in the previous study. Another study by McEwan and Knowles also produced four clusters, once again with similarities and differences to the other studies. With regard to type of offence, Hindelang and Weis found mixed support for the predicted relationship between personality type and nature of offence.

Their findings indicated that the High E-High N cluster was significantly associated with general deviancy but not with major theft and aggression. S.B.G.Eysenck *et al.* compared the P, E, and N scores of groups of offenders:

'conmen' showed lower P scores than the other groups, while property and violent offender groups had lower N scores. The groups did not differ on the E scale. McEwan and Knowles failed to show any significant variation in the types of offences committed by the personality clusters in their study. In terms of numbers of offences, McEwan compared the criminal records of the subgroups defined in the first part of his study.

The subgroup with the high P score proved to have significantly more previous convictions than the other subgroups. The weight of empirical evidence lends support to Eysenck's thesis that there is a relationship between personality and crime. Indeed, a self-report study of a range of predictors of delinquency showed that P was by far the strongest predictor. Exposition of the theory Feldman concludes that the 'Eysenckian personality dimensions are likely to make a useful contribution to the explanation of criminal behaviour'. While this may prove to be the case, a number of reservations, as Eysenck acknowledges, need to be made. The theory does not explain all crime and, with its concentration on extremes of the scale, is not applicable to all offenders.

Further, one of the theoretical bases of the theory, the link between classical conditioning and socialization, remains to be established satisfactorily. On a broader front the Eysenckian personality traits are not the only personality traits to have been described; studies have pointed to other personality dimensions which may be associated with criminal behaviour. Still further, the theory demands acceptance of a trait theory of personality which is only one of a number of ways of conceptualizing 'personality' and one which has come under fierce attack. In summary, Eysenck's theory is important, emphasizing the interaction between biological, environmental, and psychological factors. Integration of the theory into mainstream criminology, bearing in mind the various shortcomings, would be one way of bringing individual factors into more sociologically oriented views of crime.

COGNITION AND CRIME

The term 'cognition' is an imprecise one, used in a variety of ways by different authors: in general terms it refers to concepts such as memory, imagery, intelligence, and reasoning; although perhaps its most widely used meaning is as a synonym for thinking. In explanations of offending, cognition is implicit in the theories of a number of writers who suggest that various styles of thinking, such as 'impulsive' or 'concrete', are characteristic of criminal populations. The link between cognition and crime is perhaps at its most explicit in the controversial writings of Samuel Yochelson and Stanton Samenow.

In the first volume of *The Criminal Personality,* Yochelson and Samenow describe their conclusions drawn from interviews with male offenders referred to their hospital for 'determination of competency'. From these interviews, they claim to have discovered the 'criminal thinking patterns' which characterize all criminals. While cautious social scientists might exercise some restraint in accepting the conclusions of investigators who assert that 'The criminal has revealed the working of his mind to us' and 'We fractionate the criminal's mind and then synthesize it', it cannot be denied that Yochelson and Samenow present some fascinating and idiosyncratic views.

They describe a number of styles and errors of thinking—Ross and Fabiano have counted fifty-two—which define the criminal mind. These thinking patterns include concrete thinking, fragmentation, failure to empathize with others, a lack of any perspective of time, irresponsible decision-making, and perceiving themselves as victims. While there is much of interest in this work, there are a number of criticisms and shortcomings, some methodological, others theoretical. The sample used by Yochelson and Samenow is an unusual one in that it consisted of 240 persistent offenders, many of whom had been judged 'Not Guilty by Reason of Insanity'. It is questionable just how far it is possible to generalize from this sample to the remainder of the offender population. Their conclusion that all criminals share the same thinking pattern, must therefore be treated with caution. Further, as they failed to include a non-offender control group, it is not established that the thinking patterns they describe are peculiar to criminal populations. The interview method of data-gathering, while a rich source of material, does require a check for reliability and validity which is not given. Similarly, there is no indication of any attempt at standardization across interviews. At a theoretical level two principal issues arise: the first is with the concept of 'mind' and the associated assumption that thinking caused behaviour.

There are a number of theoretical variations on both mind and the primacy of cognition over behaviour, none of which is fully explored. The second issue lies in their assertion that, by processes which are not well explained, criminals are like a different breed of person. Indeed, comments of this latter type have led to charges of 'neo-Lombrosian' being levelled against this work. In summarizing the cognitive approach of Yochelson and Samenow, Ross and Fabiano express regret at the shortcomings of this work, which has led to a great deal of controversy rather than establishing a valuable contribution to clinical criminology. However, the approach of Yochelson and Samenow is not that of other cognitive models of criminal behaviour. More recent studies have looked for more explicit cognitive variations between offenders and non-offenders. Although the distinction may not be exact, Ross and Fabiano distinguish between *im*personal cognition and *inter*personal cognition.

The former is that aspect of cognition which 'deals with the physical world'; the latter is concerned with 'understanding people and their actions', sometimes called social cognition. While impersonal cognition may be a factor in the development of criminal behaviour—for example the research which points to intellectual imbalances in offender samples— Ross and Fabiano argue that interpersonal cognition may well be more important in understanding crime. In reviewing studies of social cognition with criminal populations, Ross and Fabiano described a variety of types or styles of cognition which characterize offenders. A failure in *self-control,* leading to *impulsivity,* figures repeatedly in explanations of crime. Ross and Fabiano suggest that impulsivity may be seen 'as a failure to insert between impulse and action a stage of reflection, a cognitive analysis of the situation'. This failure, they further suggest, may be due to one of a number of factors: a failure to learn to stop and think; a failure to learn 'effective thinking'; a failure to generate alternative responses; or a reflection of hopelessness. The empirical evidence is mixed. Some studies suggest that offenders are more impulsive than non-offenders others that offenders are unable to delay reward. However, other studies have not found such differences.

The difference between studies may be due to differing definitions and measures of impulsivity, and the heterogeneity of the offender population. The concept of *locus of control* refers to the degree to which individuals perceive their behaviour to be under their own *internal* control, as opposed to being controlled by *external* agents such as luck or authority figures. A number of studies have shown that offenders tend to external control, that is they explain their behaviour as being controlled by influences beyond their personal control. However, other studies have failed to show any difference in locus of control between offender and non-offender samples; while Lefcourt and Ladwig found offenders to be more *internally* controlled than non-offenders. The varied findings are probably due to two unfounded assumptions: that locus of control is a unitary concept, and that offenders form a homogeneous population.

With regard to the former point, a number of studies have shown that there are several dimensions to locus of control, such as belief in control over one's immediate environment as opposed to belief in control over political events. In terms of the latter point, locus of control within an offender population may be a function of race; type of offence, for example, violent offenders tend to external control or time spent in prison. If locus of control does have some relationship with offending, it will require rather more sophisticated research than is presently available to discover its exact role. As social perception develops so the ability to 'see things from the other person's point of view' matures and influences our own behaviour.

A long-standing finding with offenders is that they see situations only from their own perspective, not appreciating the view of the other person. This is reflected in low scores on measures of empathy and role-taking ability: although variations have been reported just as to length of criminal career and type of offence. If social perception is the ability to discriminate social cues and understand their significance, then the next step requires using these perceptions to decide upon suitable social behaviour. This requires a range of cognitive skills such as the ability to generate a range of solutions to a social problem, considering the various consequences of the different solutions, and planning the steps to achieve the different outcomes.

These cognitive skills have become more widely known as 'cognitive problem-solving' over the past few years. Several studies have found that offenders show poorer social problem solving than non-offenders. Although some doubt has been expressed about the validity of one of the measures used in some of these studies, and also about the functional relationship of these cognitive skills with offending. In total the evidence does indicate some differences in social cognition between offenders and non-offenders. However, two points require clarification: the relationship between impersonal and interpersonal cognitive abilities, particularly with regard to offender populations; secondly, and perhaps more importantly, the process by which the cognition results in offending.

It seems likely that the answer to this latter point will come from studies, not yet attempted, of social *decisionmaking* in offenders. While social decision-making in offenders has not been researched, decision-making regarding the commission of crime has received a growing amount of attention.

This line of enquiry portrays the offender as a rational decision-maker, a 'reasoning criminal'. The beginnings of this cognitive view of crime are, somewhat ironically, to be found in studies which focused on environmental rather than individual factors in explaining the crime. Simply, this view suggests that for a crime to be committed, the opportunity must be afforded for the offence to occur; the criminal is one who decides to take advantage of this opportunity. L.E.Cohen and Felson elaborated on this view of 'crime as opportunity', suggesting that for example the increase in burglaries over the past decade can be explained in terms of increased opportunity as more family members go out to work, so leaving houses empty for longer periods.

Studies have similarly investigated the effects of opportunity on car theft violence robbery and theft and vandalism. The cognitive component involves the decision-making process when the opportunity to offend arises. A crime is seen therefore as the result of the offender's consideration of the risks and costs of offending; indeed previous studies have addressed the relationship between risk perception and likelihood of offending. Cornish and Clarke summarize this view of crime:

- Its starting point was the assumption that offenders seek to benefit themselves by their criminal behaviour; that this involves the making of decisions and choices, however rudimentary on occasion these processes might be; and that these processes exhibit a measure of rationality, albeit constrained by limits of time and ability and the availability of relevant information.

Cornish and Clarke also make the distinction between criminal *involvement* and criminal *events*. The former is the process by which individuals choose to become involved in crime, while the latter refers to the short-term, immediate decisions in a given set of circumstances. Thus the approach is an interactional one, in which the offender reacts in a reasoned manner to environmental opportunities. While this represents a move away from 'dispositional' theories which focus exclusively on the offender, it does not dismiss the importance of personal variables, but rather attempts to place such variables in a wider context. As an example Cornish and Clarke work through the process of an individual's initial involvement in the crime of burglary, followed by the event decision for a specific burglary, and finally the process underlying the individual committing more and more such offences.

The initial involvement includes factors such as type of upbringing and other social variables; the event decision considers the influence of factors such as the presence of a dog or a burglar alarm on the decision to enter a particular house; while the increase in frequency is related to a growing sense of 'professionalism' in committing the crime, and accompanying changes in self-evaluation, life-style, and peer group. As well as burglary the rational choice model has been applied to shoplifting, robbery and drug use.

The rational choice model can also be applied to the decision to give up crime. In total, the traditional learning theories have concentrated upon the acquisition of criminal behaviour through reinforcement and modelling. The cognitive theories have followed this trend, but have recently considered the alternative of explaining why offending does *not* occur even when the opportunity arises. This notion of not offending is central to another group of theories which see crime as a failure to learn control behaviour.

4

Psychology and Crime: The Social Context

INTRODUCTION

Rates of crime, its seriousness, and the frequency of different types of it, all vary considerably from one country to another. That could of course be a reflection of varying definitions and recording methods rather than underlying differences. But large-scale studies suggest that in England and Wales in recent years, there have been in the region of 12–17 million crimes per annum. Those figures come from successive sweeps of the British Crime Survey. The subjectively experienced fear of crime also shows sizeable variations, but they are only circuitously related to the patterns of crime recorded in official statistics. Whatever the exact details, the upshot is that directly or indirectly, crime touches the lives of nearly everyone. Given that context, it is rarely out of the media spotlight.

Research shows that crime events take the largest single share of stories in every news medium. Furthermore, the proportion of news devoted to crime has been rising over the last 50 years. The level of saturation is such that almost everyone has an opinion, and a theory, and some evidence to back them up. Yet discussion of law-and-order inexorably reveals what could be described as an attitudinal minefield. Individuals' perspectives are more likely to be shaped by their prior attitudes and beliefs on a range of social issues than by systematic evidence concerning crime itself. Can an approach that claims to be scientific really be applicable to what most people think of as moral or political questions? In the prevalent imagery, science aims towards detachment and objectivity. Surely that prohibits an appreciation of subjective experiences, meanings, ideals, values and other elemental qualities of the human condition. On the contrary: psychology is very much concerned with those spheres. Moreover, a scientific outlook can be perfectly compatible with exploring them, and with a system of values. If psychology is to inform social action or public policy, it needs to take account of ethical and political dimensions. Nevertheless, there is a view that its methodological aspirations and close connection with biological sciences render it unsuitable for addressing social problems. If it does have a stance, its focus on individual differences leads some writers to perceive it as affiliated, intrinsically, to the conservative end of the political spectrum.

INDIVIDUAL AND COMMUNITY

Let us examine these issues first at the individual level. Working with persons who have broken the law raises a number of complex ethical questions. There is an inherent tension between providing services to meet individual needs while also attempting to serve collective or community interests. Recalling the terminology used by Garland many of the activities described earlier might make it sound as if psychology has switched its historic allegiances. While traditionally it looked like part of the Lombrosian project in criminology, perhaps it has now been assimilated into the governmental project. Psychologists help the police with their inquiries, assist courts of law in evaluating evidence, assess risk levels of offenders, and develop methods of managing them inside the penal system.

Their basic agenda is to help explain crime and find means of controlling it. In Garland's view, such a 'science of causes' is a 'deeply flawed' undertaking. And all of it is done in the service of the state! But before the idea takes off that this is one-sidedly part of a totalitarian agenda, note that much of it can also help individual citizens. It may safeguard them from being wrongfully convicted; reduce severity of punishments if they are; and protect potential victims from genuine risks of exploitation or assault. Outside criminal justice, psychology has many further uses in health, education and the workplace. Furthermore, it is possible simultaneously to meet the needs of both society *and* of the individual who has broken the law. The behaviour of those who frequently offend is evidently troublesome for the community. But much research suggests that often, members of that group are themselves very troubled people. Helping such individuals re-orient their lives can be of immense value both to them as well as to others if it effectively reduces offending.

For the 1,527 young people followed in the Denver Youth Survey, there was a strong association between numbers of self-reported problems and seriousness of offending. 'Amongst those facing only one problem, 7 per cent are serious offenders, but among those facing four problems, 85 per cent are serious offenders'. This pattern emerged for both males and females. The experience of personal difficulties across several areas of life is unfortunately sometimes accompanied by a lack of skills for addressing those problems and solving them in an effective way. For example, Wesner found poorer problem-solving skills among offenders than in a non-offending comparison sample. Whitton and McGuire gave a series of questionnaires designed to assess aspects of problems and styles of coping to young people under the supervision of youth offender teams in the Manchester conurbation, and to a matched sample of non-offenders in a secondary school.

Young offenders reported a significantly higher frequency of serious problems in their lives, and this was correlated with their numbers of previous convictions. However, in depicting the ways they coped, they showed higher rates of using fairly futile, unproductive methods, and lower rates of more active, problem-focused coping. In a study we have encountered before, Zamble and Quinsey interviewed highly repetitive adult offenders, with an average of 25 previous convictions, concerning factors that appeared to contribute to new offences. The crimes for which they were re-arrested were often preceded by difficulties in coping and by poor self-management, characterized by an absence of a positive problem-oriented approach. For example, individuals ignored problems they were experiencing, so allowing them to accumulate to intolerable levels, then adopted drastic solutions. In other research on how adult prisoners cope with problems, Zamble and Porporino found that more poorly adjusted prison inmates had more limited problem-solving skills. Morrison-Dyke found that having limited skills for solving problems was associated with homelessness among offenders with mental disorder.

Exploring the factors that were associated with giving up offending in an adult community sample, Farrall observed that 'as the total number of "problem" social circumstances facing the probationer increased, so desistance became less likely'. Many structured interventions are expressly designed to impart skills in solving personal problems but focus in addition on difficulties posed by the situations in which participants live. Programme materials often emphasize the importance of finding solutions that are most likely to work given certain constraints; depending on circumstances that may generate courses of action that involve changing external situations. Participants in this form of exercise are not extracted or dislodged from their environments. Training enables them to locate the sources of their difficulties, which does not automatically imply that problems reside solely within themselves.

ETHICAL DILEMMAS: RISK ASSESSMENT, PREDICTION AND CHANGE

The ethical tension alluded to above becomes particularly sharp in relation to assessment and prediction of risk, and different writers have taken conflicting stances on whether such a task can be performed ethically. Whether that is feasible depends on the predictive accuracy of the methods used. Some authors have designated a level of accuracy that should be reached before predictions can be ethically acceptable. Whatever that standard might be, it is important only to use the outputs from such assessments in conjunction with various other sources of information, and to inform decisions rather than dictate them. Writing reports and making recommendations are not value-free processes. The principal objective of a psychological report is to change the beliefs and influence the actions of the person who will be reading it. It is incumbent upon psychologists to pay attention to ethical dimensions arising in such work. Other dilemmas arise when contemplating the process of change. This has several interconnected aspects. The paramount question is whether participation in 'change-related activities' should be entirely voluntary, or can somehow be required by criminal justice staff. Even if we believe that someone would change if compelled to do so, is it ethical to enforce compliance?

From one perspective, the right to decide whether to participate resides solely with individuals themselves. From another, society can overrule the offender and is entitled to impose change. Having disregarded the rights of others, it is argued, he or she has forfeited the right to be left alone. We would expect that for people to make meaningful changes, for example of the immensity required when learning to control substance use, it is a prerequisite that they should participate in services on a purely voluntary basis. That is certainly the optimal arrangement. But some findings show that there are also circumstances in which a compulsory framework can be conducive to change.

Farabee *et al.* reported a review of 11 evaluation studies of treatment programmes for drug-abusing offenders. The programmes varied in the extent of legal pressure applied, but in all of them participation was coerced to some extent. Of the 11 studies, 'five found a positive relationship between criminal justice referral and treatment outcomes, four reported no difference, and two studies reported a negative relationship'. The authors challenged the orthodox view that the existence of external pressure implies that individuals lack any internal motivation to change. On the contrary, change often results from a complex interplay of internal and external factors. The authors concluded that the findings supported 'the use of the criminal justice system as an effective source of treatment referral, as well as a means for enhancing retention and compliance'. The importance of the latter was underpinned in further work by Fiorentino *et al.*. But change might not need to be coerced; it can be induced. With reference to high-frequency behaviours such as occur in substance abuse, it is possible to influence people towards change by a refined form of counselling known as *motivational interviewing*. This involves the use of a number of interactive strategies on the part of counsellors. They include, for example, encouraging clients to make statements that attribute to themselves the capacity to change, and drawing to their attention discrepancies between the things they say and the things they do.

While this is not blatantly coercive, it nevertheless raises ethical difficulties. Subtly influencing someone in this way is done without their full, informed consent and is open to the charge of being manipulative. Blackburn has discussed whether there are circumstances in which coercion could be ethically justifiable. This is based on a recognition that psychologists and other professionals working with offenders in criminal justice services are in a dual role, 'simultaneously helper and agent of social control', a conflict that can cause considerable strain.

Evidence that coercion achieves desirable ends does not in itself excuse its use. But given certain types of offence or risks of harm, 'total rejection of compulsion does not seem a viable option'.

PROFESSIONAL CODES OF ETHICS

The need to address complexities such as these has led the national psychological associations of most countries to develop and publish professional codes of ethics. Such codes are usually based on the *deontological* approach to moral reasoning: the doctrine that actions have immanent properties of rightness or wrongness independently of their consequences, and that fundamental moral values can be deduced from first principles. It is contrasted with a *utilitarian* approach in which the morality of actions is decided by their consequences or net outcomes. Although the precise contents of ethics codes vary, most enunciate several basic precepts:

- *Beneficence*: the acceptance of a responsibility or obligation to do good.
- *Non-maleficence*: the acceptance of a responsibility to avoid doing harm.
- *Autonomy*: observing individuals' freedom of thought and action, and their right to self-determination.
- *Justice*: basing actions on justice and fairness between individuals.
- *Integrity*: trustworthiness and faithfulness to commitments; acting within one's competence.

The American Psychological Association first published its code of ethics in 1953. It has since undergone several revisions. In 1995, the constituent members of the European Federation of Psychologists' Associations formulated a joint *meta-code* of ethics. Codes are binding upon members of the respective regulatory bodies, and violations of them may lead to disciplinary action. However, they cannot possibly cover all the concrete situations in which an ethical problem might surface. Some psychologists have developed problem-solving and decision-making sequences to apply in circumstances like these, an approach known as *practical ethics*.

AUGMENTING MODELS: RISK FACTORS AND GOOD LIVES

Many current developments in criminal justice programmes are derivatives of the *risk–needs* model propounded by Andrews and Bonta. Some critics contend that dissecting persons in this way represents them solely as a package of risks, a 'dissolution of the subject into a cluster of factors', so denigrating their individuality and completeness. While that misconstrues the approach in important ways, recently a few researchers have proposed major revisions to risk–needs analysis.

Some revive a long-standing assumption that in helping people to change, it may be necessary to alter the 'whole person'. Based on such a critique, Ward and Stewart have forwarded an alternative to the risk factors model, which they contend provides a sounder basis for integrating what have been called criminogenic needs within a wider analysis of motivation and change. They argue that what Andrews and Bonta term *needs* are not ones that offenders themselves would recognize. Rather, they reflect factors that other members of society would wish to change if doing so will lead to lowered rates of recidivism. Ward and Stewart propose instead that we can enrich and strengthen our understanding of need by locating it within a general model of human motivation. Within this they outline certain basic motives and 'primary human goods'. These include, for example, health, selfdirectedness, freedom from turmoil, and relatedness to or intimacy with others.

This leads to a framework for providing offender services that Ward and Stewart call the *good lives* model, in which the objective is promotion of general psychological well-being. Bonta and Andrews have retorted that risk–needs assessment encompasses a very broad range of areas, and offenders should have access to high-quality services to meet all their needs. The question is whether it is the appointed role of criminal justice services to address ones not demonstrably linked to offending. Arguably, criminal justice personnel have no clear mandate to probe factors in an individual's life other than his or her criminal acts, and to attempt more than that is invasive. Davison and Stuart distinguish *minimal goals*, the reduction of problematic behaviour, from *optimal goals*, the enhancement of other aspects of individual functioning. The relative weight given to each may have to be negotiated afresh in every case.

DESISTANCE: THE WHOLE PERSON

One of the most consistent findings in criminology, the *age–crime curve*, shows lucidly that as age increases from approximately 20 onwards, there is a substantial decline in the portion of the population committing crimes. Until recently, comparatively little was known about this process. However, several researchers have explored the reasons individuals give when they have successfully reduced their involvement in crime. One important discovery is that this is far more like a journey than a sudden event. As with the pathway into offending, it involves changes of speed and reversals of direction, as individuals' priorities and lifestyles unevenly evolve. Jamieson found that many of the young people they interviewed talked straightforwardly about growing up, maturing, and making other transitions in terms of jobs, education, partners, breaking away from offending peers, taking on responsibilities and 'settling down'. Maruna reported a series of in-depth interviews explicitly focused on desistance processes, and found that offenders need to make sense of their lives, and in doing so they construct life stories or *personal narratives* developed around specific themes. These *generative scripts* helped them to forge evolving identities within which, metaphorically speaking, they gradually become different people, or new versions of themselves, capable of acting in different ways.

In a study of the impact of probation supervision, Farrall found that the process of desistance bore relatively little relation to the efforts of supervising officers, and was much more a function of life events and circumstances. Externally, progress in desistance was associated with getting jobs, meeting partners and other key events. Others who were stuck in a pattern of offending attributed this to a 'lack of change' in their lives, meaning unsatisfactory circumstances with regard to jobs and relationships. These studies have in common an emphasis on what might be called the 'whole person' approach. While to some extent it challenges the more analytical risk factors model, the two can be complementary, as Maruna's work amply illustrates.

THE PSYCHOLOGY OF CRIMINAL BEHAVIOUR

From longitudinal and other kinds of studies, we know a great deal about the psychological makeup of offenders. We do not know about every offender, to be sure, nor about every kind of offender, but, in the aggregate, it is clear that the typical offender is not only a young male, but a young male with a particular configuration of psychological traits. Here are some highlights of this enormous empirical literature.

INTELLIGENCE

After sex and age, the single most firmly established psychological fact about the population of offenders is that the distribution of their IQ scores differs from that of the population at large. Instead of averaging 100, as the general population does, offenders average about eight points lower. Since the general population includes the lower-than-average population of offenders, the population of non-offenders alone must average someplace above 100, in order to get the general average down to 100.

The IQ gap between offenders and non-offenders must therefore be more than eight points; an informed guess puts it at about ten points. More serious or more chronic offenders generally have lower scores than more casual offenders. The relationship between IQ and repeat offending is found with IQ scores obtained even in the offender's childhood, as young as four years old. However, it stands to reason (and is supported by the data) that the population of offenders lacks not only high-scoring individuals, but very low-scoring ones as well, people whose scores are so low that they have trouble mustering the competence to commit most crimes. Moreover, a sufficiently low IQ is usually enough to exempt a person from criminal prosecution, no matter what he or she did.

The gap between offenders and non-offenders is typically larger on verbal than on performance (that is, non-verbal) intelligence tests. The more powerful predictive power of verbal ability for later criminal behaviour may already be evident in measures of linguistic development taken as early as age three, according to one Swedish study. it has been suggested that verbal intelligence is especially relevant because the essential cognitive difference between offenders and non-offenders is the one in general intelligente or "g"; it is well known that verbal scores are more dependent on g than performance scores.

Another interpretation, not necessarily inconsistent with the foregoing, is that verbal intelligence scores do better at measuring the capacity for internalizing the prohibitions that help deter crime in non-offenders. Still another interpretation is that low verbal ability is more of a disadvantage in school and in the legal job market than low performance ability and that the frustrations of failure lead to crime. Multiple offenders, as distinguished from offenders in general, also have significant deficits in logical reasoning ability per se. Whatever the reason for these patterns of differences, the methodological implications are clear: the rare study that fails to find much of an association between IQ and offending may have used non-verbal scores or scores that, for one reason or another, minimize individual differences in g.

The association between crime and IQ has been apparent since testing began in earnest. The test data just confirmed what was already long known. Deficient intelligence was accepted as a preeminent distinguishing feature of the most serious offenders within the evolving discipline of forensic psychiatry throughout the eighteenth and nineteenth centuries. The British physician Charles Goring mentioned a lack of intelligence as one of the key traits of the prison population that he described in a landmark of modern criminology early in the twentieth century. H. H. Goddard, an early leader in both modern criminology and the use of intelligence tests, concluded that a large fraction of convicts were intellectually subnormal. However, by the mid1930s, criminologists were beginning to discount IQ as a factor in criminal behaviour. They could not doubt that convict populations generally earned lower-than-average scores, because the numbers were overpoweringly clear; but they had concluded that the numbers said nothing about a real difference in intelligence between offenders and non-offenders.

They were skeptical about whether the convicts in prisons were truly representative of offenders in general; and they were dubious, at best, about what tests measured: Weren't tests just measuring socioeconomic status by other means and weren't they biased against the people from the lower socioeconomic classes or the minority groups who were most likely to break the law for other reasons? By the 1960s, the association between intelligence and crime had all but disappeared from criminology textbooks. If it was mentioned at all, it was to criticize or denounce.

Public commentary on crime has remained stuck where criminology was in the 1960s. In the meantime, most criminologists now accept not just the fact that there is an IQ gap between offenders and non-offenders, but that the gap is genuinely a gap in average intellectual level or, as it is sometimes called, "academic competence" The tables began to turn with a major review of the literature published in 1977 by two respected criminologists, Travis Hirschi and Michael Hindelang. Subsequent work has supported their conclusion that a difference in tested intelligence is among the prime discoveries of criminology.

Not only is there a gap in IQ between offenders and non-offenders, but a disproportionately large fraction of all crime is committed by people towards the low end of the scale of intelligence. For example, in a twenty-year longitudinal study of over 500 boys in a community in Sweden, 30 percent of all arrests of the men by the age of thirty were of the 6 percent with IQs below 77 (at the age of ten) and 80 percent were of those with IQs below 100. Criminology textbooks now routinely report the correlation between crime and intelligence. Some questions of interpretation are still open, but they are narrower than they used to be because the correlation itself is no longer in dispute.

What happened to shift opinion about IQ? The answer is largely a matter of the evidence. IQ has proved to be a stronger predictor of criminal behaviour than socioeconomic status (SES) or paternal education and at least as strong as race. Hence, the argument that IQ is just a cryptic measure of SES or race stumbles. IQ remains predictive within populations that are racially or socioeconomically homogeneous, as in some of the longitudinal studies I summarized. Test scores are not predictively biased against blacks or against people low in SES, contrary to the assumption that criminologists freely made in the 1960s.

Critics argue that offenders whose IQs we know are unrepresentative of the true criminal population. The smart ones presumably slipped through the net. I assume, in fact, that this is correct to some degree. If intelligence has anything to do with a person's general competence, then smart criminals should get arrested less often because they pick smarter crimes or because they execute their crimes more skillfully. But how much of a bias does this introduce into the data? Not much, seems to be the answer. The crimes we can trace to the millions of offenders that do pass through the criminal justice system and get their IQs measured or estimated account for much of the crime around us, particularly the serious predatory crime. There is no evidence for any other large population of offenders and there is barely enough crime left unaccounted for, for them to be committing. Not many, if any, Professor Moriartys are out there, brilliantly and busily committing crimes for which they are never caught.

The IQs of uncaught offenders are not measurably different from the ones who get caught, as far as we can tell from the data in hand. For example, in the New Zealand study, when caught and uncaught offenders were equated for the seriousness of the offenses they disclosed on a questionnaire, their average IQ scores did not differ significantly. If caught offenders are not as bright as offenders who are not caught, then there should have been a difference in IQ scores between these groups. In general, an IQ gap separates offenders and non-offenders among self-described offenders who haven't been caught yet, showing that the gap in the official statistics is not just a result of differential arrest rates. Differential arrests, assuming they exist, are evidently a minor factor in the aggregate data. Among those who have criminal records, there is still a significant negative correlation between IQ and frequency of offending.

Moreover, a high IQ appears to protect a person from offending, even if the other precursors are present. For example, one study followed a sample of almost 1,500 boys born in Copenhagen, Denmark, between 1936 and 1938. Sons whose fathers had a prison record were almost six times as likely to have a prison record themselves (by the time they were thirty-four to thirty-six) as the sons of men who had no police record of any sort. Having a convicted father, then, establishes a high risk of conviction for their sons. Among these high-risk sons, the ones who had no police contacts at all had IQ scores one standard deviation higher than the sons who had police contacts. Among the low-risk sons, the offenders and non-offenders had about the same IQ scores. Overall, the offenders among the sons were about seven IQ points below the non-offenders.

The protective power of elevated intelligence also shows up in the New Zealand study. Boys and girls were divided into high and low risk for delinquency on the basis of their behaviour by the age of five. High-risk children were more than twice as likely to become delinquent by the age of thirteen or fifteen as low-risk children. The high-risk boys or girls who did not become delinquent were the ones with the higher IQs. This was also true for the low-risk boys and girls: the non-delinquents had higher IQs than the delinquents.

Children growing up in troubled circumstances on Kauai in the Hawaiian chain confirm the pattern. Several hundred children were followed in a longitudinal study for several decades. Some of the children were identified by their second birthday as being "vulnerable" to behavioral disorders or delinquency. These were children suffering from two or more of the following circumstances: they were being raised in troubled or impoverished families; had alcoholic, psychologically disturbed, or unschooled (eight years or less of schooling) parents; had experienced prenatal or perinatal physiological stress. Two-thirds of these children succumbed to delinquency or other psychological disturbances. But how about the other third, the ones who grew up without becoming delinquents or disturbed psychologically? Prominent among the protective factors were higher intellectual ability scores than the average for the vulnerable group.

Personality and Temperament

As certain as it is that low IQ scores are a predisposing factor for offending and other kinds of antisocial behaviour, it is also certain that other psychological factors are involved. By the age of thirty, approximately 5 percent of the Hawaiian sample had adult criminal records. These were people who, by the age of ten, had already been disproportionately notable for their temper tantrums, aggression and bullying tendencies, irritability and dishonesty, besides their low IQs. Among those who had been otherwise vulnerable but had not succumbed to criminal behaviour, childhood personality was diagnostic. To have survived the risks, a child was likely to have been affectionate, cuddly, easygoing, even-tempered and likable, to use the very words applied to them already in infancy. At twenty months, they were alert, active and responsive, according to pediatricians and psychologists who examined the sample. A child with a sunny disposition, one that evoked affectionate and friendly responses from adults, was to a degree protected from the risks he or she was being exposed to. In the Cambridge study, the boys who did not become criminal had similar traits. Being shy in childhood, especially if not combined with aggressiveness, is also something of a shield from later offending.

In one form or another, these results echo innumerable others. Breaking the law is part of a more general disposition towards unsociable or actively antisocial behaviour that, in many cases, begins to emerge in the pre-toddler stage. As usual, however, many more children show the tendencies than become offenders; of those who become offenders, the signs were likely to have been present early in life. When offenders and non-offenders are equated for IQ, they remain distinctly different in personality or temperament.

In trying to pinpoint what these personality or temperamental differences are, however, we run into an embarrassment of riches. In discussing intellectual differences, measurement converges on IQ tests. But, for personality and temperament, there is no comparably standard measurement. This is partly because personality or temperament is inherently more complex than intelligence. For intelligence, factor analysis uncovers a single major factor, g, which accounts for at least 50 percent of all the variation in IQ among individuals. Anything that measures g is likely to look a lot like an IQ test and almost anything that plausibly measures intelligence will be saturated with g. But, as far as we know, personality or temperament is a multidimensional pie that can be cut into a bewildering array of slices. For the same reason, English contains thousands of words describing personality and temperament, but barely a dozen or so describing intellect. Because of all the ways there are to measure personality and temperament (many of which are not very reliable), the data give the impression of less consistency in the link between these traits and criminal behaviour than I believe there really is. Among the non-intellectual childhood precursors of criminal behaviour one runs into repeatedly in the technical literature are restlessness; aggressiveness; resistance to discipline; hyperactivity; attention deficits; an appetite for risk, excitement and danger; impulsiveness; coldness; shallow emotional attachments to other people a lack of commitment to social or religious mores; "problem behaviour" or "troublesomeness"; dishonesty; and a precocious tendency to experiment with sex and drugs.

In extrem form, this is a list that suggests a psychiatric disorder called antisocial personality. Offender populations indeed appear to include a disproportionate number of people with the disorder, as well as large numbers with less extreme manifestations of the symptoms. Antisocial personality almost never shows up in adulthood (barring brain injury or disease) without having been foreshadowed by antisocial behaviour in childhood.

Some personality tests ask people to answer lists of questions about their beliefs, wishes, preferences, habits, fears and self-perceptions. These "inventories," as they are often called, consistently show that the typical offender, particularly the typical serious offender, is high in antisocial tendencies and low in sociability. That is to say, a serious offender is likely to give patterns of responses similar to those given by people who have been found to be antisocial or unsociable by other means. Less consistently, but still notably, personality tests find offenders to be impulsive. They are likely to be impatient and to do poorly with requests for restraint, with situations that require deferring gratification, with tasks that are better performed slowly and methodically.

One of the precursors of offending is doing even worse in school than would be predicted by the lower-than-average IQ. This shows that the precursors include something besides IQ. To do well in school, it helps to have decent IQ scores, verbal scores especially, to accept social mores, to be able to control one's impulses, to maintain attention, or just to sit still for more than a moment or two. Just about every precursor of criminal behaviour is, in other words, at odds with what is needed to do well in school. Moreover, doing poorly in school may well be among the causes of later offending, as a person is drawn into a search for illegal gratification to compensate for the frustrations and failures in school and for a dawning recognition that legal pursuits are likewise going to be unsatisfying. Not surprisingly, some evidence suggests that poor school performance predicts criminal behaviour better than IQ per se.

TYPE OF MENTAL DISORDER AND CRIME

Thus far the term 'mental disorder' has been used without qualification, although it is apparent that it covers a range of types of behaviour and diagnostic categories. While, as discussed previously, there are difficulties with the term 'mental disorder' clearly it is necessary to have a definition, for legal purposes if nothing else. The Mental Health Act, 1983, in England and Wales divided 'mental disorder' into four categories: 'Mental illness, arrested or incomplete development of the mind, psychopathic disorder and any other disorder or disability of mind'. In practice it is the first three categories which assume the greatest importance and so these will be discussed in turn; examining both the nature of the specific disorder and its relationship with offending.

MENTAL ILLNESS AND CRIME

In truth, the term 'mental illness' causes more problems than it solves: Ashworth and Gostin note that mental illness is not defined in the Mental Health Act and therefore 'much will depend upon medical opinion'. In practice the term is used for a wide range of diagnostic categories including psychoses, affective disorders, anxiety states, hysteria, and so on. Inspection of admissions to Special Hospitals shows that by far the greatest number of mentally ill serious offenders are diagnosed as schizophrenic, with depression the next most frequent diagnosis. Does any special relationship exist between these two particular disorders and crime?

Schizophrenia

The most important indicators of schizophrenia, which would *not* all be found in one person, include disturbances of thought, perception, affect, and motor behaviour. Thought disorder refers to a disturbance of the process of making associations between thoughts. Perceptual disturbances are evinced by hallucinations, which may be visual or tactile but are most commonly auditory, typically as voices commenting or giving instructions. Affect can be flat and expressionless or alternatively it can be inappropriate such as anger without provocation, or laughter at misfortune. Finally, motor disturbances can take the form of bizarre facial grimaces, repeated gesturing, or excited agitation of the body; alternatively unusual postures can be adopted and held, in a state of immobility, for long periods. As noted, not all these behaviours would be found in the same person, although some pattern does emerge: disorganized or hebephrenic schizophrenia is characterized by hallucinations, delusions, and inappropriate affect; catatonic schizophrenia by motor disturbances; and paranoid schizophrenia by delusions of persecu-tion, incorporating 'ideas of reference' in which personal significance is continually perceived in the actions of other people. Given this range, it may well be expedient to think of schizophrenia as a group of disorders rather than a single disorder which always manifests itself in the same fashion.

While of uncertain aetiology, contemporary theories favour a complex interaction between genetic, neurochemical, and social factors as an explanation for schizophrenia. It is generally accepted that the incidence of schizophrenia is close to 1 per cent in the general population: this sets a baseline against which to compare the rates of schizophrenia in offender populations. Spry reviews the evidence on the incidence of schizophrenia and crime and notes a division in research findings: with studies of non-disordered offender groups the incidence of schizophrenia is around the 1 per cent mark with selected samples of offenders referred for psychiatric treatment, typically having committed serious offences, the incidence is much higher.

For example, Green reports that 74 per cent of a sample of fifty-eight men admitted to a Special Hospital having committed matricide were schizophrenic.

Does this suggest that schizophrenia is related to serious offences? As Spry notes, many people associate schizophrenia with crime, particularly violent crime. Indeed, there are indications that a relationship may exist between paranoid ideas and violence, and that the victims of violent attacks are often those who figured in the schizophrenic's delusions.

Crimes of this type catch the public imagination: Prins notes the case of Ian Ball, in which delusional thought processes were manifest in a plot to kidnap a member of the royal family: Prins discusses the crimes of Peter Sutcliffe, the 'Yorkshire Ripper', in which there was some controversy as to the role of his paranoid schizophrenia in the murders he committed. It should be stressed, however, that the publicity generated by these cases is in inverse proportion to their frequency; the deluded and paranoid people who commit such crimes are rare. While these extreme cases are infrequent, the finding remains that schizophrenics are slightly more likely to commit violent offences than other disordered groups or the general population.

While schizophrenia may be directly related to violence, with delusional and paranoid beliefs of apparent importance, a simple relationship between the disorder and the crime is unlikely to exist. P.J.Taylor suggests that: 'It is not unusual to find that the violent act of a schizophrenic cannot be directly explained by the current psychopathology. This does not, however, negate the relevance of the illness...social and illness variables must be considered together'. The point Taylor makes is an important one: as well as considering a causal relationship between schizophrenia and violence, attention should also be paid to the similarities in social, environmental, and organic antecedents common to both violence and schizophrenia. More recent findings by the same researcher reinforce this point. From a survey of 121 psychotic offenders, Taylor concluded that '20 per cent of the actively psychotic were directly driven to offend by their psychotic symptoms, and a further 26 per cent probably so'. When social factors such as homelessness were considered along with the nature of the crime, so that 'the direct and indirect consequences of psychosis are considered together, then over 80 per cent of the offences of the psychotic were probably attributable to their illness'.

Depression

Clinically two types of depression are distinguished: *major depression* and *bipolar disorder*. Major depression is characterized by profoundly sad mood, overwhelming feelings of selfblame, guilt, and worthlessness, appetite disturbances, fatigue and long periods of sleep, lethargy, and recurrent thoughts of death and suicide. Bipolar disorder is typified by bouts of mania as well as periods of depression: during the manic phase the individual shows elated or irritable mood, high levels of furious physical activity, goes long periods without sleep, and displays a general air of self-importance and inflated self-esteem.

Of the two, major depression is by far the most common, with estimates suggesting that 8 per cent to 11 per cent of men and 18 per cent to 23 per cent of women will be clinically depressed at least once in their life; bipolar disorder is less frequent, appearing in about 1 per cent of the population. Theories of depression incorporate a wide range of biological, cognitive, behavioural, and social factors. As with schizophrenia—or, indeed, any mental illness—there are difficulties in establishing the relationship between depression and crime.

A range of possibilities exists: the crime may have been committed because the offender was depressed; the offender may become depressed after the crime, either because of guilt or imprisonment; the offender may have been depressed when committing the crime, but the depression was not instrumental in causing the crime. In terms of a direct causal link, one of the more familiar and tragic associations between depression and crime occurs when an individual becomes convinced that life is hopeless and before committing suicide kills his or her children and other members of the family. West studied seventy-eight cases of murder followed by suicide and estimated that twenty-eight of the offenders were depressed at the time of the offence. Lawson suggests that a general pattern in certain murders by depressives lies in the 'social circumstances and pathological features of the domestic killing'.

The social circumstances involve a negative life event such as an upset in a long-term relationship, while the act itself shows no sign of planning or even malice. As well as murder, depression has been associated with other crimes including shoplifting and violence. With regard to violence, Häfner and Böker found that the violence was principally directed at relatives, suggesting similarities with the 'extended suicides'. As Howells notes, depressed in-patients are not a violent population, suggesting that the relationship between depression and crime is closely tied to social, particularly interpersonal, factors. Although most studies do not indicate which type of depression is present, it is reasonable to assume that major depression is involved.

However, McCulloch and Prins do describe a case involving a manic episode, a car salesman, and violence towards property. While Blumberg suggested that, after schizophrenia, manic depressive episodes were the disorder most commonly found in arsonists; Gunderson similarly suggested that firesetting during a manic state may be more common than is generally acknowledged. The broad picture which emerges for mental illness and crime does not really take us much further than the general evidence for 'mental disorder' and crime. Mental illness, particularly schizophrenia and depression, are found in criminal populations but the exact nature of the relationship between the two remains unclear. P.J.Taylor's work is however beginning to show how psychosis and crime may be seen as complex psychosocial phenomena, rather than in a simple relationship in which one factor has a linear causal effect on the other.

MENTAL HANDICAP AND CRIME

The Mental Health Act seeks to define a group of offenders characterized by 'arrested or incomplete development of mind which includes... impairment of intelligence and social functioning'. The Act distinguishes between 'severe' and 'significant' mental impairment although the difference between the two is not clarified. The group the Act refers to are those generally referred to as mentally handicapped, although other terms such as mentally retarded and mentally subnormal are sometimes used. It should of course be emphasized that mental *handicap* is not the same as mental *illness*. The former refers to the person's enduring level of intellectual and social ability; the latter is an episodic disturbance which does not necessarily affect intellectual functioning.

The assessment of mental handicap relies on a combination of results from tests of intellectual and social ability. While there is no legal level of IQ score by which to define impairment, in clinical assessment it is generally taken that an IQ in the region of 70 points is taken as 'borderline'. Thus a score of 70 or below, in conjunction with a low level of social functioning, may be indicative of some degree of handicap. IQ scores below 50 usually indicate a substantial degree of impairment. The 'two group theory' suggests a division between two types of mental impairment. The first is a 'normal impairment', as defined by those individuals who are at the lower end of the IQ distribution.

This may be because of family factors, including genetic endowment, or because of poor schooling or other environmental factors. While low in terms of IQ points, such individuals are usually well adapted socially. The second group are those who score very low on IQ tests and show poor social adaptation. Unlike the first group, there is usually an identifiable cause for the impairment: this may be a genetic or chromosomal abnormality such as Down's syndrome; a biological disturbance such as phenylketonuria; damage or infection *in utero,* as with rubella; birth complications such as anoxia; childhood disease like meningitis; head injury resulting in brain damage; or poisoning such as by lead, radiation, or toxic chemicals. In examining the relationship between mental handicap and crime two approaches have been used: the study of the intellectual functioning of offenders generally, and investigation of the specific offences of mentally handicapped offenders.

Before looking at the evidence it is as well to make a number of points about measuring intelligence. Most research comparing offender and non-offender groups has used IQ tests to measure intellectual ability. However, the possibility must be considered that this means of measurement introduces unwanted variance into the results: in other words, are the tests biased against offender groups? The important point is whether the standardization of the test included offenders. Standardization can be thought of as the estimation of test norms, that is, the levels or standards present in the general population.

A properly standardized IQ test should in theory always yield the same average score in a random sample from the general population. It should not, for example, be possible to score higher on an IQ test simply because, say, of age: the average score on a properly standardized test should be the same for any age level; if not, then the test is biased against some age groups. Thus if the population sample on which the test was standardized did not include offenders, then the possibility cannot be discounted that any difference in IQ between offender and non-offender groups may be due to test bias. Of course it is also the case that any differences may be due to social class, cultural, and educational differences between offender and non-offender samples.

This is not test bias, rather a reflection that intellectual performance is affected by environmental factors. To be sure that real differences in IQ exist between offender and non-offender samples it is necessary to be confident that the particular IQ test employed is not biased against offenders, and that effects due to differences in class, educational background, and so on have been controlled or allowed for in the research.

In practice the environmental variables are likely to exert a greater influence on IQ test scores than variations in standardization. Nevertheless, both points should be held in mind when considering the evidence on intelligence and offending.

Intelligence in Offender Populations

Opinion on the nature of the relationship between intelligence and crime has gone through a number of historical phases. Charles Goring, a contemporary of Lombroso, studied 3,000 English convicts and found them to be of generally low intelligence. Goring suggested that crime was therefore the result of a lack of intelligence, in turn determined by genetic factors. As criminology grew in sophistication such simplistic, unitary causes of crime were replaced by complex multidimensional theories, often with a strong sociological content. The inclusion of individual characteristics such as intelligence into such theories gradually passed out of fashion. Indeed, the occasional study suggested that there was little to be gained from such a line of investigation: Woodward calculated that on average offenders were not more than eight IQ points below the population mean—a small difference, say 92 as compared to 100.

However, in the 1960s and 1970s research once again began to suggest an association between IQ and crime. An American study by Hirschi found a significant association between IQ and self-reported delinquency, an association which remained even after allowing for the influence of race and social status. A longitudinal study of boys living in London reported by West and Farrington found a strong correlation between IQ and recidivism, with boys of lower IQ more likely to become recidivists. The correlation remained when the analysis controlled for family size and income. These and other studies led Hirschi and Hindelang to reintroduce intelligence as an important factor in understanding the development of criminal behaviour.

More recent studies have added confirmatory evidence to this line of thought. If the correlation appears reasonably strong, its meaning is less clear. West and Farrington extended their analysis and discovered that lower IQ was also associated with problem behaviour in early life, suggesting that the link between IQ and delinquency was via this earlier association. Richman *et al.* similarly showed that the IQ link with behavioural disorders could be found by 3 years of age.

It seems likely therefore that IQ and crime are associated via one or more other pathways. Rutter and Giller suggest two possible routes. The first is that low IQ leads to educational failure, which leads to low self-esteem and emotional disturbance, in turn leading to conduct disorder and criminal behaviour. While there is support for a relationship between learning disability and crime, this does not account for the findings which suggest that the associations are present at pre-school ages.

The second hypothesis is that IQ and conduct disorder share a common aetiology, the exact nature of which is open to speculation: this could be a biological, social, or familial influence; or even another individual factor such as temperament. Other research has examined the IQs of convicted offender populations.

As with all studies of offender populations, it should be remembered that these are a highly selected sample and may be unrepresentative of the general offender population, especially with regard to intelligence. Craft collated information from fifteen studies of IQ in convicted prisoners carried out between 1931 and 1952. The earlier studies show low mean IQs, ranging from a mean of 71 to a mean of 88: the most recent studies show a marked difference, all finding mean IQs of 92.

This may reflect changes in IQ tests, as well as policy changes over the decades regarding the disposal of offenders with low IQs. Although significant fluctuations in prison population IQ levels over a short period of time have been recorded.

It should be pointed out that most of the studies discussed this far are not concerned with very low IQ scores, but rather more with IQs which tend towards the 'below average' classification.

While low IQ is as common among men first convicted in adulthood as among boys first convicted as juveniles, this does *not* imply that criminals are, by definition, mentally handicapped.

Offenders may display a lower IQ on average—but this means that some offenders will have normal or above normal IQs. Further, mental handicap is as much concerned with social functioning as with IQ, but the research has mainly been concerned with intelligence. A number of studies have been concerned with very low IQ scores in offender populations. Craft reports that in convicted prisoners the percentage with IQ scores less than 70 varied from a high of 31 per cent in a 1931 study, to about 10 per cent in 1940s studies, to a low of 4.2 per cent in a 1950 study. Prins presents a similar survey, noting a high of 28 per cent of convicted offenders deemed 'subnormal' in a 1918 study, falling to 2.4 per cent in a 1964 study.

This probably reflects changes over time in the disposal of mentally handicapped offenders. More recent studies have controlled for variables such as type of test and time of testing and have found about 2.5 per cent of the prison population have IQ scores below 70. The importance of social functioning is seen in a survey by Denkowski and Denkowski of the prevalence of mentally handicapped inmates in the prisons of twenty states in the USA. From their figures on individually tested prisoners, it can be calculated that 2.25 per cent of prisoners are classified as retarded in those states which rely on IQ testing and do not use a formal means of assessing adaptive behaviour.

In the five states where IQ and adaptive behaviour was assessed the percentage of mentally handicapped prisoners is 1.28 per cent. These lower figures—in the region of 2–2.5 per cent—are similar to the incidence of mental handicap in the non-offender population. Therefore mental handicap is unlikely, in itself, to be a strong factor in the aetiology of crime: nevertheless mentally handicapped people do commit crimes —is there anything remarkable about this group?

Offending and Mental Handicap

N.Walker compared the indictable offences of 305 males ordered over a one-year period to be committed to hospital as mentally handicapped, with the offences of all other male offenders dealt with by the courts in the same year. While there were no differences in the frequency of violent and property offences, the percentage of handicapped offenders sentenced for sexual offences was six times as great as that for the other offenders. Similarly A.Shapiro found that in a sample of compulsorily detained mentally handicapped offenders, 35 per cent had committed a sexual offence.

Tutt, with a sample from a 'subnormality hospital', found that almost 16 per cent had been convicted of a sexual offence prior to admission. These rates are much higher than the expected figure for sex offences in the general offender population, which would be of the order of 3 per cent. Robertson carried out a follow-up study of the offences of a group of over 300 mentally handicapped offenders who appeared before the courts for a criminal offence and had received a hospital order and had subsequently been released into the community. Most of the offences are not unusual, although the rate of sex offences in males is relatively high.

Table. Principal Offences of Mentally Handicapped Offenders

	Male	Females
Larceny	54	60
Breaking and entering	33	9
Sexual Indecency	12	–
Soliciting	–	9
Arson	3	1
GBH/wounding	2	3
Rape	1	–
Manslaughter	1	0
Robbery	1	0

Robertson also compared the male mentally handicapped offenders with a sample of male mentally ill offenders. In personal terms, the handicapped offenders were much younger and less likely to have been married. The handicapped group had fewer hospital admissions, with about half having been in-patients prior to the Section 60 order, compared to about 80 per cent of the mentally ill group. With regard to criminal history, the handicapped group were younger when receiving their first conviction and had committed many more offences as juveniles. Despite this, the mentally ill group had more court appearances and had spent longer in prison. While the incidence of theft was similar in the two groups, the mentally ill offenders had been convicted of more violent offences such as assault and criminal damage, with more sexual offences in the handicapped group. As Robertson comments, apart from the sexual offences, the pattern shown by the handicapped offender of petty juvenile crime developing in later life to various acquisitive offences is similar to that found in the general offender population.

This contrasts sharply with the atypical pattern seen in the mentally ill population in which, as Robertson notes, 'juvenile offending is rare and where criminality may be one consequence of a general social deterioration following chronic illness'. It is, however, important to note several ways in which the mentally handicapped offender is disadvantaged compared to his or her more able contemporaries. The mentally handicapped offender may not have learned the difference between acceptable and unacceptable behaviour, therefore a 'crime' cannot be elevated to the status of a 'right' or 'wrong' act in the sense that the person knowingly transgressed the law.

The handicap may mean that the crime itself is carried out less efficiently, leading to easier detection, or the mentally handicapped person may be exploited by more able offenders. In some cases mental handicap is associated with emotional outbursts, particularly following some stressful event, which may in turn precipitate aggressive acts. A lack of social skills may mean that acts intended to be friendly are seen by others as aggressive or hostile, resulting in unfortunate consequences. A similar point may hold for sexual skills: as Craft and Craft note, the sexual experimentation of mentally handicapped people may be more visible and hence more upsetting than convention allows. Thus the high sexual offending of this group may reflect a paucity of skills in making acceptable sexual approaches; such social naivety may be seen by the 'victim' as assault and criminal proceedings are likely to follow. In the discussion of theories of mental handicap, the distinction was made between 'normal' mental handicap and those cases where the handicap results from some known, usually organic, cause. Research into mental handicap and offending has not considered this distinction: a point which may be something for future research to address as the aetiology of mental handicap in the offender may be informative theoretically, and have practical implications in terms of management and the services offered to this type of offender.

PSYCHOPATHIC DISORDER

The 1983 Act defines psychopathic disorder as 'a persistent disorder or disability of mind which results in abnormally aggressive or seriously irresponsible conduct'. As various commentators have noted, this is a less than perfect definition in that it does not specify what is meant by 'persistent', 'abnormally aggressive', or 'seriously irresponsible'. To complicate matters further, the American system varies the terminology: as Davison and Neale note, 'In current usage the terms *sociopath* and *psychopath* appear interchangeably with antisocial personality'. Given this, what characteristics identify such an ill-defined category of offenders?

Identifying the Psychopath

Cleckley identified the psychopath by listing the characteristics observed in clinical practice: these identifying characteristics place emphasis on the emotional and social emptiness of the psychopath.

Cleckley's Characteristics of the Psychopath:

- Superficial charm and good intelligence
- Absence of delusions and other signs of irrational thinking
- Absence of 'nervousness' or other psychoneurotic manifestations
- Unreliability
- Untruthfulness and insincerity
- Lack of remorse or shame
- Inadequately motivated antisocial behaviour
- Poor judgement and failure to learn by experience
- Pathologic egocentricity and incapacity for love
- General poverty in major affective reactions
- Specific loss of insight
- Unresponsiveness in general interpersonal relations
- Fantastic and uninviting behaviour with drink and sometime without
- Suicide rarely carried out

- Sex life impersonal, trivial, and poorly integrated
- Failure to follow any life plan

Hare conducted a factor analysis of data derived from the Cleckley criteria and found five factors, which offer a succinct description of the psychopath: they show an inability to develop warm, empathic relationships; an inability to accept responsibility for their antisocial behaviour; an absence of intellectual and psychiatric problems; weak behavioural control. Blackburn and Maybury performed a similar analysis on the Cleckley checklist which 'yielded results which are broadly in agreement with those of Hare in indicating that a unitary dimension describable as lack of empathy or affection pervades most of the criteria'. However, as numerous commentators have noted, many of the terms used by Cleckley are vague and imprecise, causing difficulties for clinicians and researchers alike. Hare constructed a more precise scale for the assessment of psychopathy in criminal populations: this scale is shown in full in below.

Psychopathy Checklist:

- Glinbness/superficial charm
- Previour diagnosis as psychopath (or similar)
- Egocentricity/grandiose sense of self-worth
- Proneness to boredom/low frustration tolerance
- Pathological lying and deception
- Conning/lack of sincerity
- Lack of remorse or guilt
- Lack of affect and emotional depth
- Callous/lack of empathy
- Parasutuc life-style
- Short-tempered/poor behavioural controls
- Promiscuous sexual relations
- Early behaviour problems
- Lack of realistic, long-term plans
- Impulsivity
- Irresponsible behaviour as a parent
- Frequent marital relationships
- Juvenile delinquencey
- Poor probation or parole risk
- Failure to accept responsibility for own actions
- Many types of offence
- Drug of alcohol abuse not direct cause of antisocial behaviour

Factor analysis showed that the new scale also contained five factors, similar to those found in the factor analysis of the original Cleckley checklist. Analysis also showed high agreement between the new scale and Cleckley's original criteria. Hare has subsequently shortened the list to give a *Psychopathy Checklist* for use by clinicians and researchers. The approach adopted by

Cleckley and Hare to identifying the psychopath rests on clinical observation of the defining characteristics; statistical techniques are then used to produce a reliable psychometric instrument based on the observations. A different approach to the same task is to use existing psychometric measures to define a particular 'psychopathic' personality.

The work of the British psychologist Ronald Blackburn is of particular significance here. Blackburn's original psychometric research described four types of violent offender, within which the distinction was made between *primary psychopaths* and *secondary psychopaths*. The primary group is characterized by high levels of hostility, low anxiety levels, and has few psychiatric problems. The secondary psychopaths also show high levels of hostility but with attendant anxiety, guilt, and psychiatric disturbance. Blackburn has shown that the original four groups can be described in terms of two factors, psychopathy and sociability. Primary psychopaths are high on psychopathy and sociability; secondary psychopaths also score highly on psychopathy but are low on sociability. Blackburn presents data which suggest that primary psychopaths are more likely to commit violent acts, while secondary psychopaths are more likely to commit sex offences. Hare compared a variety of assessment procedures including the checklist shown and various self-report inventories including the MMPI. Hare concludes that 'Self-report inventories simply do not sort subjects in the same way that clinical-behavioral procedures do': Hare recommends the twenty-two-item Psychopathy Checklist as a valid measure of psychopathy as it relates strongly to 'criminal activities, violence, institutional behaviour, and outcome on con-ditional release, including parole', although, as Hare points out, agreement is not perfect among such clinical assessments. Further, despite its clinical utility, this checklist approach does little towards contributing to the understanding of the aetiology of psychopathy and the development of a theoretical model of the disorder. A third level of identification is a more informal one, but none the less important for that, the criteria used by practitioners to diagnose psychopathy.

W.Davies and Feldman asked a sample of over thirty 'forensic specialists' to rate the importance of twenty-two signs of psychopathy. In summary, what has been identified about the psychopath? It is not a well-defined condition, nor is it universally popular, yet it is one which is used and cannot be ignored. A publication by the Department of Health and Social Security and the Home Office offers a pragmatic, operational definition:

- The consensus view is that psychopathic disorder is not a description of a single clinical disorder but a convenient label to describe a severe personality disorder which may show itself in a variety of attitudinal, emotional and inter-personal behaviour problems. The core problem is impairment in the capacity to relate to others—to take account of their feelings and to act in ways consistent with their safety and convenience.

While there is debate about the means of identification of the psychopath,indeed about the utility of the term psychopath, a body of research evidence has accumulated which seeks to examine a range of correlates of psychopathy. The force of this approach is that it may provide an empirical means of differentiating the psychopath from the non-psychopath and, should the distinction be established, so move towards a theory of psychopathy. The research falls into the three areas of background variables, physiological functioning, and cognitivebehavioural factors.

Background Variables in Psychopathy

The most cited aetiological variables in psychopathy are the familiar ones of family functioning, childhood behaviour, and genetic influences. W.McCord and J.McCord suggested that lack of affection and severe parental rejection were primary aetiological factors, while a longitudinal study by Robins pointed to a variety of early behavioural problems which were strongly associated with psychopathic behaviour as an adult. These problems included early referral to a child guidance clinic for theft or aggression, a history of truancy, lying, non-compliance, no signs of guilt or remorse, and general irreponsibility regarding school and family routines. As with the McCord and McCord study, family characteristics of little or no discipline were also associated with later psychopathic behaviour, as was antisocial behaviour shown by the father.

However, it should be added that this pattern of a wayward childhood is a predictor of many disorders in later life, including criminal behaviour not labelled psychopathic, as well as a range of clinical disorders from neuroses to psychoses. Therefore these findings do not point exactly to the particular antecedents of psychopathy. Some investigators have suggested that the basis of psychopathy, viewed as an extreme of antisocial behaviour, lies in genetic transmission. The evidence in support of a genetic component to antisocial behaviour, noting findings from adoption and twin studies which support the proposition. Cadoret extends this argument to psychopathy. While family, longitudinal, and genetic studies suggest various correlates of psychopathy, they do not provide all the answers: how does the genetic transmission work and what factors mediate poor parenting to produce psychopathic behaviour? An answer may lie in a suggestion made by Cantwell that adult psychopathy is associated with childhood hyperactivity, the common thread being a similar neurological abnormality of possible genetic origin. Is the key to unlocking psychopathy physiological in nature?

Physiology and Psychopathy

There is a considerable body of research evidence on physiological and psychophysiological functioning and psychopathy: For the most part investigators have concentrated on the central nervous system and the autonomic nervous system. Studies of CNS functioning have relied on the electroencephalogram, a recording of the electrical activity of the brain. A review by Syndulko pointed to the methodological difficulties of EEG studies, but nevertheless suggested high frequencies of EEG abnormality in psychopaths; the problem is, however, that not all psychopaths show EEG abnormalities, and in those that do the pattern of abnormality is not consistent.

Further, the pattern varies across situations: Hare and Jutai found abnormal EEGs when the psychopaths were resting, but normal EEGs when the psychopaths were in an active state. Blackburn found little evidence to support the notion of a general association between EEG arousal and aggression; but suggested that differences may exist between primary and secondary psychopaths. The primary psychopaths showed the lowest levels of EEG arousal, while the secondary psychopaths appeared more alert even when resting. Studies of ANS functioning in psychopaths have concentrated upon reactivity and arousal levels as indices of ANS activity. One of the most cited results from this line of research is that when resting, psychopaths have unduly *low* levels of electrodermal reactivity, but in stressful situations there are very *high* levels of cardiac reactivity. This can be viewed as a fast heart-rate indicating the 'gating out' of sensory input and so lowering cortical arousal, meaning that the psychopath is effectively 'tuning out' unpleasant environmental cues. Skin conductance is therefore low because to all intents and purposes environmental stimuli, especially aversive stimuli, are being ignored. While of interest, these physiological findings assume greater significance when considered in the context of cognitive-behavioural evidence.

Cognitive-behavioural Performance in Psychopaths

Cleckley suggested that one of the main characteristics of the psychopath was a failure to learn from experience. This poor learning is evident in the psychopath's failure to avoid the negative consequences of antisocial behaviour. A number of studies have experimentally tested this suggestion employing the technique of *passive avoidance learning* in which the subject learns to respond to anticipatory cues in order to avoid some unpleasant outcome. The findings indicate that psychopaths perform poorly on passive avoidance learning tasks: a result taken to indicate that psychopaths are in a low state of ANS arousal and are relatively anxiety-free.

The physiological evidence on ANS functioning suggests how this might occur: high cardiac arousal gates out the cues indicating the forthcoming unpleasant event, leading in turn to lower arousal and impaired avoidance learning. However, this picture becomes a little more complicated by evidence which showed an effect of the type of aversive event. When the aversive consequence of poor learning was physical pain or social disapproval the psychopaths performed poorly as compared to non-psychopathic controls; however, if the outcome was financial penalty, the psychopaths learned more efficiently than the controls. The introduction of a cognitive component might account for this difference in responding: for example some 'punishments' may have little or no meaning for psychopaths. Thus a prior cognition 'signals' a stressful event which, in turn, is gated out as indicated by the levels of physiological functioning. If the experimental learning task is made more complex by including the competing goals of monetary reward for good performance and avoiding monetary loss for poor performance, then psychopaths perform at a lower level than controls. As psychopaths are equal to controls with financial loss only, it may be that psychopaths have difficulty attending to competing contingencies once they are trying to gain a reward. Newman *et al.* employed an experimental task in which money could be gained and lost: they found that while controls were able to adjust their performance to allow for increases in the probability of losing, psychopaths failed to make such adjustments and so lost accordingly.

This pattern of behaviour is termed 'response perseveration': the continuation of the same action regardless of the consequences it produces. In other words, a failure to learn from experience. Newman *et al.* found that if a 5-second delay was forced between one response and the next, so as to interrupt response set and allow increased time to attend to feedback from the last response, then the deficit between psychopaths and controls was reduced. The reason for this effect of delay is uncertain. These learning difficulties, as demonstrated in experimental tasks, may—perhaps in conjunction with physiological variables—be related to the under-socialization and poor social performance of psychopaths.

While psychopaths may commit crimes of aggression and brutality, this type of behaviour does not seem to be specific to particular types of situations: Blackburn found that even in a hospital ward psychopaths were rated by nurses as more aggressive, more likely to use threatening behaviour to both staff and other patients, and less likely to follow institutional rules than other patients. The pattern of non- conformity to social rules and subsequent lack of remorse can be seen as a failure to learn to avoid social censure; alongside response perseveration in that the same behaviour is continually repeated regardless of the situational demands. Blackburn and Lee-Evans examined the anticipated reactions of primary and secondary psychopaths to anger-evoking situations. They found that psychopaths reported stronger anticipated reactions than controls, particularly for situations involving personal attack. The primary psychopaths anticipated less strong reactions than the secondary psychopaths: this is in accord with Blackburn's earlier suggestion that the aggression of primary psychopaths is more likely to be 'incentive-motivated', while that of secondary psychopaths is 'annoyance-motivated'.

Blackburn and Lee-Evans suggest that the cognitive processes associated with the angry reaction may be of particular importance, particularly with regard to the attentional bias in perceiving hostility in social cues. This suggestion is at odds with a view of psychopathy which suggests a lack of sensitivity to social cues in proposing that the psychopath's aggressive behaviour is in fact a maladaptive strategy in interpersonal problem-solving. In total the psychology of the psychopath is not clearly understood despite contributions such as those discussed and others from areas as diverse as ego psychology, analogies with child development, and conceptualizations in terms of an interpersonal circumplex. Indeed the psychopath remains something of a puzzle: the most reliable fact is that there are relatively small numbers as reflected in official records.

In England and Wales in 1984 there were 410 restricted patients classified as psychopathic detained in hospital. Of this number, 200 had been convicted of homicide or other offences against the person, 90 of arson, and 70 of sexual offences. The number of unclassified psychopaths is, of course, unknown. When compared to mentally ill and mentally handicapped offenders, psychopaths are much more 'criminal': they have committed more offences, particularly theft and assault; received more prison sentences; and spent more time in prison: which all suggests that the prison population may contain substantial numbers of psychopathic offenders. Thus the difficulties posed by the psychopath are numerous: the term itself is ill defined both legally and empirically; the diagnosis of psychopathy is correspondingly unreliable, but once delivered is a powerful label; and there is disagreement about the concept of psychopathy. Two strategies present themselves for resolving this state of affairs.

The first is to remove psychopathy from legal and diagnostic classifications, and there have been recommendations that this should be done, notably by the Butler Report. The second strategy is to pursue empirical research to refine the concept to a degree which allows reliable and valid classification or admits that this is impossible. To place the debate in context it is as well to remember, as Blackburn and Maybury note, 'psychopathy is a theoretical construct rather than a palpable entity'. In summary, it can be said that mental disorder and criminal behaviour do, at times, co-exist.

The nature of the relationship is altogether less clear. In some cases the relationship appears to be partially causal; however, as Taylor stresses, both disorder and crime must be placed in a social context to gain a full picture of the offence. Anticipating future research, it is unlikely that hard and fast rules will be generated regarding mental disorder and crime. It is more likely that each case will have to be considered on its individual merits to determine, in that particular instance, the nature of the relationship between the disorder and the crime. This is a point of some significance in a legal context when the court must decide on issues of responsibility in order to determine whether the offender can be held accountable and therefore punishable for their actions.

PSYCHOLOGICAL THEORIES OF AGGRESSION AND VIOLENCE

It should be noted that there is a variability in terminology in the literature: three terms are in common, sometimes interchangeable, use, *aggression, violence,* and *criminal violence*. Megargee and Siann discuss the issue of definition and have informed the meaning of the terms as used here: aggression refers to the intention to hurt or gain advantage over other people, without necessarily involving physical injury; violence involves the use of strong physical force against another person, sometimes impelled by aggressive motivation; criminal violence involves directly injurious behaviour which is forbidden by law. While concern here is with psychological theories, there are theories from other disciplines, such as anthropology and biology. A number of texts cover the full range of theories, while Mednick *et al.* review biological factors, Merikangas discusses neurological theories, and Riches details the anthropology of violence. In turning to psychological theories it is plain that there is considerable overlap with other theories. This is true of the first class of theories to be discussed, those theories which postulate some instinctual drive towards aggressive and violent behaviour.

INSTINCT THEORIES

A number of theorists have used the notion of an instinct, an innate impulse, to account for aggression and violence. Within Freud's writings, for example, there is the view that human behaviour is driven by two basic instincts, the life instinct and the death force. In the conflict between the instincts of life and death the destructive energy is displaced to the external world. Aggression can be likened to a safety valve as it reduces the energy levels within the system to acceptable levels. If the aggressive behaviour can take the form of non-destructive and socially acceptable acts, then the probability of violence is correspondingly reduced. Such cathartic release might take the form of anger or participating in acceptable aggression such as sport.

This 'neutralizing' of the aggressive instinct can go astray so that the aggression becomes 'internalized', potentially culminating in violence, murder, or suicide. Lorenz approached the study of aggression from an ethological perspective. Following observation and study of animals, Lorenz proposed that aggression stems directly from an innate 'fighting instinct'. This instinct, it is suggested, has evolved over generations owing to its benefits for the survival of the species—*homo sapiens* included. As with Freud's explanation, aggressive energy is seen as continually mounting within the individual and so has, at some point, to be vented. This venting can occur in two ways: a specific environmental aggression-releasing stimulus triggers an aggressive act; or, if the build-up of energy is not released in 'safe' amounts, a violent eruption relieves the tension. Storr sought to fuse the psychoanalytic and ethological theories of aggression. Storr agreed that aggressive behaviour stems from an instinctive impulse, biologically determined, which seeks discharge before reaching critical levels.

Storr extended the argument by suggesting that the way in which an individual manifests aggression in later life results from unconscious motivations derived from childhood emotional experiences. Further, should negative events occur in the period when the individual seeks to deal with the aggressive drive, then the psychopathological aspects of aggression—typified by depression, schizoid behaviour, and paranoia—may result from the unresolved drive. Fromm, while primarily working within a psychoanalytic tradition, argued that it is necessary to go beyond individual factors and consider the role of social, economic, and political influences in precipitating aggression and violence. The criticisms of instinct theories centre on conceptual ambiguities and a lack of empirical verification. There is little hard evidence to demonstrate an instinctual biological drive, nor do there appear to be environmental releasers of aggression in humans. Critics suggest that in the balance between innate and learned behaviour, instinct theories inadvisedly prefer biological to social forces—although Storr, for example, has attempted to meet this point.

Drive Theory

An alternative to explanations based on an innate aggressive instinct followed the development of the concept of a reac-tive drive. A 'drive' which motivates a particular behaviour, including violence, was seen as being acquired through experience rather than being innate. As the level of the drive increased so the individual is motivated to find conditions in which behaviours can take place which reduce the drive. This amalgam of ideas from psychoanalytic and early behavioural psychology as a means of explaining aggression was advanced by Dollard *et al.*. The theory proposed that if a goal was blocked and expected rewards were not forthcoming, this produces a state of frustration; the frustration instigates aggression leading to aggressive or violent behaviour.

The aggressive or violent behaviour may be directed at either the source of the frustration, or displaced to other targets which have some relationship with the primary source of the frustration. Later work pointed to the distinction between 'hostile aggression' and 'instrumental aggression': the former being where the aggression is intended to injure the victim, the latter where the aggression is simply a means to an end as in, for example, armed robbery.

Dollard *et al.*'s thesis generated a body of research work which led to a number of reformulations of aspects of the initial theory. Berkowitz proposed one such modification which has gained prominence. In contrast to the original drive theory, Berkowitz suggested that frustration produces a state of emotional arousal, or 'anger', which creates a potential for aggression.

In order for this potential to be realised, an 'anger-eliciting cue' must be present: this cue, or stimulus, takes the form of something the individual associates with aggression, such as another person's behaviour or the presence of a weapon. This view was taken a stage further with the suggestion that a strong environmental stimuli could produce aggression or violence in the absence of the prior angry state. One of the strengths of drive theory was that it offered hypotheses which could be tested experimentally. As a body of research duly amassed, it became apparent that the theory lacked full explanatory power and so attention turned to a search for new theories. As Bornstein *et al.* note: 'As a result of the deteriorating empirical status of instinct and drive theories of aggression, the social learning perspective...has grown rapidly in popularity and support in the past decade'.

Social Learning theory

Bandura suggested that there are three crucial aspects to an understanding of aggression: the *acquisition* of the aggressive behaviour; the process of *instigation* of the aggression; and the conditions which *maintain* the aggression. Social learning theory argues that acquisition of behaviour occurs through the process of learning, either through direct experience or by observation. There is empirical evidence to suggest that aggressive behaviour can be acquired through direct reinforcement, and via observation. With regard to instigation, Bandura noted that the anticipated outcome, in turn the product of previous learning, was vitally important. The anticipation, signalled by environmental cues previously associated with aggression, not only made aggression more likely, but also pointed to the potential victims of the aggression.

Alongside anticipated outcome, Bandura also suggested that aversive environmental conditions such as high temperatures, air pollution, and crowding can act to raise emotional arousal and so facilitate the instigation of aggression. A suggestion supported by recent research findings; while it has also been shown that verbal and physical provocation can have a similar effect. The effects of provocation have been explained both in terms of the anticipated consequences, such as loss of self-esteem, of failing to respond; and also in terms of the cognitive appraisal of the provocation. An act *perceived* as provocative and antagonistic is liable to increase 'angry' arousal and aggression.

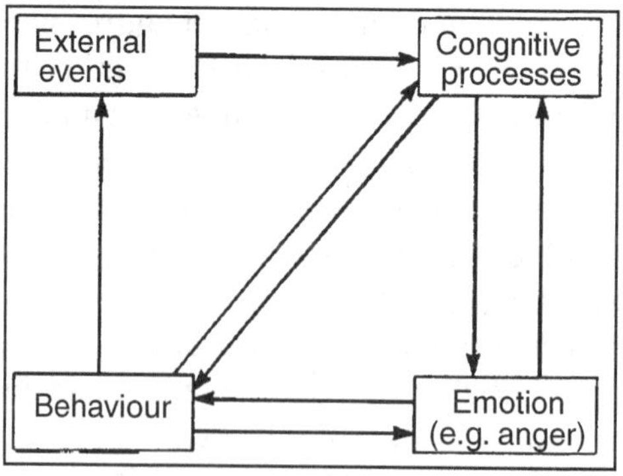

Fig. Schematic representation of the relationship between cognition, emotion and behaviour

Although as Novaco notes, there may be a reciprocal relationship between cognition and anger such that particular cognitions induce anger, while experiencing anger can lead the individual to think in an aggressive manner. Similar reciprocal relationships, as shown in Figure, may function between cognition and behaviour, and between anger and behaviour. Finally, from a social learning theory perspective, the maintenance of aggression is through the three types of reinforcement: external reinforcement, vicarious reinforcement, and self-reinforcement.

Siann makes a number of criticisms of psychological theories of aggression as detailed thus far: as a result of laboratory-based research they show a too narrow approach to aggression; they are limited by positivist methodology; and they show a poor conception of human motivation. Siann suggests that aggression might best be considered as a *social* phenomenon; a phenomenon best studied 'in the real world of perceived and actual inequalities, environmental stress and political conflict'.

Social Accounts

Toch presents the details of a series of interviews with violent men in an attempt to place violence within a social context and so move towards a 'phenomenology of violence'. Toch's work views violence from the offender's perspective, being concerned with the meaning or sense of the act for that person within the social context in which the act occurred. Toch describes different uses of violence such as alleviating tension in awkward social situations or for defending personal reputations.

Typically violence occurs when another person is seen as a threat and some action is taken to respond to the threat; the other person reacts, the instigator responds again, and the *interaction* escalates towards violence. A tradition of social research has followed this style of investigation, with recent work examining the 'rules of disorder'. This research has shown that some violence, such as between football fans, is rule-bound to the extent that it is agreed that fights should take place between equal numbers and that certain forms of fighting are not allowed. Other accounts, mainly from sociologists rather than psychologists, have concentrated even further on the social setting.

Wolfgang and Ferracuti argued that there are subcultures, usually involving young men, in which violence is the legitimate norm: the function of the violence is to provide excitement and a means of achieving status. This argument is supported by the various studies which have shown that violence is prevalent in parts of large cities, and involves a disproportionate number of young males. In accounting for these violent subcultures it has been suggested that they are the result of the anger and frustration caused by social and economic inequalities A radical criminology approach, arguing that 'violence' is defined by the powerful social classes for the purposes of social control.

Thus deaths resulting from the failure to test a drug properly, or inadequate health and safety precautions in a workplace, are not seen as 'murder', but are described as 'accidents' or 'regrettable incidents'. This strategy serves two basic functions: it deflects culpability from the privileged classes; and it locates 'real' crimes in the lower classes. As with most social accounts two problems arise: the difficulty of including the full range of social factors; and the tendency to exclude individual factors.

It is difficult to resist the conclusion that an interactive theory is required, one which seeks to place individual behaviour within a social and political context. Psychological research has contributed to both strands: in the following parts research is discussed which has examined both the situations in which violent crime occurs, and the characteristics of the violent person.

PSYCHOLOGY AND CRIME: THE SOCIAL CONTEXT

Rates of crime, its seriousness, and the frequency of different types of it, all vary considerably from one country to another. That could of course be a reflection of varying definitions and recording methods rather than underlying differences. But large-scale studies suggest that in England and Wales in recent years, there have been in the region of 12–17 million crimes per annum. Those figures come from successive sweeps of the British Crime Survey. The subjectively experienced fear of crime also shows sizeable variations, but they are only circuitously related to the patterns of crime recorded in official statistics. Whatever the exact details, the upshot is that directly or indirectly, crime touches the lives of nearly everyone. Given that context, it is rarely out of the media spotlight.

Research shows that crime events take the largest single share of stories in every news medium. Furthermore, the proportion of news devoted to crime has been rising over the last 50 years. The level of saturation is such that almost everyone has an opinion, and a theory, and some evidence to back them up. Yet discussion of law-and-order inexorably reveals what could be described as an attitudinal minefield. Individuals' perspectives are more likely to be shaped by their prior attitudes and beliefs on a range of social issues than by systematic evidence concerning crime itself. Can an approach that claims to be scientific really be applicable to what most people think of as moral or political questions? In the prevalent imagery, science aims towards detachment and objectivity. Surely that prohibits an appreciation of subjective experiences, meanings, ideals, values and other elemental qualities of the human condition. On the contrary: psychology is very much concerned with those spheres. Moreover, a scientific outlook can be perfectly compatible with exploring them, and with a system of values. If psychology is to inform social action or public policy, it needs to take account of ethical and political dimensions. Nevertheless, there is a view that its methodological aspirations and close connection with biological sciences render it unsuitable for addressing social problems. If it does have a stance, its focus on individual differences leads some writers to perceive it as affiliated, intrinsically, to the conservative end of the political spectrum.

INDIVIDUAL AND COMMUNITY

Let us examine these issues first at the individual level. Working with persons who have broken the law raises a number of complex ethical questions. There is an inherent tension between providing services to meet individual needs while also attempting to serve collective or community interests. Recalling the terminology used by Garland many of the activities described earlier might make it sound as if psychology has switched its historic allegiances. While traditionally it looked like part of the Lombrosian project in criminology, perhaps it has now been assimilated into the governmental project. Psychologists help the police with their inquiries, assist courts of law in evaluating evidence, assess risk levels of offenders, and develop methods of managing them inside the penal system.

Their basic agenda is to help explain crime and find means of controlling it. In Garland's view, such a 'science of causes' is a 'deeply flawed' undertaking. And all of it is done in the service of the state! But before the idea takes off that this is one-sidedly part of a totalitarian agenda, note that much of it can also help individual citizens. It may safeguard them from being wrongfully convicted; reduce severity of punishments if they are; and protect potential victims from genuine risks of exploitation or assault. Outside criminal justice, psychology has many further uses in health, education and the workplace. Furthermore, it is possible simultaneously to meet the needs of both society *and* of the individual who has broken the law. The behaviour of those who frequently offend is evidently troublesome for the community. But much research suggests that often, members of that group are themselves very troubled people. Helping such individuals re-orient their lives can be of immense value both to them as well as to others if it effectively reduces offending.

For the 1,527 young people followed in the Denver Youth Survey, there was a strong association between numbers of self-reported problems and seriousness of offending. 'Amongst those facing only one problem, 7 per cent are serious offenders, but among those facing four problems, 85 per cent are serious offenders'. This pattern emerged for both males and females. The experience of personal difficulties across several areas of life is unfortunately sometimes accompanied by a lack of skills for addressing those problems and solving them in an effective way. For example, Wesner found poorer problem-solving skills among offenders than in a non-offending comparison sample. Whitton and McGuire gave a series of questionnaires designed to assess aspects of problems and styles of coping to young people under the supervision of youth offender teams in the Manchester conurbation, and to a matched sample of non-offenders in a secondary school.

Young offenders reported a significantly higher frequency of serious problems in their lives, and this was correlated with their numbers of previous convictions. However, in depicting the ways they coped, they showed higher rates of using fairly futile, unproductive methods, and lower rates of more active, problem-focused coping. In a study we have encountered before, Zamble and Quinsey interviewed highly repetitive adult offenders, with an average of 25 previous convictions, concerning factors that appeared to contribute to new offences. The crimes for which they were re-arrested were often preceded by difficulties in coping and by poor self-management, characterized by an absence of a positive problem-oriented approach. For example, individuals ignored problems they were experiencing, so allowing them to accumulate to intolerable levels, then adopted drastic solutions. In other research on how adult prisoners cope with problems, Zamble and Porporino found that more poorly adjusted prison inmates had more limited problem-solving skills. Morrison-Dyke found that having limited skills for solving problems was associated with homelessness among offenders with mental disorder.

Exploring the factors that were associated with giving up offending in an adult community sample, Farrall observed that 'as the total number of "problem" social circumstances facing the probationer increased, so desistance became less likely'. Many structured interventions are expressly designed to impart skills in solving personal problems but focus in addition on difficulties posed by the situations in which participants live. Programme materials often emphasize the importance of finding solutions that are most likely to work given certain constraints; depending on circumstances that may generate courses of action that involve changing external situations. Participants in this form of exercise are not extracted or dislodged from their environments. Training enables them to locate the sources of their difficulties, which does not automatically imply that problems reside solely within themselves.

ETHICAL DILEMMAS: RISK ASSESSMENT, PREDICTION AND CHANGE

The ethical tension alluded to above becomes particularly sharp in relation to assessment and prediction of risk, and different writers have taken conflicting stances on whether such a task can be performed ethically. Whether that is feasible depends on the predictive accuracy of the methods used. Some authors have designated a level of accuracy that should be reached before predictions can be ethically acceptable. Whatever that standard might be, it is important only to use the outputs from such assessments in conjunction with various other sources of information, and to inform decisions rather than dictate them. Writing reports and making recommendations are not value-free processes. The principal objective of a psychological report is to change the beliefs and influence the actions of the person who will be reading it. It is incumbent upon psychologists to pay attention to ethical dimensions arising in such work. Other dilemmas arise when contemplating the process of change. This has several interconnected aspects. The paramount question is whether participation in 'change-related activities' should be entirely voluntary, or can somehow be required by criminal justice staff. Even if we believe that someone would change if compelled to do so, is it ethical to enforce compliance?

From one perspective, the right to decide whether to participate resides solely with individuals themselves. From another, society can overrule the offender and is entitled to impose change. Having disregarded the rights of others, it is argued, he or she has forfeited the right to be left alone. We would expect that for people to make meaningful changes, for example of the immensity required when learning to control substance use, it is a prerequisite that they should participate in services on a purely voluntary basis. That is certainly the optimal arrangement. But some findings show that there are also circumstances in which a compulsory framework can be conducive to change.

Farabee *et al.* reported a review of 11 evaluation studies of treatment programmes for drug-abusing offenders. The programmes varied in the extent of legal pressure applied, but in all of them participation was coerced to some extent. Of the 11 studies, 'five found a positive relationship between criminal justice referral and treatment outcomes, four reported no difference, and two studies reported a negative relationship'. The authors challenged the orthodox view that the existence of external pressure implies that individuals lack any internal motivation to change. On the contrary, change often results from a complex interplay of internal and external factors. The authors concluded that the findings supported 'the use of the criminal justice system as an effective source of treatment referral, as well as a means for enhancing retention and compliance'. The importance of the latter was underpinned in further work by Fiorentino *et al.*. But change might not need to be coerced; it can be induced. With reference to high-frequency behaviours such as occur in substance abuse, it is possible to influence people towards change by a refined form of counselling known as *motivational interviewing*. This involves the use of a number of interactive strategies on the part of counsellors. They include, for example, encouraging clients to make statements that attribute to themselves the capacity to change, and drawing to their attention discrepancies between the things they say and the things they do.

While this is not blatantly coercive, it nevertheless raises ethical difficulties. Subtly influencing someone in this way is done without their full, informed consent and is open to the charge of being manipulative. Blackburn has discussed whether there are circumstances in which coercion could be ethically justifiable. This is based on a recognition that psychologists and other professionals working with offenders in criminal justice services are in a dual role, 'simultaneously helper and agent of social control', a conflict that can cause considerable strain. Evidence that coercion achieves desirable ends does not in itself excuse its use. But given certain types of offence or risks of harm, 'total rejection of compulsion does not seem a viable option'.

PROFESSIONAL CODES OF ETHICS

The need to address complexities such as these has led the national psychological associations of most countries to develop and publish professional codes of ethics. Such codes are usually based on the *deontological* approach to moral reasoning: the doctrine that actions have immanent properties of rightness or wrongness independently of their consequences, and that fundamental moral values can be deduced from first principles. It is contrasted with a *utilitarian* approach in which the morality of actions is decided by their consequences or net outcomes. Although the precise contents of ethics codes vary, most enunciate several basic precepts:

- *Beneficence*: the acceptance of a responsibility or obligation to do good.
- *Non-maleficence*: the acceptance of a responsibility to avoid doing harm.
- *Autonomy*: observing individuals' freedom of thought and action, and their right to self-determination.
- *Justice*: basing actions on justice and fairness between individuals.
- *Integrity*: trustworthiness and faithfulness to commitments; acting within one's competence.

The American Psychological Association first published its code of ethics in 1953. It has since undergone several revisions. In 1995, the constituent members of the European Federation of Psychologists' Associations formulated a joint *meta-code* of ethics. Codes are binding upon members of the respective regulatory bodies, and violations of them may lead to disciplinary action. However, they cannot possibly cover all the concrete situations in which an ethical problem might surface. Some psychologists have developed problem-solving and decision-making sequences to apply in circumstances like these, an approach known as *practical ethics*.

AUGMENTING MODELS: RISK FACTORS AND GOOD LIVES

Many current developments in criminal justice programmes are derivatives of the *risk–needs* model propounded by Andrews and Bonta. Some critics contend that dissecting persons in this way represents them solely as a package of risks, a 'dissolution of the subject into a cluster of factors', so denigrating their individuality and completeness. While that misconstrues the approach in important ways, recently a few researchers have proposed major revisions to risk–needs analysis.

Some revive a long-standing assumption that in helping people to change, it may be necessary to alter the 'whole person'. Based on such a critique, Ward and Stewart have forwarded an alternative to the risk factors model, which they contend provides a sounder basis for integrating what have been called criminogenic needs within a wider analysis of motivation and change. They argue that what Andrews and Bonta term *needs* are not ones that offenders themselves would recognize. Rather, they reflect factors that other members of society would wish to change if doing so will lead to lowered rates of recidivism. Ward and Stewart propose instead that we can enrich and strengthen our understanding of need by locating it within a general model of human motivation. Within this they outline certain basic motives and 'primary human goods'. These include, for example, health, selfdirectedness, freedom from turmoil, and relatedness to or intimacy with others.

This leads to a framework for providing offender services that Ward and Stewart call the *good lives* model, in which the objective is promotion of general psychological well-being.

Bonta and Andrews have retorted that risk–needs assessment encompasses a very broad range of areas, and offenders should have access to high-quality services to meet all their needs. The question is whether it is the appointed role of criminal justice services to address ones not demonstrably linked to offending.

Arguably, criminal justice personnel have no clear mandate to probe factors in an individual's life other than his or her criminal acts, and to attempt more than that is invasive. Davison and Stuart distinguish *minimal goals*, the reduction of problematic behaviour, from *optimal goals*, the enhancement of other aspects of individual functioning. The relative weight given to each may have to be negotiated afresh in every case.

DESISTANCE: THE WHOLE PERSON

One of the most consistent findings in criminology, the *age–crime curve*, shows lucidly that as age increases from approximately 20 onwards, there is a substantial decline in the portion of the population committing crimes. Until recently, comparatively little was known about this process. However, several researchers have explored the reasons individuals give when they have successfully reduced their involvement in crime. One important discovery is that this is far more like a journey than a sudden event. As with the pathway into offending, it involves changes of speed and reversals of direction, as individuals' priorities and lifestyles unevenly evolve. Jamieson found that many of the young people they interviewed talked straightforwardly about growing up, maturing, and making other transitions in terms of jobs, education, partners, breaking away from offending peers, taking on responsibilities and 'settling down'.

Maruna reported a series of in-depth interviews explicitly focused on desistance processes, and found that offenders need to make sense of their lives, and in doing so they construct life stories or *personal narratives* developed around specific themes. These *generative scripts* helped them to forge evolving identities within which, metaphorically speaking, they gradually become different people, or new versions of themselves, capable of acting in different ways.

In a study of the impact of probation supervision, Farrall found that the process of desistance bore relatively little relation to the efforts of supervising officers, and was much more a function of life events and circumstances. Externally, progress in desistance was associated with getting jobs, meeting partners and other key events. Others who were stuck in a pattern of offending attributed this to a 'lack of change' in their lives, meaning unsatisfactory circumstances with regard to jobs and relationships. These studies have in common an emphasis on what might be called the 'whole person' approach. While to some extent it challenges the more analytical risk factors model, the two can be complementary, as Maruna's work amply illustrates.

5

Cause and Correlates of Crime

GENERAL CAUSES OF CRIME

- *Necessity of Understanding the Causes of Crime:* It is a commonplace that there can be no satisfactory control of behaviour except control based on a knowledge of the factors producing the behaviour. The experiences of the physical sciences have made that quite positive. But in most of the popular thinking, especially in connection with crime and in almost all of the formal procedure with reference to criminals there is little evidence of a realization of the truth of this commonplace.

  Our literature regarding the causes of crime is more or less interesting, but little of it is of value for purposes of control. The consideration of the causes of crime has been like a gesture or ceremony coming prior to procedure, but not influencing that procedure to a great extent. For this theoretical sociology is undoubtedly in part, at least, responsible. Graduating as it did from the philosophy of history, it has been interested in classifying the universe into factors that may conceivably affect conduct in some way or other, at some time or other. Such an analysis has value, to be sure, in securing an orientation and a general location of policies and in preventing the acceptance of unilateral explanations such as those of the economic determinists and some of the eugenists and psychiatrists. But it renders no concrete assistance in the control of crime, analogous to the assistance that is rendered in plant-breeding and animal-breeding by a knowledge of the mechanisms of heredity. Materials are just beginning to appear that give promise of the development in the near future of such a knowledge of causation as will be of direct assistance in the construction of scientific laws in the field of criminology.
- *Historical Sketch of the Explanations of Crime:* During the mediæval and early modern periods many unorganized and ephemeral

explanations of crimes were stated and accepted. Probably the principal explanation during this time was that crime was due to innate depravity and the instigation of the devil. The English indictment used as late as the nineteenth century not only accused the defendant of violating the law, but also of "being prompted and instigated by the devil and not having the fear of God before his eyes" And the Supreme Court of North Carolina as late as 1862 declared

"To know the right and still the wrong pursue proceeds from a perverse will brought about by the seductions of the evil one"

During the period when this explanation was used most frequently the conception of natural causation was not developed even with reference to such things as disease and, of course, was not developed with reference to crime. Little interest was manifested in motives, intentions, circumstances, or other immediate factors in the causation of crime. Consequently inanimate objects, insects and the lower animals were regarded as criminals and were tried with solemn dignity by the courts. A hog that had been found guilty of crime in the courts of France was pardoned by the King because of its youth. Punishments were arbitrary and unequal, with the general principle of heaping tortures on criminals in accordance with the divine example and of relying on divine interposition as the sole method of reformation.

Out of that situation developed the classical school of criminal law and criminology. Beccaria made the statement of the doctrines of this school in 1764 which has caused the school to be linked with his name. The principal object of that school was to make punishment less arbitrary and severe than it had been and it did valiant service in that way.

It contended that all persons who violate a specific law should receive the same punishment, regardless of age, sanity, wealth, position, or circumstances. This was justified on the ground that the rights of individuals can be preserved only by treating all individuals in the same way and on the ground that the punishment must be definitely determined in advance in order that it may be taken into account in the calculation of pains and pleasures that will result from violation of law.

According to this school the penalty should be just severe enough so that the pains resulting from violations of laws will exceed the pleasures. Consequently this school was not interested in an investigation of the causes of crime; it assumed that the hedonistic calculation was the sufficient explanation.

This extreme idea of equality was soon modified at two points: children and " lunatics " were exempted from punishment on the ground that they were unable to calculate pleasures and pains intelligently and the penalties were fixed within narrow limits rather than absolutely. With these modifications the classical doctrine became the backbone of the body of the law. Popular thinking and legal philosophy have both been essentially the doctrines of the classical school.

After considerable effort to prove the existence of moral insanity, to correlate crimes with economic depressions and other external phenomena and to develop experimental science in general, a decided break was made with this classical theory by a few leaders. The break appears clearly in the writings of Lombroso, started in 1876. He and his followers, known as the Italian or positive school, insisted that it was necessary to study criminals in order to deal effectively with crime.

They turned attention from crimes to criminals, as had been done, in fact, much earlier in ecclesiastical law, thus laying the basis for individualization in the treatment of criminals. Their contribution to the explanation of crime, however, consisted almost entirely in this insistence on the study of the individual criminal. For they had a poor technique for their study and were obsessed by preconceived notions of the character of the criminal. Their principal argument was that criminals constitute a born type. There are so many variations of this doctrine that, strictly speaking, it is not correct to refer to it as a doctrine of the positive school; strictly speaking, also, there is no such thing as a positive school. So far as the theory can be summarized, it is as follows:

— Criminals are by birth a distinct type.
— This type can be recognized by stigmata or anomalies, such as asymmetrical cranium, long lower jaw, flattened nose, scanty beard, low sensitivity to pain; if a person has five or more such stigmata, he is of the complete criminal type; from three to five indicate an incomplete criminal type; and less than three do not indicate criminal type.
— These stigmata show that the criminal is either a reversion to the savage type-an atavism-or else is degenerate and especially of the epileptoid type.
— Because of this nature, the typical criminal cannot refrain from crime unless the circumstances of his life are unusually favorable. One who is not a typical criminal may commit crime because of unusually unfavorable circumstances. Some of the followers of Lombroso maintained that, not only is there a born criminal type in general, but that there are special types, such as thieves,

murderers and sex offenders, that can be recognized by physical stigmata.

After much debate over this theory between Lombroso and his followers and the adherents of the French school, who claimed that crime is primarily the result of imitation, it was suggested in 1899 by Lombroso that his opponents select one hundred criminals and one hundred persons who were not criminals and make comparative measurements to determine whether there was a criminal type. The challenge was accepted and a committee appointed for this purpose, but the committee was unable to agree on procedure and the work was not performed. But one of the English prison officials, Dr. Griffiths, began such a study of the inmates of his own institution for the purpose of comparison with the non-criminal population. By changes in administration, Dr. Goring succeeded to this task and, with the help of other prison physicians and of Karl Pearson, studied more than 3000 consecutive entrants to English convict prisons during a period of about eight years. He made very careful measurements of various physical traits which Lombroso had contended were characteristic of criminals. Goring's conclusion is stated as follows:

"We have exhaustively compared, with regard to many physical characters, different kinds of criminals with each other and criminals, as a class, with the law-abiding public.... Our results nowhere confirm the evidence (of a physical criminal type), nor justify the allegation of criminal anthropologists. They challenge their evidence at almost every point. In fact, both with regard to measurements and the presence of physical anomalies in criminals, our statistics present a startling conformity with similar statistics of the law-abiding class. Our inevitable conclusion must be that there is no such thing as a physical criminal type"

Goring reported that he found about the same difference in cranial measurements between the graduates of Cambridge and the graduates of Oxford as between the criminals and lawabiding people.

A great deal of credence has been given to this theory of a physical criminal type by people who visit courts or prisons occasionally. The appearance of prisoners, of course, is strange, but it is due partly to facial expression, hair-cut, dress and other things more or less easily modifiable. Warden Osborne reports that while he was spending a week in Auburn prison as a voluntary prisoner, dressed in prison garb, some friends came through the buildings with the intention of seeing him. Though they looked directly at him, they failed to recognize him, so much was his appearance changed. Goring has proved quite conclusively that the criminals are not different anatomically as a class from other people.

The only thing that Goring found characteristic of the criminals studied was that they were from one to two inches shorter than other people of the same occupational groups and weighed from three to seven and a half pounds less and he concluded, also, that they were mentally inferior. On the basis of these findings some members of the positive school have contended that Goring really proved their thesis that the criminals constitute a type. There is justification for this contention, but, at any rule, the type that Goring found was distinctly different from Lombroso's type and does not require atavism, degeneracy, or epilepsy as an explanation.

- *Present Methods of Determining Causes of Crime.*
  - *Statistics of Crimes:* One of the earlier methods, still used to some extent, is to determine the correlation between arrests or convictions and some external condition such as temperature, price of wheat or potatoes, or the number of wage-earners unemployed. Bonger collected an immense mass of statistical materials from earlier writers to prove that there was a close correlation between economic conditions and crimes. Others have tried to prove that there is a close correlation between crimes against the person and temperature. Kropotkin even stated the following law of homicide for a particular group:

    "Take the average temperature of the month and multiply it by seven; then add the average humidity, multiply again by two and you will obtain the number of homicides that are to be committed during the month"

    The difficulties and restrictions in such a method are evident. In the first place there are no statistics that are reliable as indices of crimes committed; this is especially true of the United States, but is true also of European countries. And then this method merely locates the causes in a very general way. It may determine, for instance, that more crimes are committed against the person in hot weather than in cold weather, but it does not tell whether it is due to the effect of temperature on temper, or to a greater frequency of contacts between people in hot weather, or to a greater frequency of intoxication in hot weather, or to something else. The statistics of the American Bankers' Association show that bank burglaries increased greatly in 1919-1922 and that the increase occurred almost entirely in the central western states. It is conceivable that it might be found that in contrast with other sections, the banks that were burglarized were constructed in a more flimsy way and were less adequately protected by police and watchmen; and that, in contrast with earlier years, larger amounts of money were held in the banks and the roads were improved so that it was easier for the burglars to travel. This would, in so far, constitute an explanation of certain problems that might be raised. It would, however, not explain why some individuals robbed the banks and others did not. In general, though this method does have some values, it cannot locate causes with sufficient precision to be adequate as a method of determining the causes of crimes.

— *Statistics of Criminals:* Traits and Conditions. A second statistical method has been to study one or more traits or conditions of criminals, each considered as an isolated item, for the purpose of determining the comparative frequency of that item in the criminal and the non-criminal population. Thus mental tests are used to compare frequency of feeblemindedness in the two groups. Or an enumeration is made of the criminals who come from homes broken by desertion, divorce, or death of one of the parents, in comparison with the number of law-abiding persons who come from such homes. Similarly, colour, sex, age, nativity, alcoholism of self or parents, education and various other factors are compared. In the course of such studies many traits and conditions are compared, but each one is abstracted from the others. No pretense is made of studying any criminal as a unit and no effort is made to determine the cause of the criminality of a particular person. Goring states the reason for this:

"Our science, recognizing the protean nature of any one human soul,.the mutability and interchangeableness of all human influences, does not attempt to 'reckon with' the individual. Its methods sketch the broader outline, the cruder feature of a portrait of human beings in the mass. In more technical language, we seek to estimate the final resultant value and direction of certain universal influences and tendencies which, invisible and intangible in their action upon individuals, by the study of individuals can never be measured or appraised; but which, by their operation and interaction over a wide field and in the hearts of all people, lead in the long run to inevitable results; and become not only tangible and visible but capable of the finest definition and measurement"

Goring used this method in his elaborate study of English convicts, comparing physical measurements, weights, education, siblings, economic conditions and similar items. In the study of women delinquents in New York State, made with the assistance of the Bureau of Social Hygiene, by Misses Fernald, Hayes and

Dawley, similar methods were used and more accurate raw material or original data were secured.

It is clear that valuable information can be secured in this way. Goring disproved Lombroso's theory with complete certainty by the use of this method. It seems to be possible to measure the importance of feeblemindedness and presumably any other trait or condition that can be stated in quantitative terms for the criminal and non-criminal populations.

But there are several difficulties and inadequacies in this method.

— There is practically no information accessible regarding criminals, as such. The only information concerns prisoners. Prisoners are a selected group, of criminals and an enumeration of traits or conditions of prisoners would, presumably, yield results decidedly different from an enumeration of the same traits or conditions of all criminals. This is a difficulty that confronts any method of studying criminals, but it is more distinctly a limitation of this method than of some of the others because this method depends on mass information.

— The data regarding prisoners are doubtful in many respects. Such evident things as colour, sex and age can be determined with a fair degree of accuracy, but it is impossible to determine other things, such as nativity, home conditions, or the character of parents, without intensive investigations in the communities in which the prisoners lived prior to confinement. Goring's investigation, for instance, is decidedly unreliable on such points because he depended primarily on the statements of the prisoners, which were verified only in a small fraction of the cases by the reports of the police.

— If this method is used it is necessary to make comparisons with the general population and also with specialized occupational, racial, sex, age and other groups from which the prisoners come. But standards for the entire population and especially for particular groups are lacking for most of the important traits. Because of this it has been customary for those who used this method to enumerate their eases and then, without knowing how prevalent the same traits were in the general population, assert that the enumerated traits were the principal causes of crime. This is exactly Lombroso's defect, but it has been imitated by many investigators of the present day. For instance, it is frequently reported that a specified part of the criminal population is found, on examination, to be psychopathic and that this trait is therefore extremely important in the causation of crime. But no one knows how large a percentage of the general population would also be found, by the same tests, to be psychopathic. The logic is identical with that of an investigator who might find that 60 per cent. of the prisoners had blue eyes and assert that blueness of eyes is an extremely important cause of crime. In addition, many of the standards that we have for the general population are unreliable. It was frequently asserted that the feeble-minded person was from forty to fifty times as apt to be a criminal as the person who was not feeble-minded, but the general application of army tests revealed a much larger proportion of the population feeble-minded, as judged by mental tests. This made it clear that the former judgement had immensely exaggerated the probability of criminality of feeble-minded persons.

— It is possible to secure measurements of only a few traits or conditions and therefore this method cannot locate the causes of crime precisely. It does not explain the mechanisms by which criminality is produced. We may find, for instance, that the male is eight times as criminalistic, judged by commitments to prison, as the female.

But males are also 4.6 times as apt to be killed by lightning. Is this a sex difference, or a result of differences in occupations, or the general method of life, or something else? Or, if we find that there is a close correlation between the criminality of juveniles and the alcoholism of their parents, we want to know whether this connection is due to a constitutional defect that is responsible both for the alcoholism of the parent and the delinquency of the child, or whether the child is delinquent because the parent spends money for alcohol that ought to be used to secure necessities for the child, or because the discipline in the home is irregular or brutal, or because the status of the family is lowered. Goring's total positive conclusion from his statistical study was that the criminal is physically and mentally inferior. Even if this is true, it does not explain why the inferior person is more apt to commit crime. His correlations are, therefore, merely the beginning of an explanation, locating the field in which to look for an explanation rather than furnishing the explanation. This method seems incapable of carrying the explanation beyond the rather external factors. As Thomas has stated: "Taken in themselves, statistics are nothing more than symptoms of unknown causal processes" The mechanisms involved in the delinquency can be understood only by prying into the situations by methods that do not abstract the traits or conditions, but see them in relation to the rest of the situation. It is for that reason that Healy gave the advice

"We strongly counsel against reckoning up the total dynamic value of any cause apparently making for delinquency by regarding it as an isolated fact"

— The statistical enumeration of traits and conditions tells us that certain of these are important and perhaps measures the importance in mathematical terms. It may tell us how much more frequently children from homes broken by divorce, desertion, or death become delinquent than children from homes not so broken. But we need to know more than that: why some children from broken homes do not become delinquent and why some children from homes not broken do become delinquent. We need to know not only why feebleminded persons become criminals more frequently than normal persons (if they do), but also why some feeble-minded persons do not become delinquent and why some normal persons do become delinquent. That is, we should have information that will enable us to state that a person with such and such a nature or such and such attitudes in such and such a situation will always become delinquent. Perhaps it will never be possible to construct such laws, but it is certain that the statistics of traits of criminals will not carry us very far in that direction. The method must be supplemented by other methods.

— *Individual Case Study:* By the individual case study method the criminal rather than the trait or condition is regarded as the unit. The traits and conditions of one criminal are all studied together. It is not necessary to abstain from statistics in this method. Statistics must be used, if a general view of causation is to be secured and if the results are to be stated precisely, just as is true of any other field in which there is a combination of phenomena. The methods differ, not in that one is statistical and the other one not statistical, but in that the individual is the unit in one and the abstracted trait or condition is the unit in the other. The same traits may be studied in each method. If the importance of the home environment is determined by a comparison of the grades or indices of the homes of criminals and of non-criminals, it is not the individual case method. If the importance of the home environment is determined by a consideration of the home in relation to the rest of the situation, it is the individual case method. The comparison might be expressed better, however, if it is recalled that the purpose of the comparison of home-indices of criminals and non-criminals is to determine the importance of home conditions of specified kinds in producing delinquency; while the purpose of the individual case study is to determine how and why certain types of homes produce delinquency, how they produce delinquency, rather than how frequently they produce delinquency.

It is clear that many investigations that pass as case studies are not such in the sense here described. The study must include a sufficient investigation of the whole situation so that the traits and conditions will be understood in relation to the delinquency. A mere mental test and physical examination, for instance, is not a case study. Glueck's study of 608 prisoners in Sing Sing, to which reference is frequently made, was not a study of the kind indicated, for it included a few selected traits only, with no possibility of understanding any one of the prisoners.

Nevertheless Glueck realized the importance of complete studies, as is shown by the following statement:

"A study of causation of crime... even on the individual case involves much more than a mere diagnosis of the offender. It demands a diagnosis of the whole situation on the basis of dependable information concerning behaviour reactions, habits, mental attitudes, predilections and idiosyncrasies of the individual in his daily life"

And he pointed out that such information could best be secured by an intelligent and painstaking field inquiry, which should be supplemented by continued clinical observation within the institution. In his study of juvenile delinquents in Chicago, Healy considered the following items: family history, developmental history, environment (including home and neighborhood), mental and moral development, physical measurements, medical examination, mental tests, psychological analysis and description of delinquencies; under these heads he has a list of items covering nine pages in his book.

In the more recent studies made for the Judge Baker Foundation in Boston, Healy has included under the head of psychological studies the following: psychological examination, mental balance and personality traits. It is evident, also, that the more recent studies have been based much more on field inquiries than were the previous studies and that the relation of the delinquent to his groups has been emphasized. On the basis of such studies of the traits and situations of the delinquent, an effort is made to select the ones that seem to be instrumental in producing the delinquency. In the earlier studies by Healy, one primary and one secondary cause was selected for each case. In the later studies Healy has not attempted to do that, but gives a list of "probable direct causes" in connection with a description of the personality and background of the delinquent. The following may serve as an illustration:

- Bad companions, a delinquent group.
- Lack of good parental management, parents sickly, etc.
- Dearth of good recreational opportunities in neighborhood.
- Treatment under the law:
  - — Continuance of crowd associations through sending boy and companions to same institution,
  - — Return of boy on parole to old associations" The method used in determining the significant causal factors varies. Adler has maintained that for this purpose the important things to study are the behavioristic tendencies manifested in the past behaviour of the delinquent rather than his mental processes. Healy, on the other hand, has insisted that it is necessary to determine the mental antecedents of the delinquency, including such things as mental dissatisfactions, irritative mental reactions to environmental conditions, obsessional imagery, adolescent mental instabilities and impulsions, mental conflicts, worries or repressions, anti-social grudges, mental peculiarities or aberrations and mental defects. For this purpose he reports that the delinquent's own story is of primary importance, though this does not mean that the story must be accepted as a correct explanation of the delinquency.

This individual case study method is criticized by opponents as follows:

— Explanations are too much subject to the individual whim or prejudice of the investigator. Consequently there is danger of making much of factors that are really insignificant and neglecting factors that are very significant. The Whittier State School in California published recently in its Manual three case studies and stated their judgments as to the probable causes of delinquency in each. Miss Bronner, who has been assisting in the case studies of the Judge Baker Foundation, in a review of the Manual, stated that she did not agree with the Whittier authorities as to the probable cause in any one of the three cases. This seems to indicate that one sees in the materials of an individual case those things which fit into his own pre-existing scheme of explanation of delinquency. But the same thing is true of any statistical method of abstracted traits or conditions. And the check in both cases is the judgement of other investigators and the control that is secured by means of the knowledge.

— Most of the agencies that are making case studies are part of an administrative system dealing with delinquents and their studies must result in advice regarding procedure. Consequently there is a probability that the items which can be modified will be selected as causes, or that considerations of practicability in dealing with the offender will determine the explanation. In addition there is a tendency to introduce as a part of the causation any physical or other defect that may need to be corrected, even if it is not a significant part of the causation.

- *Study of the Criminal "in the Open":* Another method of explanation of crime is by association with criminals "in the open" It is asserted by those who have had intimate contacts with criminals "in the open" that criminals are not "natural" in police stations, courts and prisons and that they they must be studied in their every day lif outside of institutions if they are to be understood. By this is meant that the investigator must associate with them as one of them, seeing their lives and conditions as the criminals themselves see them.

  There is no doubt of the desirability of securing information in this way, but it is clearly limited by considerations of practicability. Few individuals could acquire the technique to pass as criminals; it would be necessary to engage in crime with the others if they retained a position once secured. One individual could not build upon the work of another to a very great extent. Moreover, even if these difficulties were overcome, it would still be impossible to secure information regarding the origin of most of the attitudes of the criminals, for few of them would permit interrogations regarding their earlier lives or would volunteer information regarding the factors that had made them criminals. Nevertheless the more information we can secure in this way, the less apt we are to be led astray by the other methods. So far as it can contribute, it is very valuable.

  — *Summary:* This survey of the various methods of determining causes of crime has led to the conclusion that the most important thing to know about crime is the mechanisms by which it is produced and that such knowledge can be secured best by the individual case studies. But it is necessary to realise, also, that there are values to which contributions can be made by the other methods. For some purposes it is desirable to know the comparative importance of various conditions or traits in determining criminality and this information can be secured only by a comparison of the criminal and non-criminal populations.

- *Plan for Study of Causes of Crime:* In order that we may finally arrive at an explanation of crime it is necessary that we have detailed records of the development of personalities. These need to be very detailed and pursued from early infancy to old age. Autobiographies and diaries are contributing more to the understanding of personality at the present time than any other records. But we need also the records of others who can present many phases of personality that are not apt to be written in the autobiography.

  Such records are being accumulated gradually, some of them as books or magazine articles, but most of them as records in various agencies, such as the juvenile courts, the prisons, the schools and the social welfare agencies. A few compilations and interpretations of such records have been presented to the public. There is a startling change in the whole literature in the field of welfare work and criminology in that very few articles are included which do not contain "case records"

  There should be much more effort to secure such records, not only of those who are delinquent, but of those who are not delinquent, for they both throw light on human nature and make possible an understanding of the differences in behaviour. When one considers that a bank in Chicago has a force of 60 men carrying on research work in its own field, it is evident that there should be several times that many persons engaged in personality research investigations, securing, collecting and making accessible to the public life histories of various types of personalities.

  In fact there is no reason why we should not have a continuous record of every individual in the United States. The record should begin with the birth certificate and should include much information that can be secured during the school career, including nativity, occupation of parents, apparent wealth of parents at specified times, siblings, grades in school, ability as shown by mental and educational tests, recreational interests and a general appraisal of the personality by the school teachers.

  To this should be appended various accounts written by the individual regarding his interests and attitudes. Many school children could write reliable autobiographies. A record of all children who have conduct difficulties should be secured by visiting teachers and this should include descriptions of the attitudes of children and parents and the methods used in overcoming the difficulties. Likewise the other agencies which deal with persons at points of crisis, such as the family welfare agencies, courts, prisons, psychiatric clinics, should add to this information.

At the same time it is desirable to have as much information as possible accumulated by those who come in contact with the criminals "in the open" Careful descriptions of the codes and standards of these criminals and autobiographies of criminals would be of value in understanding the general attitudes of this group.

Finally, the standards, codes and values of the "normal" society must be investigated by records of life histories and other documents. Standards of sex conduct, appreciation of variant behaviour, codes regarding the law are illustrations of the things that may be investigated. Such investigations should make it possible to construct a general science of human behaviour, of which the science of delinquency would be a part.

The statistical studies of isolated traits will continue to be of some value in locating the general fields in which search for mechanisms should be made, but the statistics of crimes in correlation with economic or other conditions will be of no value until we improve our records immensely.

CORRELATES OF CRIME

THE PERSONSITUATION INTERACTION

In our efforts to understand human behaviour it is important to consider the fact that each of us is a person functioning in a situational context. Examining this issue from a statistical standpoint, we find that in a two-way analysis of variance there are three main effects, one for variable A, one for variable B and one for the interaction between A and B. A significant interaction between these two variables connotes that the effect of one variable varies or changes at different levels of the other variable.

The primary emphasis is on the theoretical interaction thought to occur between the person and his or her environmental circumstances. Towards this end we investigate the person X situation interaction as it encompasses certain physical, social and psychological features of criminal involvement.

As we consider the nature of the person-situation interaction, our attention is drawn to the manner in which the person and situation merge to form a meaningful unit. In a study conducted some 30 years ago, Briggs, Wirt and Johnson witnessed an interaction between personality functioning and family and/or social conditions in their effect on juvenile delinquency. The outcome of this study showed that juveniles achieving high scores on MMPI scales 4 (Pd), 8 (Sc) and 9 (Ma) were more apt to engage in a variety of delinquent behaviors than other subjects.

However, the delinquency of adolescents in this group rose threefold if they had also encountered at least three separate adverse family events (for example, parental absence, economic hardship) compared to other juveniles who also elevated these three MMPI scales but had no history of adverse family conditions.

In a research study cited earlier it was determined that groups of criminaljustice experts, imprisoned offenders and general-population respondents provided a number of different answers to queries about the causes of crime. One criminal justice expert, in fact, remarked that a whole host of factors cause crime and that all of the research in the world will never be able to identify the proper causative factors. This respondent was absolutely correct in asserting that myriad factors are involved in the criminal acts of specific individuals. However, as David Rowe points out, our purpose in examining the person-situation interaction is not to expound upon the variability found in a single individual but to explain patterns applicable to the overall population.

The person X situation interaction is a focus of attention for theorists operating from a transactional or interactionist perspective. However, many such theorists believe that the person and situation are so fundamentally intertwined that their interaction defies meaningful analysis. Rowe, on the other hand, argues that while this may be true, efforts could still be directed at removing certain confounding person variations (like genetics) from the equation. Therefore, rather than concentrating on individual person or situation variables, our discussion focuses on three general behavioral domains in which person X situation interactions operate. First, however we discuss the interaction hierarchy, namely primary versus higher-order interaction.

PRIMARY VERSUS HIGHER-ORDER INTERACTION

A primary-level interaction, in the vernacular of the research scientist, occurs when the relationship between an independent and a dependent measure varies as a function of a second independent variable. Higher-order interactions, on the other hand, involve three or more independent variables. Expounding upon this conceptualization, we refer to primary-level interactions as person X situation transactions occurring relatively early in life, to be followed chronologically by higher-order interactions. Consequently, interpersonal exchanges between an infant and his or her caregiver during the first several years of life constitute a primary level of interaction, while interpersonal relationships in later childhood, some of which may involve this same caregiver, exist as higher-order interactions. The primary-level interaction frequently serves to buttress, promote and stimulate higher-order interactions.

Within the context of our present review we examine primary and higher-order person X situation interactions as they form along three dimensions: physical, social and psychological. In each case the primary-level interaction occurs when the child is very young (from birth up until age four or five). As the child approaches school age, he or she takes on greater responsibility and begins interacting with a wider network of physical, social and psychological factors. Moreover, one's primary-level interactions frequently lay the groundwork and provide the context for later, or higher-order, interactions. As we embark on this third leg of our journey through the correlates of significant criminality, the necessity of considering this amalgamation of person and situational variables will become increasingly more apparent, even to the casual observer.

THE PHYSICAL DOMAIN

Primary-Level Interaction

Primary-level interactions taking place in the physical domain position themselves around the early life task of stimulus modulation. This particular early life task subsists as an attempt by the human organism to handle the surge of environmental information and stimulation impinging upon its senses during the first several years of life. Stimulus modulation, therefore, concerns the manner in which one perceives, interprets and organizes sensory information in an effort to achieve an optimal level of physiological arousal. Turning our attention to the person and situation variables that seem to be most strongly associated with this particular primary-level interaction, we can see how the complex interplay of different person and situation variables could bring about a variety of different human behaviors.

These influences may very well be grounded in the early temperament (including the genetic inheritance) and nascent environmental experiences of the infant and young child. Although testosterone is a controversial correlate of crime, there is some evidence to suggest that it not only corresponds with aggressive behaviour but may also lead to increased levels of physical activity.

Daitzman and Zuckerman (1980), for instance, ascertained that students high in testosterone were also more likely to be high on measures of sensation seeking. Furthermore, differential testosterone levels may help explain why males are eight or nine times more likely to be involved in crime than females. By way of summary, heredity, temperament, autonomic reactivity, arousal level and testosterone are the person variables that seem most intimately tied to primary-level interactions in the physical domain.

On the situation side of the equation we find parental discipline and level of environmental stimulation. Both factors appear to play an integral role in the chain of events that lead some children to prefer higher levels of sensory stimulation than others. Likewise, it is difficult to discuss the issue of stimulus modulation without also taking into account the kinds of stimulation to which one is primarily attracted. DeMyer-Gapin and Scott, for instance, report that a group of antisocial children were initially more attentive to novel, as opposed to repetitive, stimuli but wound up habituating more rapidly to both relative to a group of neurotic children.

While a discussion of the individual person and situation variables that contribute to the evolution of stimulus modulation tendencies in children may prove interesting, we must explore the interaction of person and situation variables if we wish to fully comprehend the nature of the stimulus modulation life task. Towards this end, two independently administered studies revealed that children possessing difficult temperaments experience markedly increased rates of delinquency if raised in homes where discipline was dispensed in a less than consistent fashion. Similarly, Shostak and McIntyre observed a person X situation interaction in a subgroup of psychopathic offenders showing preference for higher levels of sensory input on the Kinesthetic Aftereffect Test, although the Zuckerman Sensation Seeking Scale (SSS) failed to differentiate between psychopathic and non-psychopathic offenders.

Several additional studies confirm that behavioral indices of sensation seeking seem particularly effective in identifying persons exhibiting features of a psychopathic life adjustment. The outcome of a study directed by Borkovec (1970) disclosed that a group of psychopathic delinquents were less aroused by a simple series of tones than groups of "normal" and "neurotic" delinquents. Along similar lines, Cox (1978) observed increased amounts of boredom and drowsiness following a brief period of isolation in college students rating high on sensation seeking and low on socialization.

Skrzypek (1969) discerned that in comparison to neurotic delinquents, psychopathic delinquents displayed greater preference for complex stimuli and novel pictures. Finally, in a study previously cited, DeMyer-Gapin and Scott (1977) verified that psychopathic children habituated more rapidly to novel stimuli and engaged in more self-stimulatory behaviour (talking, moving around) during the testing session that their neurotic counterparts.

The results of studies such as those reviewed here suggest that from a very early age individuals who eventually develop along criminal lines seek out higher levels of stimulation than most other persons. Although research on the actual nature of the interaction that presumably takes place between the person and his or her situation in effecting sensation seeking tendencies is sparse, it is likely that heredity, temperament and neurological factors on the person side and family and general environmental variables on the situation side, are involved in this drive for heightened sensory experience. The data presented in this section, combined with the early theorizing of Quay (1965), leads me to speculate that the developing criminal strives to achieve higher than normal levels of sensation and stimulation in an effort to compensate for a resting arousal level that is lower than normal. In brief, the evolving criminal requires greater modulation of stimuli in order to incur an optimal level of arousal.

Higher-Order Interaction

Table: The Person X Situation Interaction in the Physical Domain

	Person Variables	Situation Variables
	STIMULUS MODULATION	
	Genetic Factors	
	Temperament	
Primary Level Interaction	Autonomic Reactivity	Parental Discipline
	Arousal Level	Level of Environmental Stimulation
	Testosterone	
	INTERNAL-EXTERNAL ORIENTATION	
		School/Career Aspirations
	Learning	
Higher-Order Interaction	Age	Violent TV Shows
	Testosterone	Peer Interactions
	Cognitive Style	Substance Abuse
		Ambient Temparature

With experience, the aspiring criminal learns that there are numerous activities capable of providing high levels of stimulation and excitement. This awareness may be acquired through imitating the behaviour of various models or shaped by a particular schedule of reinforcement. This might then lead to the development of a particular style of thought that with time and repetition becomes self-reinforcing. An interesting possibility is that testosterone may play a role at both the primary and higher-order levels. Schalling, for instance, argues that the link between aggressiveness and testosterone differs as a function of age, the relationship tending to be somewhat stronger after puberty than before. She has also observed that high testosterone adolescent males have learned to achieve their goals by expressing anger and intimidating others.

Speaking of age, this person variable also seems to contribute meaningfully to higher-order interactions occurring in the physical domain.

Studies employing primate and human subjects indicate that stimulation-seeking tendencies peak during mid to late adolescence and follow an age pattern reminiscent of the age-crime curve.

Moreover, research on human subjects denotes that sensation seeking and criminality both decline as one proceeds through the third decade of life. These findings, coupled with the observation that one of the primary motives for crime during late adolescence and early adulthood is excitement, certainly lend credence to the hypothesis that age interacts with early stimulation-enhancement tendencies to bring about a higher-order interaction that we will henceforth refer to as internal-external orientation.

A variety of situational correlates of crime may interface with selected person variables and the early products of primary-level interaction to bring about changes in the higher-order cauldrons of the physical domain.

Predominant among the situation variables that have been investigated with higher-order physical domain interactions in the mind are school and/or career aspirations, television violence, peers, substance abuse and ambient temperature.

Glueck and Glueck (1968), for example, discovered that delinquent adolescent males ex pressed greater boredom with school and a stronger desire to enter adventurous vocations like aviation than non-delinquent male adolescents. In one longitudinally designed investigation, cognitively understimulated subjects were drawn more to "stimulating," and oftentimes violent, television shows than others. It does not take much extrapolation to decipher the implications this relationship may have for those of us interested in forming a deeper appreciation of higher-order interactions occuring in the physical domain.

Of further relevance to this issue is peers. Research suggest that peer groups not only provide delinquents with emotional support but also form a conduit through which a sense of excitement and high drama may be achieved. Drugs and alcohol would also appear to contribute to higher-order physical domain interactions to the extent that chemicals characteristically augment, alter and intensify people's perceptions of events.

Finally, certain general environmental conditions, such as ambient temperature may also enter into higher-order interactions occurring in the physical domain on the situation side of the person X situation interactive equation.

Higher-order interactions taking place in the physical domain of human experience seem to cluster around issues of personal orientation (internalization versus extemalization of parental and/or significant other messages and dictates). Consequently, an individual preoccupied with achieving an excessive level of stimulation and excitement will look towards environmental contingencies capable of providing him or her with the greatest opportunity for such experiences. The behavioral pattern associated with such tendencies apparently reflects an external rather than internal orientation.

Whereas this issue may be somewhat controversial, the preponderance of evidence on orientation and law-violating behaviour intimates that criminals, delinquents and habitual offenders are more externally oriented than non-criminals. An external orientation may therefore be a powerful precursor of subsequent criminality.

THE CRIMINAL AS A DECISION-MAKER

In July 1985, a group of researchers met in Cambridge, England, to discuss decision making and criminality. Several of the more noteworthy papers presented during the conference were subsequently published in a book edited by sociologists Derek Cornish and Ronald Clarke, under the title The Reasoning

Criminal (1986). In presenting their ideas on decision making and crime, Cornish and Clarke argued that situational variables exert an important impact, not only on the criminal event but also on the decisions the offender makes relative to his or her criminal career.

Hirschi (1986) adds that situational variables and characteristics of the individual may directly affect one's decision to engage or not engage in a specific criminal act. Basically, though, the rational approach to crime assumes that the offender seeks to benefit by way of various choices and decisions.

Criminal decisiomaking has been investigated in groups of robbers, burglars, shoplifters, commercial thieves and opiate abusers. Weaver and Carroll, for instance, explored the thinking and decision-making abilities of 17 experienced and 17 novice shoplifters by accompanying them on a trip through a local department store. They determined that both the experts and novices based their verbalized crime-no crime decisions on a simplified model of environmental risks and opportunities. Several of the more salient factors considered in this assessment were store security, physical layout, presence of bystanders and item characteristics, to include value and size. Normally, however, subjects considered no more than one or two of these factors before rendering a shoplift-no shoplift decision.

Despite the fact that experienced and novice shoplifters in the Weaver and Carroll study tended to rely on oversimplified models of the environment in rendering crime-no crime decisions, different sets of variables were responsible for deterring subjects in each group from engaging in shoplifting behaviour. Whereas fear, guilt and the possibility of apprehension characteristically deterred novices, the more experienced shoplifters were deterred only by strategic difficulties like the size of an item or the presence of security devices. Furthermore, these "experts" approached strategic difficulties as things to be overcome while novices were normally deterred in the face of any strategic roadblock. Weaver and Carroll remark that the prospect of arrest, jail, or fines rarely entered into the crime-no crime decisions of the experienced shoplifters.

The decision-making models of 113 Californian robbers were explored in interviews conducted by Feeney. Feeney found that only half his sample made even rudimentary plans before deciding to engage in the robbery that resulted in their most recent arrest and only 5 percent employed detailed plans. Interestingly, planning increased with the number of robberies committed. Similar to the experienced shoplifters in the Weaver and Carroll study, only 21 percent of the sample considered apprehension to be a risk they should concern themselves with before embarking on their most recent criminal venture. In further support of Weaver and Carroll's results, Feeney ascertained that firsttime robbers more frequently considered the risk of arrest than experienced robbers. Continuation of the criminal pattern of robbers was found to correlate positively with experience and negatively with fear of apprehension. As we might have anticipated, negative thoughts about robbery were strongest in firsttime offenders.

The decision to exit crime has also been a topic of investigation. Cusson and Pinsonneault for instance, interviewed 17 ex-robbers and reviewed several ex-offender biographies in an effort to identify the factors associated with the decision to abandon crime as a way of life. This group of former offenders advised that their decisions were based on a reevaluation of life goals and increased willingness to accept modest incomes.

Some of the specific factors mentioned by study participants as instrumental in their decision to desist from crime were shock, such as seeing one's crime partner gunned down, a gradual wearing down of the criminal drive through an accumulation of punishments and incarcerations, the problems associated with serving time as an older inmate and a building up of fear brought about by the realization that unless they changed their careers, they would be spending the remainder of their lives in prison.

As part of the reevaluation process that precedes desistence from crime, the individual begins to severe his or her ties with past criminal associates. Cusson and Pinsonneault discuss the case of one offender who resolved to move out of the city in order to avoid all contact with former inmate associates who happened to live in his old neighborhood. Though none of the respondents in their study mentioned jobs as protection against future criminal involvement, Cusson and Pinsonneault found that every one of their subjects was employed in reasonably well-paying, interesting jobs.

Steady employment may therefore reinforce the notion that honest work provides a better long-term payoff than crime. Thus, while a number of external factors enter into the decision to desist from crime, of overriding importance is a reevaluation of one's life goals and personal expectations.

CHOOSING CRIME

The economic or utilitarian approach to understanding crime places a premium on choice as a cause of crime. In its classic version, economic theory argues that people commit crimes because the benefits of such activity outweigh the costs. The complex interplay of supply and demand leads to a situation whereby the individual selects crime when the perceived utility of so doing exceeds the utility of engaging in legitimate activities.

More recently, however, additional factors have been entered into the economic equation. Block and Heineke for example, contend that wealth, the payoff of illegal activities, enforcement practices, punishment effects and the degree to which an individual is certain that a particular penalty will be administered need also be considered as a part of the utilitarian approach to explaining crime.

Like the utilitarians, Wilson and Herrnstein propose that criminal behaviour is controlled by its consequences. However, they expand the notion of reinforcement beyond the simplistic cost: benefit analyses performed by economic-minded theorists, affirming what writers like Waldo and Chiricos had been asserting since the early 1970s that choice is a perceptual process and that it is one's subjective interpretation of an event, not the event itself, which is reinforcing or punishing.

Wilson and Herrnstein further argue that the valence attached to a particular reinforcer or punisher may vary depending upon the time of day, relative satiation or deprivation of that contingency and characteristics like intelligence, impulsivity and bonding to conventional social norms. Like the utilitarian theorists, however, the essence of Wilson and Hermstein's argument is that people choose between competing criminal and non-criminal alternatives.

Suspicious of inferences made about individual-level processes like choice from aggregate-level data, Piliavin probed the impact of perceived sanctions on self-reported criminality. The results of this study, however, failed to identify a significant deterrent effect for perceived sanctions. Arguing for the necessity of aggregate-level research on choice, Heineke maintains that microlevel analyses, such as the ones conducted by Piliavin are subject to a variety of conceptual, statistical and practical limitations.

Heineke adds further that if one can demonstrate that actual rewards and sanctions are a monotonic function of perceived rewards and sanctions, the former could legitimately replace the later in research on choice. As Matsueda, Piliavin and Gartner point out in responding to this critique, however, there are at least as many problems with Heineke's argument as there are with the original Piliavin et al. study, not to mention the fact that it fails to address the problems of aggregation, measurement error and identification, all of which appear to limit the meaningfulness of economic research on criminal choice.

Two additional individual-level studies provide circumscribed support for the rational-choice explanation of crime. Witte collected data on the status of 641 men released from North Carolina prisons and witnessed modulating probabilities of crime based on permutations of variables like age and employment status; and in a study of 1,171 property offenses committed by juveniles and adjudicated by a family court in Honolulu, Hawaii, Ghali discovered that the decision to engage in certain criminal acts is a dynamic function of factors like age and history of prior court referrals. However, the fact that offending patterns vary by occupational status or criminal background is not bona fide confirmation of the rational choice position.

In fact, Paternoster in a review of research on the perceived certainty and severity of punishment, concludes that there is little evidence in support of a causal nexus between either the perceived certainty or perceived severity of punishment and self-reported criminality. If anything, asserts Paternoster, criminal involvement may be a cause of sanction-linked perceptions through modification of a person's assessment of the certainty and severity of punishment. While results such as those obtained by Piliavin and reviewed by Paternoster (1987) shed doubt on the utility of the economic approach to crime, they do not necessarily eliminate the possibility of a choice-criminal behaviour relationship. As Johnson and Payne (1986) point out, research in the field of cognitive psychology has demonstrated rather convincingly that the human ability to process, store and access information is limited.

Consequently, most of us develop heuristic strategies that facilitate memory storage and accelerate the rate at which information is retained but at the cost of increased error. Like Piliavin et al., information-processing theorists hypothesize that it is not the objective characteristics of a situation, but one's internal representation of that situation, that drives behaviour. However, because we are imperfect information processors, this internal representation embraces only part of the picture. This may help explain why choice and/or deterrence research conducted at the individual level often fails to provide support for the rational choice hypothesis.

Carroll (1978) explored this issue in a study carried out on groups of adult and juvenile offenders and non-offenders. After presenting subjects with a threeoutcome gambling task that varied along four dimensions-probability of getting away with a crime, probability of capture, the amount of money obtained if >successful, the penalty if caught-Carroll asked subjects to evaluate 72 crime opportunities. The results of this study indicate that subjects frequently based their decisions on a single dimension to the exclusion of the other three.

Though individual subjects showed consistent preferences for a particular dimension, only minor variations were noted between groups (age, criminal status). In fact, the only difference noted among the choices offered by offenders and non-offenders was that the offenders viewed all criminal opportunities as more desirable than did the non-offenders.

Based on the results of this study, Carroll (1978) concluded that a "psychological" explanation of human choice, wherein the individual makes decisions utilizing a simple, often unidimensional analysis of criminal opportunities, is more accurate than the purely "economic" interpretations of choice that portray the individual as making exhaustive, complex calculations leading to an optimal decision. Similar results were obtained in a study of British burglars. It would appear, then, that the human decision-making process is, by nature and necessity, limited. As such, we must search for research paradigms that take these imperfections into account. With the various failings of the human decision-making process clearly in mind, we turn our attention to a model of criminal choice behaviour.

A MODEL OF CRIMINAL CHOICE AND DECISION MAKING

One of the chief mistakes made by researchers utilizing computer simulations to study the process of human problem solving has been the tacit assumption that the inner workings of the human mind can be replicated by a computer. Whereas computers function on the basis of circuitry, rules and binary logic, the human learning sequence is grounded in conditioned responses, successive approximations, trial and error and the strengthening of associational bonds through repetition. While the human mind processes information less efficiently and has significantly less storage space than most modern-day computers, it is capable of several functions the computer is not. Prominent among these are the mind's capacity for ingenuity, propensity for self-evaluation and ability to act on unfamiliar information.

It would seem that the computer and human mind each possess certain strengths and advantages, although they are hardly interchangeable. There are, nevertheless, several commonalities in the way computers and human beings process information. In fact, I have taken the liberty of borrowing terms, concepts and procedures from the computer science field in deriving a model of criminal decision-making and choice. Even though the focus of the present discourse is on criminal decision making, this model seems applicable to the general human decision-making process as well.

Risk and Protective Factors. Risk factors serve to enhance the probability of a particular individual engaging in a pattern of delinquent or criminal behaviour. Protective factors, on the other hand, serve to shield one from criminogenic influences, thereby reducing one's chances of developing along criminal lines. Risk and protective factors illustrate how certain individuals may be more or less more prone to delinquent or antisocial outcomes.

They also help explain why research on person, situation and person X situation interaction variables has yielded several robust correlates of criminal involvement. Rather than causing law-violating behaviour, however, I contend that risk and protective factors interface with crime by narrowing the range of options available to an individual at any particular point in time. Risk and protective factors are often at opposite ends of the same continuum. Hence, while inadequate social bonding may leave one vulnerable to the development of later delinquency a stable mother-son relationship may protect an otherwise vulnerable child from the ravages of significant criminal involvement.

Similarly, high intelligence has been known to inoculate an individual against the temptations of a criminal lifestyle while low IQ may facilitate one's descent into a life pattern of violent criminality. Still yet another study shows that continued association with an all-male peer group at ages 18 to 19 predicts greater levels of future criminality while disengagement from an all-male peer group corresponds with decreased levels of subsequent criminality.

Data from this same longitudinal project revealed that high-risk boys who eventually went on to become recidivistic offenders had been rated as lacking in concentration at age 8, more troublesome at age 10 and were more likely to be placed in special schools at age 11 compared to high-risk boys who did not display a recidivistic pattern of subsequent criminality.

It is worth mentioning that risk and protective factors do not exist independent of other variables, but are part of a wider interlocking network within which the person X situation interaction operates. Sports, while they have been shown to exert a protective effect on black and small-town white youth, are normally ineffective in shielding urban white youth from future criminal involvement. Leisure activities, in fact, can serve to increase one's risk of future criminality under one set of circumstances and protect otherwise vulnerable adolescents from other criminogenic influences under another set of conditions.

The results of a study directed by Agnew and Petersen (1989), for instance, confirmed that time spent in unsupervised peer-oriented social activities correlated positively with delinquency, while time spent in organized leisure activities and non-competitive sports correlated negatively with delinquency. Shyness is a variable that demonstrates an even more dramatic effect, serving as a risk factor with some individuals and as a protective factor with others. McCord (1987) asserts that children rated as shy and non-aggressive by their teachers at age seven or eight were less likely to be arrested and convicted during the next 40 years, while children rated shy and aggressive were more likely to encounter legal problems during this same 40-year period.

The family seems to be a particularly powerful source of risk and protective influence. Briggs, Wirt and Johnson (1961) discerned that adverse family circumstances (for example, parental absence, economic hardship) placed male adolescents at a disadvantage in terms of subsequent delinquency development, particularly if these features were accompanied by elevated scores on three MMPI scales: 4 (Pd), 8 (Sc) and 9 (Ma).

Hathaway and Monachesi (1963), on the other hand, discovered that children achieving "adverse" MMPI configurations were protected by positive family characteristics like good communication and the presence of strong affectional ties within the family. In a cross-sectional analysis of vandalism in a northern English city, Gladstone (1980) determined that criminal behaviour was least likely in situations where the parents carefully monitored the peer-group activities of their offspring.

Positive family relationships may help protect a child against later criminality by providing an effective network of social support as well as ideas and values that inoculate the child against later criminal involvement. Negative family influences, on the other hand, tend to have a multiplicative effect on a child's risk for later delinquency. Hence, Rutter and colleagues (1975) identified six risk factors (low social status, large family size, paternal criminality, maternal psychiatric history, severe marital discord, involvement with the social service administration) that seemed to exert a synergistic effect on the behaviour of the adolescents in their study. While the presence of only one risk factor was no more criminogenic than a complete absence of risk factors, the presence of two factors increased a subject's vulnerability to delinquency fourfold, with similar multiplicative increments as the number of active risk factors mounted.

The longitudinal research of West and Farrington (1973) illustrates how risk factors elevate one's chances of engaging in later criminality without determining such behaviour. They observed that 13 percent of their sample of 400 working-class delinquents (including 17 recidivists) failed to qualify as high-risk subjects as measured by family criminality and the presence of at least two of the following six additional characteristics: born illegitimate, four or more siblings, permanently separated from one or both parents before age 15, family on welfare, residing in slum housing, under the supervision of social service administration at least once.

West and Farrington also identified a number of high-risk youth who did not engage in criminal behaviour. Though these high-risk individuals were often socially maladjusted in ways other than delinquency (for example, substance abuse, social isolation, poor work record), a few seemed to have escaped their backgrounds to become happy, successful, contributing members of society. Such findings reaffirm my original contention that risk and protective factors serve to limit and expand, respectively, one's options but do not determine one's choices.

Exacerbating and Mitigating Factors. Where risk and protective factors are designed to explain criminal involvement, exacerbating and mitigating factors are more relevant when it comes to describing specific criminal events. Consequently, they tend to be more situationally influenced than risk and protective factors. This does not mean, however, that a risk factor cannot also play an exacerbating role or that a protective factor cannot also exert a mitigating effect under a discrete set of circumstances. Drugs, for instance, not only serve to increase the possibility of criminal involvement (risk factor) but also play a significant role in the unfolding of various criminal events (exacerbating factor). Along similar lines, a strong social bond may serve to protect one from becoming involved in a criminal lifestyle while empathy for a potential victim might mitigate against committing a specific criminal act. A variable like ambient temperature, on the other hand, would seem generally restricted to an exacerbating or mitigating role in its impact on criminal outcomes.

Felson (1986) argues that the criminal event entails a convergence of person and situation variables over time and space. Assessing the contextual features of serious assault, Felson and Steadman (1983) discerned that person and choice factors, like the desire for retaliation, played a central role in serious assault and homicide. However, they also noted that specific behaviors on the part of both the victim and various bystanders influenced how the violent scenario played out. In Felson and Steadman's original study it was determined that victims were more likely to have been killed when they were intoxicated, physically aggressive, or in possession of a weapon. Follow-up analyses of these data revealed that third parties often played a role in the eventual outcome of a potentially violent event, either as antagonists or mediators.

The routine-activities approach to crime postulates that three elements must be present for a predatory criminal act to occur: a motivated offender, a suitable target and the absence of capable guardians against crime. This theory borrows liberally from the social and physical ecological perspectives and considers Hawley time-space concepts of rhythm, tempo and timing. Miethe, Stafford and Long (1987) investigated the relationship between nighttime activities away from home and crime and observed concordance in the case of property offenses but not in the case of violent crimes. They attribute the lack of a routine-activities effect for violent crime to the spontaneous nature of this category of offence. However, Kennedy and Forde (1990) explored this issue further and found that routine activities accounted for a significant portion of the variance in both violent and property crimes, but for very different reasons. Routine activities appear to exert their effect on violent crime by exposing offenders and victims to conflict situations, while they influence property crime by identifying salient criminal opportunities.

Another portentous feature of the situational context of a criminal event pertinent to exacerbating and mitigating factors is the manner in which decision alternatives are presented to the individual. Tversky and Kahneman (1981) observed that two formerly identical choice alternatives evoked markedly different preferences when phrased in slightly different ways. From these results Tversky and Kahneman concluded that the mode through which alternatives, options and possibilities are framed can have a vibrant impact on the decisions one derives. It would appear that both the situational context and the manner in which this context is presented are essential to understanding the role exacerbating and mitigating factors play in the rise of specific criminal events.

Criminal Opportunity. Our discussion of input variables would be incomplete without consideration of criminal opportunities. The study of criminal opportunities dates back to the pioneering work of Merton (1938) and Cloward and Ohlin (1960) and is particularly relevant when we examine crime rates. Weather and seasonal variations in crime doubtlessly suggest the prospect that particular crimes are more common during certain seasons or months of the year (assault during the summer for instance), when the opportunity for human interaction is more apparent. Additionally, research shows that property crimes are more prominent in developed as opposed to underdeveloped countries and in urban as opposed to rural communities and suggests that one's access to material goods is at least as important as personal and situational factors in understanding the crime of a given region, country, or area. Finally, while Newman (1972) notion of "defensible space" has been much maligned, there is qualified support for his claim that certain forms of crime can be reduced by limiting criminal opportunities via specific architectural modifications. The impact of opportunity on crime rates has been documented in research studies administered since the early 1960s. Wilkins (1964), for instance, related that a large portion of the variance in auto theft in England between the years 1938 and 1961 could be attributed to the number of automobiles available. Felson and Cohen (1977), on the other hand, discerned that burglary rates in the United States between 1950 and 1972 were a multiplicative function of three variables-proportion of the population between the ages of 15 and 24, percent of "primary individual" households and mobility of various property targets (for example, weight of the average television set), the last two of which provide increased opportunities for crime.

In a similar vein, Gould (1969) witnessed a correlation of.98 between the amount of currency available in U.S. banks and the number of bank robberies taking place between 1944 and 1965. Finally, Walsh (1978) notes a parallel between the rise of shoplifting offenses in England, circa 1950 to 1960 and a thirteenfold increase in the number of self-service grocery stores available to potential thieves.

Since it is common knowledge that one cannot steal a car that does not exist or rob a bank that is devoid of funds, what then does the study of opportunity really tell us about crime and criminals? We might answer this question by reminding the reader that a consideration of criminal-opportunity issues not only provides us with insight into the temporal, geographical and seasonal ebb and flow of crime but also furnishes us with clues crucial to comprehending specific criminal events. Opportunity restricts our access to specific criminal rewards and helps direct our attention to certain goals and away from others. Few people have available to them the opportunities for such large-scale >scams as were perpetuated by the likes of stocktrader Ivan Boesky or televangelist Jim Bakker, although the opportunity for other forms of crime can nearly always be found in an open society.

This discussion of criminal opportunity should not be construed as lending support to the misguided notion that criminals sit around waiting for a criminal opportunity to appear. Unlike most non-criminals, the career or lifestyle criminal is constantly searching for new criminal opportunities; and in a world populated by persons naïve to the ways of the criminal, such opportunities abound. Recidivistic offenders characteristically approach their environments and others in ways that differ substantially from the perspective of non-criminals.

Even when not actively pursuing antisocial plans, the habitual criminal is alert to illicit opportunities-an unlocked car door, unattended purse, or unsuspecting citizen. Like a championship football team whose defence habitually forces the opposition into turning over the ball, the high-rate offender capitalizes on whatever nascent opportunities are available in forging a criminal way of life.

This hypersensitivity to criminal opportunities was present at an early age in bank robber Willie "The Actor" Sutton:

The first day at the new school I noticed that the teacher put her pocketbook in the desk drawer. I also noticed that when we were dismissed for the morning recess she left the room too. I served to notice all of this automatically. That very first day, as we all moved down the hall towards the schoolyard, I mumbled something about having forgotten my handkerchief and slipped back into the empty classroom. It took about ten seconds to reach into the drawer of the teacher's desk, open her pocketbook and grab one of the dollar bills that lay in it.

Even though the nine-year-old Sutton saw a criminal opportunity that would have been overlooked by most non-criminals, the actual criminal events one chooses to engage in are still a function of the opportunities available to that individual at any particular point in time.

Target Selection. Cousin to the issue of opportunity is the question of target selection. Several factors are considered by offenders in identifying potential human and property targets. Some of the more popular considerations are proximity, accessibility, potential yield and timing. Given the knowledge that offenders rarely traverse a significant distance for the purpose of committing a criminal act, persons and areas in close physical proximity to the offender are at greatest risk for victimization. The accessibility of a particular target and the absence of capable guardians against crime are also frequently taken into account by offenders searching for a target upon which to unleash their antisocial inclinations. The perceived value or potential yield provided by the target is a further consideration, although offender judgments in this regard are often flawed and oversimplified. Timing enters into decisions involving target selection to the extent that certain times of the day, days of the week, or seasons of the year are more or less conducive to the commission of various criminal acts.

A potential victim's lifestyle may also influence his or her vulnerability to victimization. In the original presentation of their lifestyle theory of criminal victimization, Hindelang, Gottfredson and Garofalo examined ways in which persons leave themselves vulnerable to victimization by the company they keep and the general activities in which they engage. Victimization rates are two to three times higher in persons whose lifestyle brings them into regular contact with strangers in potentially conflict-promoting environments like discos and bars, although there is no victimization-enhancing effect for persons involved in structured social activities like organized clubs and religious functions. It seems likely, then, that certain lifestyle features of potential victims may be taken into account by offenders searching for a potential target.

Process

Once the relevant data are entered into a computer, the machine shifts into a processing mode, whereby the information is analyzed by way of existing programmes, formats and procedures. There is also a processing step in the human decision-making sequence that finds its expression in the evaluation, organization and interpretation of input data. However, unlike a computer the human decision maker does more than apply logic and rules to the information presented. First, the human decision-making process is affected by developmental factors.

Second, human problem solving is not only more flexible than the binary logic of the computer but also provides for the possibility of creative solutions that are not necessarily tied to the immediate situational context. Third, the human analytic process is less efficient and more susceptible to error than is the methodology of the computer. These three factors are critical in promoting a fuller appreciation of the information-processing stage of human decision making. Developmental Context. Just as there is a situational context (input) to human decision making, so there is also a developmental context. The humanistic notion that we are born with the capacity for free will seems as credulous as it is optimistic. It appears that the infant responds to internal drives (hunger) and external circumstances (warm ambient temperature), but does not actively choose or select one behaviour over another.

Interestingly enough, from an early age the child learns that certain behaviors are more likely to get a parental response than other behaviors. This would seem to suggest the presence of an incipient sensitivity and a budding selectivity in the actions of even the very young child.

Where a strict behaviorist might argue that an infant is "conditioned" to respond in a particular fashion and that there is no need for the intermediary concept of choice, I contend that early learning actually reflects the onset of decision-making capability. For as the child begins to realise that certain behaviors are rewarded and other actions are punished, we see the advent of internalized representations of events, situations and people.

This mental representation process is not only central to the theorizing of information-processing theorists but is also crucial in the minds of developmental psychologists like Piaget (1954). According to Piaget, a child entering into the preoperational stage of cognitive development (around age two) begins relying on internal representations through symbols, images and language. By age seven most children have graduated to the concrete operational stage, in which fundamental principles of nature such as the law of cause and effect are beginning to be grasped.

Piaget (1954) also theorized about moral development, although Kohlberg is the individual whose name is most clearly associated with this particular area of research endeavor. Building on Piaget's earlier work, Kohlberg proposed six stages of moral development embedded in three levels. There is ample evidence that younger children tend to function at lower stages of moral development than older children. However, Kohlberg's assertion that the moral reasoning skills of delinquents are inferior to those exhibited by age-matched peers has not always found confirmation in the empirical research literature. Moreover, studies show that responses on a moral dilemma task demonstrate minimal concordance with actual behaviour.

Conative development, which concerns an individual's capacity for selfcontrol, also seems relevant to our discussion on personal choice and responsibility. Mischel (1974) writes that impulse control expands with age, although the results of one study indicate that children as young as three are capable of delaying gratification. Therefore, while it appears likely that an infant does not engage in informed decision making, the capacity to choose evolves rapidly and matures in response to various changes occurring in the young child. In a review of the literature on cognitive, moral and conative development and criminal liability in children, Dalby (1985) concludes that by age 7 most children satisfy rudimentary criteria for criminal responsibility, while nearly all children are liable from a criminal justice standpoint by age 14. Dalby is quick to point out, however, that not all same-aged children are functioning at the same development level. A young child operates largely on the basis of information provided by his or her immediate environment (family members). However, as this child grows older he or she is exposed to extrafamilial sources of information through contact with peers, school officials, television and the criminal justice system. In conjunction with this evolving self-awareness comes a concomitant broadening of the options available to the individual along with an expanding ability to make informed decisions.

As such, we need to consider development variables as delimiting a person's information-processing capabilities-factors which recede in significance as the individual matures. It would also appear advisable, then, that we replace the outmoded concept of innate or absolute free will with the more reasoned hypothesis that choice behaviour unfolds and one's options expand as a function of cognitive development and a widening sphere of environmental experience.

Cost: Benefit Analysis. Decisions are characterized by three primary elements:

- A set of alternatives;
- A set of outcomes or payoffs;
- An assessment of the probability of achieving said outcomes. Economic theorists like Becker (1968) argue that the assessment of outcomes takes place in the form of a cost: benefit analysis. The human decision maker, according to Becker, weighs the relative advantages and disadvantages of committing a specific criminal act against the advantages and disadvantages of a legitimate enterprise. There are several factors that enter into the cost: benefit analysis, although one's ability to delay gratification and work for long-term benefit, referred to by Wilson and Herrnstein (1985) as one's time

horizon, is particularly vital to the eventual outcome of one's internal deliberations. Other factors that often enter into the equation include one's stated motive for engaging in crime and the fallibility of the human decision-making process, both of which are discussed later in this section. If in the end the cost: benefit ratio for crime exceeds the cost: benefit ratio for no crime then, according to economically oriented theorists, the individual will elect crime. Conversely, if the cost: benefit ratios are in the opposite direction, then the individual will select legitimate avenues of goal attainment.

While it very well may be that the human decision-making process falls along the lines of a cost: benefit analysis, there are several problems with the manner in which this process has been conceptualized by economic-minded tacticians. For one, choice appears to be a perceptual process. The deterrent value of specific punishers and the attractiveness of selected reinforcers is largely a function of how they are perceived by the individual.

What is more, there is evidence that human choice is a fallible, psychologically oriented process rather than an efficient, economically oriented process. Finally, the bulk of theorizing on the economic aspects of crime has apparently failed to take into account a number of important advances made in the field of psychology relative to the effects of specific reinforcement and punishment contingencies.

Regarding the point just made, Wilson and Herrnstein (1985) remind us that there are two types of reinforcers-primary and secondary. Primary reinforcers attain this status through satisfaction of an innate need like hunger or thirst. Secondary reinforcers, on the other hand, achieve their effect by being paired with a primary reinforcer through a process of classical conditioning.

The primary reinforcer not only lays the groundwork for such secondary reinforcers as money, material goods and prestige but also provides us with a link to the biological bases of behaviour. Various schedules of reinforcement are then formed by way of a process of operant conditioning, modeling and choice behaviour. Schedules of reinforcement take the cost: benefit process a step further by showing how the individual weighs alternatives in light of the rewards and punishments he or she has been exposed to in the past. This reinforcement history exerts a profound effect on the behaviour of the individual, since satisfaction of the drive for excitement, acceptance by antisocial peers, or rapid acquisition of material goods can be especially reinforcing, particularly if one rarely gets punished for violations of the moral code. Research, in fact, has demonstrated that fear of punishment and estimates of imminent apprehension both decline with criminal experience. This does not mean, however, that we are prisoners of our own reinforcement histories, since we all have the ability, with age, to emit behaviors that have never before been rewarded or refrain from engaging in actions that have been richly reinforced in the past.

Validation. There are multifarious reasons why people engage in criminal action. Some like the easy money, others the excitement and still others the power it seemingly provides them. Though it is difficult to organize these criminal motives into meaningful categories, to do so facilitates our understanding of the criminal decision-making process and provides an avenue through which opportunity and target selection might be paired with a specific criminal event. Validation affords the offender a psychological rationale for his or her violations of societal laws and the personal rights of others. The validation process operates on the basis of a motivational set designed to justify, direct and organize current and future displays of criminal conduct.

A study of robbers carried out by Feeney (1986) determined that 60 percent of those interviewed reported engaging in robbery as a quick means to accrue large sums of money for drugs, clothes, or late-model automobiles. The remaining subjects (40 per cent) stated that they engaged in robbery as a way of obtaining excitement, achieving a sense of power and control over others and expressing angry feelings.

In a second study, Carroll (1978) discerned that the positive aspects of a situation (money) seemed more important than the negative aspects (probability of getting caught) in directing the behaviour of criminal offenders. More recently, Walters and White (1988) discovered that the offenders in their sample gave several reasons for their involvement in crime, but one of the more common explanations was the express desire for more money.

Based more on clinical experience than research data, there are four general motives considered to be important in validating criminal activity: anger and rebellion, excitement and pleasure, power and control and greed and laziness. The anger and rebellion motive reflects the hostility, resentment and acrimony some offenders direct at the community because of a perceived sense of societal injustice.

Excitement and pleasure are prominent in the criminal activities of adolescents and young adults and provide for immediate gratification of selfcentered desires. Our third motive, power and control, reveals why some offenders put a premium on gaining power and control over others. Finally, greed and laziness can be observed in crimes inspired by the desire to accumulate material goods (to include money) as rapidly and effortlessly as possible. The validation process and the four motives that compose it, are discussed in greater detail by Walters (1990b).

Fallibility. Maultsby (1975), the founder of Rational Behaviour Therapy (RBT), asserts that we are all fallible human beings. This is particularly evident when it comes to the manner in which we analyse and process information. Alexander Pope is frequently credited with using the phrase, "to err is human"; well, it is also quite common for humans to rely on oversimplified environmental models in making decisions.

According to the results of a participant-observer study of professional shoplifters, habitual offenders weigh alternatives utilizing an oversimplified, often unidimensional, decision-making approach. This is probably one of the pitfalls into which many offenders, novice as well as professional, fall once they embrace the criminal lifestyle. To a large extent, continued involvement in lawbreaking activity augments these persons' chances of arrest in the future.

As was discussed previously, developmental factors place limits on one's ability to process information. The natural imperfection of the human decisionmaking process does much the same thing. Being human, we are subject to information loss and the drawing of erroneous inferences. This occurs, in part, because people are in the habit of considering only a portion of the relevant facts and sometimes focus on irrelevant information in rendering their decisions.

Accordingly, the human decision maker will never be as efficient as a computer, but then again, the computer will probably never be able to capture the creativity, ingenuity and charity of the human decision maker. In short, the innate limitations of the human mind need to be taken into account when examining the process of decision making, criminal or otherwise.

6

Sexual Crime

Prins notes that the number of sexual offences in England and Wales is consistently about 10,000 per year, less than 1 one per cent of all recorded crime: a figure which, as Prins suggests, is generally accepted as substantially less than the real percentage. Amir, for example, estimated that fewer than 30 per cent of rapes were reported to the police. A number of factors can lead to non-reporting of a sexual attack. The victim may not wish to face the discomfort of official questioning about the details of the crime; the victim may not want to draw public attention to the fact that she has been involved in a sex offence; the victim may fear reprisals or further attacks should she report the crime; or parents may wish to spare child victims. In some instances the victims may not perceive the forced sexual act as an assault or as rape, perhaps blaming themselves for what happened and so not reporting. There are a number of offences with sexual content: these range from acts such as exhibitionism and voyeurism, to 'victimless' crimes such as prostitution and some homosexual acts, to crimes involving attacks on women and children. In terms of serious crimes, two aspects of sexual offending have been selected for discussion —rape and sexual offences involving children. This is not to suggest that other sexual offences are not serious, indeed they are: rather that these two offences have attracted by far the greatest amount of psychological research and so illustrate the role of psychology in understanding this particular type of serious crime. Accounts of the other sexual offences not covered here can be found in Howells and West.

RAPE

A man commits rape if he has sexual intercourse with a woman who does not consent to the act. While, the prevalence of rape is not known, there are grounds for thinking that there are cross-cultural variations in the prevalence of rape. Sanday surveyed 156 societies and found almost half to be rape free. Further research has highlighted three social factors which characterize 'rape cultures': the sexes are clearly separated; there is a general subscription to male dominance; male violence is sanctioned for solving personal problems. Thus if the culture is patriarchal, giving men dominance in work, family, and sex, then men can assert their dominance in a number of ways, including rape, to maintain the submissive role of women. A number of texts are available on the cultural and political aspects of rape which provide the context for research which has focused on the rape itself and the psychology of the rapist.

Offence Analysis

With the caveat that any empirical research is limited to those cases in which the victim is willing to talk, a number of studies have analysed the situations in which rape occurs. Two American surveys found that in large cities rape is most likely to take place in the victim's home, while in small cities rape is most commonly committed in motor vehicles. This difference reflects the victimization of hitch-hikers, who are more likely to accept lifts in country areas than in large cities. These surveys also reveal that rape most frequently takes place in the hours between 8pm and 2am, and almost always in total darkness. The obvious reason for darkness is the avoidance of detection, but there may be other reasons. Bartol and Howells suggest that in the dark the offender may feel 'deindividualized', able to set aside any feelings of guilt and remorse, and view the victim as an object rather than a person. It is also possible that as alcohol and drugs are most frequently used in the evening and early hours of the morning that they may be involved in some way.

Ploughman and Stensrud carried out a detailed study of rape victimization in Buffalo, New York. Their starting-point, influenced by the notion of 'social ecology' is that: 'The circumstances under which crimes occur, including rape, appear to be neither random nor trivial but rather are socially structured phenomena that depend heavily upon the spatial and temporal organization of human activities'. In keeping with previous studies of city rape, Ploughman and Stensrud found that most offences took place in either the victim's home or the offender's home. The initial contact between victim and rapist most commonly happened on the street, typically a street in the offender's neighbourhood, often adjacent to the victim's neighbourhood. Most offences were committed between 8pm and 8am, with Saturday the most usual day; while May and November saw the greatest frequency of rapes. The demographic characteristics of the rape victim have been described in a number of studies.

The general consensus of these studies, mostly American, is that victims are young —with elderly victims very infrequent—single, have a low income, and that black women are over-represented in the victim population. With the additional finding that victims were most often students, with housewives and the employed at much less risk, Ploughman and Stensrud suggested that 'Unmarried women are more likely to be victimized than married women because of their greater exposure to potential rape situations'. It should be emphasized that these are American studies and the findings, especially regarding race, may not generalize to other countries. However, an English study did find that most victims were in the younger age range and came from a variety of occupational groups.

The demographic characteristics of the rapist have also been described in a number of studies. The rapist is typically young, generally 16 to 30 years, although it has been suggested that adolescent sex offenders may be more common than generally acknowledged. Rapists tend to come from a lower socioeconomic class, and American studies have shown an over-representation of black males convicted for rape. Alder found that almost half of a large sample of convicted rapists were or had been married, and almost 60 per cent had one or more children. It is unlikely that all rapists are psychiatrically disturbed in terms of a formal diagnosis, and therefore are not as a group psychologically 'sick' or 'psychotic' in a clinical sense. About one-quarter of arrested rapists have raped previously, with approximately one-third having a history of arrest for violent offences. It also seems likely that convicted rapists will continue to offend when released from custody: Romero and Williams found a 10 per cent recidivism rate for sexual offences in a sample of convicted sexual assaulters, although this particular sample committed as many non-violent as violent offences on return to the community. In considering this 10 per cent recidivism as measured by arrest rate, note should be taken of the finding of Groth *et al.* who, using a self-report methodology, discovered that rapists admitted to an average of over five undetected offences, with a range up to 250 undetected rapes. The surveys also show that in about one-third of cases the victim and offender are acquainted prior to the rape; although this may be an underestimation as victims related to their attacker may be less willing to report.

Ploughman and Stensrud found that when the victim knew the attacker, it was most often an acquaintance previously encountered in either the victim's or offender's home or place of work. In other cases, in decreasing order of frequency, the relationship was with a friend, neighbour, ex-husband or boyfriend, family friend, relative, and fellow employee. Does this pattern bear similarities with the notion of 'violent transactions' in which murder victims are seen as precipitative agents in their eventual death? West is blunt and to the point: noting that while in some instances rape may be 'preceded by some social interaction between the woman and the offender...this in no way justifies the man in forcing himself upon an unwilling companion'.

In any case, it is highly improbable that every rape follows a withdrawn sexual invitation. The associated view that men have sexual impulses which, once aroused, cannot be controlled, is not one which meets with general agreement among contemporary theorists. Indeed, the fact that the majority of rapes are planned in advance contradicts the view of rape as an uncontrollable, impulsive act. What may be of more importance in understanding the nature of these social encounters is the rapist's perception of the interaction in tandem with their general beliefs and attitudes towards women: these points are addressed in considering the psychology of the rapist. In a minority of cases, between 10 per cent and 15 per cent, the rapes involve more than one attacker; while in about one-quarter of rapes the attacker demands other sexual acts, usually oral sex and less often anal intercourse. In more than half the reported cases weapons are used, typically guns and knives. Given these findings, it is not surprising that along with the physical injury resulting from the forced sexual act, other serious physical injury occurs which often requires medical treatment or hospitalization. In some cases the viciousness of the attack results in severe internal injury, while in a minority of cases the rape is sadistic in the extreme, culminating in sexual murder.

Offender Taxonomies

Attempts to classify rapists have used a range of strategies such as specific aspects of the offence, characteristics of the victim, and psychiatric or legal sub-groupings. Another approach seeks to classify the act just as to the motives of the offender: thus Guttmacher described three types of rapist: the *'true sex offender'* who has a sexual motive in committing the rape; the *sadistic sex offender* for whom physical violence is of primary importance; and finally the *aggressive offender* for whom the rape is simply part of a general criminal, antisocial life-style. However, with the exception of two more recent studies, Prentky *et al.* conclude a review of these taxonomies with the comment that 'past attempts to classify sex offenders have, by and large, failed to examine comprehensively the motives of men who assault women'.

The two recommended taxonomies are those suggested by M.L.Cohen *et al.* and by Groth; Prentky *et al.* also offer a taxonomy of their own devising. M. L. Cohen *et al.* defined four types of rapists. The *displaced-aggression* rapist uses the rape to express anger and aggression, with the aim of physically injuring the victim who is typically a wife or girlfriend. The *compensatory* offender uses the rape to satisfy the need for a sexual goal, the aggression being a step towards fulfilling that aim: the rape is therefore a way of compensating for inadequacy in achieving sexual goals by conventional methods. For the *sex-aggression-diffusion* rapist the rape is a sadistic act in which the sexual and violent components of the act become fused, so that it is the victim's pain which excites sexual arousal. Finally, the *impulsive* rapist acts without planning, raping when the opportunity presents itself, as perhaps during the course of a burglary.

Table. Types of Rapist

Type	Motivation	Characteristics
Displaced aggression	Aggression	Anger, rage; physical injury
Compensatory	Sexual	Rape fantasies being acted out
Sex-aggression-diffusion	Aggression and sexual	Sadistic sexual assault and severe physical injury
Impulse	'Opportunity	Impulsive reaction to chance opportunity

From clinical observation of 500 rapists Groth described three types of rape just as to the varying degrees of hostility and control associated with the act. The *anger rape* typically follows arguments, sexual jealousies, and social rejection: the offender reports experiencing anger and rage, together with a sense of being wrongly treated, prior to the attack. In committing the sexual act the rapist uses far more force than is necessary to ensure compliance; the aim appears to be to inflict physical injury with the rape almost an afterthought, an additional way of inflicting pain. Groth estimated that 40 per cent of the sample could be classified as anger rapists.

The *power rape* is different in that sexual conquest is the goal; physical force is used only to the degree necessary to force compliance. Groth suggests that it is, however, not sexual gratification which is the goal, rather the experience of power which alleviates personal insecurities and asserts manhood and heterosexuality. Groth suggested that 55 per cent of the sample were power rapists. Finally, with *sadistic rape* sexuality and aggression are bound in a reciprocal fashion. The victim is made to suffer, typically by being tied, tormented, and often tortured; the victim's humiliation and suffering is sexually exciting, rape fuels the experience yet further. This was the least common type of rape, accounting for 5 per cent of Groth's sample. Following a study of 108 offenders, Prentky *et al.* described eight types of rapist. These eight types are defined by combinations of levels of three variables: the meaning of aggression, the meaning of sexuality, and the offender's level of impulsivity. They define two types of aggression: *instrumental* in which the aggression is used to force compliance; *expressive* in which the act is principally violent. There are four levels of meaning of sexuality: *compensatory* in which the behaviour is used to act out some sexual fantasy; *exploitative* in which the rape is an impulsive, predatory act; *displaced anger* where the sexual act is an expression of rage; *sadistic* in which the rape is an enactment of sexualaggressive fantasies.

Impulsivity is dichotomized as *high* or *low*: while differing slightly in definition just as to the level of the other two variables, the low levels are associated with offender characteristics such as shyness, introversion, and susceptibility to cues such as perceived threat; high levels are characterized by 'acting out' behaviours, low social competence, and character disorders. It is informative to compare these taxonomies with the way in which offenders view rape. Scully and Marolla interviewed 114 convicted rapists, examining the rapists' 'own perceptions of the crime and themselves'. Following the interviews Scully and Marolla described five types of rape. In the first, the rapists said that revenge and punishment were their motives: following some perceived indiscretion from their partner, the man raped another woman to get even with their wives or girlfriends.

These rapists reported extreme anger, even rage, at the time of committing the act and physically assaulted their victims. A second group saw the rape as an 'added bonus' to another crime: 'The decision to rape was made subsequent to the original intent which was burglary or robbery...after they realised they were in control of the situation'. A third group claimed they were sexually motivated in committing the rape, the rape serving to obtain what was not available or not offered. The 'date rape' frequently figured here, typical of a situation in which the man believed that the woman was sexually available—other women included in this 'available' category were those met in bars or hitch-hiking—and when his sexual advances were turned down the man took what he saw as rightfully his. Scully and Marolla described the fourth group as rapists who enjoy impersonal sex and power: the act of rape provides an experience of control and dominance which also avoids the emotions generally associated with intimacy and tenderness. Finally, a fifth group raped for recreation and adventure, typically in gangs where the rape is seen simply as another form of criminal activity. The payoffs for the rape for these offenders are very much in terms of social rewards from the gang for participating in the illegal group activity. Victims of this type of rape were typically hitch-hikers, women abducted by force from the street at night, or women who believed they had a date with one of the gang members only to be taken to a predetermined location and raped by each of the gang.

Scully and Marolla reported that the rapists admitted to little or no compassion for their victims. The majority said that after the rape they 'felt good', 'relieved', or 'nothing'; with only 8 per cent saying they felt 'guilty' or 'bad', and fewer than 1 per cent expressing any concern for their victim. These various reasons for raping contain elements of revenge, power, and opportunity similar to the taxonomies, strongly supporting the argument that rape is not simply a matter of sex. Different men rape to gain different rewards. However, while taxonomies are helpful in furthering understanding of the complexities of the act and the motivation of different rapists, they say little about the question of individual differences between rapists and non-rapists.

Unless the position is taken that all men are potential rapists, some distinction between rapists and non-rapists should exist. In looking for this difference psychological research has focused principally on three areas: the cues which are sexually arousing for the rapist; the attitudes towards women held by men who rape; and the level of social behaviour displayed by rapists.

Psychology of the Rapist

In studying sexual arousal in sex offenders penile plethysmography is the most widely used technique: simply, the methodology relies on measuring changes in penile volume and diameter in response to stimuli such as slides, audiotapes, videotapes, and selfimagery. Measurement of sexual arousal is technically sophisticated with associated technical and practical issues such as validation of the test stimuli, the subject's voluntary control of erectile response and the relationship between physiological and psychological arousal. Given these considerations, a considerable body of research has accumulated on the reactions of rapists to stimuli of varying sexual content.

The first studies of this type clearly showed that rapists were aroused by stimuli which depicted acts of non-consenting sex. Recent research has been consistent with this pattern: greater arousal to rape stimuli in rapists than in non-rapists, and greater arousal to consenting sexual scenes in non-rapists compared with rapists. These findings led to the hypothesis that rapists have a preference for aggressive sex because they find this the most arousing form of sexual behaviour. Other studies have suggested a rather different picture from that of a difference in arousal patterns between rapists and non-rapists. Abel *et al.* found that rapists were more aroused by rape scenes than non-rapists, but that the rapists were equally aroused by mutually consenting sex: if consenting and non-consenting scenes are equally arousing for rapists then this plainly argues against a preference hypothesis.

Barbaree *et al.* reported similar results to Abel *et al.* and suggested an explanation in terms of inhibition rather than preference. Both rapists and non-rapists are similarly aroused by the sexual cues present in all sexual scenes: while cues of violence or non-consent act to inhibit arousal in non-rapists, the rapist's arousal is not inhibited by such depictions. The lack of inhibition may be due to a failure to acquire inhibitory control, or alternatively a failure of inhibitory processes due, for example, to drug or alcohol use or high emotionality. Quinsey *et al.* found differences between rapists and controls in their responses to a rape scene, but also found that if non-rapists were told that arousal to deviant material was commonplace in males then high arousal levels were obtained. A series of studies by Malamuth and colleagues led Malamuth and Donnerstein to suggest two caveats to the view that normal males do not experience the same arousal as rapists to rape scenes. The first concerns the context of the rape: if the victim is shown as becoming involuntarily sexually aroused by the rape then 'normal' males become as, if not more, aroused than rapists: it is only when the victim continues to suffer that arousal remains low in normal subjects. The second point concerns individual differences: while it is tempting to dichotomize between rapists and non-rapists, the evidence suggests that while some men do not rape they report that given the right conditions—not being apprehended and punished—they would be capable of rape.

Malamuth and Donnerstein note that the arousal patterns of this third group of men, classed as 'high likelihood of raping', are very similar to that found in rapists. In keeping with the inhibition hypothesis studies have demonstrated that alcohol intoxication and anger can act to disinhibit arousal in non-rapists. A recent study by Baxter *et al.* has added a new twist to the debate in finding that '*Both* the rapists and the non-rapists…responded significantly *less* to the rape episodes than to the consent episodes'. As Baxter *et al.* note, this is not consistent with the sexual preference hypothesis, nor does it fully accord with an inhibition hypothesis.

They suggest that this novel finding may be a function of a larger sample size than in previous studies, or due to differences in rapist samples across studies. A line for research to follow which suggests itself from the present position is to test for differences in sexual arousal across one or more of the taxonomies. Howells summarizes the position: 'The complexity and ambiguity of the relationship between deviant arousal and deviant behaviour should be appreciated. Rapists may be discernible from non-rapists...but many apparently normal males may show significant arousal to deviant material'. The relationship between stimuli and arousal respose is not a simple one; however, if there is some cognitive mediation perhaps this might be evident in studies of rapists' attitudes towards women and rape. Field found a relationship between attitudes towards women and perception of rape, such that men who saw women in more 'traditional roles' were more likely to say that rape was the fault of the woman. Segal and Stermac, amending some shortcomings in Field's design, compared the attitudes towards women of rapist, non-sex offender, and non-offender groups. Segal and Stermac conclude that their results 'failed to demonstrate that rapists as a group are exclusively conservative or negative in their attitudes towards women'. Overholser and Beck compared rapists with other offender and non-offender groups using the *Attitudes Towards Sex and Violence Scales* and the *Rape Myth Acceptance Scale.*

The rapists did not differ from the other groups on either measure. Stermac and Quinsey similarly found no difference between rapists and non-rapists on a measure of attitudes towards women. Thus it appears that rapists do not hold attitudes towards women that are any different from those held by men who do not rape. Indeed, Check and Malamuth suggest that the type of attitudes commonly held by men support the feminist perspective on the general pervasiveness of rape myths and the 'normality of rape'. Moving from attitudes to behaviour, Howells made the point that 'Social competence with females is generally a necessary condition for consenting sexual behaviour with an adult and it is not difficult to see that impaired social skills might make a partner inaccessible and that, in some cases, offenders might resort to...rape as an alternative sexual outlet'.

The evidence exploring this suggestion has provided mixed results. Segal and Marshall assessed a range of social skills in rapist and control groups and found no differences between groups. Stermac and Quinsey failed to find any significant difference between rapists and other offender controls on various measures of social behaviour, with the one exception that rapists were less assertive. However, Segal and Marshall found no difference in assertiveness between rapists and matched control groups. Overholser and Beck did find skill differences: the rapists in their sample showed significantly less skilled social behaviour, particularly in the area of conversation skills. The rapists also showed significantly more anxiety, measured physiologically using GSR, during the role-plays which formed part of the study. An explanation for some of the variation in findings is that the samples in the Segal and Marshall studies were not matched for age which might have influenced some of their measures. While social skills include overt behaviour, the skill model also emphasizes the importance of social perception, both of one's own and others' behaviour. Segal and Marshall assessed rapists' perception of a heterosexual interaction and found that the rapists did not differ significantly from controls in their level of social skill, their prediction of their own ability, or on a measure of the discrepancy between the two.

It appears that the rapists are accurate in perceiving their own performance. D.N.Lipton *et al.* looked specifically at the ability of rapists to process interpersonal cues from women, particularly negative cues. This study used a newly developed measure of heterosocial perception, in which videotaped interactions of either a 'first date' or an 'intimate couple' are viewed then rated for content of affective cues such as 'romantic' and 'bad mood'. The results showed that when compared to both offender and non-offender control groups, 'Rapists displayed a significant deficit when reading women's cues in first-date interactions...comparison with violent non-rapists supported the view that the rapists' deficits are related to sexual aggression in particular rather than to aggressive behaviour in general'.

The rapists' misperceptions involved a low degree of sensitivity to negative and bad mood cues: however, it is not clear why the effect was found only for the 'first date' and not the 'intimate' scene. While these results are interesting in that they point to an aspect of heterosexual interaction in which rapists may be deficient, clearly this in itself is not an explanation for rape. As Lipton *et al.* suggest, the cognitive decision-making process following the perception is a candidate for future research, to which might be added the need to understand the development of such perceptions in both an individual and cultural sense.

SEX OFFENCES INVOLVING CHILDREN

As with sex offences involving adults, the gap between reported offences involving children and the real number of offences is unknown. Both Finkelhor and Alter-Reid *et al.* review the prevalence studies and suggest that a number of factors, such as the method of data collection and the operational definition of abuse, can influence the figures. It is generally agreed that the official figures are an underestimation: in a typical study Mrazek estimates that 10 per cent to 15 per cent of children and adolescents experience at least one incident of sexual victimization, with girls twice as likely as boys to be victims. The offence behaviour includes genital fondling, oral sex, and sexual intercourse. The majority of offenders are male, about threequarters of whom select female victims; the remainder chose male victims, with only a very small proportion victimizing both male and female children.

Offence Analysis

From interviews with individuals who had been victims of abuse as children, Finkelhor presents a picture of the act of child sexual abuse. Genital fondling was the most common type of assault for both female and male victims: this included the adult's contact with the child's genitals, using either hand or mouth, or the child's contact with the adult's genitals. Sexual intercourse was not often reported, although other activities such as masturbation and exhibitionism were frequently experienced.

The low incidence of penetration may be due to physiological restrictions: the relative size of the male sexual organ and the child's vagina or anus means that the child experiences severe pain and injury if penetration is attempted. Another explanation for the low incidence of penetration is that the majority of child abusers are not seeking adult-style relations but rather an escape to more child-like sexuality. Finkelhor also found that the majority of sexual abuse took the form of a single, unpleasant experience: the child is able afterwards to avoid the adult or tell a parent who then takes preventive action. In the other cases the contact becomes episodic, sometimes on a regular basis: Finkelhor reports an average duration of thirty-one weeks for female victims. Although typically lasting for months rather than years, some abuse spans a great deal of time—Finkelhor recorded one case which lasted for eleven years. At one time the occurrence of child sexual abuse was either denied or attributed to childhood sexual fantasy, then following recognition of the reality of abuse, the blame was attributed to the child.

The child was seen as either actively encouraging the sexual contact, or corroborating by failing to take self-protective steps. As Finkelhor suggests, this image of the child as a sexual agent is easily traced to the psychoanalytic view of the child's sexual impulses. In discussing the proposal that the child may be an active and willing partner, Finkelhor is unequivocal in his view, which perhaps represents the present consensus, that children are the recipients of sexual actions, not the initiators. He strongly maintains that any movement away from depicting the child as anything other than a victim of force and coercion is not only not helpful, but also positively destructive. It is the fear and anxiety produced by the act and threats of retribution by the offender, not compliance or corroboration, which prevent the child from telling an adult about the abuse.

The recent availability in Britain of a confidential telephone service for children to report abuse has resulted in a massive response—although it is impossible to tell what percentage of calls are genuine. The 'high risk studies' have highlighted a number of facts about the victims of child sexual abuse. Females are more likely to be victimized than males, approximately at a 2.5:1

ratio. Children are victimized at all ages from birth to 18 years with peaks of vulnerability at 6–7 years and particularly during the pre-pubescent ages of 10–12 years. However, it is possible that older children are more likely to report abuse, so the lower figures with younger children are not a source of even scant comfort. While there may be some association between social class and physical abuse of children, this does not appear to be the case with child sexual abuse. Further, there do not seem to be any ethnic differences in rates of sexual abuse, nor does the incidence appear to differ between rural and urban communities. In terms of social network, girls with few friends report more abuse, but it is unclear whether this is an antecedent or consequence of the abuse. Several family factors have been consistently associated with sexual abuse: these include living without the biological father; a mother who is disabled or ill; a mother employed outside the home; the presence of a stepfather.

With regard to aspects of family relationships as predictors of abuse, two findings are outstanding: the sexually abused child is likely to report a poor relationship with his or her parents, and the presence of a poor parental relationship, characterized by conflict and little mutual affection. In almost half the cases with female victims the abuser was a member of the family, and a further third of abusers were acquaintances. Male victims showed a different pattern, with less than one-fifth of abusers being relatives but over half acquaintances. In the remainder of cases the abuse occurred with a stranger. Given the predictive power of family functioning, it is convenient to blame the parents for the abuse. While this may be true in some cases—incest being the obvious example —it should also be recognized that parental absences and conflicts can be the result of social and economic factors. The fault, if blame is to be apportioned, may lie as much in a social structure which fails to provide adequate child care when parents are necessarily working as in the parents themselves.

Offender Taxonomies

A number of approaches to classifying child sexual abusers have been reported, focusing on either the nature of the offence or some characteristic of the offender. Groth *et al.* made the distinction between *child rape* and *child molestation*. The former offences involve violence and are seen as similar to adult rape; the latter are offences in which the child is coerced by non-violent means, and the harm to the child is psychological rather than physical. Howells made the distinction between *preference molesters* and *situational molesters*. The former have a stable primary sexual orientation towards children and are uninterested in emotional and sexual relationship with adult partners. Preference molesters, sometimes termed *pedophiles,* defend their behaviour as an acceptable form of sexual activity. The situational molesters are normal with respect to forming heterosexual adult relationships: the offence with the child is impulsive and seen by the offender as abnormal.

Lanyon suggests that the preferencesituational distinction might be better seen as a dimension of offender behaviour rather than a strict dichotomy between different offender groups. While the three groups—child rapists, preference molesters, and situational molesters—seem reasonably well defined, other dimensions are also important. There are homosexual as well as heterosexual offenders, although it is unclear whether such offenders have adult homosexual preferences.

Another oftenmade distinction is between *incestuous* and *non-incestuous offenders*: the implication being that some offenders abuse children only within their own family, while others victimize children who are not relatives. However, recent research by Abel, Mittleman, Becker, Cunningham-Rather, and Lucas casts doubt on some of the distinctions between incestuous and non-incestuous offenders. With a sample of 142 men who sexually abused their daughters, Abel *et al*. discovered that 44 per cent of the men also abused female children outside the family home; 11 per cent had also been abus-ing male children, while 18 per cent admitted raping mature women.

As Conte suggests, while it is clear that incestuous offenders are sexually aroused by children, other assumptions about this offence remain unsubstantiated. Another approach to taxonomy, similar to that used with violent offenders, attempts to generate 'profiles' of the offender using standard psychometric measures such as the MMPI. Despite a number of attempts, Conte is accurate in his comment that 'There is no currently verified profile of the typical adult who sexually abuses children'.

Psychology of the Child Sex Offender

Conte suggests five dimensions which might usefully guide the study of the psychology of the child sex offender. The first of these is the offender's *denial* of any problem: the denial may be due to a fear of lack of confidentiality; difficulty in admitting the offence in an interview setting; or the offender's interpretation of the abuse as something other than harmful. The role of denial would seem to warrant attention as it would seem likely that differences would exist between offenders who deny for reasons of shame or guilt, and those who deny any problem at all. The second dimension Conte suggests is *sexual arousal*. The research with child sex offenders has used identical methods to measure arousal as in the previously discussed studies with rapists.

The weight of evidence with child offenders suggests that there are individuals who are sexually aroused by children. Quinsey *et al*. and Abel *et al*. found that despite claims to be normally aroused by-adults, child offenders showed greatest arousal to stimuli depicting children. Abel *et al*. also found that incest offenders were aroused by pedophilic stimuli which were *not* descriptions of sexual acts with their daughters or stepdaughters. Avery-Clarke and Laws were able to identify correctly aggressive child offenders on the basis of their responses to imagined scenes of violence against children. *Sexual fantasy* is the next dimension: Conte suggests that sexual fantasy involving children paired with arousal via masturbation may be an antecedent in child sexual abuse. However, as Conte notes, there are considerable problems in gaining access to fantasies, verifying the content of fantasies, and pinpointing the aetiological role of fantasy.

The same points also apply to the next factor, *cognitive distortions,* although, if reliable, the content of such distortions is illuminating. Abel *et al*. identified seven distorted attitudes and beliefs commonly expressed by child molesters. Such cognitions may serve a number of functions: they may be a strategy for coping with guilt and remorse; a means of rationalization for future acts; or a means of denial of any abnormality.

Cognitive Distortions in child Molesters:

- Genital fondling is not really sex so no harm is done
- Children don't tell because they enjoy the sex
- Sex enchances a relationship with a child
- Society will eventually see that sex with children is acceptable
- A child enquiring about sex means he or she wants to experience sex
- Physical sex is a good means of teaching children about sex
- A lack of physical resistance means that the child wants sex

Moving from cognition to overt behaviour, *social skills* are the next factor in Conte's scheme. As with rapists, the suggestion of a link between social skills and offending rests on the assumption that a skills deficit leads to child abuse as an alternative means of achieving sexual goals.

Segal and Marshall found that the social skills of child molesters were significantly poorer than those of rapists who did not differ from control groups. Overholser and Beck also reported that child molesters were less skilled than controls. The skill deficits extended to social perception and levels of social anxiety, leading Segal and Marshall to note that 'Child molesters presented a clearer picture of heterosocial inadequacy than did rapists'. Finally, Conte suggests that a variety of variables might be collected under the general label 'other problems'. These other problems include 'alcohol or drug abuse, depression, poor self-concepts, relationship problems, impulse problems such as abuse of credit cards, and difficulty controlling or expressing anger'. To this list might be added fear of negative evaluation and highly stereotyped views of sex role behaviour.

THEORIES OF SEXUAL OFFENCES

The first point to be made is one of distinction: do sex offences require a different theory from violent offences? Current opinion holds that rape is a violent offence.

Romero and Williams tentatively make the point that:

- All forms of bodily assault committed by sex offenders, particularly sexual assaulters, should be carefully examined as parallels may exist between the two types of offence. If this is the case, then the distinction between sex offenders and violent non-sex offenders may be concep-tually weak where sexual assaulters are concerned.

Following an empirical study of almost 1,000 serious offenders, Alder is less reserved in concluding that:

- Contrary to the prior understanding of rape as the sexually motivated behaviour of a sexually maladjusted male who is likely to repeat the offence, present evidence suggests that rape may be more appropriately conceived of as one violent action in a repertoire of other non-sexual criminal behaviour.

Therefore, with the caveat that some explanation is required as to why the rapist rapes—*i.e.* why he is sexually aggressive rather than physically aggressive in a non-sexual manner—rape is probably best understood in terms of theories of violence.

If there is general agreement that rape is a violent crime, then there is also general agreement that child sex offenders, with the possible exception of child rapists, require a different level of explanation.

Finkelhor reviews theories which focus on the offender, the victim, the family, and social and cultural factors.

While these theories offer some degree of illumination, they fall prey to the criticism of attempting to fit the act to an existing theoretical perspective, rather than generating an explanatory model from data concerning the phenomenon itself.

Finkelhor has, however, begun to formulate the necessary model which seeks to integrate the diverse views and empirical data. This model consists of four complementary processes which may act in varying combinations in individual cases to create sexual interest in children. Finkelhor is at pains to stress that the four levels include individual, physiological, and sociocultural variables and concepts.

Table. Finkelhor's Model of Child Molesting

1	Emotional congruence	Children attractive because of their low dominance and male socialization to dominance; offender immature, low self-esteem, aggressive.
2	Sexual arousal	Children sexually arousing due to offender's socialization through personal experience, models, or child pornography; possibility of physiological explanation *e.g.* hormonal levels.

3	Blockage	Problems in forming adult relationships with women; related to sexual anxiety, poor heterosocial skills, attitudes towards sex,
4	Disinhibition	Offender able to overcome inhibitions through drugs, alcohol, cognitive distortion; or situational stress disrupts inhibitors.

Emotional congruence seeks to address the issue of why an individual finds children a source of emotional gratification. The suggested reasons include the child's lack of dominance, and the offender's low self-esteem and immaturity. *Sexual arousal* to children, clearly shown in a number of studies, may be due for example to learning experiences in childhood or to the use of child pornography: although Langevin and Lang cast doubts over both these factors. The offender's *blockage* in seeking adult partners may result from social anxiety or poor social skills—both of which the data support.

Finally, *disinhibition* may have a role to play, perhaps via alcohol or situational stress, in enabling the offender to overcome the conventional social and moral restraints against such behaviour. The key is the manner of male sexual socialization: he contends that men are raised to 'sexualize their emotions' so that sex is the way to achieve emotional needs. Men are taught to be attracted to younger, smaller, less dominant partners—children are simply the logical extension of this continuum, while the general lack of socially sanctioned involvement of men in childcare serves to distance them from a full understanding of children. There are two important points with regard to this model. The first is that it clearly defines areas with which future research should be concerned: that is the model is testable and open to verification, refinement, or refutation. Second, the approach does not seek to exclude or impose any particular theoretical perspective in the interpretation of the data. However, it would be anticipated that if the model is followed empirically one of the principal theoretical approaches—psychodynamic, social learning, etc. —would eventually prove able to accommodate the refined model with the greatest ease.

SEX-RELATED CRIMES

Being involved in a sex-related crime can be a complicated process because of all the details that help to define where the lines fall for the crime. There are many different types of sex crimes depending on what kind of situation was involved with the crime. The technical definitions for sex crimes can become very complicated because it's somewhat hard to define what is classified as a sex crime and what is classified as consensual sex. The area to define each type of sex-related crime can become a very grey area because of the age of consent and other details. The first thing that you should understand is that every sex crime is a crime that involves forcing someone to commit some type of sexual act without their direct consent. This means that any type of sexual act that is forced by another person could be consider a sex crime depending on the circumstances.

No matter what the person may say later, if the person said no at any time and the event still occurred, it would technically be considered a sex crime. Understanding this fact will help in any sex crime case that you may be involved with. The next factor that you should consider is that every sex-related crime will have some sort of punishment no matter what the circumstances of the event may have been. The next thing you should realise is that there many different types of sex-related crimes. Rape is considered to be a sex crime because of all the things that it entails. Rape is technically defined as forcing someone to have sexual intercourse without their consent to the actions. This means that someone is forced to have sex with another person without their consent to the actions that happened. The convictions for a rape charge as well as the consequences to go along with it can be quite severe with a lifetime of changes that will always affect your life. Some of the consequences could be jail time or even prison time as well as a rather large fine. The court can also assign you a long probation period as well as up to 1000 hours of community service time that you must complete in a certain amount of time. These are just some of the many consequences that go along with some of the other sex-related crimes as well.

PROSTITUTION

Human Rights Watch, there are approximately 15 million prostitutes in India. There are more than 100,000 women prostitution in Bombay, Asia's largest sex industry centre. Girl prostitutes in India, Pakistan and the Middle East are tortured, held in virtual imprisonment, sexually abused, and raped. Girl prostitutes are primarily located in low-middle income areas and business districts and are known by officials. Brothel keepers regularly recruit young girls. Girl prostitutes are grouped as common prostitutes, singers and dancers, call girls, religious prostitutes or devadasi, and caged brothel prostitutes. Districts bordering Maharashtra and Karnataka, known as the 'devadasi belt', have trafficking structures operating at various levels.

The women here are in prostitution either because their husbands deserted them, or they are trafficked through coercion and deception. Many are *devadasi,* dedicated into prostitution for the Goddess Yellamma. An oft-repeated cause of prostitution is poverty. But poverty is not the only reason. The helplessness of women forces them to sell their bodies. Many girls from villages are trapped for the trade in the pretext of love and elope from home, only to find themselves sold in the city to pimps, who take money from the women as commission. The other causes of prostitution include ill treatment by parents, bad company, family prostitutes, social customs, inability to arrange marriage, lack of sex education, media, prior incest and rape, early marriage and desertion, lack of recreational facilities, ignorance, and acceptance of prostitution.

Economic causes include poverty and economic distress. Psychological causes include desire for physical pleasure, greed, and dejection. Most enter involuntarily. India, along with Thailand and the Philippines, has 1.3 million childrens in its sex-trade centres. The childrens come from relatively poorer areas and are trafficked to relatively richer ones. India and Pakistan are the main destinations for children under 16, who are trafficked to South Asia. What is causing alarm both in governmental and non- Governmental Organisations circles is the escalation in trafficking of young girls, in the last decade. NGOs like STOP and MAITI in Nepal, report that most trafficking in India is for prostitution. And 60 per cent of those trafficked into prostitution are adolescent girls in the age group of 12 to 16 years. These are corroborated by a study done by the Department of Women and Children in 13 sensitive districts of Uttar Pradesh. It revealed that all sex workers who formed a part of this survey had entered the profession as young girls. Many transsexuals, called *hijiras*, are sex workers. The families of *hijiras* reject them. They face opposition from the public, and with the denial of employment, they take to begging and then enter the sex market.

Globalisation, professionalisation of trafficking syndicates, feminisation of poverty and rise in sex tourism—all have contributed to an increase in trafficking.

This problem is further compounded because of two factors: linkages of trafficking with the spread of HIV/AIDS and the clandestine nature of the activity. Studies now show that while women of all ages are more vulnerable to the infection than men, young girls are even more at risk because their genital tracts are immature. In addition, they have absolutely no control over sexual relations and sexual health. So a physical vulnerability is compounded by gender vulnerability.

The study done in 13 districts of Uttar Pradesh showed that in a sample of 1,341 sex workers, brothel-based prostitution was 793 and family-based prostitution came close at 548. Since prostitution is not legal, the police can arrest sex workers at any time. The police, whose main function is to protect and serve, turn out to be robbers, stealing the little money that these workers "earn". Interventions are increasingly based on issues like combating stigma related to HIV/AIDS, developing empowering strategies for victims and involving communities in the rehabilitation of rescued women and girls. But there is a lot that still needs to be done. Involvement of communities is of the greatest significance here since, it has been seen that their families and communities do not accept rescued women and girls. The situation becomes worse, if someone is tested positive for HIV, then she is immediately labeled a prostitute—a perception that creates a complex situation in the rehabilitation programmes. Even if trafficked returnees can avoid such treatment, they have few options for survival.

What is needed is a multi-pronged strategy, which can help in curbing trafficking and empowering communities and which also has scope for rescue and rehabilitation processes. The task is not just daunting; given the political priorities of most governments, it has not been given the importance it deserves.

CAUSES OF PROSTITUTION

- Bad company.
- Early marriage and desertion.
- Economic causes include poverty and economic distress.
- Family prostitutes.
- Ill treatment by parents.
- Inability to arrange marriage
- Lack of recreational facilities, ignorance, and acceptance of prostitution.
- Lack of sex education, media.
- Prior incest and rape.
- Psychological causes include desire for physical pleasure, greed, and dejection.
- Social customs.

Notorious red light districts of India include GB Road in Delhi, Sonagachi in Kolkata, Kamathipura in Mumbai, Budhwar Peth in Pune and Reshampura in Gwalior. There are around 2.8 million prostitutes in the country and their number is increasing, as informed by Lok Sabha. Most of the girls are brought from Nepal and Bangladesh. Young girls are trafficked from Nepal to brothels in Mumbai and Kolkata at an average age of twelve. They are trapped into the vicious cycle of prostitution, debt and slavery. By the time they are in their mid-twenties, they are at the dead end.

In modern India different kinds of prostitution is prevailing apart from prostitutes in brothel there are:

- Bar dancers
- Beat prostitutes
- Call girls
- Child prostitutes
- Escort girls
- Fricatrice prostitutes
- Gimmick prostitutes
- Religious prostitutes
- Road side brothel
- Street prostitutes

Prostitution is a problem in itself and child prostitution is making it more complex. Quoting a study on 'Girls/Women in prostitution in India', Minister for Women and Child Development Renuka Chowdhury said that out of the total number of prostitutes in the country, 35.47 per cent entered the trade before the age of 18 years. Though in cases like Gaurav jain vs. Union of India direction where given for the upliftment of prostitutes and establishment of the juvenile home for the children's of prostitutes.

THE PROSTITUTION LEADS TO MANY HEALTH PROBLEMS

In a country like India where most of the people indulge themselves in unprotected sex with prostitutes it is very difficult to eradicate the problem of AIDS. Historically, the AIDS epidemic in India was first identified amongst sex workers and their clients, before other parts of society became affected. The sex workers are themselves taking steps to combat with aids in some brothels in India for example, Sonagachi a brothel in Kolkata; where the sex workers are insisting their clients for use of condoms in order to avoid AIDS. But in all the other brothels in India social workers and NGO,s are trying to acquaint the sex workers about the ill effects of AIDS and are insisting them for using condoms

- Cervical cancer
- HIV
- Psychological disorders
- Sexually transmitted diseases
- Traumatic brain injury

STEPS THAT SHOULD BE TAKEN IN ORDER TO FIGHT WITH PROSTITUTION

- Adequate publicity, through print and electronic media including child lines and women help lines about the problem of those who have been forced into prostitution.
- Awareness generation and legal literacy on economic rights, particularly for women and adolescent girls should be taken up.
- Culturally sanctioned practices like the system of *devadasis, jogins, bhavins,* etc. which provides a pretext for prostitution should be addressed suitably.
- Formal education should be made available to those victims who are still within the school going age, while non-formal education should be made accessible to adults
- Rehabilitation and reintegration of rescued victims being a long-term.
- Recruitment of adequate number of trained counsellors and social workers in institutions/homes run by the government independently or in collaboration with non-governmental organisations.
- The Central and State Governments in partnership with non-governmental organisations should provide gender sensitive market driven vocational training to all those rescued victims who are not interested in education.

SHALL INDIA LEGALIZE PROSTITUTION

Some people opine that prostitution shall be made legal in India and accept them as a part of society because the problem of prostitution is inevitable. The benefit of legalizing prostitution in India will be that atleast as suggested, have a track record of Sexworkers as for example when dance bar in Bombay were closed most of the bar dancers migrated to Gujarat and Karnataka and other neighbouring state and started their business undercover. Legalising prostitution will see these women, who live life on the edge everywhere, gaining access to medical facilities, which can control the spread of AIDS. There is a very strong need to treat the sex industry as any other industry and empower it with legal safeguards. The practical implications of the profession being legal would bring nothing but benefits for sex workers and society as a whole. Keeping prostitution illegal also contributes to crime because many criminals view prostitutes and their customers as attractive targets for robbery, fraud, rape, or other criminal acts. The criminals realise that such people are unlikely to report the crimes to police, because the victims would have to admit they were involved in the illegal activity of prostitution when the attacks took place, now if it is legal then they will easily go and report this to police.

Benifits of legalizing prostitution are:

- Legalization of prostitution and the sex industry will stop sex trafficking.
- Legalization of prostitution will control the sex industry.
- Legalization of prostitution will decrease clandestine, hidden, illegal and street prostitution.
- Legalization of prostitution will promote women's health as they can have easy access to medical facilities which they don't have when it is illegal.
- Legalization of prostitution will protect the women in prostitution as they will have rights.
- Recognizing prostitution as an economic activity, thus enabling women in India to obtain working permits as "sex workers".
- Women in systems of Prostitution want the sex industry legalized as they are the one who suffers the most as they don't have any rights.

TRAFFICKING CRIMES OF PROSECUTION

EXPEDITING TRIAL

- Ensure timely intimation to witnesses and facilitate their appearance in the court. Delayed trials are mostly due to non-appearance of witnesses.
- Witness care requires that transport and other contingencies are taken care of.

- Provide protection to the witnesses against undue publicity
- To encourage experts to appear in the court as witnesses, it is essential to maintain their address, contact telephones, e-mail and networking. Maintaining regular personal contacts is advisable.
- Police officials who are witnesses do get transferred out. Therefore, keep an update of their addresses and contact numbers.
- Ensure liaison with the prosecutors and court staff for timely redressal of the problems and issues which come up in trial.
- Liaison between the Presiding Officer of the court, the Prosecutor and the Police official concerned is a sin-qua-non for removing all bottlenecks and ensuring early and prompt delivery of justice. Prosecutor is the officer of the court and, therefore should take initiative in ensuring this liaison.
- Prosecutor has a large role to play in the delivery of justice by bringing to the notice of the court any major flaw or deficiency in investigation. This would facilitate the court to take an appropriate decision whether to proceed further or to refer the case back to police for further/ fresh investigation or draw the attention of senior police officers/or refer the case to specialized agency like CID etc for investigation.
- S.22 ITPA provides for special courts to be constituted by the State Government or the Central Government. Prosecutor should take initiative in this direction as this is an important step in delivering justice expeditiously.
- Ensure that all facts are brought to the notice of the court. " It is as much duty of the prosecutor as of the court to ensure that full and material facts are brought on record so that there might not be miscarriage of justice".

VICTIM AND WITNESS CARE AND PROTECTION DURING TRIAL: DOS AND DON'TS

- Victims are wary of the court ambience. Do orient and counsel them. Assure them that their rights will not be violated and that their truthful version of all facts is essential for delivery of justice which is in their interest and also in the larger public interest.
- Victims require briefing on the facts of the case, especially to recall the events in a logical way. This should be done before she is put in the witness box.
- Prosecutors ought to ensure that the defence-side does not violate the rights of the victim. Embarrassing questions need to be avoided. Intervention of the court should be sought immediately to prevent any such violations.
- All efforts should be made to ensure the anonymity of the victim. Anonymity provides strength and confidence to the victim.

- Move the court for allowing in-camera trial. The Supreme Court of India has directed that in-camera trial should be extended to all cases of sexual assault on children. A screen has to be provided in the trial court so that the child victim is not exposed to the suspect and accused persons. A child counselor should be provided to assist in the court. Adequate recess should be allowed during trial proceeding so that the child victim gets rest. This is a landmark judgement in ensuring child rights and, therefore, needs to be implemented in letter and spirit. The police and prosecutors should move the trial courts for the same. _ Video conferencing is an ideal mechanism to prevent victimization of the trafficked victim. It should be done whenever possible. The Supreme Court, in its landmark decision, in State of Maharashtra vs Dr. Praful B. Desai 2003 (4) SCC 601, has underscored the validity of video conferencing and enumerated the safeguards to be ensured during the trial of cases.
- *Victim care and protection also requires the following*:
  - Depute a sensitive liaison officer with the victim, preferably a WPO.
  - Brief the victim on the facts of the case before trial starts.
  - Orient the victim to the court scenes before the trial.
  - Debrief the victim immediately thereafter.
  - Follow up on the debriefing and make required amendments.
  - If the victim speaks a different language, make arrangements for appropriate translators.
  - Ensure transportation of the victim to and fro.
  - Provide for contingency expenditures. Court has funds for this. In some states like Tamil Nadu, Government has provided special funds for this work.
  - Take care to return the victim to the concerned destination.
  - Do look after other logistics and contingencies such as providing facility for rest, easement, etc.
  - Do not forget to thank the victim/witnesses and all those who assisted in getting the victim to the court. Do ensure their safe and comfortable return.
- Post Conviction Matters requires special attention by the prosecutor. This includes the following major steps:
- Seeking enhanced punishment for repeated offences/offenders.
- Moving the court to impose fine alongwith punishment.
- Seeking compensation for the victim from the offender.
- Seeking compensation from the state.
- Taking steps for closure and eviction of brothels u/s 18 ITPA.
- Taking steps for surveillance of convicted person.
- Initiating steps for externment of the convicted person.

VICTIM/ WITNESS PROTECTION SYSTEMS

There are several constitutional, legal and administrative provisions in India for ensuring the rights and protection of witness/victim.

- Right to anonymity is a legal right
- In camera trial, u/s 327 CrPC is essential in rape crimes. The provisions of in camera trial have been extended to all crimes of sexual assault against children Therefore in camera trial should be invoked in all crimes of trafficking of children for CSE.
- Video Conference is allowed in the trial of crimes. This ensures not only anonymity but also protection to the victims and witnesses.
- Provision of free atmosphere: In Sakshi vs UOI, it was held that "the whole inquiry before a court is to elicit the truth. It is absolutely necessary that the victim or the witnesses are able to depose about the entire incident in a free atmosphere without any embarrassment. A screen or some such arrangements be made where the vctim or witnesses do not have to undergo the trauma of seeing the body or the face of the accused".
- Recess during court proceedings: In Sakshi vs UOI the Supreme Court directed that whenever a child or a victim of rape is required to give testimony, sufficient brakes should be given as and when required.
- Legal representation is a legal right. In Delhi Demostic Working Womens Forum vs UOI, 1995 (1) SCC 14.) The requirement of legal representation and counseling has been extended to the victim right from the Police Station itself.
- Victim can have Private Lawyers who can assist the Public Prosecutor and even submit written arguments, nevertheless functioning under the public prosecutor, vide Section 301(2) CrPC.
- Victim is never an accomplice.
- Right of accused to cross examine the victim/witness, though a legal right, is restricted by Sakshi judgt, in such a way that in a case of sexual assault of children, the defence cannot question the victim directly, but has to furnish the questions to the court and the court will, in turn, communicate it to the victim.
- Compensation is an entitlement of the victim for injury/loss, u/s 357 CrPC.
- Compensation can be awarded to the victim from the convicted person even if there was no fine as part of the sentence.
- Compensation can be awarded to the victim even without conviction and even during pendency of trial.
- Age assessment of the victim should be done, when in doubt, in favour of the victim. In State of Karnataka vs Majamma, it was held that even if the prosecution has not proved that the girl was less than 16 years, her own statement should be trusted and accepted.

- Delay in reporting of the case will not affect the case if reasonable explanzation is given/brought out during investigation.
- *Defective Investigation*: Flawed investigation is no ground to deny justice to the victim. "It would not be right to acquit an accused person solely on account of defect; to do so would tantamount to playing into the hands of the investigating officer if the investigation is designedly defective".
- *Prosecutrix need not be examined*: in State of Himachal Pradesh vs Mohan Misra, 1995 CrLJ 3845, the Supreme Court held that "merely because the victim girl is not examined, this can never be a ground to acquit an accused if there is evidence otherwise available proving the criminal act of the accused.
- Character and antecedents of the victim has no bearing or relevance… and can never serve either as mitigating or extenuating circumstance. No stigma should be implied against the victim/witness. 'After all it is the accused and not the victim of sex crime who is on trial in the court'..
- *On reliability*: The evidence of a victim of sexual offence is entitled to a great weight, absence of corroboration notwithstanding The rule of prudence that the evidence of a victim of sexual assault must be corroborated in material particulars has no application.
- *On corroboration*: In Punjab vs Gurmeet Singh it was held that the statement of the rape victim who was between 15-17 years, inspired confidence for acceptance and, therefore corroboration of evidence was not needed. Held that there is no legal compulsion to look for corroboration of the evidence of the prosecutrix before recording an order of conviction. Evidence has to be weighed and not counted. There is no rule of practice that there must in every case be corroboration before a conviction can be allowed to take place.
- *On discrepancy in the statement of victim/witness*: In cases involving sexual assault minor contradictions or insignificant discrepancies in the statement of the witnesses should not affect the case. It was held that the court must appreciate the evidence in totality of the background of the entire case and not in isolation.
- On medical report: In Rampal vs State of Haryana, 1994 Supp(3) SCC 656, conviction was based on the sole testimony of the prosecutrix. Though the doctor did not find any visible injuries, the court held that, there was no reason to suspect the testimony of the victim and upheld the conviction of the accused.
- Expeditious trial is an essential ingredient of reasonable, fair and just procedure guaranteed by Article 21. It is the constitutional obligation of the state to devise such a procedure as would ensure speedy trial.

- Courts need to take participative role to deliver justice to victim. "The Courts have to take a participative role in a trial. They are not expected to be tape recorders to record whatever is being stated by the witnesses. S.311 of CrPC and S.165 of Ev. Act confer wide and vast powers on presiding officers of Court to elicit all necessary materials by playing an active role in the evidence collecting process".
- *Witnesses to turn up in trial*: In order to ensure fair trial, a duty has been cast on the prosecution to produce witnesses on time. "The presence of the Investigating Officer at the time of the trial is must. It is his duty to keep the witness present. If there is a failure on the part of the witness to remain present, it is the duty of the court to take appropriate action".
- *Right to be rescued*: Section 16 ITPA provides powers to Executive Magistrates and Judicial Magistrates for directing any police officer of the rank of SI and above to rescue a person based on information received from any source. This accrues a right to the victim to notify the Magistrate, by whichever means possible, and a duty is cast on the Magistrate to ensure steps for rescue.
- *Right to restoration to a safe place after rescue:* Section 17 ITPA provides that a rescued person shall not be restored to or placed in the custody of a person who may exercise a harmful influence over the person. This section of law calls for Home verification to verify whether the original home of the rescued person is safe enough for her return.

HUMAN TRAFFICKING AND SEXUAL EXPLOITATION

There is no universally accepted definition of trafficking for sexual exploitation. The term was formerly thought of as the organized movement of people, usually women, between countries and within countries for sex work with the use of physical coercion, deception and bondage through forced debt. However, according to the Trafficking Victim's Protocol Act of 2000, movement is not an element necessary for the crime. The issue becomes contentious when the element of coercion is removed from the definition to incorporate facilitating the willing involvement in prostitution. For example, in the United Kingdom, The Sexual Offenses Act, 2003 incorporated trafficking for sexual exploitation but did not require those committing the offence to use coercion, deception or force, so that it also includes any person who enters the UK to carry out sex work with consent as having been trafficked. In addition, any minor involved in a commercial sex act in the United States while under the age of 18 qualifies as a trafficking victim, even if no force, fraud or coercion is involved, under the definition of Severe Forms of Trafficking in Persons, in the US Trafficking Victims Protection Act of 2000.

Sexual trafficking includes coercing a migrant into a sexual act as a condition of allowing or arranging the migration. Sexual trafficking uses physical or sexual coercion, deception, abuse of power and bondage incurred through forced debt. Trafficked women and children, for instance, are often promised work in the domestic or service industry, but instead are sometimes taken to brothelswhere their passports and other identification papers are confiscated. They may be beaten or locked up and promised their freedom only after earning—through prostitution—their purchase price, as well as their travel and visa costs.

The main motive of a woman (in some cases, an underage girl) to accept an offer from a trafficker is better financial opportunities for herself or her family. In many cases, traffickers initially offer 'legitimate' work or the promise of an opportunity to study. The main types of work offered are in the catering and hotel industry, in bars and clubs, modeling contracts, or au pair work. Traffickers sometimes use offers of marriage, threats, intimidation and kidnapping as means of obtaining victims. In the majority of cases, the women end up in prostitution. Also some (migrating) prostitutes become victims of human trafficking. Some women know they will be working as prostitutes, but they have an inaccurate view of the circumstances and the conditions of the work in their country of destination. Trafficking victims are also exposed to different psychological stressors. They suffer social alienation in the host and home countries. Stigmatization, social exclusion, and intolerance make reintegration into local communities difficult. The governments offer little assistance and social services to trafficked victims upon their return. As the victims are also pushed into drug trafficking, many of them face criminal sanctions.

The Yogyakarta Principles, document on international human rights law on sexual orientation and gender identity also affirm that "States shall (c) establish legal, educational and social measures, service and programmes to address factors that increase vulnerability to trafficking, sale and all forms of exploitation, including but not limited to sexual exploitation, on the grounds of actual or perceived sexual orientation or gender identity, including such factors as social exclusion, discrimination, rejection by families or cultural communities, lack of financial independence, homelessness, discriminatory social attitudes leading to low self-esteem, and lack of protection from discrimination in access to housing accommodation, employment and social services."

TRAFFICKING IN GIRLS AND WOMEN

The problem of trafficking in women for the purpose of prostitution was already known in public at the end of the 19th century. According to UN reports, girls and women from South and South-East Asia (Burma, China, Cambodia, Laos, Nepal, Taiwan, Thailand, Vietnam), East Europe (the Baltic, Ukraine) and Latin America (Brazil) are particularly at risk today. The actual number of instances is difficult to estimate however. According to local NGOs, between 200,000 and 2 million women work as prostitutes in Thailand alone.

The women are promised a well-paid job in another country. Their passports are taken away from when they cross the border and they are forced to work in brothels. They are forced to live and work in conditions similar to slaves, as a result of their debt to the traders who have taken over the costs for transport and all incidentals. The social stigmatisation, the violence and the foreign country increases the dependence of the victims. The traditional son preference, poverty, or simply trust leads the parents to sell their daughters to trader rings. Frequently, however, girls and women are forcibly kidnapped. Trafficking in women is a growing market, comparable in the meantime with the volumes traded in drugs and weapons. This market is fed by the racist and power fantasies of Western men who spend their money on possessing sexually and/or permanently available girls and women, and on the similar needs of men in each of the countries. The low social status of the women, the discrimination against the divorced, raped or widowed, as well as their poor general circumstances life (hardly any chance or finding work or getting an education), that has become even worse as a consequence of socio-economic changes in the last few years, makes a contribution to this business so scornful of human life.

What is being done against trafficking in women? Since 1904, international agreements on fighting trafficking in women exist, such as the International Agreement on Securing Effective Protection against the Trafficking of Girls of 18th May 1904. The International Agreement on Fighting the Trafficking of Girls of 4th May 1910 obliges its member states (status in 1989: 71 signing states) to make the seduction of female minors into prostitution or forced prostitution in their countries an offence against the law. An Agreement on the Suppression of Trafficking Mature Women of 1933 also exists.

Local laws to suppress prostitution are frequently and mainly oriented towards the victims, who are persecuted as illegal immigrants or illegal prostitutes, whereas the pimp is often set free after paying bail and bribing the authorities. In many EU countries a woman can only turn to the courts for help if she possesses a residents permit. Even if she is a witness in a trial, for instance, to give evidence against trafficking rings, she is threatened with extradition to her own country. Which places the women under the complete control of their pimps; criminal proceedings against traffickers are normally discontinued due to lack of evidence.

TRAFFICKING IN WOMEN AFTER SOCIALISM

The trafficking in women and girls for prostitution has recently commanded the attention of state authorities, activists and academics the world over, although it is hardly a new phenomenon. In the late 19th and early 20th centuries, increasing globalization, accompanied by population increases, urbanization, international migration, colonization and political upheaval contributed importantly to the growth of prostitution and the trafficking in women and girls around the world. European countries, China and Japan supplied prostitutes to other countries. For example, French, Polish, Russian and Italian women went to brothels in other European countries, Argentina and Brazil while Chinese and Japanese women, including women of Korean ethnicity, went to brothels in colonial holdings such as British Hong Kong, the Dutch East Indies, French Indo-China, Manchuria, Singapore and Shanghai.

Though the extent of trafficking in women and its geographic routes have changed in the last hundred years, its structural causes and organization remain remarkably stable. Then, as now, traffickers used marriage or promises of marriage to recruit women and girls; others assured them of domestic service or entertainment work abroad. Still others enticed women already engaged in prostitution who then willingly left for foreign brothels. Whatever the particularities of the recruitment method, there has been no shortage of persons ready to benefit from the availability of women and girls: from procurers who have sold them, to pimps who take portions of their earnings, to brothel madams who have kept them in debt bondage, to local policemen who have had financial and other interests in keeping the brothel system alive and well. The boundaries between trafficking, prostitution and forced labour migration are often blurred, but trafficking involves deception and coercion, whether at the point of departure when women are recruited or when they arrive at their destinations.

The contemporary trafficking involves women from across the globe. The collapse of communism that began in 1989 provided new resources—geographical and human—for the sex trade, increasingly incorporating women from Eastern Europe. One of the most striking images of the changes soon after the fall of the Berlin Wall was that of women lining the highways offering sex for sale. Political and economic liberalization as well as internal and international militarism created new opportunity structures and daunting economic uncertainties that produced both a demand for and a supply of sex workers in and from Eastern Europe. Most of these sex workers have been and are women and girls. Whether working part-time to supplement income, or full-time voluntarily in sex clubs, or forced through trafficking, prostitution is a stable, ever-expanding feature of the global service economy. But in contrast to the neon lights advertising live sex shows or lap dancing clubs, trafficked women are largely invisible, hidden from the publicly commodified sex trades.

As European borders have become more porous and labour more flexible, the commodification and exploitation of sex as a form of labour have increased in scope and global reach. The collapse of communism catapulted the former socialist countries into the global economy. The availability of cheap labour and potential markets brought multinational corporations, banks and manufacturers to the region. Directors of pornographic films and magazines as well as international sex tourism agencies also flocked to the former socialist states where there was then little threat of institutional regulation and enforcement. After the fall of the Berlin Wall, shorter distances made it easier and cheaper to move women from Eastern to Western Europe rather than from

Africa, South America or Asia. Across Eastern Europe, global secondary economic activities blossomed, including underground trafficking in persons, drugs, arms and organs.

Economic decline and increasing poverty are significant contributors to trafficking. A key feature of post-socialist change has been the restructuring of the labour market and of social inequalities. This restratification draws attention to class as a significant variable in trafficking: poverty, urban and especially rural, is a consistent factor, historically and comparatively. There appears to be a correlation between national poverty rates and sending countries. Many women engage in the diversity of 'legal' sex trade opportunities because of the potential for higher incomes unobtainable in other occupations. Still others, enticed by apparent job opportunities elsewhere or offers to become the brides of men in other countries, find themselves sold into sexual servitude. However women come to 'sell their bodies', it usually forms part of an economic strategy often endorsed by family members. Yet, they and the women in question are frequently uninformed about the risks such occupational opportunities abroad may entail.

Most recent reports on trafficking to, through and from Eastern Europe concur on the patterns of source, transit and destination countries, although the numbers presented vary considerably. The fast-tracked North Atlantic Treaty Organization (NATO) and EU accession countries, especially Poland and Hungary, are variously considered to be source, transit and destination countries. In Poland, women and girls are trafficked from further east—Russia, Ukraine, Belarus—to and through Poland. Polish women are themselves trafficked primarily to Western Europe. Hungary is generally considered more a transit than either a source or destination country, with women from further east brought to and through Hungary en route to destinations further west. However, since 1989, Budapest has become a sex trade capital, suggesting that Hungary is not viewed as a source country in large measure because so many Hungarian women work in the sex trade in Hungary itself. In 1998, Budapest had an estimated 300 sex clubs operating.

Scholars have long viewed the Balkans as the crossroads between East and West, and in the world of trafficking, they continue as such. Albania is a key source and transit country. Those being transited, mostly from Moldova and Romania, Ukraine and Bulgaria, continue on to Western Europe. UNICEF notes that "the main trafficking routes into Albania follow the arms and drug smuggling routes, through Romania, Serbia and either Montenegro or Macedonia". Romania is yet another source and transit country. Women from Moldova, Ukraine and other former Soviet countries are trafficked to Turkey, Italy, Greece and the former Yugoslavia. Romanian women have been trafficked to France, although some go voluntarily as sex workers. Bulgaria is another source and transit country. The destinations of women trafficked from or through Bulgaria vary, with Kosovo (Serbia), Macedonia and Western Europe most prevalent among them. Recently, the number of Bulgarian women trafficked has declined, possibly due to increased enforcement and a somewhat more stabilized economy. Bulgaria's NATO and current EU accession interests, as elsewhere in the region, have been influential in this process.

Since 1989, visa regulations have played an important role in the routes that traffickers use. Women from Poland, the Czech Republic and Hungary did not need visas to travel to Germany and after their admission to the EU, they may travel more freely across its borders. Entrance into the EU, including candidate countries slated for admission in 2007 such as Romania and Bulgaria, has had a discernible impact on trafficking patterns. For example, the liberalization of visa requirements for Romanians travelling to EU member states has resulted in more women being trafficked to Western Europe than to locations in the former Yugoslavia. In this respect, EU accession facilitates trafficking within and across its internal borders in the short run, although anti-trafficking efforts serve as impediments. The efforts of the Southeast European Cooperative Initiative (SECI) Regional Centre for Combating Transborder Crime are particularly noteworthy.

Western European countries are prime destination countries. Estimates of the numbers of women trafficked there vary widely. At the end of the 1990s Europol estimated that several thousand individuals were trafficked into the EU each year for the transnational sex industry and that 90 per cent originated from Central and Eastern European states. In March 2001, according to an International Organization for Migration (IOM) report, the European Commission estimated that some 120,000 women and children were trafficked annually to Western Europe. The State Department has projected numbers between 600,000 and 900,000 of persons trafficked across borders. It is difficult to assess these statistics, however, because information about their collection is rarely detailed. Whatever the actual numbers, there is basic consensus about sending countries and the destinations of those trafficked. Not surprisingly, western destination countries tend to be wealthier than the Eastern European countries from which women's journeys originate.

Militarization also plays a role and has been a key feature in the diversification of trafficking in both Bosnia and Kosovo. Wars have facilitated trafficking of women and girls, drugs and arms under the alleged auspices of competing mafias, traffickers and complicit, corrupt officials and individuals. Although Bosnia and Kosovo are comparatively poor, they have non-etheless become destination points: women from Moldova, Romania, Ukraine, and, to a lesser extent, from countries further east, such as Kazakhstan, often wind up in Bosnia. During the Bosnian war, the small town of Taszlar in Hungary saw the emergence of brothels with local and trafficked women in demand there. Within months of NATO intervention in the Kosovo war, a system of sex services was apparently flourishing. And soon after US military planes began landing in Romania's Black Sea port city, Constanta, in February 2003, in preparation for the war in Iraq, the sex trade and traffic there increased.

Nonetheless, in general, trafficking occurs independently of militarization. As in other forms of labour migration, poverty and limited economic opportunities are primary factors in the lives of women and girls who are trafficked. According to the World Bank database of World Development Indicators, mid-1990s poverty rates in Eastern Europe were above 20 per cent in some countries (*e.g.*, Moldova, Poland and Romania) and above 30 per cent in others (*e.g.*, Russia and Ukraine). Although it is hard to find statistics on the rates of individual or family poverty that are comparable across countries, economic data from the UN and the World Bank suggest a relation between trafficking patterns and economic decline. Two primary source countries—Moldova and Ukraine—are also those with notably low Gross National Incomes (GNI). Moldova falls well below the cut-off point for being categorized by the World Bank as a 'low-income country' with a 2002 per capita GNI of only $460; Ukraine barely made it above the $736 cut-off point with its 2002 per capita GNI of $770. Other sending countries, including Russia and Romania, are comparatively better off but are still classified in the World Bank's World Development Indicators Database as 'lower-middle-income economies'.

Women are disproportionately affected by poverty and limited economic options globally, including in post-socialist countries. For example, the World Bank's Gender Statistics Database showed increasing women's unemployment from 1995 to 2000 in the Czech Republic (4.8 to 10.6 per cent), Poland (14.7 to 18.5 per cent), Slovakia (13.8 to 16.4 per cent), Russia (9.2 to 13.1 per cent) and Ukraine (4.9 to 11.5 per cent). Gendered labour market shifts have generally pushed women towards lower-paid and part-time work. Furthermore, rural poverty has grown dramatically since 1989; rural women are believed to be over-represented among trafficked women.

Given these trends, it is not surprising that women's unemployment rates tend to be higher than men's in primary sending countries such as Moldova and Ukraine. The exclusion of women from the paid labour force is an ongoing process in Ukraine, where gender specifications are a customary feature of job advertising and hiring, as are preferences based on marital status. Such gendered practices exclude women from some occupations, concentrate them in others, contribute to high poverty rates and unemployment for women, and leave them vulnerable to the enticements of traffickers who can take advantage of their desire for better working and living conditions abroad. To reiterate, women are recruited from both rural and urban areas (to which rural women have often first migrated). They need not be from among the poorest of the poor, or even from among the working poor. Whatever women's individual circumstances, their overall prospects are typically limited, making promises of their dreams coming true elsewhere adequate incentive to accept plausible offers from traffickers.

We underscore that trafficking forms part of forced labour migration as well as the global service economy into which women and children from the former socialist states have been incorporated. In view of politicized international attention to trafficking, it is often difficult to imagine that women and girls remain unaware of what may await them. And, hope of a better life in the much-fantasized West is a powerful incentive for many to take risks when they are assured of alleged job or marriage opportunities. Awareness is therefore an important factor in combating trafficking, as is cooperation between governmental and non-governmental organizations in promoting it. Engaging diverse means, including advertising campaigns, church sermons and educational programmes in schools, can play an important role in enabling women to make better informed choices about opportunities and potential risks. Many such efforts presently exist. To illustrate, in Moldova, the government and the IOM have promoted a widespread campaign, using billboards and other media to advertise their message: "*nu esti marfa*" ("You're not a commodity").

But increased awareness will not eradicate trafficking. It does not combat poverty or limited job opportunities and economic prospects. Nor does it tackle the interests—and profits—that drive trafficking. International and country initiatives must address both 'push' factors (*e.g.*, poverty and gender discrimination in sending countries) and 'pull' factors (*e.g.*, the sex trade as a lucrative business for traffickers combined with ready underground sex markets in the West and across the globe), putting into practice the goals they have legislatively embraced.

Substantive and systematic research is also urgently needed which includes the development of strategies to produce reliable data on the number and demographics of women and children trafficked, detail their life experiences (through qualitative research), and analyze the relation between trafficking, prostitution, economic trends and militarization. Such information is crucial to better comprehend the dynamics and consequences of trafficking. Dialogue between specialists on migration and on prostitution must be promoted if trafficking is to be more fully conceptualized. There is presently little articulation between what are emotionally politicized and often moralizing discourses and debates about trafficking and actual practices. Given the fervour surrounding this multi-faceted issue, it is telling that research has not been at the forefront of strategies to address trafficking.

It is also telling—and paradoxical—that in the 21st century in which human rights discourses circulate widely across the globe, forms of slavery in the guise of trafficking are tacitly tolerated and, indeed, are proliferating. The interests that drive trafficking in women and children are intimately related to those driving other dimensions of trafficking, including of humans for forced labour other than sexual labour. As income disparities widen across the globe and as the service economy grows, it is ever more imperative that enduring gender inequalities in valuing women's work and recognizing women's rights be rectified. The persistent failure to do so contributes to the abusive trafficking patterns and conditions that so many claim to want to curtail. Until attention is focused on the demand side of trafficking (in all of its forms), and poverty is not a resource for profit-driven entrepreneurs the world over, trafficking will continue not only to exist but to expand.

THE PREVENTION OF HUMAN TRAFFICKING

In 1946 human rights was not a cause as prevalent as it is today. However, as the world changes, so does the United Nations. The globalization of the Universal Declaration of Human Rights, drafted by Eleanor Roosevelt and adopted by the UN in 1948, has contributed to the growing concern over human rights. Now the Human Rights Council is one of the most vital committees in the UN, discussing pressing issues such as the Israeli-Palestinian Conflict, intolerance, and human trafficking.

Every year, anywhere from 700,000-2 million men, women and children fall into the hands of traffickers in their own countries and abroad ("Women Trafficking"). Every country in the world is affected by trafficking, whether as a country of origin, transit or destination for victims. Many trafficking victims begin their journey by consenting to be smuggled from one country to another. Because of this similarity, 'smuggling' and 'trafficking' are often confused. Both involve moving humans for profit, but in the case of smuggling the crime ends on arrival in the destination country, whereas in cases of trafficking, arrival is just the beginning of enslavement.

The Protocol to Prevent, Suppress and Punish Trafficking in Persons defines human trafficking as "the recruitment, transportation, transfer, harbouring or receipt of persons, by means of the threat or use of force or other forms of coercion, of abduction, of fraud, of deception, of the abuse of power or of a position of vulnerability or of the giving or receiving of payments or benefits to achieve the consent of a person having control over another person, for the purpose of exploitation" ("UNDOC"). Exploitation includes sexual exploitation such as prostitution of others, forced labour, slavery, other forms of servitude, or the removal of organs.

Trafficking is a multistage process that brings people into slavery. First, nearly all people who are vulnerable to traffickers are poor. The desire for a better life, the need to escape conflict and oppression, and the hope for a new start, all bring people into contact with traffickers. Most trafficking victims are not kidnapped, but tricked. Often the victims will believe they are consenting to take part in a legal migration and employment; however, once the transportation begins, the victim is likely to have their travel and identity documents taken away. This leaves the victim in the control of the trafficker. Once under control, the victim begins a period of enslavement and exploitation. Finally, the trafficking ends, for some victims with death; others will be discarded when, through injury or illness, they become useless to their exploiter. Children, especially girls, trafficked into domestic service will often be thrown out on the streets when they reach their teens. For women forced into prostitution, the onset of HIV infection can mean the end of their exploitation and the beginning of their physical collapse.

However, some trafficking victims do escape; when they do, their situation can be very risky. Without knowing the language or being able to contact anyone back home, they are at the mercy of whomever they encounter. This can often lead to re-enslavement, or rough treatment at the hands of officials who should be protecting them, but only see the escaped victim as an illegal immigrant.

A recent study concluded that the most significant factors predicting human trafficking from a country, "given in order of their power to do so are the level of a country's governmental corruption, the country's infant mortality rate, the proportion of the population below the age of 14, the level of the country's food production, the country's population density, and the amount of conflict and social unrest the country suffers" ("Human Trafficking").

Trafficking also often occurs following widespread disaster, mostly because traffickers prey on the most vulnerable. Following the December 2004 tsunami that devastated Southeast Asia, an estimated 1.5 million children were affected. Their homes and towns were destroyed; their family and friends were gone. Many have had nothing to eat or drink and no place to sleep. "It is easy to see how young victims of a natural disaster become targets to those perpetrating one of the world's worst disasters. The destruction affords the 'perfect opportunity' for traffickers in Indonesia to sell children into forced labour and sexual slavery in neighboring countries such as Malaysia and Singapore" (McGarvey), UNICEF spokesperson John Budd told the BBC. He also confirmed reports of text messages distributed around Asia advertising orphans for sale. According to the United Nations, the trafficking of children is a lucrative business; it ranks third in the world (behind drugs and arms sales) in terms of the money it generates.

No one debates that human trafficking is wrong and must be combated at all levels. This means of enslavement is occurring all over the world as victims are transported, brought under violent control, and exploited for profit by criminals. There is no debate about the basic nature of trafficking, that victims are flowing from poor countries to richer countries to meet the demand for cheap and controllable labour. Trafficked people are enslaved in agriculture, sweatshops, criminal activities such as selling and transporting illegal drugs, and many other types of work. There is controversy within the area of human trafficking; however, and it focuses on just one type of exploitation. The key question concerns whether prostitution, in and of itself, constitutes a form of slavery.

This controversy over prostitution has focused on human trafficking because at times the word 'trafficking' has been used only to describe transporting and forcing women into prostitution. At the end of the 19th century, there was significant official concern in Europe and North America over the 'white slave trade' (again primarily concerned with the enslavement of 'white' women into prostitution), and much less concern over the continuing enslavement into other types of exploitation or the trafficking of other ethnic groups. Today, significant debate continues over the best way to respond to prostitution, and because many human trafficking victims are forced into sexual exploitation, they are in the spotlight.

On one side of this argument are individuals and groups, primarily women's groups, who believe that all prostitution is tantamount to slavery. This side is sometimes called the 'abolitionists' because their ultimate aim is the complete eradication of prostitution. On the other side are individuals and groups who believe that a person can sometimes reasonably decide to engage in prostitution. Their position is that many women have few or no options for earning a living and that if prostitution is the best of the bad choices available, then they should be protected and allowed to do this 'sex work'. Both sides point to the overarching conditions of poverty, sexism, discrimination, violence against women, and lack of education as factors that push a woman towards prostitution. A key difference is that abolitionists consider these factors, plus the potentially violent control exercised by pimps, to be *forcing* a woman into prostitution. Those who might call prostitution 'sex work'. argue that prostitution can be a reasonable if unappealing *choice* for a woman given these factors. Fundamentally, the debate rages over whether women have truly chosen or can truly choose to engage in prostitution.

In some countries where prostitution is legal, such as Germany, people can and do choose to prostitute themselves. The legal prostitution system in Germany, advocates suggest, provides a safer alternative to unregulated prostitution in other nations. "The government regulates brothels across the country, requiring safety standards, clear accounting, and workplace safety. Brothels employ security guards and use video cameras to ensure the safety of all employed prostitutes" ("2006 World Cup"). Because German brothels require these security and safety measures, supporters of the system argue that women are less at risk of receiving poor treatment from a boss, known as a 'pimp'. Nevertheless, trafficking is still an issue and countries like this can serve as transport countries, putting surrounding states at higher risk of trafficking.

Trafficking is not only prevalent in Third World countries and states that allow prostitution; it has occurred in the United States too. Beginning in 1995, a well-educated deaf woman named Adriana Paoletti masterminded a scheme to trick deaf Mexicans to come to New York City. Promised good jobs and a chance to support their families at home, more than 50 men and women were recruited. Upon arrival in the US, the reality of their enslavement descended upon them. All 50 of them were crammed into two apartments, and they received little food. During the day they were sent to the subway and street corners to sell trinkets for a dollar. "Their deafness was used to increase sympathy in passers-by, but it also served as a wall of silence that allowed them to be hidden in plain sight. Thousands of people passed these enslaved workers each day, but their inability to communicate meant that they could not call for help" (Sexton). They would be left on the streets up to 20 hours a day, and then picked up and returned to the two small apartments where they would sleep on the floors. At the apartment, enforcers waited to count up the money they had earned in that day. If the sum was too small, the deaf Mexicans would be beaten; some were held down while given electric shocks from a stun gun. Their terror went on for months, until finally four of the men scribbled a note and took it into police station. This case along with several others is what pushed the US to establish its anti-trafficking laws in 2000.

Thus far governments have done little to monitor, detect, and prevent trafficking. This is mainly because the victims have no way to communicate their enslavement, and law enforcement usually sees them as illegal immigrants. In the past few years the United Nations Human Rights Council (UNHRC) and the General Assembly have composed multiple resolutions on the topic of human trafficking.

These documents focus on the prevention of human trafficking and the care of the victims after the fact. The resolutions urge "Member States that have not yet done so to consider ratifying or acceding to, as a matter of priority, the United Nations Convention against Transnational Organized Crime and the Protocol to Prevent, Suppress and Punish Trafficking in Persons, Especially Women and Children, supplementing the United Nations Convention against Transnational Organized Crime, taking into consideration the central role of those instruments in the fight against trafficking in persons, and urges States parties to those instruments to implement them fully and effectively". They also call upon "concerned Governments to allocate resources, as appropriate, to provide access to appropriate programmes for the physical, psychological and social recovery of victims of trafficking, including thorough job training, legal assistance in a language that they can understand and health care, including for HIV/AIDS, and by taking measures to cooperate with intergovernmental and non-governmental organizations to provide for the social, medical and psychological care of the victims". Along with the United Nations there are various NGOs (non-governmental organizations), such as Free the Slaves and Shakti Samuha, working to combat human trafficking.

Free the Slaves is the main American organization working to end slavery across the globe. It is the sister organization of Anti-Slavery International, the world's oldest and original human rights organization. Founded in 2000, Free the Slaves runs liberation and rehabilitation projects overseas, collaborates with other anti-slavery organizations through funding and networking, raises public awareness of contemporary slavery, promotes slave-free trade, aids policy makers in enforcing and drafting new legislation to prevent slavery, and continues research to understand forms of slavery and devise ways to eliminate it. In recent years, Free the Slaves has teamed with eight grassroots groups in Ghana, Haiti, India, and Nepal. With these groups, Free the Slaves has convinced slaveholders in Ghana to release children they had forced to dive to untangle fishing nets, often resulting in drowning. 20 children were released in the last few months alone, with parents provided with skills training to improve their incomes, More than 4,000 slaves in India were encouraged to free themselves and then move into sustainable livelihoods, while creating community vigilance committees in areas rampant with child trafficking. In just the past 18 months, these committees have brought forward more than 2,300 trafficking cases. The anti-trafficking organization Shakti Samuha began in 996 when 500 girls and women were rescued from slavery in Indian brothels during widespread police raids. It is run by Nepalese women who have been rescued from slavery and forced prostitution in India and returned to Nepal. Having struggled to reclaim their lives, they are reaching out to help other returning trafficking survivors by providing shelter, legal aid, vocational training, and counselling. They have also set up groups for adolescent girls based in poor communities to spread the message about the dangers of trafficking. Now they are reaching out to rural districts where this crime is prevalent, helping women make a united stand against the traffickers. Shakti Samuha is different from other groups that help trafficking survivors, as it places the highest value on self-empowerment. Its aim is to give a stronger voice to women who have been violently exploited and are now in danger of being rejected by their own communities. Shakti Samuha feels that if women and girls are given safe shelter, counselling and practical help, they can find their own ways to rebuild their lives.

The international community has continually become more aware of the effects human rights issues have on the world, and in recent years we have seen these disputes causing violence and wars. Overall, the UNHRC continuously works with governments and other organizations to alleviate cruel treatment of trafficking victims around the world. Vulnerability due to language barriers, gender inequality, poverty, and other causes of susceptibility often leads to trafficking, and the UNHRC strives to eliminate this vulnerability.

PREVALENCE OF TRAFFICKING IN WOMEN

How common is trafficking in women and girls? Trafficking in persons, particularly women and children, impacts nearly every country. The problem has increased in recent years. Because of its hidden nature, it is difficult to determine the precise magnitude of the problem of trafficking in women. As is the case with other forms of violence against women, victims are often reluctant to report or make the fact of the violence known publicly. On the other hand, media reports frequently give estimates of numbers of women trafficked into the commercial sex industry for various regions and countries. Such statistics vary widely and are frequently unreliable or inaccurate. Furthermore, the methods by which such statistical data are gathered are seldom included, and statistics are generally not disaggregated by the sex of the victim.

The United States Department of State Trafficking in Persons Report for 2003 estimates that 800,000 to 900,000 people are trafficked across international borders annually. According to the report, millions of people around the world live in situations of forced labour and commercial sexual exploitation. The United Nations Population Fundstates that "[s]tatistics about trafficking are unreliable for a number of reasons, including the clandestine nature of the activity. However, rough estimates suggest that between 700,000 to 2 million women are trafficked across international borders annually. Adding domestic trafficking would bring the total much higher, to perhaps 4 million persons per year."

The problem of trafficking in women for the purpose of sexual exploitation is particularly significant in the countries of the CEE/FSU region. Poverty, the lack of opportunities for women and the opening of borders are the primary factors contributing to the growth of trafficking in women from these countries to Western Europe. For example, the Ukrainian government estimated in 1998 that 400,000 women had been trafficked from the Ukraine in the past decade. Ukrainian non-profit organizations and scholars believe this number is even greater.

CAUSES AND RISK FACTORS

The various factors that contribute to trafficking are sometimes categorized as 'supply side' factors, such as the feminization of poverty, and 'demand side' factors, such as weak border controls in destination countries. Frequently, it is a combination of these factors that pushes women and girls into situations in which they are exploited and become victims of trafficking. Effective strategies to eliminate trafficking necessarily involve addressing multiple contributing factors.

While this analysis is useful in explaining the complex nature of trafficking, the factors that play a role in trafficking are actually interdependent and interconnected. Some factors, such as military conflict, do not fit neatly into either the 'demand' or 'supply' side of trafficking, but nevertheless have contributed to this problem in some regions. For example, internal conflicts force people to leave their home country, which may encourage trafficking across borders. At the same time, an increase in military personnel in a specific region also increases the 'demand' for women to be brought from outside to work in the commercial sex industry.

EFFECTS AND CONSEQUENCES

According to the United Nations Population Fund, "perhaps 4 million persons per year" are trafficked. Women who have been trafficked may suffer from serious physical and mental health problems. Physical abuse can result in serious injuries and lasting health problems; trafficking victims may also contract life-threatening diseases, such as HIV/AIDS or tuberculosis.

Victims of trafficking may also face serious legal consequences. They may be detained or deported for immigration violations that are the result of being trafficked. Victims may also face prosecution for other criminal offenses that were committed as a direct result of being trafficked.

Although trafficking most directly affects individual victims, it also has broader consequences. Trafficking directly affects the societies from which victims are removed, resulting in cultural and economic losses, and threatening public health. Citing Paul Holmes, author of the *Regional Anti-Trafficking Law Enforcement Manual for South-Eastern Europe*, the United Nations Development Programme estimates that trafficking generates at least US $7 billion a year and, after drugs and weapons, has become the third largest criminal business worldwide. These profits may be used to further fund organized crime activities.

PROTECTION, SUPPORT AND ASSISTANCE OF VICTIMS

A comprehensive strategy for combating trafficking must always consider the safety of the victims. Non-governmental organizations (NGOs) and state agencies that work with repatriated victims of trafficking should also address the multiple difficulties women face when they attempt to reintegrate. Victims of trafficking require comprehensive assistance in both destination and transit countries. Victims are always entitled to the protection of their basic human rights, and any measures adopted to protect victims should take into account age, gender and any special needs.

Victims of trafficking face a range of needs, including physical and mental health care, job training and employment issues, housing issues and, possibly, childcare. Victims need access to a range of support services such as medical, housing, and legal assistance. Child victims also require special protection. The types of services and assistance required by trafficking victims varies somewhat depending on whether the victim is still in the destination country or has returned to her country of origin.

Under principles of international law, States are obligated to provide adequate support for victims of crimes. The United Nations Declaration of Basic Principles of Justice for Victims of Crime and Abuse of Power states that victims are entitled to access to the justice system and prompt redress. Regarding assistance, the Declaration states: "Victims should receive the necessary material, medical, psychological and social assistance through governmental, voluntary, community-based and indigenous means.... Victims should be informed of the availability of health and social services and other relevant assistance and be readily afforded access to them." Victims of trafficking need access to accommodation, financial assistance, physical, sexual and psychological health care and support, and independent health, legal, and social counselling. Access to services should not be contingent on a victim's willingness to cooperate with authorities. Services should be timely and adequately funded. Victims should receive counselling about the benefits of sexual health examinations where appropriate, but such examinations should not be made mandatory. Victims should not be housed in detention centres, but instead should have access to shelters or other forms of accommodation.

In order to provide victims with access to services, governments may need to ensure that inter-governmental organizations and NGOs are adequately funded to assist in meeting the needs of victims. Such organizations play a critical role in providing services to victims. In 2001, the Office for Democratic Institutions and Human Rights (ODIHR) of the Organization for Security and Cooperation in Europe (OSCE) published a *Reference Guide for Anti-Trafficking Legislative Review*, which is also available in Russian and Serbian. The *Reference Guide* includes detailed information about existing legislation that ensures protection of and assistance for victims of trafficking and also describes the role of NGOs:

> [NGOs] are an important source of information on the phenomenon of trafficking and do an enormous amount of work to ensure that the basic needs of victims are met.... Effective and continuous victim assistance and protection requires that states provide relevant NGOs with sufficient resources and training opportunities. Effective victim assistance and protection also require well-functioning co-operation between NGOs and state authorities.
>
> NGOs can play an important role in identifying the type of services needed by the victim, providing referrals, assisting the victim in making appointments with and visiting health care professionals and, in some cases, through the direct provision of services. In the destination country, a victim's most immediate need may be for safe accommodation and legal counselling to assist with immigration issues. Many NGOs have responded to the need for safe accommodation by creating temporary shelters for victims of trafficking. While trafficking victims in the destination country may be in acute need of medical or psychological treatment, they also frequently require long-term medical care when they return to the home country. NGOs that work closely with victims and know of

their specific needs can advocate for the continuation of services for the victim in her country of origin.

Victims of trafficking need assistance in dealing with the legal consequences of trafficking. Victims should not be detained, charged, or prosecuted for entering the destination country illegally or participating in illegal activities where such activities are the direct consequence of their situation as victims of trafficking. In addition, victims need assistance in navigating the legal system of the destination country. This means providing victims with information about their rights in a language that they can understand, and allowing victims an opportunity to present their views and concerns. Victims should also be provided with work authorization and social benefits for the duration of their stay in a country. Because victims may not be able to safely return to their home countries, victims should be allowed to apply for permanent residence in the destination country.

Child victims of trafficking should be identified and helped appropriately. Children should have access to education or vocational training. Child witnesses in judicial proceedings may require special accommodations.

Even after a victim of trafficking has been returned to her home country, the need for protection and assistance continues. The process of reintegration can be enormously difficult for trafficking victims. Rehabilitation programmes should include all of the services in the context of destination countries: shelter, financial assistance and health care. In addition, in order to reintegrate and begin new lives, trafficking victims can benefit from education programmes, such as job training or vocational skills courses.

NGOs can also provide support for victims of trafficking through advocacy for protection of victims' rights. For example, three leading NGOs, the Global Alliance Against Traffic in Women, the Foundation Against Trafficking in Women and the International Human Rights Law Group, collaborated on the drafting of Human Rights Standards for the Treatment of Trafficked Persons, which enumerates concrete actions that governments should undertake to fulfil their obligations to protect and assist victims of trafficking.

PREVENTION OF TRAFFICKING IN WOMEN

Trafficking is a complex problem that requires a multifaceted approach. Frequently, anti-trafficking initiatives at the state level have focused on legal reform and prosecution. As the Organization of Security and Cooperation in Europe (OSCE) points out, however, "effective anti-trafficking strategies should never be restricted to post-trafficking criminal prosecutions. States are also obliged to take adequate measures for the prevention of trafficking."

Prevention of trafficking in women requires examining the factors that contribute to the problem as well as providing education to potential victims. Both government and non-governmental programmes should identify women who are at risk for trafficking and provide them with the tools necessary to find work abroad without putting themselves at risk. At the same time, more far-reaching programmes that address gender inequalities in the labour market are needed to combat trafficking in women. The United Nations High Commissioner for Human Rights produced a report entitled "Recommended Principles and Guidelines on Human Rights and Human Trafficking" in 2002. It identifies demand as a root cause of trafficking; saying, "[S]trategies aimed at preventing trafficking should take into account demand as a root cause. States and governmental organizations should also take into account the factors that increase vulnerability to trafficking, including inequality, poverty and all forms of discrimination and prejudice."

Within the broad category of prevention, government bodies and non-governmental organizations (NGOs) should take both a short-term and long-term approach to addressing trafficking. Short-term actions include education and awareness-raising initiatives. Medium and longer-term projects include lobbying efforts to change national laws, training and technical cooperation projects for law enforcement and the judiciary and improving the social and economic position of vulnerable women.

INTERNATIONAL LAW ON TRAFFICKING IN WOMEN

The United Nations obligates States to refrain from committing human rights violations and also to take positive steps to ensure that individuals are able to enjoy their human rights. A State's legal obligations are articulated in human rights instruments, such as treaties and conventions. The UN also drafts politically-binding documents that do not have the force of law, such as declarations and resolutions, but which nevertheless represent important guidelines on States' obligations.

The United Nations addresses trafficking in women from various directions. First, the UN human rights instruments apply to women and men equally, and are relevant to the kinds of abuses that women suffer in cases of trafficking. In addition, the UN international standards on the treatment of crime victims also obligate States to protect victims of trafficking.

Second, of the types of violence against women addressed by this site, trafficking in women was perhaps the first to receive the attention of the UN as a transnational crime. This chapter, therefore, includes a historical overview of the UN conceptualization of trafficking, prior to the emergence of an international women's human rights movement. Third, the UN treaties and resolutions that articulate the rights of women are applicable to the situation of trafficking and define trafficking as a form of gender-based violence. Since the early 1990s, all major UN instruments on States' commitment to ensure women the full enjoyment of their human rights and their protection from violence have included specific obligations to combat trafficking in women.

Fourth, the UN Convention Against Transnational Organized Crime entered into force in September 2003. The accompanying Protocol to Prevent, Suppress and Punish Trafficking in Persons, Especially Women and Children received its 40th ratification in September 2003 and entered into force on December 25, 2003. The Trafficking Protocol contains the international consensus definition of trafficking and sets forth State obligations to prevent trafficking, to protect victims and to prosecute perpetrators of trafficking.

Finally, at its 60th session in April of 2004 the United Nations Commission on Human Rights (UNHCHR) appointed a Special Rapporteur on Trafficking in Persons, Especially Women and Children for the explicit purpose of focusing on the human rights of victims of trafficking from a global perspective. The Special Rapporteur's mandate is to take action on violations committed against trafficked persons, to undertake country visits to understand specific situations and make recommendations to prevent and combat trafficking, and to submit annual reports to the Commission on his/her activities as special rapporteur. To do so, the rapporteur's job is to gather and exchange information from governments, non-governmental organizations and victims of trafficking in order to propose appropriate measures to prevent and remedy trafficking violations. Working within the major international instruments and definitions of trafficking, the Special Rapporteur publishes reports and take up cases where individual or widespread rights abuses have occurred.

So far, the Special Rapporteur, Ms. Sigma Huda, has released two reports. One, entitled "Integration of the Human Rights of Women and the Gender Perspective", challenges that trafficking continues to be treated as a "law and order problem" and examines the human rights implications of trafficking. The other reports on a mission to Bosnia and Herzegovina.

CHILD SEXUAL ABUSE

Sexual abuse is defined as "all sexually oriented conduct, commentary or gestures, intentional and repeated, not desired or accepted freely by their object, for whom it is an imposition, a humiliation or attack on their dignity". The term *abuse* includes physical as well as non-physical acts. There is enough evidence to suggest that it often receives wider familial sanction. It is institutionalised in various forms, ranging from long hours of labour, often within and outside the home, denial of food, neglect of ailments and verbal abuse to physical violence by the husband and sometimes other family members. Far more difficult to acknowledge are problems caused by the narrow definition of sexuality as a means of perpetuating control over their minds and bodies in a conjugal relationship. Legally child sexual abuse is interpreted as 'rape' of a child who is below 16 years of age and rape as defined in Indian Penal Code is penetration without her consent.

However, in Indian law has interpreted and defined rape as penile-vaginal penetration. This definition is inadequate as in most of the child sexual abuse cases, Sakshi has worked with, there has been no sexual penetration. Child sexual abuse is the physical or mental violation of a child with sexual intent.

Thus Narang, 1998 defines child sexual abuse as follows:

- An adult exposing his/her genitals to a child or persuading the child to do the same.
- Adult touching a child's genitals or making the child touch the adult's genitalia
- An adult involving a child in pornography which includes exposing a child to pornographic material.
- An adult having oral, vaginal or anal intercourse with a child
- Any verbal or other sexual suggestion made to a child by an adult
- An adult persuading children to engage in sexual activity

Kemps sexual abuse is defined as "the involvement of dependent, developmentally immature children and adolescents in sexual activities they do not really comprehend, to which they are unable to give informed consent, or that violate the social taboos of family roles. Sexual abuse is defined as any sexual misuse of the child by a care-taking adult.

Sexual abuse includes incest, oral-genital contact; sodomy, molestation, digital manipulation and so on. RAHI includes exploitative sexual activity, whether or not they involve physical contact, between a child and another person, who by virtue of his power over the child due to age, strength, position, or relationship uses the child to meet his or her own sexual and emotional needs to the definition of child sexual abuse. The act though sexual in nature is also about the abuse of power and the betrayal of trust.

A child's dependency needs for nurturance, touch, caring, caressing, and the like are not the same as adult sexual desires. The adult or older person completely disregards the child's own developmental immaturity and inability to understand sexual behaviours. The act, therefore, is not only a gross violation of the child's body but also of the trust implicit in a care giving relationship. Child sexual abuse, just as to the report is any sexual contact between a child and an adult.

The contact covers a wide range of behaviours. It may or may not involve physical contact, force or violence, but always involves coercion. It can also include fondling of the breast or genitals, rape, oral sex, and/or sodomy.

It can also include an adult demanding that a child touch his/her genitals either directly or through clothing. Non-physical sexual contact also includes exhibitionism, obscene talk or pornography.

Child sexual abuse takes place in all cultures, races and in every strata of the society. Both males and females are sexually abused. Girls however, are abused more frequently and over a longer period of time. Findings based on research done at Sakshi as well as international statistics on child sexual abuse indicate that at least 2 out of 4 girls and 1 out of 6 boys are victims of sexual abuse. A study carried out by a Bangalore based NGO, Samvada, in 1994 of 348 girls from Karnataka, revealed that 83 per cent of the respondents had experienced some form of child sexual abuse.

The preliminary report of an ongoing survey of Sakshi with about 650 girl students indicates that about 60 per cent of the girls had experienced some form of abuse till the age of 15 years. Out of these 60 per cent, about 20 per cent had suffered abuse by close relatives. DCP S.B.K.Singh reported in a daily newspaper, 'The Pioneer', that 85 per cent of the rape cases registered in the District during 1997, involved persons known to the victims.

The World Health Organisation, one in every ten child is sexually abused. In a 1980 study of 1000 victims of child abuse, A.B.Dave, et al found that 81 per cent could be classified as victims of physical abuse, 7 per cent of what the authors call neglect, 9.3 per cent of sexual abuse and 2.7 per cent of emotional abuse. None of these categories can be treated as exclusive and it is important to note that studies of this kind are extremely difficult to undertake. This particularly so in the area of sexual relations where the overall attitude of secrecy and suppression which governs any discussion or reference to sex making it difficult to come to any definite conclusion on the extent of sexual abuse of children. Yet of available figures, of almost 10,000 reported rapes in 1990, an alarming 25 per cent are of girl children below the age of 16 and about a fifth are those under ten. A recent analysis done by the Crimes Against Women Cell, Delhi Police, points out that of the 143 rape cases registered between January and June 1992, 107 or almost 75 per cent were in the age range 7 - 18 years. Forty of the rapists were immediate neighbours and seven were relatives.

Conversations with those in charge of the cell indicate that such cases are on the increase. Sixty per cent of 650 school girls questioned in a survey said they had suffered abuse, close relatives having abused twenty per cent of them. The word perpetrator is used in relation to the person or people who are directly abusing a child or children. Although this can be applied to the person responsible for any other form of mistreatment, it tends to relate to those committing child sexual abuse.

It is not used to refer to other adults who may have played a role but were not directly involved, such as a non-abusing parent who might have been aware of the abuse but unable to intervene. In most cases, the abuser is known to the child family friend, sibling, relative, servant, teacher and so on. There have also been cases where the abusers have been very close relatives—father, grandfather, brother and uncle. The abuser is usually an older person who is in some position of trust and/or power vis-avis the child. Even though both men and women can sexually abuse a child, most abusers are male.

The abuser violates a relationship of trust with the child. They may use tricks or threats to persuade the child to take part in a sexual activity. The abuse generally takes place in the child's home or the abuser's home. Given that the abuser is often known to the child and usually has both access to as well as authority over the child, the abuse does not commonly involve physical violence and generally continues over a long period of time. The abuser uses threats or blackmail to warn the child against telling any one about the abuse. This may be the primary cause for the child's silence.

Child sexual abuse is on the increase because of the responses to it and towards the victims. One of the response being denial of its existence and disbelief: Many people with whom Sakshi has interacted, deny any existence of child sexual abuse especially within a family. The concept of Indian families is perhaps the most sensitive and revered.

Therefore, it is difficult to believe that sexual abuse in the families really happens. For them, if at all the concept of child sexual abuse exists, it is limited to a particular class. The popular belief is that it is very rare and happens only in low class families. Even if some people believe that child sexual abuse exists, there is denial publicly as it is difficult for them to deal with the fact that it is prevalent in our traditional Indian families.

Due to ignorance, denial of its existence, and inability of adults to deal with the subject, the child is met with disbelief when he/she finally summons up the courage to confide in someone about the experience and trauma of being sexually abused. Thus the child is forced to suffer in silence giving the abuser greater power over the child. Sexual abuse is shrouded in shame and secrecy. Sexual organs or any reference to sex is considered to be shameful. Children are not given proper answers when they ask questions about sexual organs.

They get the messages that certain body parts are dirty and they should never be talked about. So, when a child is abused, there is total silence. The child knows that there is something wrong going on, yet the child does not have the language or the words to express it. There is loneliness because the child cannot talk about it to anybody and does not know whom to approach. This hampers disclosure and thus the abuse continues. In families where parents/relatives accept and realise that a child has suffered sexual abuse, the child is forced into silence given the culture of privacy, family prestige and family unity. The child generally does not receive much support from the family as they do not want the matter to be disclosed and the family name exposed. Thus the abuser is not confronted and the child is encouraged to 'forget' the traumatic experience. The child and her future are sacrificed for the image of the family. A healthy environment is a family situation where family communication is clear, direct and specific and rules are flexible.

Children can freely approach elders or adults with questions or concerns about sexual experiences in the full knowledge that the adults concerned will address these issues with the child's welfare in mind.

In this situation no trusted older individual violates the child's person and the child feels the freedom to say no to potential abusers and report the incident with full confidence that he or she will be protected. Families in which incest occurs often appear to be like any other family. However, they are riddled with secrets and psychological stress. Incestuous families tend to be closed, inward families lacking in any real emotional connection to people outside the family.

These families often have a history of problems for several generations, which increase the potential for incest. Frequently the mothers of abused children were themselves molested as children. Many victims assume that being dominated and treated poorly by the offender is just a fact of life and not something to be challenged. However it is vital to note that, while family influences may contribute to incest, the dysfunction itself cannot cause an individual to become sexually abusive. However, the situation makes it easier for the symptoms to play themselves out.

The offender is the sole person responsible for the abuse. In some cases, the mothers do not want to take action against the abused as they are constrained by the status of the abuser within the family, for example; a father. Economic dependence, low self esteem, lack of power within the family, incapacity to accept the responsibility of single parent and moral shame of the act keep the mother quite Members of voluntary organisations says that a mother would often suppress and wish away the event, not only because of a sense of shame and outrage, but also out of fear of reprisals from her husband, son, or other relatives.

In 1992–93, there were eight cases of rape and molestation reported by mothers to Crime Against Women Cell in Delhi. Officials at the cell pointed out that this was a significant development as hardly any such instances were reported earlier. At the same time, wives expected the police to merely caution their husbands; filing a case against them would be unheard of.

Society constantly judges women including young girls and children. They are made to feel responsible, guilty or persecuted. Girls are very scared of this judgement, and of being exposed, which forces them into silence. Abusers are aware of this societal attitude towards women and this becomes their power. Society's attitude enables them to go scott-free. Child sexual abuse is usually dismissed because in most cases it is not 'rape' as defined by law. It is met with disbelief and girls are accused of being destructive when the complaint is against a family member.

In cases where there is no penile penetration or when rape cannot be proved due to inadequate evidence, the accused is charged for 'outraging the modesty of a woman' where they may be sentenced only for a period of six months of two years. In most cases, the accused are acquitted in absence of adequate laws on child sexual abuse and inadequate interpretation of existing laws. The court room environment is hostile and girls are humiliated over and over again. This poses to be a major obstacle for girls who want to file a complaint against their abuser.

The effects of child abuse are long lasting and are carried into adulthood leaving deep scars on the personality of the abused. Healing is an important process and must begin as early as possible. Singh has pointed out that child sexual abuse triggers a host of complexities in the child's psyche. Periodic bouts of low self esteem, sexual dysfunctioning, guilt are some of the problems that arise out of child sexual abuse and which continue to haunt the individual well into adulthood.

Sexual abuse is not the only childhood experience that causes difficulty for people as they mature. Long term effects are often identical to those of other early developmental setbacks. The difference however is that most of them can be talked about freely and without involving embarrassment. The person who is sexually abused in childhood is faced with the taboo of talking about it.

Most former victims keep their experiences a secret for many years. Consequently their emotions are likely to run very deep and when they eventually surface the effects can be devastating. The abuser conveys the message that the abuser's needs come first and so it destroys the basis for child-adult trust. Victims of sexual abuse grow up without a sense of protection and security, something that is essential for them to build inner strength and venture into new experiences.

As a result, they also have difficulty in trusting others and forming relationships. Survivor's sexual activity as children were dominated by perpetrators emotional needs and selfish orientation towards sexuality. Tension, fear, betrayal, pain and mistrust coloured the victim's sexual awakening. Consequently, as adults, the sexual behaviour of survivors is severely impacted. They face issues such as sexual maladjustment, abstaining from sex or compulsively seeking it out.

Adult women victimised as children are also more likely to manifest depression, self destructive behaviour, anxiety, feelings of isolation, low self esteem, a tendency towards substance abuse, over-eating and various other addictions. The most disturbing effect of child sexual abuse is that the worst scars are on the emotional and mental health, which may show up as unidentifiable symptoms. Children are prone to a variety of psychological and behavioural disturbances caused by the trauma of abuse. These include bed wetting, nightmares, sleep disorders, depression, anxiety, running away from home, multiple personality disorders, low self esteem caused by guilt and shame.

Many children also develop a negative attitude towards their body as they blame themselves for the abuse. Renu, victim of sexual abuse began hating herself and her body. She started eating constantly, as she wanted to look ugly and so that she would not fall prey to abuse again. Thus it can lead to disturbing the child's relationship with her sexual identity/sexuality and she can fall anywhere in the spectrum, which extends from promiscuity to frigid.

It effects her self worth and the future interactions that she will have, especially with men. Shobha Srinath NIMHANS, points out to a fact that a young child below ten may not always be aware that her sexual violation is in fact qualitatively different from thrashing and abuse; it is only with the onset of puberty that she becomes aware of her sexuality.

In fact in an environment where physical contact, both affectionate and abusive, by relatives of both sexes is not uncommon, child rape needs to be viewed a little differently from the rape of a post-pubertal girl. Not unexpectedly, the families rarely talk about the rape of their young daughter: when the rapist is a father or brother, the chances of reporting is even lower. A victim of incest may attempt suicide, may have bouts of panic attack and depression.

The child may not even confide in the parents. He adds that, the wide prevalence of the crime can be gauged by the fact that just as to a study, 16 per cent of the patients being treated for genito-urinary symptoms in the dermatology and sexually transmitted diseases department of a public hospital in New Delhi, were below 14 years of age. The child feels three Ds—dirty, damaged and different. There is a lot of anger, shame and guilt involved. There are suicidal tendencies, drug addiction and alcoholism. They also exhibit self-mutilating behaviour and have panic attacks and depression. At times the impact plays itself out in certain compulsive behaviour like over-eating, bulimia, anorexia nervosa generally seen in abused girls. There would be a slump in academic performance, increased temper tantrums, "different" conduct with some members, exhibition of sexual awareness in crude manner which are indicators of abuse. Most often children do not have the language to describe sexual activity.

It is difficult for a child to articulate his or her experience. Moreover, they are extremely traumatised as they try to make sense of what has happened to them. Hurt and fear of disclosure or punishment are the initial responses that prevent a child from speaking out. Hence it is very important to cultivate openness within the immediate family where the children can confide in their parents without the fear of ridicule or reproach. Parents can look for certain telltale signs and reactions to find out how safe their children are, says Singh,

- The child tries to stay away from friends and people he was close to earlier. This could be due to guilt that has flooded his little conscience.
- He or she may seem depressed. Depression itself may not be easy to gauge in children but it is translated into more expressible emotions such as being irritable, withdrawn and listless
- The child may resume bed-wetting if he or she has stopped it. Sometimes he or she can get incontinent while awake.
- He or she may avoid a particular individual and show fear when forcibly made to come face to face with this person. This person could be abuser or someone who looks like him.

- Difficulty in concentrating or failing tests at school
- Sudden use of sexual language and swear words.
- Sexual exploitation or exploration of other children.
- Irritation in throat and bladder infections.
- Sexually transmitted infections.

CHILD PROSTITUTION AND TRAFFICKING

The UN Special Rapporteur on the sale of Children, Child Prostitution and Child Pornography defines Child Prostitution as the sexual exploitation of a child for remuneration in cash or in kind, usually but not always organised by an intermediary. Thus the violence against the girl child acquires a new dimension in the sale of young girls below the age of 18 for prostitution and trafficking.

To curb this, the Suppression of Immoral Trafficking Act, later modified to the Prevention of Immoral Trafficking Act has been passed. Prostitution in India is a ₹ 40,000 crore annual business. It has been estimated that 30 per cent of the sex workers are children, who earn ₹.11,000 crore. This has been reported by a study by the Centre of Concern for Child Labour.

At present the number of child prostitutes in India is between 270,000 and 400,000, with the number of children in "commercial prostitution" increasing at the rate of 8–10 per cent per annum. The practice of child prostitution is in blatant contravention of the UN Declaration on the Rights of the Child, endorsed by the "National Policy for Children" of the Ministry of Social Welfare, Government of India. Principle 9 of the Declaration states: The child shall be protected against all forms of neglect, cruelty and exploitation. These shall not be the subject of traffic in any form." Poverty and deprivation, coupled with a low status in society for girls is a primary factor for child prostitution. It is well known that prostitution exists in the Third World because of poverty. A UNICEF Report, children are often required to work to supplement their meagre incomes. Thus in a country like India, child prostitution in most cases stems from child labour. Prostitution is often viewed as an avenue providing easy money, which seems attractive for families steeped in poverty.

Dr. K.K.Mukhpadhyay from Delhi School of Social Work, University of Delhi, in his presentation based on surveys he conducted for the Government of India, said that young girls in India were taken away from their parents in poor backward and drought affected districts of the country for purposes of trafficking. These were also states with gender inequality and low literacy rates. The trafficking network was well organised in these areas. He found in his survey that about eighty per cent of the girls who were in this profession entered it as children and due to difficult circumstances, such as poverty, illiteracy, ignorance, and deception. The increasingly consumerist society only further complicated the situation. Children are often hired out or sold by their families to agents who may or may not reveal the true nature of the work offered. The agent may promise a job as a domestic servant or factory worker at a wage many times higher than is customary in rural areas.

A sum which is large in the eyes of the family, may be handed over to them, and the child is obligated to work to pay off the debt. Some young girls are deceived by young urban boys who go to villages.

The biys conduct fake marriages with these girls, bring them to the cities and sell them to the brothels. On the economic front, it must be noted that development policies and patterns of development promoting tourism, industrialisation, rural to urban migration particularly of males generate a demand for commercial sex. In such a situation, the developing countries bear the brunt of the problem. Economic disparities within countries, and between countries and regions fuels the demand for trafficking from low income to high income areas. In addition, population mobility has been facilitated by globalization and liberalization as they have opened borders and relaxed controls. Such a scenario gives a spurt to tourism which leads to 'sex tourists' from the West journeying East with the purpose of exploiting children.

Goa has become one such haven for paedophiles and people indulging in child prostitution. There are at least 400 minors in the locality involved in the trade. Further, there is no respite in the situation as the existence of minors is often hidden on receiving a tip off about the raids. There are also instances of the arrest of 25 odd girls and their being summarily released subsequently, once their ages have been found to be above 18. The exploitation is shown in the fact that a girl below the age of 16 is available for ₹ 300- ₹ 500, justifying for Goa the name of 'India's Bangkok'. Men who travel to the Third World for 'sex with children', argue that there is nothing new in going abroad to escape the moral strictures at home. This phenomenon is further enhanced by the growing demand for very young girls with a premium on virgins. A research scholar with the Department of Criminology at Madras University, the fear of AIDS often makes the Western 'sex tourist' to seek virgins.

Such a demand is catered to by large markets in Bombay and Hyderabad also. Child prostitution in India is further aggravated by the presence of social conventions and myths prevailing in society. It is popularly believed that sex with a virgin is a cure for venereal and other diseases. Moreover, a reason for the rise in child trafficking can be attributed to the myth that having sexual intercourse with a child would protect the client from AIDS. This was stated at a workshop organised by UNICEF on "The Rights of the Child". With the low levels of education and literacy, such myths are only perpetuated.

It is well known that the female sex is further disadvantaged due to the inadequate educational and employment opportunities, gender disparities in access to opportunities and the lack of social safety nets. Social conventions play an important role in the continuance of the phenomenon of child prostitution. These include child marriages, polygamy, dowry and social stigma against single, unwed, divorced women and girls who have been sexually abused.

Children, especially young girls, in these circumstances are especially vulnerable to the prostitution racket. There have been instances of girls being driven into the sex trade following traumatic sexual experiences during childhood, including rape. If, in the case of Shahida of Kozhikode, it was the violence inflicted by her father's younger brother followed by molestation by her cousin and then rape, Lakshmi's tale of woe began when she was raped by her step father at age 8 and her further sexual exploitation for food when she left home.

Prostitution thus becomes a viable option for children who have been abandoned, for those from disrupted families and for those who are financially supporting their families. The prevalence of traditional and religious practices in some communities that consist of dedicating girls to gods and goddesses serve to encourage child prostitution. The evolution of the *Devadasi* cult can be traced to a period earlier than the entry of *Aryans* in India.

The cult appears to be a relic of the *Dravidian* matriarchal society. It exists today in India with many regional variations. This social convention condemns nearly 5 to 10 thousand girls every year to a life of sexual servitude and subsequently into prostitution. The *devadasi* girls form 15 per cent of the total women in prostitution in India. In the border districts of Maharashtra and Karnataka states, their per centage in prostitution is nearly 80 per cent. The striking fact is that all of them have entered prostitution in an extremely organised manner. This process involves first making the girl a *devadasi* and then legitimising her entry into prostitution with the help of 'religion'.

The practice receives sanction from mythology and was once supported by feudal land owning systems. Social backwardness is the most closely linked factors to both *devadasis* and prostitutes. It is known that ethnic minority, "scheduled castes" and "other backward classes", indigenous people, hill tribes, refugees and illegal immigrants are particularly susceptible to the racket. Interestingly, the "signs" used to identify the chosen child are those of ill health - white patches of eczema, leprosy and even mental retardation. Researchers now speculate whether prostitution was one lucrative way of making use of such otherwise "worthless children".

Among those involved in child prostitution, it is the street children who are most vulnerable to it. The problem of street children is primarily the outcome of four circumstances—poverty, non-existence of a supportive social and economic structure, rapid urbanisation leading to chronic housing shortage and the growth of slums and an oppressive home environment. The prevailing situation is aggravated by the lack of awareness of legal rights, the exploited situation of the victims and the absence of a channel for seeking redress.

In the presence of the growth of trans-national crime and expansion of drug trafficking networks, weak law enforcement mechanisms, exploitation by corrupt law enforcers and officials are the order of the day. On paper, prostitution *per se* is not illegal and hence there are loopholes in the law that ensure a person goes scot-free even if he sells a minor girl to a brothel, provided there is a stamped receipt. The erosion of traditional family systems and values and the pursuit of consumerism encourages sale of children.

The National Commission for Women identifies sexual glorification by the electronic media as one of the prime reasons for minors in prostitution. In 1991, the Central Social Welfare Board conducted a study on Child Prostitution. Among the causes of entry to prostitution, economic distress accounted for 41 per cent; desertion by spouse = 24.5 per cent; deception = 11.9 per cent; social customs = 5.35 per cent; family tradition = 5 per cent; kidnapping and abduction = 2.25 per cent.

The study also indicates that many of the young girls join, emulating the example of girls who have joined the trade and as a consequence are living well. It has also been shown that most prostitutes are forced to remain in their professions due to police highhandedness and the clout of local henchmen. This makes chances of rescue and rehabilitation very slight. It has been found in 1994 that India has four lakh child prostitutes. The Bangalore based NGO "Equations", about 20 per cent of India's 2 million prostitutes are below the age of 15. Bombay city alone is believed to have 40,000 child prostitutes.

The flesh trade in India is liberally replenished from Nepal, which is believed to contribute an estimated 20,000 young girls every year. The survey conducted by the Central Social Welfare Board in 1991-92 in the cities of Bombay, Calcutta, Delhi, Madras, Hyderabad and Bangalore shows that 15 per cent are below the age of 15 at the time of entry and 25 per cent are minors in the age group of 16-18 years. However, among the various studies conducted, there does appear to be some discrepancy in their findings.

A study on prostitution in Delhi has challenged the findings of a report by the National Commission for Women on child prostitution. While the NCW says that children form 60 per cent of the prostitutes in the Capital's main sex market at G.B. Road, the study by Jan Shakti Vahini figures it as low as 7 per cent. On a similar note, very few cases of child sex workers have been reported in the state of Kerala.

However, just as to the study conducted by Loyola College of Social Sciences on "Girl Children in Prostitution", this does not imply their total absence; it merely indicates that locating them is difficult. Violence against prostitutes is of two kinds, argued Mr Dasgupta, and relates to violence at the workplace. Girls are sold by their parents or procured by abductors. A good number, about 25 per cent to 30 per cent are known as *chukris* in Calcutta.

These women who are sold by their parents or husbands are severely beaten and tortured into submission. As a rule they have to pass on all their earnings to the keepers and any deviation from this norm is also countered with violence. Lack of space accounts for the presence of keepers in a big way.

However those with a place of their own face yet another problem: *Goondas* toughs) forcefully seek entry into the women's houses and assume the role of the pimps. They live off their earnings and, in case of resistance, get violent. Data revealed that clients were the least prone to use violence. Mr Dasgupta's study showed that 75 per cent of women in the prostitution industry are from West Bengal, of whom a third are from Murshidabad, Birbhum and Burdwan or the Radh area.

The Radh are a has traditionally sent girls to Calcutta for prostitution. What is important here is the prevalence of child marriage and child widows. When they returned to their parent's home, as they were considered burdens, they were sent off to Calcutta to work as housemaids or prostitutes. Earlier, these women came from Kulin Brahmin and Kayastha families, nowadays they are from all castes. Micro studies conducted by Prerana, Mumbai, conducted 10 focus group interviews of five children in each group reveals that the age of becoming a prostitute was under 18 for 90.3 per cent of the girls, the average age being 16 years.

When dealing with child prostitution, the best possible available indicator as to its prevalence is the incidence of AIDS and sexually transmitted diseases in the age group below 18. UNAID, one in every two women in Mumbai's brothels was infected by 1993 and one in every three attend STD clinics. Nationally, it estimates that the incidence of HIV was 25 per cent among women in prostitution and 10 per cent among clients.

Sudden increases in the number of kidnappings and abduction of young girls and their subsequent adoptions could possibly be indicators of the practice of child prostitution. The National Crime Records Bureau reported a 100 per cent increase in kidnappings in the last two years. Often, young girls are kidnapped from their homes. 60 per cent of these children are forcibly "married", and then hidden by the brothel owner until they reach the "profitable" ages of 9-13 years.

7

Corporate Crime

DEVELOPMENT OF ECONOMIC CRIME

ECONOMIC CRIME DEFINED

The lack of agreed upon definitions regarding economic crime and computer crime, has resulted in a paucity of data and information on the size and scope of the problem. There are no national mechanisms, such as the Uniform Crime Reports, for the reporting of economic crimes by law enforcement. Academics have not been able to agree on definitions and have for the most part continued to focus on white-collar crime. White-collar crimes require that the perpetrator be a person of status who has opportunity because of his position in an organization. This definition, while seminal in the 1940's, is inaccurate today and impedes agreement on more contemporary definitions.

Based on Sutherland's limited definition, all other crimes are viewed as newer versions of conventional crimes. Thus, the true nature of the amount of economic crime is buried in the statistics of more conventional crimes.

For example, credit card fraud is typically classified as a larceny instead of access device fraud. In 1995 the National Fraud Investigation Center undertook the task of creating a classification system that would be able to categorise and classify fraud information in a dynamic and hierarchical structure. The Fraud Identification Codes (FIC) were designed hierarchically to allow classification of each type of fraud in order of importance, and thus, provide the ability to add and modify types as it became necessary. Four levels of classification were developed, from the most general to the more specific: Class, Sub-class, Type and Sub-type. The following groups reviewed and recommended changes to the FIC: The Uniform Crime Reporting Division of the FBI, The National Incident Based Reporting System of the FBI, The White Collar Crime Division of the FBI, the American Bankers Association Check Fraud Unit, and the Secret Service.

The FIC system currently has over 600 classified types of fraud including 11 classes, 75 subclasses, over 350 types and over 175 sub-types. Without a framework and a single reporting center, economic crime statistics will continue to be fragmented estimates of the true extent of the level of the crimes.

A system such as the FIC codes could provide the logical format for a national Programme to gather data on economic crimes. In order to address the issue of economic crime in the United States, it is necessary to adopt a definition for the purpose of this white paper.

The definition as suggested, follow is:

- Economic Crime is defined as an illegal act (or a constantly evolving set of acts) generally committed by deception or misrepresentation (fraud) by someone (or a group) who has special professional or technical skills for the purposes of personal or organizational financial gain or to gain (or attempt to gain) an unfair advantage over another individual or entity.

This definition provides for the inclusion of more contemporary crimes and methods in situations where the individual is not a person of status in an organization or even employed by the organization. It does not refer to these types of crimes as non-violent, as most definitions of white-collar crimes do.

Increasingly, organised crime groups have used economic crime to fuel their enterprises, such as arms trafficking, drug smuggling, and terrorism, and have used violence to further their ends.

TYPES OF ECONOMIC CRIMES AND DEVELOPMENT OF STATUTORY LAW

There seems to be no limit to the types of economic crimes and the methods of committing them. However, certain crimes are unique to certain industries. For example, cloning applies to the wireless telecommunication industry and currency transaction reporting applies primarily to the banking and financial services industry. The discussion that follows relates to specific economic crimes in nine different areas and the laws enacted by Congress that proscribe the illegal conduct.

MAIL AND WIRE FRAUD: GENERIC FRAUDS AND SWINDLES

The mail fraud statute was enacted in 1872. The law was designed specifically to enable special agents of the U.S. Mail to investigate frauds and swindles perpetrated through the use of the mail system and to seek federal prosecution for such offenses. Because it applies to "any scheme or artifice to defraud, or for obtaining money or property by false pretenses, representations or promises," the statute has been used to prosecute fraudulent insurance claims, fraudulent loan applications, securities frauds, and an unlimited variety of frauds and swindles.

It frequently is applied to new types of fraudulent acts in those situations where Congress has not had the opportunity to enact a specific statute to deal with the crime. Because mail fraud has generic appeal, it applies to conventional economic crimes in the eight areas on which this report focuses. The crime of mail fraud is committed by depositing or receiving matter with or from the Postal Service or a private interstate carrier or causing matter to be delivered by the Postal Service or such carrier for the purpose of furthering the fraudulent scheme.

There is no monetary threshold necessary for prosecution, although federal prosecutors informally may decline to handle minor cases. The wire fraud statute is patterned after the mail fraud statute. It proscribes the use of interstate communications by wire, radio or television to perpetrate a scheme or artifice to defraud. The statute is generic in application and applies to a wide range of criminal activity across industries.

Courts have not limited the reach of the statute to land line telephone communications; the statute has been applied to wireless communications using microwave technology, in part. Because transactions over the Internet usually involve interstate communications by telephone wire or cable, the wire fraud statute will continue to serve as an effective law enforcement and prosecutorial tool to combat cyber crimes against all major industries.

BANKING INDUSTRY: FINANCIAL INSTITUTION CRIMES

Like mail and wire fraud, the bank fraud statute applies generically to any scheme to defraud a financial institution or any fraudulent act designed to obtain money or property from a financial institution. The statute currently defines a financial institution as any depositary institution insured by the FDIC, as well as credit unions and the Federal Reserve Bank. Unlike mail or wire fraud, which are limited to the medium of communication, the bank fraud statute applies to any fraudulent scheme designed to obtain money or property from the financial institution, including check forging, check kiting, stolen checks, credit card fraud, fraudulent loan applications, student loan fraud, and embezzlement.

The financial statement statute applies to any fraudulent statement made to a financial institution for the purpose of obtaining money or property in the custody or control of the institution. The quintessential financial statement fraud is a false statement made in an application for a loan or to obtain credit from a financial institution.

The Continuing Financial Crimes Enterprise (CFCE) statute was enacted in 1990 and is designed to impose criminal sanctions for large-scale frauds committed upon financial institutions, such as the massive frauds upon the savings and loan industry. A CFCE is a series of violations of numerous sections of title 18 of the U.S. Code, as well as the crimes of mail and wire fraud, if they affect a financial institution, committed by one who organises, manages or supervises the enterprise, and receives $5 million in gross receipts from the enterprise over a 24-month period. It is limited to financial institutions as victims, but would include a series of credit card frauds, if those crimes were charged under 18 U.S.C. § 1341, 1343 or 1344.

The computer fraud statute currently prohibits accessing a "protected computer" without authority, or in excess of authority, to obtain information or to obtain something of value, hacking into a protected computer and transmitting a Programme, information, code, or command with the intent to damage the computer, or transmitting in interstate commerce any threat to cause damage to a protected computer in order to extort something of value. Because a "protected computer" includes a computer "exclusively for the use of a financial institution" or if not exclusively used, a computer "used by or for a financial institution and the conduct constituting the Offence affects that use by or for the financial institution", the statute applies to specific criminal conduct directed at bank computers or computerised data storage facilities. The money laundering statutes were enacted in 1986 as part of the Money Laundering Control Act.

These sections apply to the conduct of the customer of a financial institution who deposits the proceeds of criminal activity with the bank and uses the bank to layer or launder those proceeds and to facilitate the transportation of the proceeds into or out of the country. Banks providing online services and electronic wire transfers are particularly susceptible to such conduct.

In 1970, Congress enacted the Bank Secrecy Act, also known as the Currency and Foreign Transaction Reporting Act, to curb the laundering of cash through banking institutions. That Act requires the filing of currency transaction reports (CTR's) for any deposit or withdrawal of cash exceeding $10,000. Subsequent amendments to the Act require the filing of reports for the transportation of currency or monetary instruments exceeding $10,000 into or out of the U.S., cash transactions exceeding $10,000 at casinos or as part of business transactions, and for suspicious activity transactions. The Treasury Department has promulgated several regulations providing the details of the reporting requirements, which apply to both electronic fund transfers and online banking transactions. The Racketeering Influenced and Corrupt Organizations (RICO) statute has application to mail fraud, wire fraud, bank fraud, currency transaction reporting violations and money laundering because they are predicated acts constituting racketeering activity. RICO provides an effective law enforcement weapon against those who engage in a pattern of racketeering activity and victimise a financial institution, or those financial institutions that engage in a pattern of racketeering activity.

CREDIT CARD CRIMES

In addition to mail and wire fraud, Congress has enacted two laws that specifically address the traditional means of committing crimes involving a credit card. The credit card fraud statute prohibits the sale, use or transportation of a counterfeit, altered, stolen, lost or fraudulently obtained credit card in a transaction affecting or using interstate or foreign commerce, or furnishing money obtained through the use of a counterfeit, altered, stolen, lost or fraudulently obtained card, or the receipt or concealment of goods or tickets for interstate or foreign transportation obtained though the use of such a card.

Federal courts disagree whether this crime can be committed without a plastic card. Because online transactions involve the use of the credit card number and not the card itself, it is unclear whether section 1644 applies to online transactions. The access device statute, however, defines an "access device" to include a card or an account number. This statute prohibits the production, use or trafficking in counterfeit credit cards or account numbers, the possession of 15 or more counterfeit cards or account numbers, producing, trafficking in or possessing equipment used to produce counterfeit cards, without authority from the card issuer, offering a card or selling information regarding applications to obtain cards, or attempts or conspiracies to commit any of the acts regarding credit cards or account numbers.

HEALTH CARE FRAUD

Prior to 1996, federal prosecutors employed generic crimes such as the false statements statute, false claims statute, mail fraud statute or wire fraud statute to prosecute those charged with engaging in conduct encompassed by the term "health care fraud." In some instances, prosecutors were able to use laws created to address specific methods of committing health care fraud relating to the Medicare and Medicaid Programmes, such as the false claims statute, the anti-kickback statute, and the self-referral statute.

In 1996, Congress enacted the Health Insurance Portability and Accountability Act (HIPAA), which created five distinct health care fraud crimes. This enactment was significant in that it imposes criminal penalties for health care frauds perpetrated upon private health care benefit plans, as well as Medicare and Medicaid. "Health care fraud" under HIPAA is committed by executing or attempting to execute a scheme or artifice to defraud any health care benefit Programme or fraudulently obtaining the money or property of a health care benefit Programme.

HIPAA also proscribes the theft or embezzlement of funds, securities, premiums, property and other assets of a health care benefit Programme, concealment of a material fact or fraudulent statements in connection with the delivery or payment of health care benefits or services, and the obstruction of or interference with the communication of records relating to a violation of HIPAA to a criminal investigator. Additionally, a conspiracy to violate any of those offenses also is a crime. Federal financial statement fraud and false claims fraud have limited application to the health care industry because the victim in those statutes is the government. The enactment of HIPAA significantly enhances the prosecutorial arsenal available to combat health care fraud committed by traditional means because the victim of those crimes are health care benefit Programmes, which include private health insurance plans. The

Act, however, does not address a myriad of other cyber crimes that are health care related, for example, pharmaceutical fraud, web sites that fraudulently purport to provide medical advice, and phony web sites. The only statutory tool currently available to prosecute such conduct effectively is the wire fraud statute.

INSURANCE FRAUD

Most fraudulent conduct impacting upon the insurance industry constitutes application fraud or claims fraud. These frauds may be committed by the insured, an agent or employee of the company, a third party, or as is more often the case, a conspiracy between two or more of those groups.

Historically, insurance fraud has been the subject of state regulation. Nevertheless, federal jurisdiction and laws may be invoked where the fraudulent activity constitutes a mail or wire fraud, which is frequently the case. Applications for insurance are commonly sent through the mail or processed online over the Internet. Proofs of loss, bills, invoices and receipts submitted in support of an insurance claim typically are transmitted to the insurer by mail or by fax transmission. Further, a continuing pattern of such activity may constitute a RICO crime. Federal law also regulates the conduct of persons or entities engaged in the business of insurance.

It imposes criminal sanctions for:

- The embezzlement or misappropriation of premiums, money or other property of insurance companies,
- The making of false statements or reports to an insurance regulatory agency or official involving the overvaluing of land, property or security for the purpose of influencing action by that agency,
- Making false entries in any book, report or statement of the insurance company to deceive the company or an insurance agency or official regarding the financial solvency of the business,
- Engaging in the insurance business by any person convicted of a felony involving dishonesty or a breach of trust, and
- Threatening, influencing or obstructing the administration of law in any pending proceeding before an insurance regulatory agency or official.

There is no published decision to date regarding prosecutions under this section. Section 1034 authorises the U.S. Attorney General to seek civil penalties or injunctions for violations of section 1033.

Securities Fraud

Congress created numerous securities fraud crimes by enactment of the Securities and Exchange Act of 1934. The major anti-fraud statute is section 10(b) of the Act, which is codified at 15 U.S.C. § 78j (b). That section and Rule

10b-5, which was promulgated by the Securities Exchange Commission, prohibit the use of any instrumentality of interstate commerce or stock exchange or mail for the commission of a fraudulent act, scheme or artifice to defraud, or the making of a false statement in connection with the purchase or sale of a security. Although that statute and rule have served as an effective prosecutorial weapon in combating securities fraud and insider trading, the statute was not drawn with the Internet and e-trading in mind.

Telecommunication Fraud

Fraud impacts all sectors of the communications industry—telephone, wireless, and cable. The types of fraud are numerous: toll fraud, including "clip-on" and "shoulder surfing" methods, call-sell operations established by organised crime groups who engage "phreaks" to hack into phone line, subscription fraud, which frequently also involves identity theft, PBX fraud, which also involves call-sell operations, calling card fraud, remote call forwarding, and computer terrorism/sabotage.

Because these frauds frequently encompass interstate wire communications, the wire fraud statute is an effective legal weapon to combat telecommunication fraud. The principal fraudulent activities impacting upon the wireless communication industry are subscription fraud and cloning. Subscription fraud occurs when an individual applies for and obtains a wireless telephone account.

Because a fraudulent application customarily involves the use of a counterfeit or stolen credit card or account number, or a stolen means of identification, the credit card fraud, access device fraud, and identity fraud statutes are available for the prosecution of such Behaviour. Most wireless service providers currently encourage customers to apply by accessing their web site. The wire fraud statute serves as an additional prosecutorial weapon to combat online subscription fraud. Cloning entails the theft of an electronic serial number (ESN) and mobile identification number (MIN) assigned to a legitimate wireless phone, and the installation of those numbers on a stolen phone. Once accomplished, the cloned stolen phone behaves like the phone owned by the legitimate customer, and the monthly bill for charges are sent to the legitimate customer.

The access device statute specifically proscribes the theft of ESNs and MINs, the production or use of a cloned phone, and the possession, use, production or trafficking in scanning receivers or hardware or software utilised to clone phones for the purpose of obtaining unauthorised wireless services. Although cloning a phone and the use of a cloned phone historically has not involved the Internet, technology is now in place to enable wireless access to the Internet. The access device statute should continue to be an effective legal weapon to combat the use of cloned phones for Internet access.

Additionally, the computer fraud statute may also apply to such conduct. Congress initially sought to regulate abuses committed by the telemarketing industry by enactment of the Telephone Consumer Protection Act of 1991. That Act provides for statutory damages for each violation, but does not impose criminal sanctions. In 1994, Congress enacted the Senior Citizens Against Marketing Scams (SCAMS) Act. The SCAMS Act imposes criminal penalties for telemarketing frauds involving wire communications, including conspiracies to commit such crimes, and enhanced sentences where senior citizens are victimised. Because Internet scams encompass the use of wire communications in part, the wire fraud statute will remain an effective legal weapon for the prosecution of scammers.

INTELLECTUAL PROPERTY AND COMPUTER CRIME

The computer fraud statute seeks to address conduct involving the use of computers to perpetrate the crime and computers as the victims of crime.

The statute imposes criminal penalties for:

- Accessing a computer without authorization to obtain classified federal information to be used for the benefit of a foreign nation.
- Accessing a computer without authorization to obtain the financial record of a financial institution, issuer of a credit card, consumer reporting agency or federal agency.
- Accessing a government computer without authorization and affecting the government's use of the computer.
- Accessing a protected computer (a "protected computer" is a computer either used in interstate or foreign commerce or exclusively for the use of a financial institution or the U.S. government) without authorization and with the intent to defraud and obtaining anything of value through that fraudulent act.
- Transmitting a Programme, information, code or command and intentionally causing damage to a protected computer.
- Accessing a protected computer and causing damage.
- Trafficking in any password that can be used to access a computer if the trafficking affects interstate or foreign commerce, or "such computer is used by or for the Government of the United States."
- Transmitting any threat to cause damage to a protected computer in order to extort money or other thing of value.

To the extent that credit card account numbers constitute computer data on various e-commerce web sites, accessing the computers or peripheral equipment for the purposes of unlawfully obtaining and trafficking in stolen account numbers may also constitute computer fraud. A recent example of such conduct is the hacker identified as Maxim who attempted to extort $100,000 from CD Universe and, when the threat failed, posted credit card account numbers that he had obtained from CD Universe's web site on another web site. Because the use of a modem involves a wire communication, the wire fraud statute applies to the use of a computer to commit crimes, including credit card transactions, online banking, online insurance fraud, etc. Prior to 1996, the principal federal weapon designed to combat the theft of trade secrets was the Trade Secrets Act.

That statute prohibits the unauthorised disclosure of confidential information by government employees. Prosecutions for trade secret theft that victimised the private sector were based on the National Stolen Property Act, which was not particularly effective because it did not encompass intangibles (soft property) within its protective embrace, or the mail or wire fraud statute. The Economic Espionage Act of 1996 attempted to cure previous deficiencies by imposing criminal penalties for economic espionage by or for foreign government and for the theft of trade secrets from public and private sector sources. Moreover, the 1996 statute defines the theft of trade secrets to include a misappropriation committed by any means, as well as the receipt of trade secrets. The Trademark Counterfeiting Act of 1984 imposes criminal penalties for the intentional trafficking in counterfeit goods and services, *i.e.,* those goods and services that bear a stolen trademark. Congress first imposed criminal sanctions for copyright infringements in 1897. Since that time, the statute has been amended on numerous occasions as Congress attempted to provide more protection to the copyright holder. Notably in 1992, the Copyright Felony Act added protection against large-scale computer software privacy, and in 1997 Congress enacted the No Electronic Theft Act, which removed the requirement that the perpetrator derive a financial gain from the infringement.

Identity Theft

The federal identity fraud statute prohibits the unlawful production, possession, transfer or use of a "means of identification" of another person to commit or abet any federal crime or state felony crime or to defraud the federal government. The statute defines a "means of identification" as any name or number used to identify an individual, including an access device.

Because access devices include a credit card account number, the crime of identity fraud encompasses the use of another person's credit card account number, as opposed to use of the plastic card itself. The statute also includes other devices as "means of identification," including a passport, birth certificate, driver's license, social security number, taxpayer identification number, unique electronic identification number, and unique biometric data, such as a fingerprint, voice print, retina or iris image. By 1999, twenty states had enacted identity theft statutes. Many other states prosecute identity theft under criminal impersonation statutes. The success of identity theft prosecutions under those impersonation statutes depends upon the language of each statute.

VICTIMS OF ECONOMIC CRIME

CONSUMERS

Very few studies on fraud victimization have been conducted. Two that studied telemarketing are Harris and Associates and a study by the American Association of Retired Persons. The most comprehensive study to date is the National White Collar Crime Center's National Public Survey on White Collar Crime. The study's goal was, "to present a picture of what the average American thinks about white collar crime."

Its survey of 1,169 households throughout the United States found that:

- Over 1 out of 3 households had been victimised by white collar crime in the last year.
- Widely held opinions concerning the profile of typical white collar crime victims are divorced from the actual profile of victims found by recent research on victimization.
- There is a disparity between how Americans believe they will react if victimised and how they do react when they are actually victimised.
- Less than 1 in 10 victimizations were ever reported to law enforcement or consumer protection agencies.
- The public has a deep concern with increasing the apprehension and sanctioning of white collar criminals.

Consumer victimization usually results in three types of losses: privacy, good credit status, and funds or assets. Consumers are concerned that personal information disclosed to companies with which they do business may be compromised. Such compromises include unauthorised access and/or by the company's employees, lack of security to protect the information, providing the information to third parties, and the maintenance of accurate information. Any one of these breaches could result in the consumer's personal information falling into criminal hands, which could easily result in identity theft. Other consequences range from damage to an individual's credit rating to the loss of funds and/or assets.

INDUSTRY

The victimization of industry falls into four categories:

1. Profit losses
2. Damage to reputation
3. Loss of continuity of business
4. Loss of intellectual property

According to The Credit Risk Management Report, "The average organization loses more than $9 a day per employee to fraud and abuse. The average organization loses about 6 percent of its total annual revenue to fraud and abuse committed by its own employees. Fraud and abuse costs US organizations more than $400 billion annually."

Early on, many corporations were able to take the position that fraud was a cost of doing business, and could make it up by passing the cost of fraud to the consumer through increased prices. In more competitive markets this is not possible. In those cases when the bottom line is hit hard by fraud, executives are less reluctant to commit funds to fraud management and computer security.

While big business can sustain a major loss to fraud, many small businesses have suffered severely and in some cases have gone out of business as a result of their fraud losses. This often occurs because these small organizations cannot afford sophisticated hardware and software to prevent and detect fraud. Because corporations are afraid that reporting fraud may damage their reputation, they are reluctant to do so.

They fear legal retaliation if they share or disclose too much, and are afraid that their consumers and stockholders will lose confidence in them. The actual amount of corporate victimization is not known, because of the unwillingness of corporations to report or admit that fraud has affected them. Many e-Businesses are concerned about the continuity of their business. That is, they do not want their services to customers to be disrupted. Although security remains a significant concern for business, consumers are paramount in e-Commerce; they want to shop quickly with no hassles. Recent distributed denial of service attacks on web sites such as e-bay and Amazon.com point to the vulnerabilities of e-Commerce. The lack of security and the intrusion of criminals (fraudulent element) both impede the growth of e-Commerce.

Intellectual property theft – in the form of trademark infringement, cyber squatters, typo squatters, trade-secret theft, and copyright infringement – has increased as Internet use and misuse has risen. It occurs across the seven industries detailed here, as well as most other businesses. "According to the American Society for Industrial Security, American businesses have been losing $250 billion a year from intellectual property theft since the mid-1990's."

GOVERNMENT

Government suffers from several forms of victimization, much like corporations do, including theft of intellectual property, theft of assets, and loss of reputation. Several cases have been in the news where United States secrets have been compromised or potentially compromised.

These events have tarnished the reputation of several government agencies by pointing out the lack of, or loose, security procedures. Numerous federal governmental web sites have been defaced by hackers, including the CIA, FBI, and the United States Department of Justice.

Several reports of intrusions have occurred with government computers. In many of these cases, systems have been penetrated, but no classified information was accessed. Fraud, waste, abuse, and mismanagement are generally reported together.

While it is hard to get a handle on their size and scope, the Senate Governmental Affairs Committee, chaired by Senator Fred Thompson (R-Tennessee) reported on January 26, 2000, that "In 1998 alone, $35 billion in taxpayer dollars was lost due to government waste, fraud, abuse, and mismanagement."

WAGING THE WAR ON ECONOMIC CRIME

LAW ENFORCEMENT

On the federal level, numerous regulatory and law enforcement agencies are authorised to combat specific economic crimes, including the Federal Bureau of Investigation (FBI), United States Secret Service (USSS), the United States Postal Inspection Service, Securities and Exchange Commission (SEC), and United States Customs.

Each of these agencies has jurisdiction over the following economic crimes/ fraud.

- *FBI*: health care, financial institution, intellectual property, telemarketing, securities/commodities, bankruptcy, insurance, computer, and Internet
- *Secret Service*: credit card, cellular, and computer
- *Postal Inspector*: mail and consumer
- *Securities and Exchange Commission*: insider and online trading, stock manipulation, and fraudulent stock offerings
- *United States Customs*: money laundering, cyber crimes, including child pornography and the importing of dangerous substances

On the international level, Interpol recently announced its intention to become active in the investigation of international computer crimes. Interpol announced on June 30, 2000 that it is establishing an international intelligence network to inform the public and private sectors of impending cyber attacks and potential targets for malicious hacks.

The intelligence information will be relayed to Interpol by Atomic Tangerine, a venture consulting firm, using technology (Net Radar) developed by SRI International, the parent company of Atomic Tangerine. Local law enforcement capabilities for combating economic crime vary depending on the size and location of the department, and the allocation of resources. Some larger municipalities and state law enforcement agencies have formed economic and computer crime units. As resources, training, and awareness of the intensity of the problem increase, it is likely that more of these units will be formed.

NATIONAL FRAUD CENTER

The National Fraud Center (NFC) is an internationally recognised leader in global customised fraud and risk management solutions. Formed in 1982, its original mission was to combat insurance fraud, which, at that time, was becoming a societal concern. Since then the NFC has earned a reputation for combining expert knowledge and technology to produce solutions to fraud problems for vertical industries and the government. "Technological solutions developed with NFC's expertise have saved clients tens of millions of dollars." The NFC has an in-depth understanding of how economic crime affects businesses, consumers, and government agencies, as its researchers collect and analyse fraud data continuously.

ECONOMIC CRIME INVESTIGATION INSTITUTE

The Economic Crime Investigation Institute (ECII) was formed in 1988 by Dr. Gary R. Gordon, then Director of the Economic Crime Investigation Programme at Utica College of Syracuse University, and Mr. John Martin, Esq., then Chief of Internal Security for the United States Department of Justice. Part of the Institute's mission is to support education and research in the areas of economic crime and computer security, by advising Utica College faculty on formal academic Programmes for pre-professional students and professionals in the field of economic crime investigation.

Its other goal is to develop the ECII into the premier educationally focused institute, providing a national forum that brings together all interested parties to develop solutions to economic crime problems faced by society. The ECII strives to provide a forum for individuals in government, corporate America, and higher education to discuss current economic crime issues and to promote the dissemination of information on economic crime and its investigations. The Economic Crime Investigation Institute's annual conferences are its primary way of accomplishing this.

NATIONAL WHITE COLLAR CRIME CENTER

A non-profit organization that receives federal grant funding from the Bureau of Justice Assistance, Department of Justice, the National White Collar Crime Center (NW3C) "provides a nationwide support network for enforcement agencies involved in the prevention, investigation, and prosecution of economic and high-tech crime." Founded in 1980, the Center's focus is to support state and local agencies, using their needs as a guide for the projects and endeavors the NW3C undertakes.

In addition to its state-of-the-art financial and computer crime training course development and delivery, new projects include the development of the National Fraud Complaint Management Center (NFCMC) to leverage technology in the management of economic crime complaints and to bring added value to the prevention, investigation, and prosecution efforts surrounding complaints. A significant part of this project is the establishment of the Internet Fraud Complaint Center (IFCC) in partnership with the Federal Bureau of Investigation. The IFCC represents a unique approach to the growing problem of fraud on the Internet. The NW3C has also been selected to serve as the Operations Center for the National Cyber crime Training Partnership (NCTP), an initiative of the United States Attorney General, headed by the Computer Crimes and Intellectual Property Section of the Justice Department.

THE NATIONAL COALITION FOR THE PREVENTION OF ECONOMIC CRIME

A non-profit organization established in 1996, the National Coalition for the Prevention of Economic Crime (NCPEC) provides support services to businesses in their fight against economic crime. Its mission is to reduce incidents of economic crime through cooperative, information-sharing efforts. Current training Programmes include instruction on fraud management, operational and strategic fraud management techniques, financial investigations practical skills, basic data recovery and analysis and instruction on how to use the Internet as an investigative tool. Hosted in partnership with the NW3C, the NCPEC has established an annual national conference entitled the Economic Crime Summit which brings together academics, government, private corporations, victims' interest groups, prevention specialists, and others to examine methodologies and share ideas to address economic crime on all levels.

INTERNET FRAUD COUNCIL

The Internet Fraud Council, a division of the National Coalition for the Prevention of Economic Crime, is composed of organizations from around the world that are interested in the prevention, investigation, and prosecution of Internet fraud. The Internet Fraud Council's mission is to provide research, education, best practices, and tools for the prevention of economic crime committed using the Internet.

INTERNET FRAUD COMPLAINT CENTER

The Internet Fraud Complaint Center (IFCC) is a partnership between the Federal Bureau of Investigation (FBI) and the National White Collar Crime Center (NW3C). IFCC's mission is to address fraud committed over the Internet. For victims of Internet fraud, IFCC provides a convenient and easy way to alert authorities of a suspected criminal or civil violation. For law enforcement and regulatory agencies, IFCC offers a central repository for complaints related to Internet fraud. The data from this source can then be analysed to identify and quantify fraud patterns, as well as statistics on the current fraud trends.

The IFCC's ultimate goal is to reduce Internet fraud victimization. As stated on its web site, "Long term benefits of this Programme will be substantial. Not only will its efforts reduce the amount of economic loss by Internet fraud throughout the United States, it will enable state and local law enforcement professionals to develop and successfully prosecute criminal Internet fraud cases. IFCC will also serve as the catalyst that allows law enforcement and regulatory authorities to network and share fraud data."

INDEPENDENT CORPORATIONS AND PRIVATE SECTOR INDUSTRY COALITIONS

As a result of limited law enforcement resources, corporations on their own or in cooperation with industry coalitions, such as BITS, the technology group for the Financial Services Roundtable, have had to initiate strategic economic crime management plans and investigative groups. There is a growing level of frustration among these corporations, because the monetary thresholds for law enforcement even to investigate a case, let alone prosecute, can be very high, depending on the jurisdiction.

Coupled with this, is increased legislation requiring corporations to institute anti-fraud Programmes and compliance departments. While the protection of corporate assets and their consumers should be their responsibility, there are several consequences to this arrangement. Many economic crimes go unreported, fewer prosecutions of these offenses occur, and perpetrators tend to be fired rather than prosecuted, leaving them free to move on to another organization and continue their victimization.

IMPACT OF TECHNOLOGY ON ECONOMIC CRIME

The growth of the information age and the globalization of Internet communication and commerce have impacted significantly upon the manner in which economic crimes are committed, the frequency with which those crimes are committed, and the difficulty in apprehending the perpetrators. A recent survey conducted by the Gartner Group of 160 retail companies selling products over the Internet reveals that the amount of credit card fraud is twelve times higher online than in the physical retail world. There is no reason to believe that this figure is unique to the credit card industry. Another recent study indicates that the number of search warrants issued by the federal government for online data has increased 800 per cent over the past few years. Technology has contributed to that increase in four major respects—anonymity, security (or insecurity), privacy (or the lack of it) and globalization. Additionally, technology has provided the medium or opportunity for the commission of traditional crimes.

Criminals continue to make false statements in credit applications submitted over the Internet, bank employees continue to embezzle funds by wire transfer or account takeover, and swindlers continue to misrepresent products at auction sites over the Internet. However, it is the widespread use of technology and the Internet for business transactions and communications, and the confluence of anonymity, security, privacy and globalization that have exposed the public and private sectors to an alarming new array of cyber attacks. In addition to their inability to prevent such attacks, both government and the private sector lack effective enforcement tools and remedies to bring the perpetrators to justice. Technology and the Internet have contributed to the growth of economic crime in each of the identified industries in similar ways.

Anonymity enables the criminal to submit fraudulent online applications for bank loans, credit card accounts, insurance coverage, brokerage accounts, and health care coverage or to construct a counterfeit web site in order to establish an inflated value for publicly traded stock in order to sell the stock at a falsely inflated price ("pump and dump" schemes). Anonymity also enables employees to pilfer corporate assets. For example, bank employees can embezzle money through electronic fund transfers and employees of credit card issuers can capture account numbers and sell them to outsiders, electronically transferring the account numbers to the coconspirators.

Further, anonymity provides enhanced opportunities for two types of perpetrators—the organised crime mobster and the teenage hacker. Security, or the lack of it, enables criminal hackers to disrupt e-commerce in several ways. They can engage in denial of service attacks, compromise payment systems in online banking, penetrate web sites and extract credit card account numbers for resale or as ransom for the extortion of cash from the card issuer, or hijack a web site for the purpose of stealing the identity of the e-commerce merchant, directing the proceeds of sales to the hijacker. Privacy protections enable thieves to take advantage of the benefits of anonymity, while hampering the efforts of law enforcement and private sector fraud investigators to track the thieves. Lastly, the Internet enables communication and commerce to occur beyond or without borders, presenting significant problems in the prevention, investigation and enforcement of those crimes.

BANKING

There is no pending legislation that specifically addresses frauds in connection with online banking. The Internet provides fertile ground for those intending to defraud financial institutions. Because the online customer is anonymous, the risk of fraud is greater. Projected increases in the volume of online transactions and repeal of the Glass-Steagall Act, which has expanded the types of institutions that may provide banking services, could increase the exposure to cyber attack. Congressional focus is currently on cyber laundering, specifically the electronic transfer of funds into U.S. banks from sources outside the country and subsequent transfers by those banks to cyber laundering havens. On the regulatory side, the Federal Trade Commission and other agencies have proposed regulations dealing with the privacy of financial data, the circumstances when disclosure may be made, and the conditions precedent to such disclosures.

Those regulations, which are scheduled to take effect on November 13, 2000, require financial institutions to provide privacy notices to consumers, limit the disclosure of non-public personal information to non-affiliated third parties, and allow consumers to opt-out of certain restrictions. The Electronic Signature in Global and National Commerce Act, which became law on July 1, 2000, is a major effort to facilitate the consummation of contracts, including agreements with banking and financial institutions, electronically. While the Act facilitates e-Commerce, it provides yet another opportunity for the theft of a significant aspect of one's identity—the signature. The Act contains no provision imposing criminal sanctions for the theft or piracy of one's signature. The access device statute should be amended to include electronic and digital signatures as a "means of identification. Additional legislation is essential to reduce the risks presented by anonymity and database insecurity, including prescribed authentication procedures and encryption protections.

CREDIT CARD

The use of credit cards for online retail purchases, as well as for online gambling and to gain access to pornography and child pornography sites, is expected to increase exponentially. Online transactions are not conducted face-to-face; therefore, the merchant cannot identify the customer in the traditional manner. The increased volume of online transactions and the absence of face-to-face interaction provide greater opportunity for fraud, including identity theft for the purpose of conducting an online transaction.

While substantive laws provide ample redress for the criminal use of credit cards (and debit cards) in cyberspace, the implementation of new technologies for credit purchases, such as smart cards and electronic wallets, may raise issues regarding the applicability of existing criminal statutes. Those statutes should be amended to prohibit the theft or fraudulent sale, distribution or possession of a counterfeit, stolen or fictitious account number regardless of whether that account number is used in connection with a plastic card, electronic wallet or other form of digital storage.

The amendment should also state that the crime applies to the theft by computer of account numbers or information that could be used to identify an account number. There is currently no pending legislation that would regulate the use of credit cards for online transactions. However, S. 699, the Telemarketing Fraud and Seniors Protection Act, would amend the wire fraud statute to include schemes or artifices to defraud, perpetrated via Internet communications. Because credit card fraud can be prosecuted under this statute, the proposed legislation would enhance significantly the enforcement arsenal for credit card fraud. Further, the proposed Identity Theft Protection Act of 2000 would strengthen protection against fraudulent practices committed with stolen credit cards.

That Act requires the card issuer to confirm any reported change of address and notify the cardholder of any request for additional cards. It also requires credit-reporting agencies to inform the card issuer if the address on the application for a credit card is different than the address shown in the consumer's records. Section 4 of the Act would also add a requirement that, upon the request of the consumer, a consumer reporting agency must include a fraud alert in the consumer's file and notify each person seeking credit information of the existence of that alert. That Act would provide significant protection from the technological identity theft.

HEALTH CARE

Currently, there is no pending legislation designed to address health care frauds committed in cyberspace. Future legislative attention should focus on the attributes of the Internet and e-commerce that promote fraudulent activity in the provision of health care products and services.

INSURANCE

There currently are no pending federal laws or regulations that address insurance fraud committed in cyberspace. Historically, regulation of the insurance business has been the province of the states. The 1999 Gramm-Leach-Bliley Act, which repealed the Glass-Steagall Act, enabled financial institutions to provide a variety of services, including insurance. The federal government should establish broad legislation designed to regulate and secure the online sale of insurance products.

Arguably, the only effective weapon at the disposal of federal prosecutors is the wire fraud statute. Additional legislation that requires secure connections and seeks to prevent fraudulent activity regarding online insurance applications and claims should be a priority. Moreover, because the Internet is an instrument of interstate commerce, Congress should rethink that portion of the Gramm-Leach-Bliley Act which leaves the regulation of issues such as the use of non-public information by insurance companies to the state regulators. Federal involvement in this area would provide uniform regulation and would not subject financial institutions that provide banking, securities and insurance products to a different regulatory scheme for the offering of insurance products.

SECURITIES

The Internet is an instrument of interstate commerce. Thus, section 10(b) of the Securities Exchange Act of 1934 and Rule 10b-5 provide criminal sanctions for fraudulent acts committed in cyberspace involving the purchase or sale of securities. Also, the mail fraud and wire fraud statutes provide an additional weapon for the prosecution of frauds and swindles involving securities.

Again, substantive criminal laws provide ample sanction for fraudulent conduct impacting upon the securities industry. The Securities Exchange Commission is, however, faced with the difficult task of detecting and investigating securities frauds committed in the online venue. It has created a new enforcement unit to deal specifically with online trading and frauds committed with respect to securities, but legislation is required to assist investigators in the detection and investigation of such frauds. The Online Investor Protection Act of 1999, S. 1015, would be a start in that direction.

TELECOMMUNICATIONS

Section 699, The Telemarketing Fraud and Senior Protection Act would amend the wire fraud statute to prohibit fraudulent telemarketing practices over the Internet. That statute should be further amended to prohibit fraudulent conduct over the Internet transacted in part through a wireless connection.

INTELLECTUAL PROPERTY AND COMPUTER CRIME

Although existing criminal laws will continue to provide effective weapons to combat cyber crimes committed upon the traditional service industries that offer their services and products through e-commerce, Congress and the global community must move swiftly to provide an effective array of substantive laws designed specifically for Internet transactions. That array should include laws and treaties to provide law enforcement and the private sector with the tools essential for the detection and investigation of cyber crime.

Some Congressional attention has focused on peripheral issues such as privacy and encryption, and there are signs that Congress is beginning to address Internet-specific issues. Five pending Congressional bills suggest that Congress is aware that law enforcement must be equipped with adequate resources and remedies to combat cyber crime. A High Tech Crime Bill was introduced on February 24, 2000 by senators Charles Schumer and John Kyl.

This bill proposes amendments to the computer fraud statute that would include fraudulent acts committed upon "protected computers" in the United States, by persons in foreign countries and would include damage done to computers and computer systems irrespective of property damage losses. That amendment would encompass damage caused by, for example, denial of service attacks.

The proposed bill also would amend 18 U.S.C. § 3123 (c), enabling law enforcement to employ trap and trace devices to assist in the investigation of computer attacks. The Internet Security Act of 2000, introduced in April 2000 by Senator Leahy, would expand the jurisdictional scope of the computer fraud statute to include international hacking. It would amend section 3123 to enable law enforcement to employ trap and trace devices, impose encryption standards, and authorise the prosecution of juvenile hackers. It would also appropriate $25 million for each of the next four fiscal years for law enforcement training Programmes in computer fraud investigations. Both bills seek to react to recent attacks upon e-Commerce sites, including the denial of service attacks. The Internet Integrity and Critical Infrastructure Protection Act of 2000, introduced on April 13, 2000 by Senator Hatch, co-sponsored by Senator Schumer, would impose criminal penalties for cyber hacking committed by persons under 18 years old, create a National Cyber Crime Technical Support Center to serve as a resource center for federal, state and local law enforcement and assist them in the investigation of computer-related crimes, and provide the implementation of computer crime mutual assistance agreements in order to enable reciprocal assistance for foreign authorities.

Also on April 13, 2000, Senator Hutchinson introduced S. 2451 that would increase the criminal penalties for computer fraud committed in violation of 18 U.S.C. § 1030 and establish a National Commission on Cyber security to study incidents of computer crimes and the need for enhanced methods of combating such crimes. Finally, on May 9, 2000, Congressman Boehlert introduced the Law Enforcement Science and Technology Act of 2000, co-sponsored by Congressman Stupak. This bill would establish an Office of Science and Technology in the Office of Justice Programmes of the Department of Justice.

The mission of that office would be:

- To serve as the national focal point for work on law enforcement technology; and
- To carry out Programmes to improve the safety and effectiveness of, and access to, technology to assist Federal, State and local law enforcement agencies.

The bill would direct the appropriation of $40 million for regional National Law Enforcement and Corrections Technology Centers, $60 million for research and development of forensic technologies and methods to improve crime laboratories, and $20 million for the testing and evaluation of technologies. Additional governmental attention must be focused on extradition and mutual assistance treaties that will enable the United States to prosecute cyber crimes committed by international terrorists and hackers.

FUTURE NEEDS AND CHALLENGES

LAW ENFORCEMENT TRAINING

Specialised training in the areas of economic and computer crime, and how they affect specific industries, as well as computer forensics, needs to continue to increase for law enforcement personnel. Without an understanding of how specific industries function, it is difficult to investigate or prosecute economic crimes. New career paths within law enforcement organizations could be established before promotions and reassignments drain agencies of their limited skilled personnel in technically sophisticated areas. Often, individuals develop expertise and then are promoted or reassigned, making it necessary to train new people from ground zero. Unless the individuals who have expertise, experience, and contacts in industry are given an incentive to stay in their units, this cycle will continue and the investigation and prosecution of economic crime will not increase or improve.

LAWS, REGULATIONS AND REPORTING SYSTEMS

In the United States, government (federal, state and local), with limited exceptions, has allowed self-regulation of the Internet. Government regulation has, for the most part, focused on cyber crimes that are not economic crimes, such as child pornography and cyber stalking.

Fortunately, that attitude appears to be changing. There are numerous bills pending in Congress that address criminal frauds committed on the Internet, identity theft, and issues involving Internet security and attacks upon web sites. This legislation should use language that will be easily adaptable to future technological changes to help deter future economic crimes. However, there are other gaps in legislation. There are many regulations that require businesses to protect themselves by working to prevent fraud (*i.e.* know your customer). However, the government sends conflicting signals when it will not assist in prevention efforts by cleaning up regulations and enacting new supporting laws, as well as providing prosecutorial support. Current government regulations covering certain industries prohibit companies from sharing information with each other. This eliminates the possibility of an instrument, such as a central database of fraud, which companies could use in their procedures for preventing and detecting fraud. It is important that legislation addressing this be written and passed. Other legislation is also necessary, such as laws that keep pace with the changing nature of credit card payment and online payment systems.

PUBLIC-PRIVATE PARTNERSHIPS

No one group will be able to solve the complex problem posed by economic crime. Coalitions of private and public groups need to work together to combat economic and cyber crime. As more of these alliances develop, there will be more resources available to reverse the trend of economic crime. College and universities need to revamp their existing Programmes, *e.g.* criminal justice, accounting, computer science, or create new ones to meet the changing needs of society in this area.

At this time there are only two undergraduate Programmes and one graduate Programme addressing these issues – the Economic Crime Investigations Programmes at Utica College (Utica, NY) and Hilbert College (Hamburg, NY) and the Economic Crime Management Master's Programme at Utica College. These Programmes are supported by advisory boards consisting of individuals at the top of their fields from the credit card, banking, insurance, and telecommunications industries, as well as representatives from government agencies, such as the U.S. Secret Service and the FBI. Further Congress, through the Identity Theft Assumption and Deterrence Act requires the FTC and industry to work together. Presidential Directive 63 required industry and government to work together in combating Internet/e-commerce fraud.

BALANCING PRIVACY INTERESTS

The growth of e-commerce and the creation of new law enforcement techniques to combat cyber crime raise critical issues concerning consumer, business and governmental privacy. The protection of individual privacy, while considered almost sacred, in the world of economic and cyber crime can actually work to the criminal's advantage. The new FBI tool, Carnivore, is an attempt to gather intelligence information, without compromising privacy.

According to the FBI's web site,

- In recent years, the FBI has encountered an increasing number of criminal investigations in which the criminal subjects use the Internet to communicate with each other or to communicate with their victims. Because many Internet service providers (ISP) lack the ability to discriminate communications to identify a particular subject's messages to the exclusion of all others, the FBI designed a diagnostic tool, called Carnivore.
- The Carnivore device provides the FBI with a "surgical" ability to intercept and collect the communications which are subject of the lawful order while ignoring those communications which they are not authorised to intercept.
- This is a matter of employing new technology to lawfully obtain important information, while providing enhanced privacy protection.

Carnivore provides law enforcement with the ability to keep pace with the technical advances in communication. However, this tool raises "Big Brother" concerns for the public. The controversy that Carnivore has evoked in its infancy points to the issue of trust that government, industry, and society as a whole need to resolve. BITS, Financial Services Roundtable adopted privacy principles in late 1997 that are guidelines for banking industry self-regulation concerning privacy. Industry, in general, sees self-regulation as preferable to government rule.

The BITS policy includes guidelines in each of these areas.

- Recognition of a customer's expectation of privacy
- Use, collection, and retention of customer Information
- Maintenance of accurate information
- Limiting employee access to information
- Protection of information via established security procedures
- Restrictions on the disclosure of account information
- Maintaining customer privacy in business relationships with third parties
- Disclosure of privacy principles to customers

Several other industry organizations are developing similar guidelines. Their aim is to have self-regulation rather than government intervention. By informing customers of privacy policies, industry is attempting to engender their trust. There is a delicate balance between protecting one's privacy, legitimate business use of personal data, and fraud prevention. However, the use of personal data for fraud prevention and interdiction is beneficial to society. Therefore, fraud and risk management exceptions should be built into any and all laws, regulations, and policies. In fact, the use of personal data for identity theft prevention directly reduces the number of identity theft victims. Further, many industries (*i.e.* insurance, banking and securities) require fraud prevention through regulation to protect consumers, customers, shareholders, and employees. Effective authentication in an e-commerce transaction is not possible without the use of independent, personal verification data. Authentication is critical to the growth and confidence of e-commerce. Fraudsters have quickly learned to defeat our technical systems.

If they are allowed to opt out of databases, they will rapidly exploit our vulnerabilities to the financial detriment of the general public. Global cooperation is also needed in this area. The United States must take a leadership role in fostering cooperation throughout the global community in the development of uniform laws, meaningful and comparable privacy policies, effective assistance to prosecutions by foreign countries, and a sharing of information.

The U.S. already has surrendered a leadership role in the areas of privacy and information sharing. The European Union developed a comprehensive privacy directive applicable to all member nations in 1995, and the European Parliament recently refused to allow its member nations to share data and non-public information with the U.S. With respect to information sharing, Interpol has announced its intention to provide private industries throughout the world with intelligence information regarding the vulnerability of those industries or specific companies to cyber attacks. At this point, the global community perceives the U.S. as a reluctant partner, not a leader.

GLOBAL INTERACTION AND COOPERATION

For the past two decades, the international community has focused on the development of extradition treaties, mutual legal assistance treaties, and sanctions to combat the proliferation of money laundering crimes on an international scale. The international focus for the next two decades must be directed Towards Internet crime and cyber crime. That focus cannot be limited to procedural remedies. Many countries lack substantive laws specifically designed to combat computer and Internet crimes.

For example, the alleged perpetrators of the "Love Bug" virus in the Philippines could not be charged with a substantive crime because no computer crime laws had been enacted in that country. The international community must maintain a more aggressive and comprehensive approach to cyber crime, including treaties that provide for uniform laws on cyber crime and cyber terrorism. That approach should be inspired and led by the United States.

On April 27, 2000, the Council of Europe released a draft version of its proposed International Convention on Cyber-Crime. In 1989 and 1995, the

Council encouraged member governments to revise or adopt laws specific to the challenges of computer crime. However, a binding legal agreement is now considered necessary to harmonise computer crime laws and to step up investigations and ensure effective international cooperation. The Council hopes to adopt the Convention by September 2001.

The Convention draft requires each signatory nation to adopt legislation or other measures with respect to five categories of crimes:

1. Offenses against computer data and systems;
2. Computer-related forgery;
3. Computer-related fraud;
4. Child pornography; and
5. Copyright and intellectual property offenses.

The Convention draft also contains uniform provisions for searches and seizures of computers and computer data, extradition, and mutual legal assistance procedures. The United States has participated in the negotiations preliminary to the release of the Convention draft. The Computer Crime and Intellectual Property Section (CCIPS) of the Department of Justice assisted in the drafting process. U.S. government agencies, including the Department of Justice, plan to seek legislative support for the Convention. In addition, the Group of Eight (G8) nations have discussed economic crime and cyber crime during recent annual summits in London and Moscow. The issue again appeared on the summit agenda for the July meeting in Okinawa.

CCIPS chairs the G8 subgroup on high-tech crime. The OECD has made recommendations for industry and government to work together in order to combat money laundering. Guidelines have been established for authentication and "know your customer Programmes". Congress needs to address, both from a domestic and global perspective, current law enforcement tools that are needed for investigations and prosecutions in the digital environment.

Although Congress has enacted laws that facilitate global e-commerce, for example, the Electronic Signature in Global and National Commerce Act, it has not considered legislation focusing upon the investigation and enforcement of crimes committed in the e-commerce venue. For example, law enforcement needs judicial guidance, but preferably legislative authorization, regarding the search and seizure of computers and peripheral equipment, eavesdropping with new technological devices, and the preservation and presentation of digital evidence. Without Congressional initiative, state and federal courts will continue on a path of conflicting decisions that inhibit effective law enforcement investigations and effectively paralyse U.S. cooperation with foreign governments.

CONCLUSION: TRENDS AND OBSERVATIONS

According to the National White Collar Crime Center's National Public Survey on White Collar Crime, FBI statistics indicate that, for the period from 1988 to 1997, arrests for violent crimes decreased, but the arrest rate for crimes having to do with fraud and embezzlement increased dramatically. As is evident from this study, this trend is sure to continue, and to grow, as technology facilitates the emergence of cyber crime. As a result of the burgeoning of e-commerce, cyber crime has become prevalent, and it will soon be difficult to differentiate among traditional economic and cyber crimes. Reporting of economic and cyber crime is problematic and grossly underestimated, as is apparent from the reluctance of corporations to report fraud losses and activity. The FBI's Uniform Crime Report should be revised to include specific economic crimes, following the Fraud Identification Codes established by the National Fraud Center.

Until such a means of reporting is implemented and the stigma of fraud victimization is removed, this problem will not be solved. Uniform and thorough reporting is necessary in the war on economic and cyber crime; resources for investigation and prosecution will naturally follow as the enormity of the problem unfolds. Preventing, detecting, investigating, and prosecuting economic crimes must become a priority, in order to lessen their impact on the economy and the public's confidence. Law enforcement, as it stands now, is in danger of slipping further behind the highly sophisticated criminals. New resources, support for existing organizations, *e.g.* The National Fraud Center, The National White Collar Crime Center, The Internet Fraud Council, and The Economic Crime Investigation Institute, and innovative solutions are needed to control this growing problem in America and the world.

This is not to say that the focus should be entirely on economic crime to the detriment of investigation and prosecution of violent crime. Certainly, it would not be in society's best interest to have violent crime increase, while economic crime decreases. However, it has often been questioned and argued whether the psychological and financial impact of economic crime on its victims is as great or greater in many instances as violent crime.

Rather, higher priority must be given to the provision of necessary resources and the passage of relevant legislation to counter the near-epidemic impact of economic crime on American society and the world. This can only be accomplished with the cooperation of the private, public, and international sectors. All stakeholders must be more willing to exchange information on the effect economic and cyber crime has on them and the methods they are using to detect and prevent it. No one sector holds all the resources, tools or solutions. In fact, in many instances, industry has more resources than government, but must be motivated and authorised to partner and communicate. All parties must be willing to work together to effect change in existing laws and regulations and to promulgate new initiatives. The "victims" need to follow the lead of the "criminals" and organise themselves, so that the organised "bad guys" are not operating in a lawless environment, where culpability is at a minimum.

8

Computer Crime

COMPUTER RELATED CRIMES

This category covers a number of offences that need a computer system to be committed.

Unlike previous categories, these broad offences are often not as stringent in the protection of legal principles, including:

- Computer-related fraud;
- Computer-related forgery, phishing and identity theft; and
- Misuse of devices.

FRAUD AND COMPUTER RELATED FRAUD

Computer-related fraud is one of the most popular crimes on the Internet, as it enables the offender to use automation and software tools to mask criminals' identities. Automation enables offenders to make large profits from a number of small acts. One strategy used by offenders is to ensure that each victim's financial loss is below a certain limit. With a 'small' loss, victims are less likely to invest time and energy in reporting and investigating such crimes. One example of such a scam is the Nigeria Advanced Fee Fraud.

Although these offences are carried out using computer technology, most criminal law systems categorise them not as computer-related offences, but as regular fraud. The main distinction between computer-related and traditional fraud is the target of the fraud. If offenders try to influence a person, the offence is generally recognised as fraud. Where offenders target computer or data-processing systems, offences are often categorised as computer-related fraud. Those criminal law systems that cover fraud, but do not yet include the manipulation of computer systems for fraudulent purposes.

Online Auction Fraud

Online auctions are now one of the most popular e-commerce services. In 2006, goods worth more than USD 20 billion were sold on eBay, the world's largest online auction marketplace. Buyers can access varied or specialist niche goods from around the world. Sellers enjoy a worldwide audience, stimulating demand and boosting prices. Offenders committing crimes over auction platforms can exploit the absence of face-to-face contact between sellers and buyers. The difficulty of distinguishing between genuine users and offenders has resulted in auction fraud being among the most popular of cyber crimes.

The two most common scams include:

1. Offering non-existent goods for sale and requesting buyers to pay prior to delivery; or
2. Buying goods and asking for delivery, without intention to pay.

In response, auction providers have developed protection systems such as the feedback/comments system. After each transaction, buyer and sellers leave feedback for use by other users as neutral information about the reliability of sellers/buyers. In this case, "reputation is everything" and without an adequate number of positive comments, it is harder for offenders to persuade targets to either pay for non-existent goods or, conversely, to send out goods without receiving payment first. However, criminals have responded and circumvented this protection through using accounts from third parties. In this scam called "account takeover", offenders try to get hold of user names and passwords of legitimate users to buy or sell goods fraudulently, making identification of offenders more difficult.

Advance Fee Fraud

In Advanced Fee Fraud, offenders send out e-mails asking for recipients' help in transferring large amounts of money to third parties and promise them a percentage, if they agree to process the transfer using their personal accounts. The offenders then ask them to transfer a small amount to validate their bank account data (based on a similar perception as lotteries – respondents may be willing to incur a small but certain loss, in exchange for a large but unlikely gain) or just send bank account data directly.

Once they transfer the money, they will never hear from the offenders again. If they send their bank account information, offenders may use this information for fraudulent activities. Evidence suggests that thousands of targets reply to e-mails. Current researches show, that despite various information campaigns and initiatives advance fee frauds are still growing – with regard to the number of victims as well as with regard to the total losses.

COMPUTER RELATED FORGERY

Computer related forgery describes the manipulation of digital documents - for example, by:

- Creating a document that appears to originate from a reliable institution;
- Manipulating electronic images (for example, pictures used as evidence in court); or
- Altering text documents.

The falsification of e-mails includes the scam of "phishing" which is a serious challenge for law enforcement agencies worldwide. "Phishing" seeks to make targets disclose personal/secret information. Often, offenders send out e-mails that look like communications from legitimate financial institutions used by the target. The e-mails are designed in a way that it is difficult for targets to identify them as fake e-mails. The e-mail asks recipient to disclose and/or verify certain sensitive information. Many victims follow the advice and disclose information enabling offenders to make online transfers, etc.

In the past, prosecutions involving computer-related forgery were rare, because most legal documents were tangible documents. Digital documents play an ever more important role and are used more often. The substitution of classic documents by digital documents is supported by legal means for their use *e.g.*, by legislation recognising digital signatures.

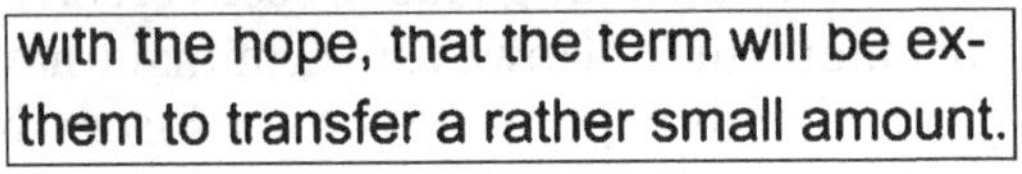

Fig. Compared to the Falsification of Classic Documents, Electronic Data can Rather Easily be Manipulated. Technical Solutions Such as Digital Signatures can Prevent Unrecognised Manipulations.

Criminals have always tried to manipulate documents. With digital forgeries, digital documents can now be copied without loss of quality and are easily manipulated. For forensic experts, it is difficult to prove digital manipulations, unless technical protection is used to protect a document from being falsified.

IDENTITY THEFT

The term identity theft–that is neither consistently defined nor consistently used–describes the criminal act of fraudulently obtaining and using another person's identity. These acts can be carried out without the help of technical means as well as online by using Internet technology.

In general the offence described as identity theft contains three different phases:

1. In the first phase the offender obtains identity-related information. This part of the offence can for example be carried out by using malicious software or phishing attacks.
2. The second phase is characterised by interaction with identity-related information prior to the use of those information within criminal offences. An example is the sale of identity-related information. Credit card records are for example sold for up to 60 US dollars.
3. The third phase is the use of the identity-related information in relation with a criminal offence. In most cases the access to identity-related data enables the perpetrator to commit further crimes. The perpetrators are therefore not focusing on the set of data itself but

the ability to use them in criminal activities. Examples for such offence can be the falsification of identification documents or credit card fraud.

The methods used to obtain data in phase one cover a wide range of acts. The offender can use physical methods and for example steal computer storage devices with identity-related data, searching trash ("dumpster diving") or mail theft. In addition they can use search engines to find identity-related data. "Googlehacking" or "Googledorks" are terms that describe the use of complex search engine queries to filter through large amounts of search results for information related to computer security issues as well as person information that can be used in identity theft scams. One aim of the perpetrator can for example be to search for insecure password protection systems in order to obtain data from this system. Reports highlight the risks that can go along with the legal use of search engines for illegal purposes.

Similar problems are reported with regard to file-sharing systems. The United States Congress discussed recently the possibilities of file-sharing systems to obtain personal information that can be abused for identity theft. Apart from that the offenders can make use of insiders, who have access to stored identity-related information, to obtain that information. The 2007 CSI Computer Crime and Security Survey shows that more than 35 per cent of the respondents attribute a percentage of their organization's losses greater than 20 per cent to insiders. Finally the perpetrators can use social engineering techniques to persuade the victim to disclose personal information. In recent years perpetrators developed effective scams to obtain secret information (*e.g.* bank account information and credit card data) by manipulating users through social engineering techniques.

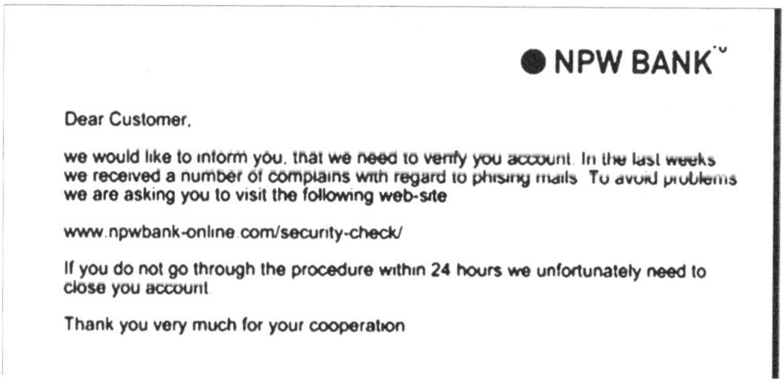
NPW BANK

Dear Customer,

we would like to inform you, that we need to verify you account. In the last weeks we received a number of complains with regard to phising mails. To avoid problems we are asking you to visit the following web-site

www.npwbank-online.com/security-check/

If you do not go through the procedure within 24 hours we unfortunately need to close you account.

Thank you very much for your cooperation

Fig. Phishing Mails are Used to Obtain Secret Information (Such as Account Information, Password and Transaction Numbers) from Targets. This Information can be used by Offenders to Commit Offences.

The type of data the perpetrators target varies. The most relevant data are:

- *Social security number (SSN) or passport number*: The SSN that is for example used in the United States is a classical example of a single identity-related data that perpetrators are aiming for. Although the SSN was created to keep an accurate record of earnings it is currently widely used for identification purposes. The perpetrators can use the SSN as well as obtained passport information to open financial accounts, to take over existing financial accounts, establish credit or run up debt.

- *Date of birth, address and phone numbers*: Such data can in general only be used to commit identity theft if they are combined with other pieces of information (*e.g.* the SSN). Having access to additional information like the date of birth and the address can help the perpetrator to circumvent verification processes. One of the greatest dangers related to that information is the fact that it is currently on a large scale available in the Internet – either published voluntarily in one of the various identity-related fora or based on legal requirements as imprint on web sites.
- *Password for non-financial accounts*: Having access to passwords for accounts allows perpetrators to change the settings of the account and use it for their own purposes. They can for example take over an e-mail account and use it to send out mails with illegal content or take over the account of a user of an auction platform and use the account to sell stolen goods.
- *Password for financial accounts*: Like the SSN information regarding financial accounts is a popular target for identity theft. This includes checking and saving accounts, credit cards, debit cards, and financial planning information. Such information is an important source for an identity thief to commit financial cyber crimes.

Identity theft is a serious and growing problem. Recent figures show that, in the first half of 2004, 3 per cent of United States households fell victim to identity theft. In the United Kingdom, the cost of identity theft to the British economy was calculated at 1.3 billion British pounds every year.

Estimates of losses caused by identity theft in Australia vary from less than 1 billion USD to more than 3 billion USD per year. The 2006 Identity Fraud Survey estimates the losses in the United States at 56.6 billion USD in 2005.

Losses may be not only financial, but may also include damage to reputations. In reality, many victims do not report such crimes, while financial institutions often do not wish to publicise customers' bad experiences.

The actual incidence of identity theft is likely to far exceed the number of reported losses. Identity theft is based on the fact that there are few instruments to verify the identity of users over the Internet. It is easier to identify individuals in the real world, but most forms of online identification are more complicated. Sophisticated identification tools (*e.g.,* using biometric information) are costly and not widely used. There are few limits on online activities, making identity theft easy and profitable.

MISUSE OF DEVICES

Cyber crime can be committed using only fairly basic equipment. Committing offences such as libel or online fraud needs nothing more than a computer and Internet access and can be carried out from a public Internet café. More sophisticated offences can be committed using specialist software tools. The tools needed to commit complex offences are widely available over the Internet, often without charge. More sophisticated tools cost several thousand dollars. Using these software tools, offenders can attack other computer systems at the press of a button.

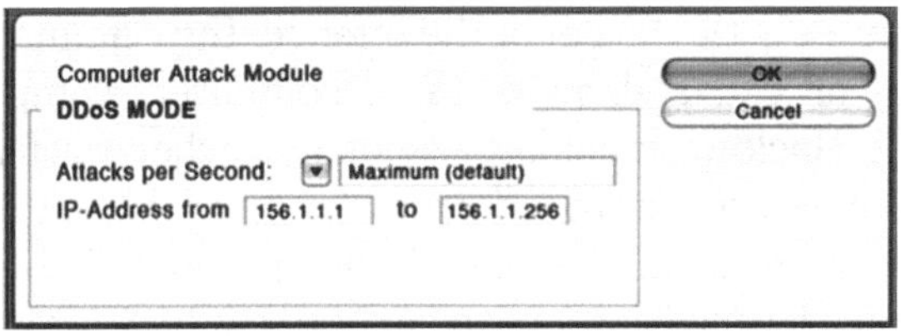

Fig. A Number of Tools are Available that Enable Offenders to Automate attacks against all Computer Systems Using IP-addresses Within a Predefined IP Range. With the Help of Such Software, it is Possible to Attack Hundreds of Computer Systems within a few Hours.

Standard attacks are now less efficient, as protection software companies analyse the tools currently available and prepare for standard hacking attacks. High-profile attacks are often individually designed for specific targets.

Software tools exist to:

- Carry out DoS attacks;
- Design computer viruses;
- Decrypt encrypted communication; and
- Illegally access computer systems.

A second generation of software tools has now automated many cyber-scams and enables offenders to carry out multiple attacks within a short time. Software tools also simplify attacks, allowing less experienced computer users to commit cyber crime. Spam-toolkits are available that enable virtually anybody to send out spam emails. Software tools are now available that can be used to up- and download files from file-sharing systems. With greater availability of specially-designed software tools, the number of potential offenders has risen dramatically. Different national and international legislative initiatives are being undertaken to address cyberscam software tools–for example, by criminalising their production, sale or possession.

TYPES OF COMPUTER CRIME

We begin by providing an overview of cyber-crime and criminal techniques used to penetrate protected computer networks. The CFAA, how it is applied, and how it has changed over the past decade. Then we will look at other laws that are on the books that the federal government uses to control computer crimes. Due to the international nature of cyber-crimes, we discuss briefly some of the international cooperative developments.

A computer can be the target of the offence, the tool used in the offence, or may contain evidence of the offence. An understanding of the different uses of a computer will provide the foundation of the application of the criminal statutes. The computer is an indispensable tool for almost all cyber-crimes. However, as more devices are enabled to communicate with the Internet, the hackers arsenal of tools is likely to multiply.

When a computer is the target of the offence, the criminal's goal is to steal information from, or cause damage to, a computer, computer system, or computer network. Hacking, cracking, espionage, cyber-warfare, and malicious computer code viruses are common forms of crimes that target the computer. The perpetrators range from teenage "cyber-joyriders" to organized crime operations and international terrorists. According to a survey conducted by Michael G. Kessler and Associates Ltd., a New York security firm, computer theft of proprietary information is committed by discontented employees (35 per cent), outside hackers (28 per cent), other U.S. companies (18 per cent), foreign corporations (11 per cent), foreign governments (8 per cent), and miscellaneous (10 per cent).

The computer may also be a tool of the offence. The criminal uses the computer to commit a traditional crime, such as counterfeiting. For example, a counterfeiter that used to engrave plates to create the counterfeit currency can now use sophisticated graphic computers with advanced colour printers. An example of a computer used to perpetrate a traditional crime is the extortion attempt by George Matos Rocha from North Carolina. Mr. Rocha was charged with bombing three home improvement stores and subsequently threatened the retail chain to continue the bombings unless he received $250,000. Using the Internet, Mr. Rocha set up a bank account in Latvia and instructed the company to wire the extortion money to his Latvian account. The FBI was able to identify the account and trace its origin back to the United States with the help of his Internet Service Provider. Mr. Rocha pleaded guilty in December to explosives charges and extortion. He could have faced life in prison.

Computers can also be incidental to the offence, but are nevertheless important because they contain the evidence of a crime. Money launderers, for example, may use a computer to store details of their laundering operation instead of relying on paper accounting records. Child pornographers' computers are often seized as the key evidence that the defendant produced, possessed, received, and/or distributed child pornography.

DENIAL OF SERVICE

A Denial of Service ("DoS") attack is a rather primitive technique that overwhelms the resources of the target computer which results in the denial of server access to other computers. There are several different techniques that hackers use to "bring down" a server. As the network administrators learn how to limit the damage of one technique, hackers often create more powerful and more sophisticated techniques that force system administrators to continually react against assaults. In order to understand how to apply the law to these attacks, a basic understanding of the anatomy of the attacks is necessary.

There are basically three main network exploits that are used to overwhelm a system's server: SYN Flood Attacks, UDP Flood Attacks and ICMP Flood Attacks. Each technique exploits a weakness in the way computers communicate amongst each other over the Internet. A basic understanding of the TCP/IP Internet protocols is helpful to differentiate between the techniques.

Internet Protocols

The Internet is a network of computers that are connected so they can exchange information amongst each other. The computer that is asking for information from another computer is the "client" and the computer that is receiving the request is the "server." When the client wants to receive information that is located on the server, it sends a request for the information. However, the computers must establish a connection before data can be exchanged.

The server needs to know who it is going to send the information to and needs to make sure the client computer is ready to receive the information. This is considered a "3-way handshake." The first part of the handshake occurs when the client computer sends a message to the server with a "SYN flag" that tells the server how to identify it. Second, upon receiving the request, the server will send out its own identification number, called an Initial Sequence Number ("ISN") in a SYN for this request and an acknowledgement ("ACK") of the client's request.

In the third part of this "handshake," the client computer receives the SYN and ACK from the server and sends back the ACK with the server's numbers, like a secret code the two of them share so the server can keep track of multiple clients. Now the data transfer can take place. In summary, the client sends a message to the server, the server sends back a message to the client that the server is "awake" and ready to process the requests, then the client sends back an acknowledgement that they are ready. This may seem redundant, but the need to establish the connection on both sides is very important because the data is broken up into small pieces by the server and sent out over the Internet to the client. The client needs to know how to organize the data puzzle as the packets arrive and the client also needs to know if any packets are missing. As each piece of the puzzle arrives, the client lets the server know the piece has been received, so the server knows if it has to re-send it.

TCP/IP stands for Transmission Control Protocol and Internet Protocol. Basically, the TCP is the workhorse of the communication on both sides. If a file is requested by the client, the server locates the file on its computer and breaks the file into tiny pieces. The tiny pieces are called datagrams. Each datagram is "wrapped" in a bundle of instructions that tells it where to go. These little bundles are called "packets." The TCP assigns a sequence number to every byte transferred so it can track what it has sent and eliminate the need to duplicate sending the same piece twice unless the piece is lost somewhere along the line to the client. The "packet header," contains the sequence numbers that also tells the client the next sequence number to expect after each packet, so the client can start arranging the packets and conduct a rolling inventory. The TCP acts as a digital shipping and receiving department. The job of the Internet Protocol ("IP") is easier. The IP's job is to route the packets across the Internet to the client. Each computer on the Internet has an IP address that tells the computers where the other is located.

The IP address is very similar to a zip code. For example, a zip code that begins with a 9, belongs to an address located on the west coast of the United States. If the next number is a 4, the location is in the San Francisco area, and so on until the precise region is located. However, to parallel the IP addresses, each house in the zip code area would be assigned a number, instead of an address. So when a client or server sends a packet out over the Internet, the packet is "routed" through many other servers to reach its final destination. The IP tacks on the numerical address and ships it out, hoping the packet arrives where it is supposed to go. If the server does not receive a response that the packet was received on the other end, the IP can send an error message to the client, called an Internet Control Message Protocol, or ICMP, letting the client know that the packet did not get there. It is this system of trust and cooperation between the computers that is exploited by a denial of service attack.

SYN Flood Attacks

One of the weaknesses in the system is the amount of SYN requests the TCP can handle. When the TCP receives more requests than it is programmed to handle, it puts the other incoming SYN requests in a queue. When the queue is filled to capacity, there is no more room to put the other incoming SYN requests and they are turned back. Hence, they are "denied service."

Another technique is to slow down the TCP process by making the TCP wait for all of the ACKs it sent out to be acknowledged by the client. When the attacker sends a message to the server requesting data, the server sends out a SYN and an ACK and waits to hear back from the attacker's client, as part of the third part of the 3-way handshaking. However, the attacker has "spoofed" his return address so that the server sends a "self-addressed and stamped" envelope to an address that is either false or belongs to a computer that is not responding. If enough of these "spoofed" SYN messages are sent, the server is paralyzed by its wait for non-existent confirmations. "SYNK" is a common SYN flood programme that is widely downloadable on the Internet.

UDP Flood Attacks

User Datagram Protocol ("UDP") flood attacks work in very much the same manner as the SYN Flood attacks. In a server, the UDP provides information about the server to other computers, such as the server's local time, echo, chargen, etc. When the server is hit with multiple requests for information about itself, the server can be quickly overwhelmed by its inability to process so many UDP packets. The result is total consumption of the server's processing power and bandwidth, thereby "denying service" to others who are trying to access the server. The problem is multiplied when a hacker connects one computer's chargen port with another's echo port. The result is the generation of a massive amount of packets that overwhelm the system and render it useless.

ICMP Flood Attack

The Internet Control Message Protocol ("ICMP") flood attack is also similar to the above flood attacks. The ICMP is used to handle errors and "pings."

Pings are small "feelers" that are sent out to other computers to see if they are turned on and connected to the same network. Ping is also used to determine if there is network congestion and other network transport problems. When a ping packet is sent to an IP broadcast address from a computer outside of the remote computer's network, it is broadcast to all machines on the target network. The ICMP attack begins when a large number of forged ping requests are sent to a broadcast address on a third-party's server. These packets contain the return address of the intended victim. The flood of ping requests causes the targeted server to answer with a flood of responses which can cause both the target site and third-party sites to crash.

A variation on the ICMP attack is the "Ping of Death." The Ping of Death is a large ICMP packet that is sent to the target server. The target receives the ping in fragments and starts to re-assemble the packets as they arrive. However, the completed size of the packet is larger than the buffer, or than the room the computer has allocated to such packets, and the computer is overwhelmed, often resulting in the server shutting down or freezing up.

HACKING : COMPUTER CRIME

Hacking means finding out weaknesses in a computer or computer network, though the term can also refer to someone with an advanced understanding of computers and computer networks. Hackers may be motivated by a multitude of reasons, such as profit, protest, or challenge. The subculture that has evolved around hackers is often referred to as the computer underground but it is now an open community. While other uses of the word hacker exist that are not related to computer security, they are rarely used in mainstream context. They are subject to the long standing hacker definition controversy about the true meaning of the term hacker. In this controversy, the term hacker is reclaimed by computer programmers who argue that someone breaking into computers is better called a cracker, not making a difference between computer criminals (black hats) and computer security experts (white hats). Some white hat hackers claim that they also deserve the title hacker, and that only black hats should be called crackers.

CLASSIFICATIONS

Several subgroups of the computer underground with different attitudes use different terms to demarcate themselves from each other, or try to exclude some specific group with which they do not agree. Eric S. Raymond (author of The New Hacker's Dictionary) advocates that members of the computer underground should be called crackers. Yet, those people see themselves as hackers and even try to include the views of Raymond in what they see as one wider hacker culture, a view harshly rejected by Raymond himself. Instead of a hacker/cracker dichotomy, they give more emphasis to a spectrum of different categories, such as white hat, grey hat, black hat and script kiddie. In contrast to Raymond, they usually reserve the term cracker for more malicious activity. According to a cracker or cracking is to "gain unauthorised access to a computer in order to commit another crime such as destroying information contained in that system". These subgroups may also be defined by the legal status of their activities.

WHITE HAT

A white hat hacker breaks security for non-malicious reasons, perhaps to test their own security system or while working for a security company which makes security software. The term "white hat" in Internet slang refers to an ethical hacker. This classification also includes individuals who perform penetration tests and vulnerability assessments within a contractual agreement. The EC-Council, also known as the International Council of Electronic Commerce Consultants has developed certifications, courseware, classes, and online training covering the diverse arena of Ethical Hacking.

BLACK HAT

A "black hat" hacker is a hacker who "violates computer security for little reason beyond maliciousness or for personal gain". Black hat hackers form the stereotypical, illegal hacking groups often portrayed in popular culture, and are "the epitome of all that the public fears in a computer criminal". Black hat hackers break into secure networks to destroy data or make the network unusable for those who are authorised to use the network. They choose their targets using a two-pronged process known as the "pre-hacking stage".

- *Part 1*: *Targeting*: The hacker determines what network to break into during this phase. The *target* may be of particular interest to the hacker, either politically or personally, or it may be picked at random. Next, they will port scan a network to determine if it is vulnerable to attacks, which is just testing all ports on a host machine for a response. Open ports—those that do respond—will allow a hacker to access the system.
- *Part 2*: *Research and Information Gathering*: It is in this stage that the hacker will visit or contact the target in some way in hopes of finding out vital information that will help them access the system. The main way that hackers get desired results from this stage is from "social engineering", which will be explained below. Aside from social engineering, hackers can also use a technique called "dumpster diving". Dumpster diving is when a hacker will literally search through users' garbage in hopes of finding documents that have been thrown away, which may contain information a hacker can use directly or indirectly, to help them gain access to a network.
- *Part 3*: *Finishing The Attack*: This is the stage when the hacker will invade the preliminary target that he/she was planning to attack or steal. Many "hackers" will be caught after this point, lured in or grabbed by any data also known as a honeypot (a trap set up by computer security personnel).

GREY HAT

A grey hat hacker is a combination of a Black Hat and a White Hat Hacker. A Grey Hat Hacker may surf the Internet and hack into a computer system for the sole purpose of notifying the administrator that their system has been hacked, for example. Then they may offer to repair their system for a small fee.

ELITE HACKER

A social status among hackers, *elite* is used to describe the most skilled. Newly discovered exploits will circulate among these hackers. Elite groups such as Masters of Deception conferred a kind of credibility on their members.

SCRIPT KIDDIE

A script kiddie (or skiddie) is a non-expert who breaks into computer systems by using pre-packaged automated tools written by others, usually with little understanding of the underlying concept—hence the term script (*i.e.* a prearranged plan or set of activities) kiddie (*i.e.* kid, child—an individual lacking knowledge and experience, immature).

NEOPHYTE

A neo-phyte, "n00b", or "newbie" is someone who is new to hacking or phreaking and has almost no knowledge or experience of the workings of technology, and hacking.

BLUE HAT

A blue hat hacker is someone outside computer security consulting firms who is used to bug test a system prior to its launch, looking for exploits so they can be closed. Microsoft also uses the term BlueHat to represent a series of security briefing events.

HACKTIVIST

A hacktivist is a hacker who utilises technology to announce a social, ideological, religious, or political message. In general, most hacktivism involves Web site defacement or denial-of-service attacks.

ATTACKS

A typical approach in an attack on Internet-connected system is:

- *Network enumeration*: Discovering information about the intended target.
- *Vulnerability analysis*: Identifying potential ways of attack.
- *Exploitation*: Attempting to compromise the system by employing the vulnerabilities found through the vulnerability analysis.

In order to do so, there are several recurring tools of the trade and techniques used by computer criminals and security experts.

SECURITY EXPLOITS

A security exploit is a prepared application that takes advantage of a known weakness. Common examples of security exploits are SQL injection, Cross Site Scripting and Cross Site Request Forgery which abuse security holes that may result from substandard programming practice. Other exploits would be able to be used through FTP, HTTP, PHP, SSH, Telnet and some web-pages. These are very common in Web site/domain hacking.

TECHNIQUES

- *Vulnerability scanner*: A vulnerability scanner is a tool used to quickly check computers on a network for known weaknesses. Hackers also commonly use port scanners. These check to see which ports on a specified computer are "open" or available to access the computer, and sometimes will detect what Programme or service is listening on that port, and its version number.

- *Password cracking*: Password cracking is the process of recovering passwords from data that has been stored in or transmitted by a computer system. A common approach is to repeatedly try guesses for the password.
- *Packet sniffer*: A packet sniffer is an application that captures data packets, which can be used to capture passwords and other data in transit over the network.
- *Spoofing attack (Phishing)*: A spoofing attack involves one Programme, system, or Web site successfully masquerading as another by falsifying data and thereby being treated as a trusted system by a user or another Programme. The purpose of this is usually to fool Programmes, systems, or users into revealing confidential information, such as user names and passwords, to the attacker.
- *Rootkit*: A rootkit is designed to conceal the compromise of a computer's security, and can represent any of a set of Programmes which work to subvert control of an operating system from its legitimate operators. Usually, a rootkit will obscure its installation and attempt to prevent its removal through a subversion of standard system security. Rootkits may include replacements for system binaries so that it becomes impossible for the legitimate user to detect the presence of the intruder on the system by looking at process tables.
- *Social engineering*: When a Hacker, typically a black hat, is in the second stage of the targeting process, he or she will typically use some social engineering tactics to get enough information to access the network. A common practice for hackers who use this technique, is to contact the system administrator and play the role of a user who cannot get access to his or her system. Hackers who use this technique have to be quite savvy and choose the words they use carefully, in order to trick the system administrator into giving them information. In some cases only an employed help desk user will answer the phone and they are generally easy to trick. Another typical hacker approach is for the hacker to act like a very angry supervisor and when the his/her authority is questioned they will threaten the help desk user with their job. Social Engineering is so effective because users are the most vulnerable part of an organization. All the security devices and Programmes in the world won't keep an organization safe if an employee gives away a password. Black Hat Hackers take advantage of this fact. Social Engineering can also be broken down into four sub-groups. These are intimidation, helpfulness, technical, and name-dropping.

- *Intimidation:* With the angry supervisor, the hacker attacks the person who answers the phone with threats to their job. Many people at this point will accept that the hacker is a supervisor and give them the needed information.
- *Helpfulness:* Opposite to intimidation, helpfulness is taking advantage of a person natural instinct to help someone with a problem. The hacker will not get angry instead act very distressed and concerned. The help desk is the most vulnerable to this type of Social Engineering, because they generally have the authority to change or reset passwords which is exactly what the hacker needs.
- *Name-Dropping:* Simply put, the hacker uses the names of advanced users as "key words", and gets the person who answers the phone to believe that they are part of the company because of this. Some information, like web page ownership, can be obtained easily on the web. Other information such as president and vice president names might have to be obtained via dumpster diving.
- *Technical:* Using technology to get information is also a great way to get it. A hacker can send a fax or an e-mail to a legitimate user in hopes to get a response containing vital information. Many times the hacker will act like he/she is involved with law enforcement and needs certain data for record keeping purposes or investigations.

• *Trojan horses*: A Trojan horse is a Programme which seems to be doing one thing, but is actually doing another. A trojan horse can be used to set up a back door in a computer system such that the intruder can gain access later. (The name refers to the horse from the Trojan War, with conceptually similar function of deceiving defenders into bringing an intruder inside.)

• *Viruses*: A virus is a self-replicating Programme that spreads by inserting copies of itself into other executable code or documents. Therefore, a computer virus behaves in a way similar to a biological virus, which spreads by inserting itself into living cells. While some are harmless or mere hoaxes most computer viruses are considered malicious.

• *Worms*: Like a virus, a worm is also a self-replicating Programme. A worm differs from a virus in that it propagates through computer networks without user intervention. Unlike a virus, it does not need to attach itself to an existing Programme. Many people conflate the terms "virus" and "worm", using them both to describe any self-propagating Programme.

- *Keyloggers*: A keylogger is a tool designed to record ('log') every keystroke on an affected machine for later retrieval. Its purpose is usually to allow the user of this tool to gain access to confidential information typed on the affected machine, such as a user's password or other private data. Some keyloggers uses virus-, trojan-, and rootkit-like methods to remain active and hidden. However, some key loggers are used in legitimate ways and sometimes to even enhance computer security. As an example, a business might have a keylogger on a computer used at a point of sale and data collected by the keylogger could be used for catching employee fraud.

INTELLECTUAL PROPERTY AND COMPUTER CRIME

Although existing criminal laws will continue to provide effective weapons to combat cyber crimes committed upon the traditional service industries that offer their services and products through e-commerce, Congress and the global community must move swiftly to provide an effective array of substantive laws designed specifically for Internet transactions. That array should include laws and treaties to provide law enforcement and the private sector with the tools essential for the detection and investigation of cyber crime.

Some Congressional attention has focused on peripheral issues such as privacy and encryption, and there are signs that Congress is beginning to address Internet-specific issues. Five pending Congressional bills suggest that Congress is aware that law enforcement must be equipped with adequate resources and remedies to combat cyber crime. A High Tech Crime Bill was introduced on February 24, 2000 by senators Charles Schumer and John Kyl.

This bill proposes amendments to the computer fraud statute that would include fraudulent acts committed upon "protected computers" in the United States, by persons in foreign countries and would include damage done to computers and computer systems irrespective of property damage losses. That amendment would encompass damage caused by, for example, denial of service attacks.

The proposed bill also would amend 18 U.S.C. § 3123 (c), enabling law enforcement to employ trap and trace devices to assist in the investigation of computer attacks. The Internet Security Act of 2000, introduced in April 2000 by Senator Leahy, would expand the jurisdictional scope of the computer fraud statute to include international hacking. It would amend section 3123 to enable law enforcement to employ trap and trace devices, impose encryption standards, and authorise the prosecution of juvenile hackers. It would also appropriate $25 million for each of the next four fiscal years for law enforcement training Programmes in computer fraud investigations. Both bills seek to react to recent attacks upon e-Commerce sites, including the denial of service attacks. The Internet Integrity and Critical Infrastructure Protection Act of 2000, introduced on April 13, 2000 by Senator Hatch, co-sponsored by Senator Schumer, would impose criminal penalties for cyber hacking committed by persons under 18 years old, create a National Cyber Crime Technical Support Center to serve as a resource center for federal, state and local law enforcement and assist them in the investigation of computer-related crimes, and provide the implementation of computer crime mutual assistance agreements in order to enable reciprocal assistance for foreign authorities.

Also on April 13, 2000, Senator Hutchinson introduced S. 2451 that would increase the criminal penalties for computer fraud committed in violation of 18 U.S.C. § 1030 and establish a National Commission on Cyber security to study incidents of computer crimes and the need for enhanced methods of combating such crimes. Finally, on May 9, 2000, Congressman Boehlert introduced the Law Enforcement Science and Technology Act of 2000, co-sponsored by Congressman Stupak. This bill would establish an Office of Science and Technology in the Office of Justice Programmes of the Department of Justice.

The mission of that office would be:

- To serve as the national focal point for work on law enforcement technology; and
- To carry out Programmes to improve the safety and effectiveness of, and access to, technology to assist Federal, State and local law enforcement agencies.

The bill would direct the appropriation of $40 million for regional National Law Enforcement and Corrections Technology Centers, $60 million for research and development of forensic technologies and methods to improve crime laboratories, and $20 million for the testing and evaluation of technologies. Additional governmental attention must be focused on extradition and mutual assistance treaties that will enable the United States to prosecute cyber crimes committed by international terrorists and hackers.

INTERNET FRAUD

The best source of information concerning the growing incidence of fraud committed on the Internet is the Internet Fraud Complaint Center (IFCC), a partnership between the National White Collar Crime Center (NW3C) and the Federal Bureau of Investigation (FBI).

The following findings are taken from the IFCC's 2001 Internet Fraud Report:

- From January 1, 2001 – December 31, 2001 the IFCC's web site received 49,711 complaints. This total includes many different fraud types and non-fraudulent complaints, such as computer intrusions, SPAM/unsolicited e-mail, and child pornography. During this same time period, the IFCC referred 16,775 complaints of fraud, the majority of which was committed over the Internet or similar online service.

The total dollar loss from all referred cases of fraud was $17.8 million, with a median dollar loss of $435 per complaint.

- Internet auction fraud was by far the most reported offence, comprising 42.8 per cent of referred complaints. Non-deliverable merchandise and payment account for 20.3 per cent of complaints, and Nigerian Letter fraud made up 15.5 per cent of complaints. Credit/debit Card fraud and Confidence fraud (such as home improvement scams and multi-level marketing) round out the top five categories of complaints referred to law enforcement during the year. Among those individuals who reported a dollar loss, the highest median dollar losses were found among Nigerian Letter Scam ($5,575), Identity Theft ($3,000), and Investment fraud ($1,000) complainants.
  - The Nigerian Letter Scam is defined as a correspondence outlining an opportunity to receive non-existent government funds from alleged dignitaries that is designed to collect advance fees from the victims. This sometimes requires payoff money to bribe government officials. While other countries may be mentioned, the correspondence typically indicates "The Government of Nigeria" as the nation of origin. This scam has run since the early 1980's and is also referred to as "419 Fraud" after the relevant section of the Criminal Code of Nigeria, as well as "Advance Fee Fraud." Because of the scam, the country of Nigeria ranks 2nd for total complaints reported at the IFCC on businesses by country.
- Nearly 76 per cent of alleged fraud perpetrators are individuals (as opposed to businesses), 81 per cent are male, and half reside in one of the following states: California, Florida, New York, Texas, and Illinois. While most are from the United States, perpetrators have a representation in Canada, Nigeria, Romania and the United Kingdom.
- The amount loss by complainants tends to be related to a number of factors. Business victims tend to lose more than individuals and males tend to lose more than females. This may be a function of both online purchasing differences by gender, and the type of fraud the individual finds themselves involved in. While there isn't a strong relationship between age and loss, proportion of individuals losing at least $5,000 is higher for those 60 years and older than it is for any other age category.
- Electronic mail (E-mail) and web pages are the two primary mechanisms by which the fraudulent contact took place. Nearly 70 per cent of complainants reported they had e-mail contact with the perpetrator.

The primary federal statute used to prosecute Internet fraud is 18 U.S.C. § 1343, which provides that:

Whoever, having devised or intending to devise any scheme or artifice to defraud, or for obtaining money or property by means of false or fraudulent pretenses, representations, or promises, transmits or causes to be transmitted by means of wire, radio, or television communication in interstate or foreign commerce, any writings, signs, signals, pictures, or sounds for the purpose of executing such scheme or artifice, shall be fined under this title or imprisoned not more than five years, or both. If the violation affects a financial institution, such person shall be fined not more than $1,000,000 or imprisoned not more than 30 years, or both. The following essay by Jonathan Rusch, Special Counsel for Fraud Prevention in the Fraud Section of the Criminal Division at the U.S. Department of Justice, describes in more detail the types of fraud frequently perpetrated through the Internet and the Justice Department's efforts – relying on section 1343 and other statutes – to stop them.

Fraud Involving Online Auctions

Online auction fraud typically involves several recurring approaches. The most common approach appears to be the offering of some valuable item, such as computers, high-priced watches, or collectible items, through a known online auction site. The individuals who are informed that they are successful bidders send their money to the seller, but never receive the promised merchandise. In a variation of this approach, the criminals send counterfeit merchandise in place of the promised merchandise. A third approach involves the criminal contacting losing bidders in a particular online auction, informing them that additional units of the item on which they bid have become available, and taking the bidders' money without delivering the items.

Consumers interested in a particular auction sometimes want to learn if other buyers have had favorable experiences with the purported seller in that auction. Major auction sites like eBay and Amazon.com allow legitimate customers to provide feedback on their experiences with particular sellers. Criminals, however, can also use false e-mail identities to provide "shill feedback" — false favorable information about themselves — to make it appear that they are satisfied customers and to give consumers a false sense of security about that auction.

In a recent prosecution, United States v. Denlinger, No. 00CR573IEG (S.D. Cal. filed Feb. 28, 2000), the defendant used online auction sites to offer Beanie Babies for sale, but failed to deliver the products after receiving the victim's money. He used various "screen names" (or aliases) in sending e-mails to prospective victims, and provided them with screen names and e-mail addresses of persons he falsely described as "references." In fact, those screen names were assigned to the defendant, so that when victims e-mailed the "references," the defendant responded with messages that gave victims false and favorable information about his own reliability and trustworthiness as a seller. The defendant also used two techniques to prevent victims from contacting him directly: he gave victims a pager number and falsely told them it was his home telephone number; and he asked them to send their payments to various commercial mail receiving agencies, which he falsely told them was his home address. His scheme defrauded more than 200 victims of nearly $50,000. (The defendant, after pleading guilty to mail and wire fraud, was sentenced to twelve months imprisonment and $46,701 in restitution.)

Fraud Involving Online Retail Sales

One category of fraud that overlaps with auction fraud is fraud in online retail sales of goods and services. The IFCC reports that so-called "nondeliverable" merchandise accounts for 22 percent of all referred complaints. One approach to retail fraud has involved placing banner advertisements on an auction site that offers the same types of goods being auctioned. Prospective buyers who click on the banner advertisement are taken to a different Web site that is not part of the auction site, and that offers none of the protections that leading auction Web sites have adopted for their members. Another approach involves using unsolicited commercial e-mail ("spam") to lure prospective victims to a Web site which purports to sell items of the same type that are available through well-known online auction sites.

In retail sales of services, some criminals have taken advantage of the complexities of the Internet's operations to compel or mislead consumers into visiting their Web sites. In United States v. Kashpureff, 98CR0218 (E.D.N.Y. filed March 19, 1998), the defendant operated a Web site, AlterNIC, that competed with the InterNIC Web site for domain name registration. He wrote and placed software on that Internet that caused persons who wanted to visit the InterNIC Web site to be involuntarily redirected to his Web site. Ultimately, he pleaded guilty to a violation of the computer fraud statute, 18 U.S.C. § 1030.

In United States v. Lee, No. 99-00560 SOM (D. Haw. filed Dec. 9, 1999), the defendant knew that the Hawaii Marathon Association operated a Web site with the Uniform Resource Locator (URL) "www.hawaiimarathon.org" to providc information about the Marathon and enable runners to register online. Although he had no affiliation with the real Hawaii Marathon, he copied the authorized Marathon Web site, and created his own Web site with the confusingly similar name, "www.hawaiimarathon.com." Runners who came to his Web site thinking that it was the real Hawaii Marathon site were charged a $165 registration fee — $100 more than the real site charged for entry. The defendant also operated another Web site where he sold Viagra over the Internet without a prescription. (The defendant later pleaded guilty to wire fraud and unlawful sale of Viagra, and in February 2001 was given a split sentence of ten months imprisonment.)

Investment Fraud

Another major category of online fraud is investment fraud. The Securities and Exchange Commission (SEC) has reported that it receives between 200 and 300 online complaints each day about possible securities fraud online. While the major types of online securities fraud generally parallel traditional securities fraud schemes, market manipulation schemes are a frequent focus of enforcement actions.

"Pump-and-Dump." The most widely publicized form of online market manipulation is the so-called "pump and dump" scheme. In a "pump and dump," criminals identify one or more companies whose stock is thinly traded or not traded at all, then adopt various means to persuade individual online investors to buy that company's stock. These means can include posting favorable, but false and misleading, representations on financial message boards or Web sites, and making undisclosed payments to people who are ostensibly independent but who will recommend that stock. Once the price has increased sufficiently, the participants in the scheme — who may be company insiders, outsiders, or both, sell their stock, and the stock price eventually declines sharply, leaving uninformed investors with substantial financial losses. While an outsider who merely expresses his opinions about the worth or likely increase or decrease of a particular stock may not be committing criminal fraud, outsiders or insiders whose conduct extends beyond mere advocacy to manipulation of markets for their personal profit by giving the public false and misleading information may violate securities fraud statutes and other criminal statutes.

In one pump-and-dump case, United States v. Aziz-Golshani, No. 00-007-GAF (C.D. Cal. filed Jan. 4, 2000), two defendants manipulated the stock of a bankrupt company, NEI Webworld, Inc. They posted messages on several financial message boards, falsely stating that NEI was going to be taken over by a California company, and, with the help of a third individual, bought 130,000 shares of NEI before their manipulations resulted in a dramatic price increase. In an attempt to conceal their identities, the two defendants and their confederates used computers at the UCLA Biomedical Library to post the false reports. An SEC amended complaint charged that the defendants and another individual had also engaged in similar manipulative conduct concerning the securities of eleven other issuers in 1999. (In January, 2001, both defendants were sentenced to fifteen months and ten months imprisonment, respectively).

"Cybersmear." The converse of the "pump and dump" is the "cybersmear." A "cybersmear" scheme is organized in the same basic manner as a "pump-and- dump," with one important difference: the object is to induce a decline in the stock's price, to permit the criminals to realize profits by short-selling. To accomplish a sufficiently rapid decline in the stock's price, the criminal must resort to blatant lies and misrepresentations likely to trigger a substantial sell off by other investors.

In United States v. Moldofsky, No. S100CR388 (RPP) (S.D.N.Y. convicted March 8, 2001), the defendant, a day trader, on the evening of March 22, 2000, and the morning of the next day, posted a message nearly twenty times what was designed to look like a Lucent press release announcing that Lucent would not meet its quarterly earnings projections. For most of those postings, he used an alias designed to resemble a screen name used by a frequent commentator on the Lucent message board who had historically expressed positive views of Lucent stock. He also posted additional messages, using other screen names that commented on the release or on the message poster's conduct. On March 23, Lucent's stock price dropped more than 3.7 percent before Lucent issued a statement disavowing the false press release, but rose by 8 percent within ten minutes of Lucent's disavowal.

In United States v. Jakob, No. CR-00-1002-DT (C.D. Cal. indictment filed Sept. 28, 2000; pleaded guilty Dec. 29, 2000), the defendant engaged in even more elaborate fraudulent conduct to effect a "cybersmear." After he tried to short-sell stock in Emulex, but found that the market was bidding up the price, he wrote a press release falsely reporting that Emulex was under investigation by the SEC, that Emulex's Chief Executive Officer was resigning, and that Emulex was reporting a loss in its latest earnings report. He then caused his former employer, a company that distributed online press releases, to send it to major news organizations, which reported the false statements as fact. When Emulex stock rapidly declined, the defendant covered his short-sale position by buying Emulex stock and realizing nearly $55,000 in profits. He also bought more Emulex stock at lower prices, and sold when the stock had recovered most of its value.

One notable feature of online market manipulation schemes is the speed with which the scheme's participants can induce dramatic, though short-term, fluctuations in stock prices, and can realize substantial profits by correctly timing their purchases and sales. In Aziz-Golshani, during the week of November 9, 1999, the defendants bought their NEI stock at prices ranging from 9 cents to 13 cents per share. On November 15, 1999, NEI stock opened at 9:00 a.m. Eastern time at $8 per share, and within 45 minutes had risen to $15 5/16 per share. Less than a half-hour later, NEI stock had dropped to approximately 25 cents per share. By selling when the stock price was still high, the defendants realized profits of more than $360,000. In Jakob, once the false press release was distributed, Emulex's stock price dropped in less than one hour from more than $110 per share to approximately $43 per share, and the trading volume of Emulex stock increased significantly as individual traders sold off the stock at notably lower prices. The defendant realized nearly $55,000 in profits from his short sale, and additional profits of nearly $187,000 as the stock price rebounded.

Payment Card Fraud

One of the fastest-growing categories of Internet fraud is payment card (*i.e.*, credit card and debit card) fraud. One Internet research firm, Meridien

Research, predicted in January 2001 that online payment-card fraud worldwide will increase from $1.6 billion in 2000 to $15.5 billion by 2005.

Online credit card fraud causes substantial problems for online merchants. Initially, many online merchants were defrauded when people, using others' credit card numbers, ordered merchandise and had it shipped to foreign locations that were clearly different from the addresses of the true credit card holders. Under the policies that major credit card issuers established, merchants must bear the losses for online purchases, which qualify as "card- not-present" transactions. As a number of merchants took defensive measures, such as installing software designed to flag possibly fraudulent online transactions, some criminals changed their methods to request shipment of the goods they ordered with others' credit card numbers to United States addresses. Confederates then sell or ship those goods to another location.

To commit online payment-card fraud, criminals need access to valid payment-card numbers. One means of acquiring them is the unlawful accessing of e-commerce Web sites. Within the past year, several computer intrusions that made possible the downloading of tens of thousands, if not millions, of credit card numbers — such as the exposure of more than 3 million credit cards at Egghead.com — have received worldwide attention in the media.

A number of Internet credit card schemes involve computer hacking as the means of accessing the numbers. For example, in United States v. Bosanac, No. 99CR3387IEG (S.D. Cal. filed Dec. 7, 1999), the defendant was involved in a computer hacking scheme that used home computers for electronic access to several of the largest United States telephone systems and for downloading thousands of calling card numbers (access codes).

The defendant, who pleaded guilty to possession of unauthorized access devices and computer fraud, used his personal computer to access a telephone system computer and to download and transfer thousands of access codes relating to company calling card numbers. In taking these codes, the defendant used a computer programme he had created to automate the downloading, and instructed his coconspirators on how to use the programme. The defendant admitted that the loss suffered by the company as a result of his criminal conduct was $955,965. He was sentenced to eighteen months' imprisonment and $10,000 in restitution.

Identity Theft and Fraud

Online payment-card fraud is closely related to the problem of identity theft and fraud. The Federal Trade Commission (FTC) reports that its Consumer Sentinel Web site, which provides law enforcement with access to more than 300,000 complaints about all types of consumer fraud, has received more complaints about identity theft and fraud than any other category of consumer fraud. While identity theft can be committed in furtherance of many types of crime, a number of recent federal prosecutions have combined identity theft and Internet fraud. In United States v. Christian, No. 00-03-SLR (D. Del. filed Aug. 3, 2000), two defendants obtained the names and Social Security numbers of 325 high-ranking United States military officers from a public Web site, then used those names and identities to apply for instant credit at a leading computer company and to obtain credit cards through two banks. They fenced the items they bought under the victims' names, and accepted orders from others for additional merchandise. The two defendants, after pleading guilty to conspiracy to commit bank fraud were sentenced to thirty-three and forty-one months imprisonment and restitution of more than $100,000 each.

Similarly, in United States v. Wahl, No. CR00-285P (W.D. Wash. sentenced Oct. 16, 2000), the defendant obtained the date of birth and Social Security number of the victim (who shared the defendant's first and last name and middle initial). He then used the victim's identifying information to apply online for credit cards with three companies and to apply online for a $15,000 automobile loan. He actually used the proceeds of the automobile loan to invest in his own business. (The defendant, after pleading guilty to identity theft, was sentenced to seven months' imprisonment and nearly $27,000 in restitution).

Business Opportunity Fraud

Business opportunity or "work-at-home" schemes are also making their way onto the Internet. In United States v. Shklowskiy (C.D. Cal. sentenced June 9, 2000), the defendants used the Internet to harvest e-mail addresses and send more than 50 million unsolicited e-mails ("spam") to offer people a "work-at-home" opportunity that promised tremendous returns in exchange for a $35 "processing fee." Approximately 12,405 individual victims sent money to what they thought were various businesses, but in fact, were postal mailboxes. As part of the scheme, the defendants forged the e-mail headers in their "spam" to make it appear that the e-mails were coming from an Internet service provider, BigBear.Net. As a result of the header forgery, when approximately 100,000 recipients of the spam responded with complaints by e-mail, the unexpected large volume of e-mails caused BigBear.Net's computer file servers to crash or cause disruptions in their service to customers. BigBear.Net had to hire three temporary workers for nearly six months to respond to the large numbers of complaints. (Ultimately, two defendants, after pleading guilty to conspiracy to commit mail and wire fraud, were sentenced to twenty seven months' imprisonment and restitution of $104,000 to fraud victims, including BigBear.Net).

The Response to Internet Fraud

As the case examples above indicate, more and more United States Attorneys' Offices are pursuing significant cases of Internet fraud. The cases being prosecuted tend to show that the criminal statutes that apply to other types of white collar crime — conspiracy, mail and wire fraud, credit card fraud, securities fraud, money laundering, and identity theft — are equally applicable to various forms of Internet fraud. In addition, a variety of existing sentencing guidelines enable federal prosecutors to seek higher sentences in appropriate cases of Internet fraud. These include enhancements for mass-marketing (USSG § 2F1.1(b)(3)), identity theft (USSG § 2F1.1(b)(5)(C)), conducting a substantial part of a scheme from outside the United States (USSG § 2F1.1(b)(6)(B)), large numbers of vulnerable victims (USSG § 3A1.1(b)(2)(B)), and use of a special skill (USSG 3B1.3; compare United States v. Petersen, 98 F.3d 502, 506-08 (9th Cir. 1996), with United States v. Godman, 223 F.3d 320, 322 (6th Cir. 2000)).

HACKING

Computer crime often involves illegally accessing and damaging computers. Illegally accessing and damaging computers runs the gamut from the mischievous to the malicious. This section first addresses hacktivism, a relatively benign form of illegal access and damage to computers undertaken for a political purpose. Hacktivism includes web defacement, web sit-ins, and denial-of-service attacks. The discussion then shifts to more malicious denial-of-service attacks; worms and viruses, which propagate destructively through the Internet; and finally systems hacking.

Hacktivism

As Palestinian rioters clashed with Israeli forces in the fall of 2000, Arab and Israeli hackers took to cyberspace to participate in the action. According to the Middle East Intelligence Bulletin, the cyberwar began in October, shortly after the Lebanese Shi'ite Hezbollah movement abducted three Israeli soldiers.

Pro-Israeli hackers responded by crippling the guerrilla movement's web site, which had been displaying videos of Palestinians killed in recent clashes and which had called on Palestinians to kill as many Israelis as possible.

Pro-Palestinian hackers retaliated, shutting down the main Israeli government web site and the Israeli Foreign Ministry web site. From there the cyberwar escalated. An Israeli hacker planted the Star of David and some Hebrew text on one of Hezbollah's mirror sites, while pro-Palestinian hackers attacked additional Israeli sites, including those of the Bank of Israel and the Tel Aviv Stock Exchange. Hackers from as far away as North and South America joined the fray, sabotaging over 100 web sites and disrupting Internet service in the Middle East and elsewhere.

The Palestinian-Israeli cyberwar illustrates a growing trend. Cyberspace is increasingly used as a digital battleground for rebels, freedom fighters, terrorists, and others who employ hacking tools to protest and participate in broader conflicts. The term "hacktivism," a fusion of hacking with activism, is often used to describe this activity.

Hacktivists see cyberspace as a means for non-state actors to enter arenas of conflict, and to do so across international borders. They believe that nation-states are not the only actors with the authority to engage in war and aggression. And unlike nation-states, hacker warriors are not constrained by the "law of war" or the Charter of the United Nations. They often initiate the use of aggression and needlessly attack civilian systems.

Hacktivism is a relatively recent phenomenon. One early incident took place in October 1989, when anti-nuclear hackers released a computer worm into the US National Aeronautics and Space Administration (NASA) SPAN network. The worm carried the message, "Worms Against Nuclear Killers....Your System Has Been Officically [sic] WANKed....You talk of times of peace for all, and then prepare for war." At the time of the attack, anti-nuclear protesters were trying (unsuccessfully) to stop the launch of the shuttle that carried the plutonium-fueled Galileo probe on its initial leg to Jupiter. The source of the attack was never identified, but some evidence suggested that it might have come from hackers in Australia.

In recent years, hacktivism has become a common occurrence worldwide. It accounts for a substantial fraction of all cyberspace attacks, which are also motivated by fun, curiosity, profit, and personal revenge. Hacktivism is likely to become even more popular as the Internet continues to grow and spread throughout the world. It is easy to carry out and offers many advantages over physical forms of protest and attack.

The Attraction to Hacktivism

For activists, hacktivism has several attractive features, not the least of which is global visibility. By altering the content on popular web sites, hacktivists can spread their messages and names to large audiences. Even after the sites are restored, mirrors of the hacked pages are archived on sites such as Attrition.org, where they can be viewed by anyone at any time and from anywhere. Also, the news media are fascinated by cyberattacks and are quick to report them. Once the news stories hit the Internet, they spread quickly around the globe, drawing attention to the hackers as well as to the broader conflict. Activists are also attracted to the low costs of hacktivism. There are few expenses beyond those of a computer and an Internet connection. Hacking tools can be downloaded for free from numerous web sites all over the world. It costs nothing to use them and many require little or no expertise.

Moreover, hacktivism has the benefit of being unconstrained by geography and distance. Unlike street protesters, hackers do not have to be physically present to fight a digital war. In a "sit-in" on the web site of the Mexican

Embassy in the United Kingdom, the Electronic Disturbance Theater (EDT) gathered over 18,000 participants from 46 countries. Hacktivists could join the battle simply by visiting the EDT's web site.

Hacktivism is thus well-suited to "swarming," a strategy in which hackers attack a given target from many directions at once. Because the Internet is global, it is relatively easy to assemble a large group of digital warriors in a coordinated attack. The United Kingdom-based Electrohippies Collective estimated that 452,000 people participated in their sit-in on the web site of the World Trade Organization (WTO). The cyberattack was conducted in conjunction with street protests during WTO's Seattle meetings in late 1999.

Another attraction of hacktivism is the ability to operate anonymously on the Internet. Cyberwarriors can participate in attacks with little risk of being identified, let alone prosecuted. Further, participating in a cyberbattle is not life-threatening or even dangerous: hacktivists cannot be gunned down in cyberspace.

Many hacktivists, however, reject anonymity. They prefer that their actions be open and attributable. EDT and Electrohippies espouse this philosophy. Their events are announced in advance and the main players use their real names.

Web Defacement and Hijacking

Web defacement is perhaps the most common form of attack. Attrition.org, which collects mirrors and statistics of hacked web sites, recorded over 5,000 defacements in the year 2000 alone, up from about 3,700 in 1999. Although the majority of these may have been motivated more by thrills and bragging rights than by some higher cause, many were also casualties of a digital battle.

Web hacks were common during the Kosovo conflict in 1999. The US hacking group called Team Spl0it broke into government sites and posted statements such as, "Tell your governments to stop the war." The Kosovo Hackers Group, a coalition of European and Albanian hackers, replaced at least five sites with black and red "Free Kosovo" banners.

In the wake of the accidental bombing of China's Belgrade embassy by the North Atlantic Treaty Organization (NATO), angry Chinese citizens allegedly hacked several US government sites. The slogan "Down with Barbarians" was placed in Chinese on the web page of the US Embassy in Beijing, while the US Department of Interior web site showed images of the three journalists killed during the bombing and crowds protesting the attack in Beijing. The US Department of Energy's home page read:

"Protest USA's Nazi action!...We are Chinese hackers who take no cares about politics. But we can not stand by seeing our Chinese reporters been killed which you might have know [sic]....NATO led by USA must take absolute responsibility....We won't stop attacking until the war stops!"

Web defacements were also popular in a cyberwar that erupted between hackers in China and Taiwan in August 1999. Chinese hackers defaced several Taiwanese and government web sites with pro-China messages saying Taiwan was and always would be an inseparable part of China. "Only one China exists and only one China is needed," read a message posted on the web site of Taiwan's highest watchdog agency. Taiwanese hackers retaliated and planted a red and blue Taiwanese national flag and an anti-Communist slogan, "Reconquer, Reconquer, Reconquer the Mainland," on a Chinese high-tech Internet site. The cyberwar followed an angry exchange between China and Taiwan in response to Taiwanese President Lee Teng-hui's statement that China must deal with Taiwan on a "state-to-state" basis.

Many of the attacks during the Palestinian-Israeli cyberwar were web defacements. The hacking group GForce Pakistan, which joined the pro-Palestinian forces, posted heart-wrenching images of badly mutilated children on numerous Israeli web sites. The Borah Torah site also contained the message, "Jews, Israelis, you have crossed your limits, is that what Torah teaches? To kill small innocent children in that manner? You Jews must die!" along with a warning of additional attacks.

Hacktivists have also hijacked web sites by tampering with the Domain Name Service so that the site's domain name resolves to the IP address of some other site. When users point their browsers to the target site, they are redirected to the alternative site.

In what might have been one of the largest mass web site takeovers, the anti-nuclear Milw0rm hackers joined with the Ashtray Lumberjacks hackers in an attack that affected more than 300 web sites in July 1998. According to reports, the hackers broke into the British Internet service provider (ISP) EasySpace, which hosted the sites. They altered the ISP's database so that users attempting to access the sites were redirected to a Milw0rm site, where they were greeted by a message protesting the nuclear arms race. The message concluded with "Use your power to keep the world in a state of PEACE and put a stop to this nuclear bullshit."

Web Sit-ins

Web sit-ins are another popular form of attack. Thousands of Internet users simultaneously visit a target web site and attempt to generate sufficient traffic to disrupt normal service. A group calling itself Strano Network conducted what was probably the first such demonstration as a protest against the French government's policies on nuclear and social issues. On December 21, 1995, they launched a one-hour Net'Strike attack against the web sites operated by various government agencies. At the appointed hour, participants from all over the world pointed their browsers to the government web sites. According to reports, at least some of the sites were effectively knocked out for the period.

In 1998, EDT took the concept a step further and automated the attacks. They organized a series of sit-ins, first against Mexican President Ernesto Zedillo's web site and later against US President Bill Clinton's White House web site, the Pentagon, the US Army School of the Americas, the Frankfurt Stock Exchange, and the Mexican Stock Exchange. The purpose was to demonstrate solidarity with the Mexican Zapatistas. According to EDT's Brett Stalbaum, the Pentagon was chosen because "we believe that the US military trained the soldiers carrying out the human rights abuses." For a similar reason, the US Army School of the Americas was selected. The Frankfurt Stock Exchange was targeted, Stalbaum said, "Because it represented capitalism's role in globalization utilizing the techniques of genocide and ethnic cleansing, which is at the root of the Chiapas' problems. The people of Chiapas should play a key role in determining their own fate, instead of having it pushed on them through their forced relocation....which is currently financed by Western capital."

To facilitate the strikes, the organizers set up special web sites with automated software. All that was required of would-be participants was to visit one of the FloodNet sites. When they did, their browser would download the software (a Java Applet), which would access the target site every few seconds. In addition, the software let protesters leave a personal statement on the targeted server's error log. For example, if they pointed their browsers to a non-existent file such as "human_rights" on the target server, the server would log the message, "human_rights not found on this server."

When the Pentagon's server sensed the attack from the FloodNet servers, it launched a counter-offensive against the users' browsers, redirecting them to a page with an Applet programme called "HostileApplet." Once there, the new applet was downloaded to their browsers, where it endlessly tied up their machines trying to reload a document until the machines were rebooted. The Frankfurt Stock Exchange reported that they were aware of the protest but believed it had not affected their services. Overall, EDT considered the attacks a success. "Our interest is to help the people of Chiapas to keep receiving the international recognition that they need to keep them alive," said Stalbaum.

Since the time of the strikes, FloodNet and similar software have been used in numerous sit-ins sponsored by EDT, the Electrohippies, and others. There were reports of FloodNet activity during the Palestinian-Israeli cyberwar. Pro-Israel hackers created a web site called Wizel.com, which offered FloodNet software and other tools before it was shut down. Pro-Arab hackers put up similar sites. The Electrohippies have been criticized for denying their targets' right to speech when conducting a sit-in. Their response has been that a sit-in is acceptable if it substitutes the deficit of speech by one group with a broad debate on policy issues and if the event used to justify the sit-in provides a focus for the debate.

The Electrohippies also demand broad support for their actions. An operation protesting genetically modified foods was aborted when the majority of visitors to their site did not vote for the operation.

Denial-of-Service Attacks

Whereas a web sit-in requires participation by tens of thousands of people to have even a slight impact, the so-called denial-of-service (DoS) and distributed denial-of-service (DDoS) tools allow lone cyberwarriors to shut down web sites and e-mail servers. With a DoS attack, a hacker uses a software tool that bombards a server with network messages. The messages either crash the server or disrupt service so badly that legitimate traffic slows to a crawl. DDoS is similar except that the hacker first penetrates numerous Internet servers (called "zombies") and installs software on them to conduct the attack. The hacker then uses a tool that directs the zombies to attack the target all at once.

During the Kosovo conflict, Belgrade hackers were credited with DoS attacks against NATO servers. They bombarded NATO's web server with "ping" commands, which test whether a server is running and connected to the Internet. The attacks caused line saturation of the targeted servers.

Similar attacks took place during the Palestinian-Israeli cyberwar. Pro-Palestinian hackers used DoS tools to attack Netvision, Israel's largest ISP. While initial attacks crippled the ISP, Netvision succeeded in fending off later assaults by strengthening its security.

NEW COMPUTER CRIME LEGISLATION

Senators Charles Schumer and Jon Kyl have introduced new legislation, S 2092, aimed at addressing some of the perceived weaknesses in the CFAA. The three main provisions addressed by this new legislation propose the following: trap and trace orders, federal jurisdiction requirements, and sentencing.

First, the new legislation would make it easier for cyber-investigators to obtain "trap and trace" orders. "Trap and trace" devices are used to capture incoming IP packets to identify the packet's origins. Due to the ease with which hackers are able to "spoof" their true origin, the most effective way to reconstruct the path of a virus, DoS or hacking assault is to follow a chain of trapping devices that logged the original malicious packets as they arrived at each individual router or server. In the case of a single telephone company, it has been relatively easy for investigators to obtain trap and trace orders. According to Congresswoman Scott of Virginia, "one communication is being carried by several different [ISPs], by a telephone company or 2, local or long distance, by a cell company or 2, and soon enough by a satellite company or 2." Once the segment of the route goes beyond the court's jurisdiction, investigators must then go to the next jurisdiction and file a request for a trap and trace order for the next segment. The new legislation would authorize the issuance of a single order to completely trace an on-line communication from start to finish.

The second provision would lower the monetary barrier for federal jurisdiction. Currently, the CFAA requires a damage threshold in excess of $5,000. However, the $5,000 is often difficult to establish when there is no fixed monetary value to the information. For example, how do you put a price on the value of medical records? Also, investigators must currently wait for a damage assessment before they can initiate an investigation, which can cause expensive delays. The new legislation would permit federal jurisdiction at the outset of an attack. Crimes that exceed $5,000 will still be treated as felonies. However, attacks that cause less than $5,000 in damage would be defined as misdemeanors. Finally, the legislation clarifies what is included in the calculation of "damage," making it easy to reach the $5,000 threshold. It provides for the costs of responding to the offence, the damage assessment costs, restoration costs, and any lost revenue or costs incurred from the interruption of service.

The third provision would modify the strict sentence directives contained in the Antiterrorism and Effective Death Penalty Act of 1999 which required a mandatory incarceration for a minimum of six months for any violation of 18 U.S.C. § 1030(a). Some hacking crimes have gone unprosecuted because the six month sentence was considered excessive. The new legislation would provide lesser sentences for lesser crimes, helping to ensure that all levels of hacking cases will be prosecuted.

Finally, the proposed legislation would make juvenile perpetrators fifteen years of age and older eligible for federal prosecution in serious computer crime cases at the Attorney General's discretion.

However, the proposed changes have raised privacy concerns. A report written by the President's Working Group on Unlawful Conduct on the Internet entitled "The Electronic Frontier: the Challenge of Unlawful Conduct Involving the Use of the Internet" has raised the concerns of privacy advocates. The groups are particularly concerned about the potential for trap and trace abuse by authorities. The American Civil Liberties Union ("ACLU"), would like to raise the standards for trap and trace devices, rather than lower them. According to the ACLU, law enforcement currently only needs to overcome "minimum obstacles" to obtain trap and trace devices. The ACLU is concerned that an expansion of the government's power to obtain trap and trace orders will enhance the government's power to "surreptitiously intercept even more personal electronic communications." The current standard for a trap and trace order is that the investigator must assert in writing to the court that the information is "relevant" to an ongoing investigation. According to the ACLU, the "judge to whom the application is made *must* approve the application, *even if he disagrees* with the assertions of law enforcement."

Additionally, the ACLU is concerned that an expansion of the substance of the orders will erode privacy. The ACLU speculates that an expansion of the powers "might allow law enforcement agents to access a variety of data, including dial-up numbers, Internet Protocol ("IP") addresses, electronic mail logs, uploaded files, and so on.... without a court order."

The CFAA is broad enough to cover most computer crimes. The Act protects government and private computers against inside and outside threats to information, fraud, and damage. Continued pro-active legislative changes to keep the Act up to date in the escalating cyber-war between secure web sites and hackers will be critical to maintaining the integrity of our increasingly inter-networked society.

One challenge in the near future will be the expansion of devices that are able to access the Internet. For example, as televisions become "web-enabled," allowing users to access the Internet from their televisions, will televisions be considered "high-speed data processing devices" as defined under the Act's "computer" definition? Would passwords taken from the television's cookie storage be protected under the Act? As Wireless Application Protocol ("WAP") brings the Internet to hand-held devices and mobile telephones, will the devices and telephones be considered "protected computers"? Will refrigerators that are wired to the Internet be covered? Cyber-crime prosecutors are also facing the difficulty of attacks that originate overseas beyond their jurisdiction. If part of a hacking trail is routed overseas, unless the U.S has an agreement with the foreign jurisdiction, that trail could lead to a dead end if investigators do not have access to the server's logs. The world of individual national jurisdictions will need to address the increasingly borderless crimes committed in cyberspace. However, the CFAA provides a solid foundation upon which we can develop new cyber-crime laws for the coming century.

9

Crime and Punishment: Theory and Types

INTRODUCTION

The effect that psychologically based interventions have been shown to be effective in reducing criminal recidivism, probably forms the single most important reason for the current resurgence of interest in psychology in criminal justice. We also saw that the most frequently used strategy when responding to offenders, so widespread and firmly established that it could be called the standard or mainstream approach to criminal conduct, is the use of punishment. However, the outcomes of its use are far from satisfactory. There are few instances in which it has been shown to 'work' in the sense of serving to ensure that those who have committed criminal offences do not do so again. Almost certainly, professionals working in various criminal justice settings may be able to cite anecdotal instances where that occurred.

But they tend to be the exceptions; and for the most part punishment of offenders singly fails to achieve its publicly appointed objectives. The bulk of the findings available indicate either that its effects are virtually non-existent, or that in some instances it actually makes matters worse. Put another way, it is on balance unproductive, and it can often be counter-productive. As suggested, examine this issue in more detail. To do so the stage is divided into four sections. First, it is helpful to make some conceptual distinctions, as there are different rationales underpinning punishment, and confusing them with one another can make it difficult to judge both arguments and evidence. Second, as suggested, survey and scrutinize a range of findings that call into question the value of punishment as an effective way to achieve the goals that the law proclaims for it, and citizens notionally expect of it. Third, the assumption that punishment ought to work appears to be deeply embedded in many people's thinking; it is almost a part of the taken-for-granted fabric of social life. It is important then to propose an explanation of why people's expectations of it are tantamount to an illusion. This will draw on relevant findings from psychological research. Finally, given the confounding state of affairs in which one of society's chief weapons in the 'war on crime' abjectly misses its intended target, as suggested, briefly discuss why, despite the evidence, it goes on being applied.

Our habit of thinking that punishment is the answer to crime is so deeply ingrained that, whenever bad news concerning crime hits the streets, there are nearubiquitous demands for even more of it. For example, in the wake of the publication of the annual Criminal Statistics for 2002 showing an increase in crime rates, there were once again calls for greater use of severe sanctions against offenders. The phrases used are familiar and well-worn: 'crack down', 'get tough', 'show less understanding', 'teach the culprits a lesson', 'turn up the heat'. Debates concerning 'law and order' seem to exist on a single dimension along which opinions are expressed. The language typically casts the issue in terms of a polarity between 'hard' and 'soft' in our basic disposition towards crime and criminals. The 'hard' end of the scale is purportedly grounded in a more realistic picture of what people are like.

Those who commit crimes are bad; they are unlikely to change unless compelled to do so. They need to be dealt with more strictly, and the only way to do it is to make the costs of crime higher, or its consequences as unpleasant as possible. At the 'soft' end, there is perhaps a belief that people who commit crimes are no different from anyone else; they have the capacity to live decent lives and to reform themselves, but they have grown up in adverse surroundings, and need to have better opportunities given to them. Such liberalism is discredited when it is discovered that some offenders reportedly 'get away with it' by being dealt with in ways that are thought too lenient. Evidence that even prison sentences do not deter is interpreted by many as proving that prisons are too much like 'holiday camps' and punishments should be more severe. Worse still, some offenders seem to be virtually rewarded for their crimes, for example when staff of residential centres take them on outdoor pursuits trips, in one infamous instance overseas. Within this debate, while the precise phraseology changes slightly over time, the underlying arguments remain the same.

PUNISHMENT

The possible preventive and corrective that will first occur to the reader are punishment and the threat of punishment. The meaning of this term, as many understand it, is deprivation of anything that is considered desirable: life, property, freedom, comfort of body and mind, convenience, etc., when such deprivations are inflicted on account of misdoings. As thus employed the meaning is quite too broad. For when a wayfarer takes the life of a bandit who has just now advanced as if to shoot him or to inflict a blow upon his head his act is not in the category of punishments.

The parent's prohibition against his child's attendance at a party given by roustabouts in whose company the youngster has hitherto fallen into evil ways is not punishment. The judge who places a youthful offender into the charge of a juvenile protective association is not administering punishment even though the young misdemeanant chafes under the restrictions that are thus imposed upon his freedom of action. Once more, the adult who has murdered his neighbour and has been committed to the State Hospital for mental diseases has not been punished for having taken a life.

But if any one of these hypothetical persons has received one or another of the impositions that have been mentioned because the parent or court believes that pain or embarrassment that goes with treatment carries with it will "teach the culprit a lesson," that the memory of it will dissuade him in the future from committing crimes or misdemeanors; if the injured person (or one acting for him) makes an imposition upon the offender "to get even with him"-in any of these cases we have an illustration of punishment. Thus the attitude of the individual who makes the imposition, whether in his private or official capacity, determines whether the act of imposition is in the category of punishment or not. The sufferer does not invariably make this distinction. But sometimes he does so, as when a child "takes it" from his parent or teacher-even though "it" may be a severe correction, because the administrator is not "nasty" about the matter. Even so the child is only recognizing the attitude of his elder.

He is probably not distinguishing between "punishment" and "correction" nor between either of these and "guidance" or "teaching" or "measure for improvement" In any case he is "getting it" or taking his "rap" And the case is probably not much different in relation to adult offenders against the criminal law-the great majority of them at any rate. But the "rap" in home, school, or prison may leave grouches and resentments behind it that make mischief in the future, or it may not. That is the important thing.

It makes little difference whether we call it "punishment" or something else. Whatever urge there is to erase that term from our vocabulary is academic and not practical from the offender's viewpoint.

THEORIES OF PUNISHMENT

Whatever theory of punishment is generally held in a given period affords some indication of the attitudes of administrators and of the people at large towards the offender; and these attitudes determine the manner and spirit of our penal measures.

In the first place it will be sufficient with little more than a mention to pass what may be called the transcendental theories. First there is the theological theory that every criminal act is an offence against God, who must be appeased by the infliction of pain upon the evil-doer. Secondly, the expiatory view which is that the offender is befouled by reason of his act and must be cleansed by the healing influence of pain. And in the third place there is the aesthetic view according to which the commission of a crime and the existence of a criminal disturb a certain balance or satisfactoriness in social relations which is analogous to the destruction of the beauty of a picture. We are satisfied when we have turned our back upon the ugly picture and have cast it away from us. This is closely akin to the doctrine that punishment is only for revenge and has no function whatever except to afford those who inflict punishment-or those in whose name it is inflicted-a sense of satisfaction in having reacted hostilely to the criminal.

Each of the foregoing theories makes punishment an end in itself. It is not primarily for the advantage of the public nor of the criminal himself. For even the expiatory view that looks towards purifying the wrong-doer makes expiation a process that must take place in the nature of things. It is not for any advantage that purification may bring to the individual who is making expiation, except possibly in an incalculable future state.

Moreover, the biology and psychology of the twentieth century cannot hold by these doctrines. And we unavoidably think of punishment as in some way a medium by which we hope to attain an advantage that lies in large measure outside the person who applies punishment and him who receives it; and an advantage that is completely removed from the narrow circles of satisfaction that one experiences as a result of striking back. And so we come to those theories that justify punishment on the ground that it offers some practical good to the people at large or to the state.

In the first place is the theory that punishment is justified by its reformatory effect upon the one who receives it. The offender is regarded as morally sick and as needing a cure. Punishment affords the cure and the cure becomes manifest in the offender's resolve never again to transgress the law; to lead an upright life and in every way to bring forth the fruits of true repentance.

Reformation of the criminal is an end that is greatly to be desired. If it is once secured the public is fully protected against the reformed one because he will never offend again and obviously there would be no recidivists if each offender were to be reformed by the infliction of punishment after his first offence.

But the theory foredooms any system of punishment to failure before it is attempted. Perhaps the criminal has reformed completely and immediately after the commission of his act. If so there is nothing that punishment can accomplish that has not already been accomplished without it. Moreover, if the criminal, caught red-handed, says he has reformed and that he is truly repentant, there is nothing that a consistent reformatory theorist can do but withhold his hand from punishment. For it is only the future behaviour of the criminal that is competent to demonstrate whether he is truly reformed or not. Conceivably one might successfully "reform" any number of times.

According to the theory of disablement, punishment has done its perfect work when it has made it impossible for the criminal to offend a second time. Disablement may be effected by putting the criminal to death or by putting him away where he can do no harm. This may be considered as a complement to the reformatory theory and as applicable to those who are incorrigible and therefore not reformable.

In the next place is the theory that punishment justifies itself by reason of its deterrent effect. It deters the culprit from putting himself again into a position in which he may bring upon himself such suffering as his present punishment carries with it. This is only a practical matter. It has nothing to do with reformation of character. Moreover, punishment deters not only the culprit who endures it, but others who look on and who might otherwise drift into a criminal career. Reformation and disablement are for the offender himself. There is the first consideration in the mind of the one who imposes punishment. There the effect of punishment is ended except that the public is spared depredations that he might otherwise commit in the future. But the deterrent effect of punishment is conceived as extending not only to the offender himself, but to the public at large, while at the same time it shields the public from future damages. Indeed, the probability of its deterrence upon people generally is most prominent in the minds both of the leaders and of the rank and file. "Why wait till the horse is stolen before we lock the barn?" The defender of the theory of deterrence would try to prevent the act by showing to the world what has happened at any rate to one who has stolen a horse, for example.

It is sometimes urged that the theory of the preventive value of punishment relies for its success only upon base motives of fear which is disorganizing and not constructive. But in the first place no human motive is necessarily and thoroughly base everywhere and all the time. There is nothing base about fearing a boa-constrictor; or if there is-let us be base! And if punishment be interpreted as a symbol of an outraged sense of public welfare-welcome, fear of punishment! If that is treasonable, reflect that in our own personal experience (save in abnormal cases) a disorganizing state of fear impends the organization of a better state.

To the motive of deterrence from criminal acts add that of protection of the public-of the state-in the exercise of those functions that have been guaranteed in our political economy and we have the theory of the purpose of punishment that holds the stage today. Punishment is an infliction of some sort of deprivation upon a wrong-doer-a criminal for our purpose-to the end of preventing him from offending or injuring in the future as he has done in the past and for the purpose of deterring others from following in his wayward footsteps. This deterrence or prevention may be by way of reformation, of disablement, or by any other route. It is of less consequence by what way it comes to pass, so long as the public is protected. Protection is the major consideration that justifies punishment and it must be had at all cost.

EFFICACY OF PUNISHMENT

And now we must enquire what is the utility of punishment? It must be measured, if at all, by its elimination of crimes. This is bound to be an exceedingly difficult question to answer because there is no state in which there is no punishment. We cannot therefore compare the effects of its presence with the effects of its absence. And even if we had two states that were unlike in respect to the presence and absence of punishment it is very likely that they would not be found alike in all other important respects. If we make the answer to this question depend upon our introspections we are bound to report that punishment is efficacious as a preventive. How efficacious it is, of course, is a different question. No one who has driven a motor can doubt the validity of this proposition. In other words nearly every man and woman in the United States over the age of eighteen is able to affirm it.

Every one of us is familiar with the warning to motorists: "State Laws Enforced" And it is exceedingly doubtful that any one is entirely neglectful of the warning unless-and this is an important exception-nobody is looking. And the driver is very likely to satisfy himself at least that nobody is looking before he speeds up and runs into a "speed trap" Or if the street sign is wanting and one has heard of one's neighbor's having been haled into court and fined for driving at too high speed one is likely not to bear down hard upon the gas lever.

Of course, we would be better satisfied with ourselves and with the race if the threat of punishment implied in the roadside placard were unnecessary; if there were only "Be Careful" placards and if these were proven to be as efficacious as any other warning: if "Straight Road Ahead" were just as conducive to conservative driving as "State Laws Enforced" It may be that "Be Careful" is efficacious. But there is no gainsaying that "State Laws Are Enforced" is practical also. And until-if ever-a clear advantage can be shown for a preventive measure that carries with it no threat of penalty we shall not give up the threat-actual or implied.

And we shall still cling to the old-fashioned conviction that the fear of the law is wholesome and constructive; that obedience to law, even because of fear of consequences, may, according to the laws of habits and their integration, help to yield a good grade of citizenship and may, therefore, be remedial in respect to natures so weak that they may fall into criminal ways if, indeed, they have not already done so.

We may be permitted once more to appeal to the evidence of introspection. The question whether severe penalties are not much more effective than light ones is usually answered thus: light penalties, promptly and certainly inflicted, are more effective than heavy penalties tardily or uncertainly applied. While it is impossible to suggest a measure of the "more" or "less," the statement is undoubtedly correct. Men are not deterred to any appreciable degree, apparently, from riding in automobiles and from driving them by reason of the fact that hundreds are known to be killed in such vehicles. They eagerly take the chance. But what would be the effect if 100 per cent, or even 90 per cent, of those who choose such means of transportation were promptly snuffed out by one means or another connected with the operation of the car? No one would be foolhardy enough to attempt it. It need not be elaborately demonstrated that there is something appalling about the certainty and promptness of a disagreeable consequence.

It is very often pointed out that there are in the United States about ten times as many homicides per unit of population as in England and it is probable that the disparity in the murder rates is not far different from this. It is usually alleged that the difference is due to the much greater degree of promptness and certainty of punishment in England than in the United States. There are many delays and loop-holes in the criminal procedure in the United States. When one has been arrested and charged with felony there are still many chances that he will not even be brought to trial or that if he is brought to trial at all it will be so late that witnesses will have disappeared. So the threat of punishment in his case carries along with it a zest-inspiring gambler's chance.

But the difference between England and the United States is not traceable solely to greater and less celerity of arrest, trial and punishment of the guilty. It has been attributed also to the racial ingredients of the populations. The racial composition of the English population is practically uniform, whereas the population of the United States is a conglomerate. The nation's homicide rate, so far in excess of that of England, may be swollen by the excessively high rate in one or two racial or alien national groups. Thus in the whole registration area in the United States in 1922, the homicide rate among whites was 5.6 per 100,000. The rate among the colored element in the population was 34.7. Among industrial policy holders of the Metropolitan Life Insurance Company, only tuberculosis and pneumonia rank higher than homicide as causes of death of young-adult Negro males. The homicide rate of Chinese in the registration area of the United States in 1921 was 155.6 per 100,000.

Florida has a homicide rate twenty-two times as high as Vermont. And it is doubtless much saner to attribute the difference, not to differences in manner of punishment between the states respectively nor to laws and procedure, but to the large Negro population in Florida and the lack of it in Vermont. This is suggested by the fact already alluded to that over the whole registration area in the United States the homicide rate among Negroes is approximately seven times as high as among the whites.

Moreover, it appears that the great death rate from homicide in this country is largely due to group quarrels within the races. According to the police report, forty-one Negroes were murdered in Chicago during the year 1921-1922 and thirty-three of them were murdered by other Negroes. Seventy-one Italians were murdered in that city in the same year and sixty-seven of the murders were committed by Italians. In Washington, D. C., from 1915 to 1919 eighty-seven Negroes were murdered-eighty of them by other Negroes. If we should exclude killings in race riots and murders resulting from quarrels among members of races that have no more than begun to come into contact with the culture of the land, we should probably find our homicide and murder rates approximating to those of England.

We have thus gone into these matters relating to our much mooted unfavorable comparison with England to suggest that the difference as to celerity and certainty of punishment between the two countries is by no means the only existing difference that could account for a variation in murder and homicide rates. There is still another factor that almost unquestionably plays a part affecting the difference of rate we have been discussing. England is an ancient civilization. Obedience to authority and respect for the representative of law have there become a firmly fixed attitude or set. The laws will be observed there with a matter-ofcourse-ness that does not prevail in a newer and rapidly expanding civilization.

TREATMENT IN PRISON AND REFORMATORY

It is not necessary here to enter upon the history of imprisonment for crime, nor of its abolition in any particular instances. Suffice it to say in this place that the maximum of punishment-maximum in the sense of severity and degree of deprivation-is probably in every period of history near the upper limit that public sentiment and opinion will tolerate; and that its form too lies within the region of the tolerable from the viewpoint of public opinion.

The wretched conditions of congregate prisoners in England seized the minds of Englishmen in the latter portion of the eighteenth century and the beginning of the nineteenth through the efforts of John Howard and Elizabeth Fry, among others. The result was the building, at many places in England, of jails and prisons for cellular confinement. Simultaneously, the same development, carried over from England, was occurring in Pennsylvania under the aegis of the Quakers. But imprisonment in cells as it was being developed in England and in Pennsylvania implied, not the use of a tiny space only large enough to accommodate a cot and a stool, but a sizable room connecting with an out-door space, all of which was to be occupied by one solitary prisoner.

The aim of the promoters of solitary confinement was a worthy one-to protect the prisoner against moral contamination by his associates and, moreover, to give him the best opportunity to reflect upon his past and to resolve to do better. But the result was not what had been anticipated. Mental disorder among solitary prisoners threatened to become the rule. Few natures can endure it for a long period. Culprits are likely to emerge from it with their fitness for normal community life reduced rather than improved. The result has been a modification of solitary confinement-even its elimination except as applied to a relatively few especially incorrigible prisoners.

The commodious cell, in the English sense, was supplanted by the central steel cell block, with one cell above another and each one large enough for little more than a cot and a chair. All the cells composing the block were surrounded by a corridor and that in turn, by a great wall with barred windows set high, through which light is admitted to the corridors and cells. Outside this wall are the more or less extensive grounds and shops and enclosing all a high, guarded wall. The structure as a whole expresses the idea of a compromise between cellular and congregate confinement.

It provides congregate life in the course of the day and solitude at night when prisoners are locked in their places. This was the "Auburn " system as distinguished from the "Pennsylvania" system, because in the city of Auburn was its most conspicuous example for many years following 1816, when the State of New York passed a law that provided for the construction of a prison in that city-a prison that was finally built along the lines that have been indicated above. There was a violent struggle between the partisans of the Pennsylvania and the Auburn systems respectively until 1860. The latter, however, gained the upper hand and became the typical American system. In Europe, on the contrary, it was the less successful competitor for the field.

The issue of the controversy had very important consequences in America, for it facilitated the development of prison labour.

PRISON LABOUR

Solitary confinement without occupation, as it was at its inception, is a doubly unnatural state; it is difficult in such a case and in our generation especially, to provide work that will be useful as a builder of character. Early attempts were made to correct the deficiency by providing "the wheel" This was constructed after the fashion of a water-power wheel. While he grasps a bar above him, the prisoner treads the wheel below. He must keep going or be suspended by his arms till, out of sheer exhaustion, he falls into a depth beneath him. "The crank" expressed a similar motive on the part of prison managers. It was safer than "the wheel" The prisoner was made to stand by the wall and to turn a crank revolving a wheel against greater or less resistance; several thousand revolutions in the morning and other thousands in the afternoon. Each of these activities is on a par with moving a pile of stones from one side of the yard to the other and immediately back again for no other purpose than to be busy.

The fundamental objection to every activity such as these is that no man would choose any one of them for himself, at any rate not for more than the satisfaction of a momentary curiosity. Human occupation is purposive. One of us might tread a thousand steps upon "the wheel" to estimate the limit of human endurance in such a situation and so to satisfy a scientific interest; in other situations we will be active merely for the pleasure that the activity itself affords; in others, for the reason that it brings them into pleasurable association with persons like themselves. In still another situation, we are active for the purpose of making a living.

There are thousands of variations. But the work we have to do in our normal relations is within the limits of the tolerable and the absorbing in so far as we see through it to some advantage that it will bring to us and that we cannot otherwise attain. When this condition prevails, our work is constructive in the sense that it is the means for building character. Whenever the desirability of the results to be gained by the activity wanes or disappears it loses its absorbing quality, fails to call out our coördinated effort, activity becomes sporadic or slovenly at best and character is no longer in the building. It no longer carries healing in its wings and the society that fails to provide constructive activity for its prisoners, to that extent forfeits the protection that should come from the regeneration of the prisoners, nearly 100 per cent of whom will ultimately be released in a fit condition physically.

More than one-half of those who are admitted to our prisons in a given year are under 25 years of age. In other words, they are within the period of life in which men generally are acquiring their professional and occupational attitudes. Obviously the prison should take advantage of this situation.

The late Mr. John L. Whitman, when he was Superintendent of the House of Correction in Chicago, once wrote to the author describing the revolutionary change of attitude that occurred in prisoners in his charge when, in 1910, he was employing large numbers (and prisoners alone) in the construction of a new cell-house to replace an old one that had outlived its usefulness and respectability.

They were transformed from a howling mob to a group of respectable laborers. And as Mr. Whitman interpreted it, it was only because they were made to feel that they were doing a great constructive work, a great service to the City of Chicago, affording relief to a long line of others who, following them, would be "doing time" there. Mr. Whitman lost no opportunity to remind the men of the great work they were carrying through and this provided a strong motivation.

The effects as Mr. Whitman saw them were so much to be desired that he immediately began to develop many other forms of coöperative labour in the House of Correction, including the salvaging of junk accumulated from the city streets and alleys. The whole scheme was remunerative from the angle of institutions and once more the prisoner's labour was dignified, for the worker was at least helping to carry his own load.

It is difficult to allow the least doubt that the men's experience in these coöperative enterprises was somewhat of a rebuilding factor in their lives and hence, to some extent, a deterrent of future criminal behaviour on their part. It is easier to believe this than to prove that it is true, but we cannot fail to accept it unless we are ready to cancel our assent to the proposition that worthy attitudes grow from constructive labour and that these attitudes are practical determiners of behaviour.

Many prison systems have become highly organized for promoting labour within penal institutions. Numerous forms of industry have been fostered; for example, in addition to agriculture, the manufacture of binder twine, sign tags, shoes, clothing, tobacco, tin utensils and furniture. Two systems have developed: one that provides for the disposition of prison-made goods in the open market and the other, the "state use" system, that limits the market to institutions maintained by the state or by municipalities within the state. In either system, the maintenance and discipline of prisoners, the physical conditions of labour and the sale of products may be under the control either of the state or of private parties. In the former case the state is engaging directly in the business of manufacturing and selling; in the latter the state leases to a private individual or corporation, who undertakes maintenance, discipline, control of labour conditions and sale of product.

He sells the product of the industry where he can and for what price he can command. Under the contract system, the situation differs only in that the contractor is not allowed responsibility for maintenance and discipline. In either case, the state is but indirectly engaged in the manufacture and sale of goods. But leasing has practically gone out of existence; the contract system has grown unpopular owing to abuses that have easily crept into it and the state is becoming more and more directly engaged in business for the purpose of supplying public institutions with furniture, tools, shoes, clothing, printed forms, bread and articles of whatever description which would otherwise be purchased in the open market from private manufacturers.

This is "state use" Moreover, the state, in many instances, is supplying food for public institutions from the penal farms and is employing men on public works such as roadways and buildings. The following table indicates the trends in respect to the management of the prison labour problem over a period of nearly forty years ending in 1923. A more recent survey by the Department of Commerce shows that no great change has occurred since 1923.

The use of prison labour to obtain its maximal remedial value and consequently its greatest ultimate protective value to the communities into which the prisoners will finally be discharged, implies such a knowledge of every prisoner who is to be employed as will indicate the occupations to which he has the best chance for making adaptation. Only by putting him into that particular occupation may we be assured that the best in him will be brought out and that a healthy attitude towards work will be developed. At the same time, it implies a knowledge of what each occupation demands of one who would follow it successfully. Moreover, it is implied that the state will supply in its prisons opportunity for a considerable variety of forms of productive work to match at least a large proportion of the patterns of capacities for work that are represented among the individuals in the prison population. In order to make such assignment possible, all of the work of the prison has been analyzed into the groups of jobs or places of employment. Each of these jobs has been analyzed to determine the most effective way to perform the work and the personal qualifications required of the worker for each stage. As examples of the latter, we have cases where the requirements, for instance in the printing industry, would call for educational experience equivalent at least to two years in high school. There are other jobs in printing where the only requirement is that of the ordinary fifth grade grammar school education.

This continuous analysis of the prisoners coming into the institution and the analysis of the work to be performed in existing industries in and about the prison, naturally led to the division of our prisoners into five general groups, arranged in the order of their experience qualifications. In like manner, the work to be performed at the prison was divided into five general classes with various sub-divisions. The constant study of each individual gives us a constant inventory of the human end of our problem.

The constant fitting of the right man to the right job leads to a constant analysis of the sufficiency and adequacy of our industries. It has naturally forced us to expand our industries and to add industries in order to provide training better suited to the particular inmates of the smaller numbers in each group. Examples of the analysis of our population and of our industries are shown in the analyses and charts attached to this address as addenda.

OCCUPATIONAL DIVISION AND EXPANSION

There are numerous cases of occupational division and expansion. Here are a few examples:

The enlargement of the printing industry from a few hand-fed presses and hand-setting equipment naturally led first to the introduction of mechanical type-setting machines, then to highly developed ruling machines, then to more highly specialized printing presses, then to modern folding machines, then to a binding department and finally to the introduction of a thoroughly modern up-to-date vestibule school for the training and development of men in this line.

The development of the building trade training has grown from carpenter and steam fitting work of the simplest kind until today we have one of the most modern wood-working plants for the production of different grades of office furniture, sashes, doors, interior wood trim and exterior wood cornice for buildings. We also have a modern cement products training school and industry, producing concrete back-up blocks and cinder concrete blocks for partitions in State buildings.

Out of this work has also grown the most modern programme of building thoroughly modern up-to-date concrete highways, using the most modern machinery to the utmost. In this field, we differ from other governmental bodies with which we are acquainted, in that we have been able to train prisoners and to employ engineers, so that we have been able to compete with the best modern highway contractors in building modern highways in record time at fair competitive prices, where the men get a training at work at which they can be employed successfully afterwards, pay their own board and keep, receive wages which are set aside for the benefit of themselves and families and go out of the prison able to support themselves in a selfrespecting manner.

In like manner, in our tailoring school and industry, in our foundry school and industry, in our shoe manufacturing school and industry, in our shoe repairing school, as well as in our plant for manufacture of automobile markers and other tags, we have been able to carry out this same scheme of training, development, expansion and placement. Our mechanical school and industry is doing machine design and mechanical work second to none.

In the balmiest days of contract labour in New Jersey, only a part of the prison population was employed and the gross earnings to the State were $148,000. The State permitted the contractor to use shops, power, heat, light, etc., without cost to him, so that the real income to the tax-payers was considerably less than $148,000.

In the first year of State Use, the earnings of the industries reached $153,000. Prisoners were paid a wage consistent with their efforts. The Prison was rid of the detrimental influences of some of the representatives of the contractors. Both free labour and private capital, as well as the prisoners themselves and the State, benefited by the change. For the year ending June 30, 1924, the State Use sales for all State Use industries amounted to $536,000. Inventory of stock, goods in process and manufactured reached $452,000, which represented an increase of $63,000 for the year. The increase of sales for the year was $34,000.

The total number employed in State Use industries, including highway construction and farm work, has reached 1050. But the pecuniary profit or loss incident to prison labour is a secondary consideration. The fundamental thing is the development of desirable attitudes through the agency of socialized industry or by whatever other means it may be brought to pass.

It is an open question whether private or state control of labour in prisons is the better for this purpose. Once the prison officials have determined in what type of occupation the prisoner can best be engaged in view of his interests, intelligence and aptitudes, by reference to an analysis of his personal qualifications and such jobs as are available and when they have set him to work, the next essential is that he put into it everything he has got. That implies discipline. Now it may not be true of necessity, but it seems to be true, nevertheless, that privately managed industry is distinguished for its efficiency. On the whole-though there are exceptions-production per prisoner per day is greater under the contract system than under any other.

Generally speaking, one would say that this suggests a situation in which desirable attitudes towards work are more likely to develop than in those other situations in which production is less. It bears repeating that any system is good so long as it is controlled in such manner as to engage the worker's capacities and interests. Therein is embodied the principle that the psychiatrist puts to use in his effort at reconstruction of the shattered personalities that seek his aid. It follows therefrom that the practical ideal is not a prison that supports itself on the product of labour within its walls-not even a prison industry that supports itself-but an institution in which forms of labour are selected for each prisoner with a view to stimulating continuous, systematic and interesting activity.

This suggests, in the next place, the desirability of a considerable diversification of occupations. The restriction of markets for prison-made goods, therefore, which will be effected by such legislation as the Federal law known as the Hayes-Cooper Act may be a blessing in disguise. For as it prohibits the sale of such goods out of the state in which they are made, it is likely to stimulate the development of many small industrial processes to take the place of a few large ones such as the manufacture of shoes and clothing.

PUNISHMENT DISPENSATION

The pivotal agent in the dispensation of justice is the criminal court, and the main means of doing so at its disposal is the sentence it is able to impose. Sentencing is a complex process with several interlinked aims. This is the field of penology, and one with which traditionally, psychology has had little connection. There are several reasons for punishing offenders but they are generally condensed into three principal justifications for its use: *retribution, incapacitation* and *deterrence*.

RETRIBUTION

The concept of retribution is also a complex one, and different approaches to it emphasize different elements.The fundamental principle at stake is that when an individual offends against society, this causes harm to society, giving us an automatic right, even a duty, to inflict pain on the offender as a result. The basis of this comes from within the philosophical tradition of *deontology*, a theoretical framework that achieved its fullest development in the thought of the eighteenth-century German philosopher Immanuel Kant. Within this, morality is codified in a set of prescripts, which, in turn, are derived from higherorder abstract rules that are viewed as virtually axiomatic. This is not concerned with outcomes at an individual level, but with the principled administration of justice. One facet of it is the idea of censure, in which society through the agency of the court utters a statement of disapproval, and acts on it through its treatment of the offender. This is contained in the popular notion of 'just deserts'. It takes its crudest form in the *lex talionis*, the law of retaliation, where the punishment corresponds to the crime. A subtler and more analytic version is subsumed in the concept of *proportionality*. This approach is not primarily concerned with instrumental effects or outcomes; the cycle of crime and societal retribution is, as it were, complete in itself.

INCAPACITATION

Incapacitation refers to the possibility of crime control by removing from offenders the ability to commit crimes. This entails punishing them by imposing restrictions on their freedom to act. The most obvious means of doing this is incarceration in prisons or other secure residential settings. Thereby, offenders are removed from society and from situations in which they have opportunities to steal cars, break into houses or commit assaults. Liberty can be restricted to varying degrees within community penalties, too, for example by prohibiting individuals from attendance at football matches, or placing them under home curfews monitored by electronic tags. These measures almost certainly prevent crimes those individuals would have committed in the short term. And undoubtedly, there are sound justifications for the restraint or incapacitation of persons who are inflicting serious or repeated harm upon others.

However, the extent of incapacitation effects is limited. One aspect often overlooked is that many crimes are 'displaced' into prison where, for example, substance abuse and assaults are by no means uncommon. With regard to the crime-preventive effects of incapacitation, criminologists have constructed elaborate models for its evaluation. Doing so entails, for example, projecting from data on the numbers of dwellings broken into by the average burglar in a year, and estimating the number of crimes then prevented by sentencing larger numbers of house burglars to imprisonment. While the logic of this appears straightforward, it turns out to be a proportionately very expensive method of reducing crime. For example, applying such a model to England and Wales, Tarling concluded that even if the prison population were to be increased by 25 per cent, the net effect on the rate of crime would be a reduction of just 1 per cent.

DETERRENCE

A third declared intention that underpins the sentencing process, and our main focus here, is that it should alter criminal behaviour by attempting to manage its consequences. This is the core of what is entitled the *utilitarian* or *consequentialist* rationale for punishment as a response to crime. It is founded on the idea that legal sanctions will have an impact on those made subject to them. Punishment is thought to be one route towards rehabilitation of the offender. This set of expectations is sometimes referred to as deterrence theory. Deterrence effects can be sub-divided into different kinds of intended outcomes. Gibbs defined and clarified some of the terms used in this area, noting first the conventional distinction between *specific* and *general* deterrence.

The former refers to the influence of punishment on the individual made subject to it: if you are punished for committing a crime, you will be less likely to do it again. The latter refers to the wider impact this is assumed to have on others and in the community as a whole: if you are punished for committing a crime, many other people will be less likely to commit one, because we don't want the same thing happening to us. Stafford and Warr argued that the distinction between specific and general deterrence is difficult to sustain in other than broad and abstract terms. In everyday reality for most actual and potential offenders, there is likely to be a complex interplay between individual and general deterrence effects.

The convicted prisoner is aware of both the sentence imposed upon him or her, alongside a wider knowledge that these are the penalties likely to be incurred by anyone else who commits these crimes. Conceptually, however, in analysing deterrence effects, it can be useful to keep these anticipated outcomes separate in one's mind. A second and less familiar type of distinction outlined by Gibbs is between *absolute* and *restrictive* deterrence. The former refers to a situation in which an individual contemplates a crime but does not commit it for fear of being punished. Note that this refers to more than just the fact that no crime has been committed: for deterrence to occur, individuals must have considered the crime but not proceeded with it. The latter refers to the possibility that highly active offenders reduce their frequency or severity of offending to lower the likelihood of being caught. Gibbs gives the example of a driver exceeding the speed limit, but only by a certain amount so as to keep the risk of detection to a minimum. Wright and Decker carried out an ethnographic study of highly active house burglars.

They found that their respondents were not susceptible to deterrence to the extent of simply not committing their crimes. But while inside premises they sometimes left without taking too much, sacrificing higher rewards in order to reduce their time at risk of discovery. They were wary of the possibility of 'getting greedy' in the course of a burglary and being tempted to stay longer than they otherwise would. Something similar may happen with drink-driving offences, where many drivers are over the legal alcohol limit but perhaps only marginally so. It may help to explain why those committing armed robberies in building society offices select one target per location then move elsewhere; or some patterns of sexual offending, where despite strong urges to offend perpetrators confine themselves to situations in which they can best control access to their victims.

Gibbs also set out in detail a theory of the hypothesized linkages in deterrence theory between 'objective' features of sentences on the one hand, and 'subjective' or 'perceptual' features on the other, together with their hypothesized causal relationships to rates of crime. Objective properties are those that might be measured by a government statistician or a researcher in criminology, showing for example rates of detection or arrest for different types of crime, or the numbers of offenders successfully prosecuted who are then sent to prison. Subjective or perceptual properties are those which are visible to an individual offender, who may be unaware of statistics of police detection rates but well aware of friends who have escaped arrest for specific misdemeanours. The real operative factors in decision-making by would-be offenders are likely to be the latter rather than the former. The characteristics of deterrence measures include their certainty, celerity, severity and scope.

Certainty refers to the likelihood of legal punishment as a result of committing a crime; *celerity* to the amount of time that lapses between an offence being committed and an official sanction being imposed; *severity* to the magnitude of a punishment or the estimated amount of pain or discomfort a convicted offender would endure; while *scope* refers to the relationship between types of crimes defined in statute books and types of punishments imposed by the courts. In each case, these features may be objective, certainty for example being the proportion of crimes of a specific type that result in formal punishment; severity being measured as the amount of a fine or length of a prison sentence. Alternatively, they may be perceptual, reflecting individual offenders' estimates of the chances of being caught or of just how bad it would be for them if they were.

EVIDENCE FOR DETERRENCE EFFECTS

Returning to our central theme, in general terms it is a traditional expectation of sentencing practices that they should deter individuals from committing crimes. Outside the realm of penology and legal philosophy, this is also an expectation of the citizenry-at-large. Much has been written about whether the public believe that the courts are too lenient or too punitive, and it is widely thought that the news media play a pivotal role in shaping perceptions of this, for example by giving more publicity to sentences that are thought too lenient than those that seem unduly harsh.

These influences notwithstanding, more soberly conducted opinion surveys do not show the public to be as punitive or as vengeful as is often alleged; on the contrary, they are often firmly in favour of rehabilitation. It is nevertheless commonly assumed that there is a widespread, fundamental belief that crime and punishment belong together; that the latter brings home to the individual what he or she has done and thereby engenders appropriate change. If that exepectation is indeed widespread, how well-founded is it? There are seven types of evidence that are potentially relevant to the question of whether deterrence measures in criminal justice have an impact on recidivism. In what follows as suggested, examine each of them in turn.

They are:

- The effects of sentencing, as judged from criminal statistics;
- Relationships between imprisonment and crime rates;

- Effects of enhanced punishments;
- Meta-analytic reviews of outcome studies;
- Controlled trials of deterrence measures;
- Self-report surveys;
- Research on the death penalty.

THE IMPACT OF SENTENCING

A first source of doubt regarding the impact of punishment arises from official statistics of offender re-convictions. In the United Kingdom, the effectiveness of sentencing has traditionally been assessed by employing large-scale criminological data on the sequelae of different court 'disposals'. During the 1990s, this exercise achieved a higher level of sophistication by applying the tools of statistical prediction. It is now fairly well established in criminology that rates of criminal recidivism among groups of offenders can be predicted with a reasonable degree of accuracy on the basis of a combination of certain key variables.

They include gender, age at first offence, current age, number of previous convictions, number of previous incarcerations and type of current offence. This process of prediction is limited to aggregate data and cannot be extrapolated for use at the individual level. In the United Kingdom, the Home Office, through its Research Development and Statistics Directorate, developed an instrument of this kind, the Offender Group Reconviction Scale. The original version of this scale was employed for the prediction of discretionary conditional release and also to enable comparisons to be made between different types of court sentences. A second, refined version has since been developed, which allows prediction over a wider age range and for specific offence types, though only in very broad categorical terms. The advent of this measure thus allowed comparisons to be made between custodial and community penalties, respectively. One longstanding problem is that simple comparisons between raw rates of re-conviction following different types of court disposals are not valid or meaningful, due to prior differences in risk levels between groups. For example, if people sent to prison are regularly found to be poorer risks for re-conviction, it is hardly surprising if larger numbers of them are later re-convicted than those subject to other disposals.

Thus 'any attempt to compare the effectiveness of sentences through the simple comparison of reconviction rates is likely to produce very misleading results'. These difficulties were resolved by Lloyd and his associates, who reported on a carefully controlled comparison of the four main types of sentence used by the criminal courts for more serious offences. In England and Wales, when this study was done, these were imprisonment, community service orders, probation orders and probation with additional requirements. The *actual* rates of re-conviction over two years following release from prison or discharge from community penalties were compared with the *predicted* rates: those which would be expected on the basis of offenders' previous criminal histories.

Lloyd and his colleagues found some interesting differences between the groups given different types of sentence. But the real import of their data lies in the side-by-side comparison of predicted with actual rates within each sentence type. In no case was this difference larger than 3 per cent. 'When account was taken of background variables and pseudoreconvictions, most of the differences between the disposal groups disappeared'. In other words, the rate at which individuals re-offended was very close to the rate at which they were probably going to re-offend, regardless of the type of sentence imposed upon them. The sentence of the court had no clear differential impact on the outcome. It could be argued that it is a virtual irrelevance. Walker and Padfield expressed similar dismay at the result: 'the differences between expected and actual percentages are disappointingly small'. When similar analyses are done across successive years, fairly consistent patterns emerge.

This powerfully bears out the trend originally found by Lloyd and his colleagues. Summarizing these trends, Kershaw concluded that 'After taking into account all relevant factors, there is no discernible difference between the effect of immediate custody and community penalties on reconviction rates'. We might reasonably have expected that some suppressant effect of the more punitive sanction, imprisonment, would emerge from these figures, especially given almost unanimous acceptance of a necessary and desirable link between 'crime and punishment'. On the contrary, the findings imply that the sentencing system has a virtually negligible impact on criminal behaviour, certainly as far as the perspective of utilitarian justice is concerned.

IMPRISONMENT AND CRIME RATES

At any one time, only a fraction of those committing crimes in society is apprehended and punished. Yet the public visibility of this process is held to act as a general deterrent for the remainder of the population, including those likely to offend. If general deterrence operates to an extent that justifies its central position in society, there should be some association between the activity of the criminal justice system and the total amount of crime. The broadest, though possibly weakest, kind of evidence pertaining to this comes from studies of the relationship between the numbers of persons incarcerated in a society and its general rate of recorded crime.

For example, where opportunities have been available to monitor recorded levels of crime across periods when rates of incarceration were steadily changing, no clear relationship materializes, even allowing for possible time-lags. This emerges particularly in studies of, and projections based upon, the increased use of incarceration in parts of the United States. Reviewing the evidence bearing on this point up to 1997, Nagin described the conceptual and other difficulties posed in researching this question, but could find no study that can be taken seriously as demonstrating a deterrence effect of imprisonment on general rates of crime. Furthermore, recent research has failed to establish any relationship, in a direction that would be predicted by deterrence theory, between lengths of prison sentences and rates of recidivism. Gendreau *et al.* have systematically reviewed this area in a report for the Solicitor General of Canada.

The research group reviewed 23 studies yielding 222 comparisons of groups of offenders who spent longer versus shorter periods in prison. The groups were similar on a series of five risk factors. Contrary to what would be predicted by deterrence theory, offenders who served longer sentences had slight increases in recidivism of between 2 and 3 per cent; there was a small positive correlation between sentence length and subsequent rates of re-conviction. Incidentally, even Robert Martinson, in his widely cited and highly influential paper which gave 'very little reason to hope that we have in fact found a sure way of reducing recidivism through rehabilitation', also concluded that there was no evidence of an association between recidivism and sentence length. The foregoing review integrated information from many sources and was conducted on a mammoth scale. But smaller-scale research, for example on the comparative impact of fines and short jail sentences on rates of drinking and driving, have not unequivocally shown that the deterrence effect of the latter is necessarily any more powerful than that of the former.

Another frequently heard claim regarding deterrence is that it is more likely to work with 'white-collar' crimes, committed by mainly middle- or upper-class offenders. Weisburd and Chayet followed the criminal careers of 742 offenders convicted of such crimes. The sample, which was divided into those who received and those who did not receive prison sentences, was followed up for a total of more than ten years. There was no observable effect that could be attributed to specific deterrence.

ENHANCED PUNISHMENTS

During the 1970s, the proclaimed failure of education, training or psychotherapy to have their intended impact on criminal recidivism has been associated with a shift towards a more punitive stance in a number of legislatures. Particularly in the United States, from that decade onwards there was a progressive move towards harsher punishments and 'turning up the heat' on offenders. At an institutional level, such sentences included the use of boot camps and shock incarceration. In the community, intensive supervision, electronic surveillance, random drug testing, curfews and various permutations of each were tried and tested. Primary studies and evaluations of 'enhanced' and intermediate punishment therefore flourished during the 1980s and 1990s as the use of these types of sanction became more widespread. This created opportunities for controlled trials, in which more severe punishments were compared with standard punishments or 'business as usual' within the criminal justice system. Participants in the stricter forms of treatment were sometimes allocated randomly, on other occasions selected on a voluntary basis. Analysis of outcomes in such studies is made difficult by the fact that although the harshness of punishment was intensified, in many cases additional elements of education, counselling and other types of rehabilitative activity were also introduced. Petersilia and Turner reported an evaluation of intensive supervision in probation and parole conducted in 14 American states. A sample of nearly 2,000 individuals across numerous sites was allocated randomly to experimental and control groups.

Follow-up evaluation found no impact of the more intensive and restrictive supervision, which in some agencies included close surveillance, electronic monitoring, random drug testing and other innovations, on recidivism. The only positive result along these lines to emerge was an association between clients' participation in drugs and alcohol counselling and subsequent reductions in re-offending rates of the order of 10–20 per cent. However, the possibility that this was due to a selection effect could not be eliminated. Nevertheless, Petersilia was led to conclude that 'The empirical evidence regarding intermediate sanctions is decisive: Without a rehabilitation component, reductions in recidivism are elusive'. Examining this and other evaluations of intermediate punishment, Gendreau *et al.* concluded that none of the hoped-for goals of reduced prison numbers, reduced costs or reduced recidivism were delivered by these programmes. A more recent evaluation of the effectiveness of electronic monitoring in Canada, taking account of participants' risk levels, also drew negative conclusions.

Bonta and his colleagues judged that the effectiveness of electronic monitoring 'as a true alternative to incarceration and reducing recidivism has yet to be demonstrated... If one is interested in reducing recidivism, then offender treatment, rather than sanctions, is the most promising approach'. For institutionally based sanctions, a similar large-scale evaluation was undertaken of the impact of shock incarceration or 'boot camps' for the US National Institute of Justice. Here, boot camp inmates were compared with other prisoners, prison parolees or probationers at a number of sites in eight states. Again, however, the results were not supportive of deterrence theory. The impact on recidivism was concluded to be 'at best, negligible... based on the totality of the evidence, boot camp programmes did not reduce offender recidivism'. This overall finding is very close to that obtained from evaluation of detention centres designed to deliver a 'short, sharp shock' in the United Kingdom in the early 1980s.

Evaluation of this initiative concluded that 'the introduction of the pilot project regimes had no discernible effect on the rate at which trainees were reconvicted. A number of ways in which effects on reconviction might have been masked were considered and discounted'. In a further test of deterrence effects, MacKenzie *et al.* have recently reported a review of 29 evaluative studies of correctional boot camps. The authors found that there was 'an almost equal odds of recidivating between the boot camps and comparison groups'. On the basis of their review, they therefore concluded that, 'in our overall metaanalysis of recidivism, we found no differences between the boot camp and comparison samples... the results of this systematic review and metaanalysis will be disappointing for many people... boot camps by themselves have little to offer as far as moving offenders away from criminal activities' is concerned. In both institutional and community settings, then, while the innovations being researched here were ones designed to impose stiffer penalties on offenders, no useful effect of this escalation in toughness was found. Where positive outcomes were observed, they were usually associated with an investment of time and effort in rehabilitative activities.

META-ANALYTIC REVIEWS

The findings from large-scale reviews of 'offender treatment' were surveyed. Some of the meta-analytic reviews described there included studies of criminal sanctions. We noted that the estimated 'grand mean' across all reviews, of the order of an approximately 10 per cent reduction in recidivism levels, was probably diminished to some extent by the incorporation of studies that reported predominantly zero or negative effects. The average effect size was, in other words, dragged down by these particular results. Reviews that have examined criminal sanctions separately within a wide range of approaches to intervention have typically found deterrence-based programmes to have zero or negative effect sizes. One meta-analysis specifically designed to dissect the relevant literature on community-based intermediate punishments yielded negative conclusions regarding the impact of the initially much-lauded enhanced punishments. In their reviews of 135 outcome studies of surveillance, 'smart sentencing' and other measures of this type, Gendreau *et al.* found a mean effect size just below zero.

DETERRENCE ON TRIAL

The studies just discussed involved evaluation of changes in sentencing practices in criminal justice services where many other factors that were operating could not be easily or satisfactorily controlled. A possibly more robust approach is to examine deterrence effects when these have been directly manipulated, though published reviews of this field are hard to find. Sherman has reviewed studies in which the effect of deterrence practices has been evaluated using randomized designs. The use of randomization in this context clearly raises ethical issues. The focus here is upon those circumstances where it has been feasible to evaluate the use of criminal sanctioning because offenders were randomly allocated to experimental and control conditions. Of 21 studies included in Sherman's review, 14 found no differences in recidivism between experimental and control samples. In five studies, increased severity of penalties resulted in increased recidivism. Only two studies showed any impact of punitive sanctions. In one, this effect was observed only in some sub-samples and not across the experimental group as a whole. The remaining report, by Sherman *et al.*, focused on the effect of arrest and brief incarceration on perpetrators of domestic violence in Minneapolis. However, subsequent extension and replications of this study at other sites obtained mixed results, so much so that the question of whether arrest should be mandatory for spousal abuse has been re-opened by other authors. For example, in another study responding to 1,200 cases of domestic violence in Milwaukee, criminal justice intervention in some cases precipitated further harm. Short-term arrest had an initial deterrence effect, but had a criminogenic effect in the following 12 months; full arrest with many more hours detention made no difference either way. On that basis, alongside other factors, it has been argued that the nature of legal decisions made should be tailored to the circumstances and demands of each individual case.

The most comprehensive attempt to catalogue the potential impact of punitive sanctions as specific deterrents was undertaken by Weisburd *et al.*, who compiled a 'Registry' of randomized experiments. The Registry provides details of a series of 68 studies published between 1951 and 1984 involving random allocation to different levels of criminal justice sanction. The definition of the word 'sanction' was very broad, and encompassed both heightened levels of strictness in terms of prison, probation or parole, as well as other experiments in which rehabilitative activities were included in traditional sanctioning procedures. Of the 68 studies available, 44 reported no differences between experimental and control samples. Only two showed apparently better outcomes for interventions that could be construed as more punitive. In neither case did the authors report statistical significance and the conclusions they drew were based solely on apparent trends in the data.

In the remaining 22 experiments, rates of recidivism, parole violation or other similar outcomes favoured experimental over control groups. However, in all the latter studies, the increased 'sanction' consisted of provision of individual counselling, participation in group treatments such as social skills training, or other forms of intervention that entailed sanctioning only in the respect that participation was non-voluntary. Though defined as sanctions for the purpose of the Registry, and involving some coercion in terms of limits on an offender's freedom, these interventions contained few if any elements that would ordinarily be considered directly punitive. In another context, that of work with substance-abusing offenders, coercion into treatment has been shown to have effects equivalent to voluntary participation, and the provision of services within such a framework may not be intrinsically punishing. Another type of research though in a similar vein has more direct bearing on the question of general than of specific deterrence. Sherman reviewed a series of 18 studies of the impact of police 'crackdowns' on rates of crime. Crackdowns were defined as combinations of three tactical elements: increased police presence, greater use of sanctions and threats of increased sanction certainty, conveyed through the media. That is, the police announced to the public that they would be working more intensively on certain types of crime, that people were more likely to be arrested and would be more severely dealt with by the courts. In six of the studies, crackdowns were short-term and most of these experiments focused on illegal parking, drink-driving and other 'distinctly middle-class' vehicle-related offences. In five studies in this group, residual effects of deterrence were observed; in other words, the effect continued after police 'back-off' or lifting of the crackdown. The remaining experiments were longer-term, and focused on offences such as drug sales and trafficking. However, only two of the 12 studies in this category obtained residual effects. In another two studies, there was disturbing evidence that other kinds of crimes had increased.

SELF-REPORT SURVEYS

This category of evidence could be regarded as relatively weaker than some of the others discussed here, since it involves reliance on the verbal reports of people already convicted of crimes, some of whom may be dishonest, and indeed have convictions for offences involving dishonesty. However, there is no reason to believe that participants have anything to gain or lose just as to how they respond to questioners in research of this kind. Some investigators have focused on the reactions of individuals arrested and then punished for crimes, inviting them to comment on the extent to which their experience of the process might be likely to deter them from future offending. Other researchers have focused more closely on patterns in individuals' thinking in the period immediately before committing offences.

Some of this work has been based on interviews with offenders during which they have been asked to describe their offending behaviour in some detail. The types of offences committed by those taking part in these research studies varied considerably in seriousness, from shop theft and vehicle-taking to drug-trafficking and armed robbery. As suggested, return to these studies a little later in the stage. In a series of surveys, Klemke and his colleagues collected self-report information on shoplifting by teenagers. Young people were interviewed at two points several months apart. Researchers found little evidence of deterrence in preventing repeated acts of shoplifting by this age group. While only a small proportion of those arrested was apprehended a second time, a far higher proportion admitted to further acts of theft. Thus the experience of arrest appeared to have had little impact on their behaviour.

Conversely, although we cannot rule out the possibility that another proportion was deterred, other factors such as increasing age and maturation could also have explained their desistance.

The impact of arrest has also been investigated in some of the longitudinal studies. In the Denver Youth Survey, Huizinga *et al.* collected data on the relationship between ongoing involvement in offending and experience of being arrested by the police. First, they found that the majority of offenders whatever their level of seriousness were not arrested at all. Second, for those who were, their delinquent behaviour did 'not appear to be well described by their arrests'. That is, the more serious offenders were rarely apprehended for their gravest offences: they were more likely to be detained for a fairly minor offence. Third, the majority of cases showed either no change in behaviour or an actual worsening of behaviour following arrest; and 'in only 8 per cent of the cases was the serious offending rate of the arrested juvenile less than the matched control... being arrested is not a very strong deterrent against future delinquent behavior'.

THE DEATH PENALTY

Research on the most extreme of sanctions, capital punishment or 'judicial execution', self-evidently has no bearing on the question of specific deterrence, but may provide evidence on the effectiveness of this extreme measure as a general deterrent. The presumption that it is a deterrent is certainly invoked as a rationale for imposing it. Among the 71 countries that still retained its use up to the year 2001, 'the most common political justification is the belief that it has a unique general deterrent capacity to save further innocent lives or reduce significantly other capital offences'. Of course, the issue of the death penalty is a highly emotive one and attitudes towards it are primarily influenced by a range of ethical and political beliefs, rather than by evidence bearing on its outcomes. But as this evidence has nevertheless been collected and is relevant to the present discussion, it is included in this survey. Such research as is available has failed to find that the availability of the death penalty as a sentencing option has any clear suppressant effect on rates of the most serious crimes, such as homicide, including the murder of police or prison officers. Some researchers claimed to have found deterrence effects in the United States for the period 1935–1969, to the extent of calculating a ratio of executions to numbers of lives saved. But other researchers who have analysed the same data or attempted to replicate the analyses with other data sets have ultimately dismissed such claims.

In a global survey conducted on behalf of the United Nations, Hood compared different countries allotted to discrete categories just as to their pattern of usage of capital punishment over a 40-year period. Some countries or states were *retentionist*–they had retained the use of the sentence throughout that period. Others were *abolitionist*–they either had not used it throughout the same period, or had at some point halted its use. Others, most notably all states of the USA, had a period when execution was not used, but following which its use was reinstated. Analysis of the data for rates of serious crimes such as homicide under these different jurisdictions yielded no evidence that capital punishment was associated with reductions in their frequency. The assumed effects of capital punishment in suppressing rates of homicide or violent crime have proved similarly elusive even when side-by-side comparisons are made between roughly equivalent localities differing only in their usage of it.

They also fail to appear in other circumstances predicted by general deterrence theory, for example where effects might be amplified through the publicity given to executions. Even in the state of Texas, 'by far the most active death penalty state' analysis of crime statistics for the period 1984–1997 has found no relationship between the execution rate and the murder rate. One other kind of evidence might seem only tangentially relevant to the points at issue here but is nevertheless worth considering. Does the potential threat of sudden death at the hands of a fellow citizen dissuade individuals from committing crimes? McDowall *et al.* tested the widely held view that possession of lethal weapons acts as a general deterrent to crime. Such an argument is often forwarded in defence of widespread gun ownership in the United States. McDowall *et al.* analysed five sets of crime data covering periods before and after significant changes in levels of gun ownership.

In two of these cases, following an apparent upsurge in serious crimes, police forces offered training to citizens in the use of firearms, and levels of ownership increased. In one instance in the town of Kennesaw, Georgia, a law was passed making it a legal requirement for every household to maintain a firearm. In two other cases, new laws were passed in local communities prohibiting the sale or ownership of handguns. Extended time-series analysis of rates of the target offences showed no impact of these changes. This was despite widely publicized claims that guns made a difference; based, as McDowall and his colleagues showed, on misleading analyses of data over short and unrepresentative periods of time.

THE FAILURE OF PUNISHMENT THEORY

We have probed among several sources for evidence of the deterrence effects supposedly associated with the administration of official punishment. Those effects seem to be absent or so weak as to be invisible, though the evidence is perhaps not conclusive enough to say they simply don't exist. But given the centrality and assumed importance of the crime– punishment connection, are we not entitled to expect a pattern rather stronger than we have found? The most appropriate overall conclusion from this search appears to be that punishment just does not work.

Such an assertion may be thought to require firmer support. In most people's minds, the aphorism of 'crime and punishment' is so firmly embedded that one seems to follow the other as a near-necessity. Two kinds of psychological evidence can be adduced that help to elucidate the failure to realise suppressant effects from punitive sanctions in the criminal justice system. The lack of evidence concerning their effectiveness can be understood on a behavioural and a cognitive level.

STRATEGIES AND METHODS OF BEHAVIOUR CHANGE

Punishment can be effective as a means of changing behaviour, and it is people's everyday appreciation of this–supposed clear-cut 'common sense'–that perhaps leads them to expect that a similar outcome will be obtained in the larger setting of the criminal justice system. The evidence surveyed suggests the latter is not what happens. This apparent contradiction can be resolved when we look at other research showing that punishment only works when certain conditions are met in its application. Behavioural psychologists have traditionally drawn a distinction between two broad strategies for altering patterns of behaviour, with particular reference to the reduction of some type of activity agreed to be socially undesirable–in this case, criminal recidivism. *Eliminative* strategies are based on the expectation that problem behaviour can be suppressed or even eradicated by linking it to negative consequences for the individual. In behaviour modification, examples of such procedures include punishment and aversive conditioning.

In criminal justice, this consists instead of deterrence-based sentences or punitive sanctions. As we have seen, they include financial penalties and restriction of liberty to varying degrees, including the use of custody, surveillance, shock incarceration or the imposition of demanding physical regimes. *Constructional* strategies, by contrast, are based on the proposal that a reduction of socially undesirable behaviour can be achieved more efficiently, and more ethically, through the building of new 'repertoires' of action. Rather than making the immediate consequences of an act unpleasant, in a constructional system effort is directed towards increasing the frequency of alternative behaviours through which goals can be achieved. If the new behaviours are designed to be incompatible with the problem behaviour, they can even wholly replace it. This can be done through a variety of methods, such as behavioural skills training, attitude change, education, employment and other forms of intervention. Punishment and other eliminative strategies have consistently been shown to be a much weaker method of behaviour change than constructional techniques involving positive reinforcement and variations upon it. The provision of rewards for increasing certain types of behaviour, or developing skilled responses, proves to be a much more dependable method of behaviour change than aversive conditioning or other measures designed primarily to reduce the rate of a behaviour.

BEHAVIOURAL ANALYSIS OF PUNISHMENT

In behavioural research, there is a large number of studies with a direct bearing on the issue. In the mid-1990s, Gendreau estimated that cumulatively, the pertinent research literature amounted to more than 25,000 source references. Its findings, obtained primarily but by no means exclusively from laboratory studies, establish fairly firmly a number of features of punishment. The conditions necessary to make it 'work' or achieve its optimum effects have been reviewed by a number of authors as have aspects of the ethical implications of using it. The first is that for punishment to achieve maximum effectiveness it should first be inevitable or unavoidable; escape should be impossible, or the chances of it very remote. Second, it should be administered immediately following the 'target' behaviour, or at least with maximum possible speed or celerity.

Third, for best effects it should be applied at a high level of severity. Fourth, even when these conditions are satisfactorily met, punishment may still fail to be effective when the individual being punished cannot resort to alternative behaviours for pursuing a desired goal. It is extremely difficult, if not actually impossible, to fulfil these requirements sufficiently well in the complex real-world environment of the criminal justice system, or in the lifestyles of those who regularly come into contact with it as offenders. First, only a surprisingly small fraction of criminal behaviours results in punishment, if the latter is taken to mean significant loss of liberty.

The objective chances of being arrested, convicted and then punished for a crime are, from the standpoint of the well-informed offender, reassuringly low. With reference to the United Kingdom, Home Office figures have suggested that on average only 2 per cent of all offences committed result in a conviction. Following conviction, only one in seven indictable offences leads to a custodial sentence. This yields an approximate probability of being sent to prison for a crime of one in 300.

That means, with no need whatsoever to resort to a calculator, the other 299 offences go virtually unpunished. Similar figures can be cited for the United States: based on the National Crime Survey, Felson estimated that only ten burglaries per 1,000 result in a custodial sentence, with the corresponding figure for larceny even lower at three per 1,000. Using the terminology borrowed earlier from Gibbs, the certainty factor is a long way from being operative. Second, when punitive sanctions are administered, this usually occurs after a gap of weeks or months following the occurrence of the offence. During that period, many other behaviours occur, from among which the individual's offence behaviour cannot be extracted and linked to punitive consequences. You may know that being locked up today is a consequence of the burglary you committed six months ago, but it is now rather late for this punitive consequence to set up a conditioned reaction in your nervous system.

To reduce this period to any meaningful degree would require a massive expansion of police, court and penal services. So much so that, for the government treasury, there would be no money left over for anything else. Third, court sentences are graded on a loose scale of severity known colloquially as the 'tariff'. Yet this bears only a fairly lax and uncertain relationship to the seriousness of crimes. The vagaries of sentencing decisions have been much lamented within penology, and for many offenders it is not until sentence is finally pronounced that they know for sure what their fate will be. But despite calls from some segments of society for heavier sentences, including the restoration of corporal punishments and the death penalty, many citizens have reservations about the use of exclusively severe sanctions. For example, the implementation of 'three strikes' policies in the United States has been surrounded by considerable controversy. The use of draconian methods may well have a dramatic impact.

It has been reported that 'the most effective drug control policy of modern times' was that practised by the Taleban militia during the latter part of their reign over Afghanistan in 2000–2001. The use of harsh punishments against poppy farmers, which included blackening their faces, parading them in the streets, imprisonment and the threat of 'eradication', reduced the global supply of heroin by 65 per cent. Even in the context of widespread abhorrence of heroin use, it is doubtful whether many people would see such extreme measures as justified. Finally, given the goal-directed nature of much crime and the limited personal resources and life circumstances of many persistent offenders, it is unlikely that many alternative courses of action are readily available to them; though certainly efforts can be made to increase the range of such options. In all these respects, official punishment departs markedly from the required parameters, in behaviourist parlance, of an effective 'aversive conditioner'.

Some time ago Moffitt posed the question of whether findings from laboratory research can be extrapolated to the more complex, uncontrolled circumstances of criminal justice services. Examining evidence pertaining to the principal dimensions of this, Moffitt concluded that while significant gaps remained in the existing research, 'awareness of the principles of punishment may be of use to the deterrence theoretician'. Some might hope that such an awareness could allow application of deterrence-based on learning theory principles. 'Achieving such optimal conditions in real-world correctional settings, however, is problematic'. The cumulative evidence merely attests to the difficulty of applying punishment in correctional settings in ways that would approximate to those needed for it to accomplish its stated objectives.

COGNITIVE FACTORS

One of the gaps identified by Moffitt in respect of punishment effectiveness was 'the role of human cognitive and verbal abilities in attenuating delay of punishment'. Evidence from other sources suggests that in this respect, too, there are major obstacles to ensuring that deterrence can be applied effectively through the criminal justice system. Perhaps reflecting the actual nature of the circumstances in which they operate, for most individuals contemplating an offence the perceived or subjective chances of being punished are probably very low. Research on perceptual characteristics of sentencing policies supports the validity of the triad of conditions identified by Gibbs–certainty, severity and celerity–as key elements in deterrence.

On the other hand, most research suggests that deterrence plays only a fairly weak part in suppressing potentially criminal behaviour as compared with positive attachments to social norms and institutions. Using data from a sample of 298 inner-city youths in the age range 13–17, Foglia found that there was no relationship between self-reported delinquency and perceived risk of arrest. However, involvement in delinquency was related to 'internalized norms' assimilated through contact with peers, and experiences of parental discipline. To make these generalizations more concrete, let us draw an everyday parallel.

Most people are presumably aware in general terms of the possibility of being arrested and eventually punished should they break the law. Why does this not have the effect of stopping some individuals from committing crimes? Imagine that each morning you commute to work in your car. You appreciate, at some level of consciousness, the possibility that you could be involved in a collision. You may even know that in an average year in most European countries, several thousand people die in road traffic accidents, and many more are seriously injured. However, you drive off because you don't think it will happen to you. If the thought does enter your mind, other ideas will counter it, reflecting your confidence that you are a careful driver, you do not take risks, you have a car with good safety features. The divergence between a kind of 'blanket' versus a 'here-and-now' awareness, between long-term and short-term risks or satisfactions, arises in many types of situation.

It occurs when we attempt to lose weight, to quit smoking or drinking, to comply with an exercise regime, to revise for an exam... or write a book. Now transpose this to a situation where someone is poised to commit a crime. He or she is perfectly aware, in what we might call loose or distant terms, of the possibility of being caught: arrested, charged, convicted, punished, even imprisoned. For crimes of any notoriety, there might be stories in the local newspaper, perhaps the added humiliation of being photographed by the press, or filmed by a TV news team going into court. In metaphorical terms, you could say this is at the back of everyone's collective mind. But for it to have a decisive influence on behaviour, it would need–continuing the metaphor–to come more to the forefront. Studies of several different types of offence indicate that the prospect of arrest is not in the foreground of people's thinking in the moments before embarking on a criminal act.

This clearly applies in the case of offences that result from strong feelings of anger or aggression leading to acts of violence; and also where offending is associated with addictive substance abuse. In these instances, people are not in control of themselves and they are not looking very far into the future. They are dominated by 'here-andnow' thinking. Findings from a number of studies based on in-depth interviews, or *in vivo* observational work, suggest that prior to committing an offence, most individuals are preoccupied with the implementation of the act, rather than deliberating upon the consequences should they be caught. There is comparatively little research on this issue, but what is available suggests that in the period immediately preceding a criminal act, such regulatory mechanisms as might activate a self-deterrent process are not engaged or are deliberately 'switched off'. Studies of property offences of varying levels of seriousness indicate that the prospect of arrest is not salient during these crucial moments. They include the project by Carroll and Weaver in which high-frequency shoplifters walked around Chicago stores, thinking aloud and recording their thoughts on tape via a lapel microphone. Their cognitions were exclusively focused on the immediate situation, with no evidence of ongoing concern over the possibility of arrest. By contrast, the thoughts of a group of aspiring shoplifters were pervaded by apprehensive images of arrest, shame and other negative repercussions.

Light *et al.* interviewed young people involved in vehicle-taking on a deprived Bristol housing estate. Their accounts of their offences and motivations contained little indication that the prospect of being caught was a manifest feature of their thinking. Turning to other types of offence, when Bennett and Wright invited professional burglars to describe the factors that influenced their decisionmaking and selection of suitable targets, again no obvious thoughts of deterrence consequences were uppermost. While minimizing risk was one factor in their decisions, their cognitive processing had gone beyond a stage where the possibility of punishment carried any meaningful force. This parallels the findings of Wright and Decker with house burglars in the city of St Louis, Missouri.

Most of their interviewees 'consciously refused to dwell on the possibility of getting caught', a process which effectively 'robbed the threatened sanctions of their deterrence value'. All were aware of this potential outcome, though they perceived the objective chances of it as slim. Some denied that such thoughts were active at the time of committing an offence. Most, however, engaged in a kind of self-discipline to dismiss such ideas from their minds. For a few, there was even a belief that thinking about getting caught made it more likely: a superstition they called 'burning bread on yourself'. One efficient way to banish all these doubts was simply to focus on the task and the success that awaited at the end. Similarly in their interviews with a series of 88 prisoners convicted of armed robbery, Morrison and O'Donnell found their thinking preoccupied with planning and executing the offence, despite the real danger, having launched on this particular path, of being confronted with armed police. Comparable findings were obtained by Corbett and Simon in their study of attitudes towards a variety of road traffic offences. Whether their self-disclosed offence frequency was high or low, all offenders were more or less equally eager to avoid getting caught.

But high-rate offenders 'dwelled upon their beliefs about the relatively low risk of apprehension to facilitate their decisions to break the law'. These results are complemented by others from a study by Zamble and Quinsey of the processes involved in recidivism. The researchers interviewed and obtained detailed information from a series of 311 male repeat offenders returning to prison following a further re-conviction. Offences were typically preceded by personal crises, difficulties in coping and poor self-management. These men's problems had accumulated to intolerable levels, yet they rarely applied a positive problem-oriented approach.

For some an offence was a by-product of stressful events, for others a bungled attempt to escape their ongoing problems. Again there was little evidence that the potential legal consequences of criminal activity played any significant part in determining the paths they took. The overall and compelling message from all of these findings is that, hovering on the brink of a criminal act, would-be law-breakers are not for the most part in what Walker called 'deterrable states of mind'. Rather, they are in what Wright and Decker called a state of 'psychosocial encapsulation': a 'qualitatively different state of mind' inside which 'the potentially negative consequences of their actions become attenuated'.

Carroll and Weaver discussed their own findings and others in the context of a model of *bounded rationality* in which individuals apply reasoning processes, but within a narrow and circumscribed frame of reference which maps onto only one segment of the situation in which they are acting. Similarly, research on aggression typically shows that for affective or angry aggression, the type likely to manifest itself in most fights, individuals are influenced by very short-term motivations and lose sight of longer-term consequences. That increased severity of penalties does not have the deterrence effect of instilling fear is additionally demonstrated by research on drug-trafficking. As lawenforcement strategies have become progressively more intensive and punishments more severe, offenders have simply redoubled their efforts and increased the flexibility of their methods. Finally, it is likely that for punishment to have an influence on individuals it must also appear comprehensible to them.

Criminological researchers have shown that many individuals can account for their illegal actions in terms that make them acceptable. This entails employing elaborate cognitive mechanisms such as the techniques of neutralization. These function to isolate individuals from the consequences of their actions, to help them avoid responsibility, and to perceive the experience of punishment as unfair. It may be that many people's expectations that punishment will serve its purpose are based on inferring from 'common sense knowledge' that suffering pain as a result of our actions will stop us from doing something. That may be derived partly from the experience of growing up and being chastised by parents; source of the ancient adage 'spare the rod and spoil the child'. Ironically, however, punishment does not appear especially effective on that level either.

Research suggests that the main elements of parenting that contribute most to whether children are well or badly behaved are expressions of warmth and support, parents' levels of interest through monitoring what children are doing, and their use of inductive reasoning when exercising discipline and explaining rules. In the absence of warmth, or at lower levels of it, the use of corporal punishment is associated with an increased risk of delinquency among young people. This was shown, for example, in a cross-cultural study of American and Taiwanese families by Simons *et al.,* using as a measure the proportion of disciplinary encounters that involved physical punishment. While the patterns found were slightly different between the two cultural settings, overall 'our analyses provided little evidence that corporal punishment serves to deter adolescent conduct problems'.

DETERRENCE EFFECTS

It appears to be widely accepted that the existence of punitive sanctions in society contributes to the maintenance of order through the suppression of criminal activity among the population. It is equally plausible, of course, that the continuation of law-abiding behaviour by most citizens most of the time is a function of other factors such as positive reinforcement or reward for socially approved behaviour, and informal social controls exercised within proximate social groups. Conversely, for those who have become marginalized as a result of previous involvement in crime, punitive sanctions may have become diluted in their effects. These dimensions of deterrence may be illustrated by comparing the outcomes of studies reporting success and failure among deterrence-based interventions.

In some circumstances, certain kinds of sanctions can be shown to work. This applies, for example, to the use of random drugtesting in conditions in which there is a great deal at stake for those found using drugs. Borack has described the impact of such procedures in the US Navy. This study employed baseline estimates of frequency of drug use obtained from general population studies. In the Navy, a positive drug test results in dismissal. Under conditions in which a randomly selected 20 per cent of the personnel were subjected to urinalysis per 30-day period, a suppressant effect of 56.5 per cent was obtained. When the variable of uncertainty is manipulated in circumstances where potential offenders may risk significant loss, similar findings emerge.

Extensive studies in Australia concerning the suppressant effect of random breath-testing on rates of vehicle accidents have also yielded evidence firmly supportive of its efficacy. In a follow-up of 700 men arrested for domestic violence, Thistlethwaite *et al.* found that even if imprisoned, only those with a high 'stake in conformity' were less likely to re-offend. 'Conformity' for this purpose was measured by a complex scale taking into account aspects of employment, education, residence and marital status. By contrast, little effect of deterrence was observed in a study by Baron and Kennedy of the sentencing of homeless street youths. As these authors noted, 'perceptions of sanctions differ depending upon one's position in the social structure'. These very different studies illustrate the polarities of deterrence effects. While the naval recruits described by Borack had much to lose by testing positive for drugs, the reverse was true for the homeless, impoverished youths studied by Baron and Kennedy. Perceptual deterrence appears to have some fairly enduring characteristics.

In a study using data from the US National Youth Survey, Massoglia and Macmillan found evidence of considerable steadiness in the perceived certainty and severity of sanctions across a three-year period between late adolescence and early adulthood. Massoglia and MacMillan called this 'legal subjectivity' and concluded that it is 'reasonably reliable over time and highly stable' and is 'developed in the early part of the life course through childhood socialisation and experience and then likely remains part of one's psychological toolkit for the remainder of the life course'. The totality of evidence cannot then support the claim that deterrence is never effective, or that no-one has ever been prevented from further offending by criminal sanctions. 'Glimmers of a deterrence effect pop up once in a while'.

In all likelihood there is a proportion of any sample of offenders who will be deterred by official punishments. Similarly, as Gibbs has asserted, it may be that deterrence works widely in its restrictive form, in which some offenders hold back from unmitigated indulgence in crime, so as to reduce possible exposure to arrest. The extent of any such effect is probably unmeasurable. The question posed is whether specific deterrence effects are of sufficient reliability or generalizability to form the basis for a systematic policy, let alone one that is accorded the cardinal place in society's overall response to criminal behaviour. Considering ways in which deterrence effects might be manipulated, the available evidence points to certainty as the most promising instrumental variable. Complete certainty is of course impossible to ensure. Even increased probability of arrest is difficult to attain, but comparatively small increases in the perceived risk of arrest may be sufficient to deter. This direction may present the likeliest route for increasing the efficacy of deterrence. Von Hirsch *et al.* have reviewed evidence that changes in the perceived uncertainty of punishment can have marginal deterrence effects. When studies have been conducted on the relationship between probability of conviction and rates of certain crimes, most have found a negative correlation. By contrast, evidence of achieving effects by varying the severity of punishment remains exceedingly weak, making it all the more ironic that this is so commonly advocated as the solution to the 'law-and-order problem'. Other evidence showing some initial deterrence effects of sanctions has been reviewed by Nagin.

The most suitable interpretation of these findings is that they are due to manipulation of the perceptual certainty variable. For example, the passing of the British Road Safety Act in 1967 and the introduction of the 'breathalyser' test had an immediate impact on rates of fatal road accidents at night. The effect was, however, temporary and, as in the other studies reviewed by Sherman, was followed by a phenomenon he called *deterrence decay*. The introduction of similar legislation in Norway and Sweden had no parallel effect, though as we saw the Australian experiments with random breath-testing proved more positive.

One suggestion for building on the results obtained is to maintain ambiguity and uncertainty by the constant creation of novelty. This would place an onus on the police and other justice agencies to be ceaselessly inventive and innovative in finding new ruses through which to convince the public that the probability of arrest was higher than it objectively is. But even this might only work with certain types of offences or offenders. Such deterrence effects as have been found have been harder to reproduce with more serious types of crime and are less likely to be obtained with more experienced offenders. Paradoxically, the results of some studies suggest that 'the criminally uninitiated had unrealistically high expectations of sanction risks and... experience with offending caused them to lower their unrealistically high expectations'. In other words, when deterrence works it appears most likely to do so with the people who need it least, and least likely with the people who need it most! To boost certainty on any meaningful scale, however, would entail an injection of resources that few societies if any could afford. Take the example given by Felson of the policing of Los Angeles County, California, which then had a population of nearly nine million. Based on the area of the city, the number of properties to be protected and the availability of police on foot patrol, Felson calculated that the average house, shop, restaurant or office in LA is under visible police protection for an average of 29 seconds per day.

This throws into perspective the idea that crime will be reduced if police numbers can be expanded. Usually, calls for the latter are proportionately quite modest; so let us imagine that the number of 'Bobbies on the beat' is suddenly *doubled*. That would mean each property in LA could now be offered not quite one minute of police coverage each day. 'Doubling the number of police in a U.S. metropolis is like doubling a drop in the bucket'. Felson regarded the possibility of protecting property through increased policing as a fairly grotesque illusion, which he dubbed the 'Cops-and-courts fallacy'. We saw that a commentary published by Martinson has been widely considered to have played a seminal part in casting doubt on the value of rehabilitation, and of ushering in an era of greater punitiveness.

Martinson's conclusion was that treatment added nothing to what he called 'the networks of criminal justice'. The only conclusion that can seriously be sustained by all the available data is surely just the opposite. Legal frameworks and networks are essentially ineffective for their proclaimed purposes with regard to convicted offenders. Perhaps it is only by the addition of services that entail active, constructive interventions that criminal justice personnel will be likely to achieve the avowed aims of the entire process.

INEFFECTIVE–BUT INDISPENSABLE?

In summary, the evidence reviewed here cumulatively suggests that punishing offenders simply fails to achieve what is informally assumed, and officially pronounced, to be one of its central goals. On the surface, this might at first be thought to be a purely sociological question. Here are several sets of data–on rates of conviction or imprisonment, rates of crime, and the like–which are aggregate social statistics, and which can be studied closely to test ideas about whether one might have a causal effect upon the other. I hope that this stage has clarified why, to make sense of any such connection, or as it transpires the absence of one, psychological variables need to be taken into account.

That a supposedly intelligent society continues to employ a method that so singly fails to accomplish its goals, causes other kinds of pain, and incidentally entails considerable monetary cost, could be seen as irrational. To put it bluntly, when we say it will deter offenders from crime, we are simply kidding ourselves. But from a sociological standpoint it may well be that punishment serves other symbolic functions for society, related to group cohesion, shared morality or civil governance. From that perspective, it is viewed as imperative to avoid falling into what Garland called 'the trap of thinking of it solely in crime-control terms'. Nevertheless, some philosophers have argued that whether or not punishment can be justified is at least partly an empirical question. Crime-control and the creation of a 'safer society' is one of the stated roles of government, and a keenly debated theme in the manifestos of most political parties.

Punishment is usually perceived as one of the key implements in delivering it. Hence, the incongruity of its continued use alongside evidence that it fails to serve that purpose merits systematic inquiry. It is difficult to imagine that in other fields of policy, such as health, education or employment, so ineffective a procedure could be so avidly pursued in the face of so much evidence of its futility. The argument that punishment is somehow an intrinsic feature of human symbolic relations, and therefore cannot be changed, is similarly unimpressive. Because something always has been so in society is no guide to whether it should continue to be so. Were that the case, the power of monarchs, the subjugation of women, the right to enslave the conquered, would all have remained unchallenged. The philosopher Ted Honderich argued some years ago that punishment could be justified if it were, among other things, 'economically preventive of offences'. We would have moral grounds for continuing to use it if it secured 'the reduction of distress at an economical rate'. Based on all the findings reviewed earlier, punishment does not reduce and may well worsen the problem which it is designed to cure.

The following conclusion reached by Gibbs appears as accurate now as when first written: 'The bulk of findings indicate that offenders are not deterred when punished. More precisely, numerous researchers have reported either that recidivism is greater for offenders who have been punished the most severely or that there is no significant relation between punishment severity and recidivism'. Summarizing evidence from controlled trials of sanctions outlined earlier, Sherman endorsed the same viewpoint: 'The prevailing wisdom that punishment deters the future crimes of those punished is contradicted by the majority of the experimental evidence... the most frequent finding from randomized experiments is that sanctions make no difference'.

Note that the latter two statements were both written some time ago, and before the publication of considerably larger volumes of evidence reinforcing the same essential point, and subsumed in the meta-analytic reviews. More recently, considering the relationship between punishment and motivation to change, Hollin has acknowledged that punishment can be shown to serve the purposes of retribution and incapacitation. However, viewing it as a deterrent, he concludes that 'examination of the evidence with regard to *general* deterrence suggested that there is very little consistent support for the proposition that punishing offenders inhibits the antisocial behaviour of other members of society... Moving from general to *specific* deterrence, it is also doubtful whether punishment motivates long-term behaviour change at the individual level'.

Bibliography

A.M. Bagulia: *Child and Crime*, SBS Publication, Delhi, 2006.

Anil Kumar: *Criminology: Principles and Concepts*, Ancient Publishing House, Delhi, 2011.

Anjana Singh: *Crime and Criminology*, ABD Publishers, Delhi, 2011.

Asha Srivastava: *Encyclopaedia of Criminology and Forensic Science*;, Anmol, Publication, Delhi, 2008.

B.R. Sharma: *Bank Frauds - Prevention and Detection - Including Computer and Credit Cards Crimes*, Universal Law Publication, 2009.

Govind Singh: *Anatomy of Crime and Criminology*, Cyber Tech Publications, 2013.

Govind Singh: *Anatomy of Crime and Criminology*, Cyber Tech Publications, 2013.

James Vadackumchery: *Police Criminology and Crimes*, Kalpaz, Publication, 2002.

K.D. Gaur: *Criminal Law and Criminology*, Deep and Deep, Publication, Delhi, 2002.

Kalpana Kannabiran and Ranbir Singh: *Colonialism, Criminology and Human Rights in India*, Sage, Publication, Delhi, 2008.

Kamal Dua: *Community Pharmacy: Basic Principles and Concepts*, PharmaMed Press, 2012.

Lokesh Rana: *Encyclopaedia of Criminology*, Anmol, Publication, Delhi, 2006.

M.C. Gupta, K. Chockalingam and Jaytilak Guha Roy: *Child Victims of Crime : Problems and Perspectives*, Gyan, Publication, Delhi, 2001.

Masudul Choudhury: *Principles and Concepts of Corporate Banking*, Cyber Tech Publication, Delhi, 2012.

Nageshwar Singh: *Psychology and Crime*, RBSA Publishers, 2013.

Neela Gokhale and Rachna Yadav: *Research Methods in Criminology*, Shree Publication, Delhi, 2007.

P. Sinha: *International Encyclopaedia of Crime, Criminology and Mafia*, Anmol, Publication, Delhi, 2008.

Parvesh K. Atri: *Readings in Crime and Criminology*, Anmol, Publication, Delhi, 2004.

Paul T Augastine: *Combating Cyber Crime*, Crescent Publication, Delhi, 2007.

Prafullah Padhy: *Crime and Criminology*, Isha Books, Delhi, 2006.

Praveen Kumar: *Communal Crimes And National Integration: A Socio-Legal Study*, Readworthy Publication, Delhi, 2011.

Rajan Nagia: *Cyber Laws and Computer Crimes*, Cyber Tech Publication, 2009.

Ram Ahuja: *Criminology*, Rawat, Publication, 2000.

Ramakant Purvi: *Handbook of Criminology*, Dominant, Publication, Delhi, 2006.

Sheikh Hafizur Rahman Karzon: *Theoretical and Applied Criminology*, Palal Prokashoni and Empowerment Through Law of the Common People (ELCOP), 2008.

Surendra P. Singh: *Encyclopaedia of Criminology*, Reliance, 2002.

Swati Bhattacharjee: *A Unique Crime : Understanding Rape in India*, Gangchil, Publication, 2008.

Uttam Kumar Singh: *World Encyclopaedia of Criminology*, Jnanada Prakashan, 2009.

Warr: *Companions in Crime: The Social Aspects of Criminal Conduct*, Cambridge Univ Press, 2004.

Index